"Human Resource Management (HRM) has become a global agenda. While there are differences by country, there are similar principles that apply worldwide. This outstanding set of cases demonstrates how 31 countries deal with the array of human capability (talent, leadership, organization, and HRM) issues that exist around the world. The cases offer relevant, specific, and compelling insights that will be useful for business and HRM leaders who want to deliver stakeholder value through human capability."

Dave Ulrich, *Rensis Likert Professor, Ross School of Business, University of Michigan; Partner, the RBL Group*

The Global Human Resource Management Casebook

The third edition of *The Global Human Resource Management Casebook* provides a wide range of international teaching cases exploring contemporary human resource management (HRM) challenges. Each case focuses primarily on one country and illustrates a critical HRM issue confronting managers and HRM practitioners. This real-world application provides students of HRM with a unique opportunity to examine how key HRM theories and ideas translate into practice.

The case studies emphasize the national and cultural contexts of HRM, providing readers with a global understanding of HRM practices like recruitment, reward systems, diversity, and inclusion, as well as recent developments including the impact of the COVID-19 pandemic, remote working, sustainability, and digital transformation. In this edition, the editors and authors have made significant updates to reflect recent developments in the field and cover a broader range of countries. The authors also delve into new industries including consulting, energy, healthcare, IT, and education. With 31 international cases followed by further reading and learning resources, this extensive collection is an invaluable resource for any student seeking to explore contemporary HRM on a global basis.

Liza Castro Christiansen is a Visiting Senior Fellow at Henley Business School, University of Reading, United Kingdom.

Michal Biron is an Associate Professor and Head of the MBA program at the School of Business Administration, University of Haifa, Israel.

Pawan Budhwar is Professor and Associate Deputy Vice Chancellor International, Aston Business School, Aston University, Birmingham, United Kingdom.

Brian Harney is a Professor at DCU Business School, Dublin City University, Ireland.

Routledge Global Human Resource Management Series

Edited by David G. Collings, Trinity College Dublin, Ireland, Elaine Farndale, Penn State University, USA, and Fang Lee Cooke, Monash University, Australia

The Global HRM Series has for over a decade been leading the way in advancing our understanding of Global HRM issues. Edited and authored by the leading and highest-profile researchers in the field of human resource management (HRM), this series of books offers students and reflective practitioners accessible, coordinated and comprehensive textbooks on global HRM. Individually and collectively, these books cover the core areas of the field, including titles on global leadership, global talent management, global careers, and the global HR function, as well as comparative volumes on HR in key global regions.

The series is organized into two distinct strands: the first reflects key issues in managing global HRM; and the second comparative perspectives in human resource management.

Taking an expert look at an increasingly important area of global business, this well-established series has become the benchmark for serious textbooks on global HRM.

The Publisher and Editors wish to thank the Founding Editors of the series – Randall Schuler, Susan Jackson, Paul Sparrow and Michael Poole.

Dedication: The late Professor Michael Poole was one of the founding series editors and the series is dedicated to his memory.

https://www.routledge.com/Global-HRM/book-series/SE0692

Global Leadership (third edition)
Research, practice, and development
Mark E. Mendenhall, Joyce S. Osland, Allan Bird, Gary R. Oddou, Michael J. Stevens, Martha L Maznevski, and Günter K. Stahl

Macro Talent Management
A Global Perspective on Managing Talent in Developed Markets
Vlad Vaiman, Paul Sparrow, Randall Schuler and David Collings

Macro Talent Management in Emerging and Emergent markets
A Global Perspective
Vlad Vaiman, Paul Sparrow, Randall Schuler and David Collings

Global Talent Management (second edition)
Edited by David G. Collings, Hugh Scullion and Paula M. Caligiuri

International Human Resource Management (sixth edition)
Policies and Practices for Multinational Enterprises
Ibraiz Tarique, Dennis R. Briscoe and Randall S. Schuler

Performance Management Systems (second edition)
A Global Perspective
Arup Varma, Pawan Budhwar and Angelo DeNisis

The Global Human Resource Management Casebook

THIRD EDITION

Edited by Liza Castro Christiansen, Michal Biron, Pawan Budhwar, and Brian Harney

Routledge
Taylor & Francis Group

NEW YORK AND LONDON

Cover design: © Getty Images

Third edition published 2024
by Routledge
605 Third Avenue, New York, NY 10158

and by Routledge
4 Park Square, Milton Park, Abingdon, Oxon, OX14 4RN

Routledge is an imprint of the Taylor & Francis Group, an informa business

© 2024 selection and editorial matter, Liza Castro Christiansen, Michal Biron,
Pawan Budhwar and Brian Harney; individual chapters, the contributors

First edition published by Routledge 2011
Second edition published by Routledge 2017

ISBN: 978-1-032-30881-4 (hbk)
ISBN: 978-1-032-30880-7 (pbk)
ISBN: 978-1-003-30709-9 (ebk)

DOI: 10.4324/9781003307099

Typeset in Minion
by Deanta Global Publishing Services, Chennai, India

Access the Support Material: www.routledge.co.uk/9781032308807

Contents

Part I: Western Europe   1

Part II: Scandinavia   41

Part III: Central and Eastern Europe   73

Part IV: Mediterranean, Middle East, and Africa   133

Part V: Asia and the Pacific Rim   197

Illustrations

TABLES

FIGURES

Contributor Biographies

AUSTRALIA

Helen De Cieri (MA, PhD). Professor of Management at Monash Business School, Monash University, Australia. Helen is currently the Director of Research for the Department of Management. Her research is focused on relationships between human resource management, workers' well-being and mental health, and organizational performance.

Karin Sanders (PhD). Professor of Human Resource Management and Organizational Psychology at the School of Management & Governance, UNSW Business School in Sydney Australia. In addition, she is Senior Deputy Dean of Research & Enterprise at the UNSW Business School. Her research focuses on the human resource (HR) process approach, in particular the impact of employees' understanding and attributions of HR practices on their attitudes and behaviors.

AUSTRIA

Wolfgang Mayrhofer (PhD). Full Professor at WU Vienna, Austria. He previously has held full-time positions at the University of Paderborn, Germany, and at Dresden University of Technology, Germany, and conducts research in comparative international human resource management and work careers, spirituality, management, and religion, as well as systems theory and management.

Katharina Pernkopf (PhD). Research Associate at WU Vienna, Austria. She conducts research at the interface of organizational institutionalism and HRM, in particular, theoretically focusing on convention theory.

Astrid Reichel (PhD). Full Professor, Head of the HRM group and the Department of Business' Deputy Head at the University of Salzburg, Austria. She mainly researches how institutions and technology in the context of organizations shape HRM in organizations.

BOTSWANA

Dorothy Mpabanga (PhD). Associate Professor in the Department of Political and Administrative Studies, in the Faculty of Social Sciences, at the University of Botswana. Prof. Mpabanga teaches at both undergraduate and graduate levels and supervises research students at undergraduate, graduate, and post-graduate levels. Her research focuses on public sector management and reforms, human resource management and development, diversity management, project management, and NGO management.

CANADA

Sylvie Guerrero (PhD). Professor at the University of Quebec at Montreal. Her research focuses mainly on employees' retention, skills development, and the career of high potentials.

Ewan Oiry (PhD). Full Professor and PhD supervisor at École des Sciences de Gestion – Université du Québec à Montréal, Montréal, Canada. He teaches human resource management, competency management, and human-technology interactions in HR, and develops research on these topics.

Ariane Ollier-Malaterre (PhD). Management Professor and the Director of the International Network on Technology, Work and Family (INTWAF) at the University of Quebec at Montreal (ESG-UQAM), Canada. Her research examines digital technologies and the boundaries between work and life across different national contexts.

CHILE

Andrés Raineri (PhD). Associate Professor at the School of Business at Pontificia Universidad Católica de Chile. He lectures in courses in human resource management and organizational change management at graduate, undergraduate, and executive education programs, and conducts research on the same topics.

COLUMBIA

Jaime Andrés Bayona (PhD). Associate professor at the Business Department, Pontificia Universidad Javeriana in Bogotá, Colombia. He currently teaches human resource management and corporate social responsibility at undergraduate and postgraduate levels. His research interests are related to sustainable HRM and the intersection between philosophy and HRM.

Luisa Fernanda Maya (MA). Senior Human Resource Manager in Open English, Colombia.

CYPRUS

Nicoleta Nicolaou Pissarides (BSc, MSc). Senior University Officer, Medical School, University of Cyprus. Her current research interests include employee relations, equality, performance evaluations, use of innovation and knowledge, business evaluation, and human resource management.

Eleni Stavrou (PhD). Professor of Management and Director of MSc in Human Resource Management (HRM) at the University of Cyprus. Her research interests include work-life issues, strategic and comparative human resource management, and inter-generational transitions in family firms.

DENMARK

Liza Castro Christiansen (MBA, DBA). Visiting Senior Fellow at Henley Business School, University of Reading, in the United Kingdom. Liza teaches the Executive MBA module "Reputation and Responsibility" and is a supervisor in the Executive MBA and Doctor of Business Administration programs. Her research focuses on HR strategy and business strategy alignment, HR competencies, leadership during change, and diversity and inclusion.

FINLAND

Adam Smale (PhD). Professor of Management in the School of Management at the University of Vaasa, Finland. He is a member of the human resource management research group, conducts case-based teaching on executive MBA programs, and is currently serving as Dean of the school. His research interests lie in international HRM, especially HRM, talent management, and careers in multinational corporations.

FRANCE

Thierry Colin (PhD). Full Professor at the University of Lorraine, IAE Nancy Management School, and CEREFIGE, in France. He is responsible for the master's degree in human resource management. His research focuses on organizational routines, competence management, and industrial relations.

Benoît Grasser (PhD). Full Professor at the University of Lorraine, IAE Nancy Management School, and CEREFIGE, in France. He has taught extensively in bachelor's and master's courses in human resource management, and has been the supervisor of several degrees in this field. He is now Vice President for Research at the University of Lorraine.

Fabien Meier (PhD). HR Director Europe/Asia in the aerospace industry.

Ewan Oiry (PhD). Full Professor at École des Sciences de Gestion – Université du Québec à Montréal, Montréal, Canada. He teaches human resource management, competency management, and human–technology interactions in HR, and develops research and publishes articles on these topics. He supervises numerous PhDs.

GERMANY

Marion Festing (PhD). Professor of Human Resource Management and Intercultural Leadership at ESCP Business School's Berlin campus. Marion's research interests include international human resource management and talent management in various institutional and cultural contexts as well as a specific focus on diversity and inclusion.

GREECE

Maria Vakola (PhD). Professor at Athens Business School, Athens University of Economics and Business in Greece. She is the Director of the MSc in Human Resource Management. Her research interests include the psychology of organizational change, employees' reactions to change, individual differences, and silence at work.

HUNGARY

Katalin Balog is a PhD candidate at MATE University in Hungary.

Zsolt Barna is a PhD candidate at MATE University in Hungary.

Tamás Tibor Hámori is a PhD candidate at MATE University in Hungary.

József Poór (DSc, CMC). Full professor at J. Selye University in Slovakia, Honorary Professor of University Pécs Hungary, and Visiting Professor at BBU-University Cluj, Romania.

Katalin Szabó (PhD). Associate Professor and Deputy Director of the Institute for Organizational and Tender Coordination at the Hungarian University of Agriculture and Life Sciences (MATE) in Hungary.

ICELAND

Ingi Runar Edvardsson (PhD). Professor in Management and former Head of the School of Business at the University of Iceland. His research interests include human resource management, knowledge management, outsourcing, and SMEs.

Ivo Rothkrantz. Director of Strategy & Development at Marel.

INDIA

Radha R. Sharma (PhD). Professor, OB/HR, Dean, Research & Industry–Academia Linkages, and Chair at the Centre on Responsible Management & Sustainable Development at New Delhi Institute of Management, India. Her research interests are within gender equity, executive burnout, EI, competencies, and sustainability.

ISRAEL

Michal Biron (PhD). Associate Professor and Head of the MBA program at the School of Business Administration, University of Haifa (Israel), and a Fellow at the Humboldt Foundation (University of Münster, Germany). Her current research interests include flexible work arrangements, stress and burnout, team processes, and employee–supervisor relations.

Hilla Peretz (PhD). Senior Lecturer at the Department of Industrial Engineering and Management, Braude College (Israel), and an incoming visiting fellow at Tobin College of Business (St. John's University, New York). Her research interests encompass international, comparative, and cross-cultural human resource management.

ITALY

Silvia Bagdadli (PhD). Associate Professor of Business Organization and the Director of the Master of Science in Organization and HRM (MasterOP) at Bocconi University (Milan, Italy). She is Professor of Organization, HRM and Leadership at SDA Bocconi, the Business School of Bocconi University. She conducts research on careers, talent, and HR management, with an interest in the intersection of individual and organizational perspectives.

Martina Gianecchini (PhD). Associate Professor of Human Resource Management at the University of Padova (Italy). She is Director of the Executive Master's in Human Resource Management at CUOA Business School (Altavilla Vicentina, Italy). Her main research interests are career management and labor market dynamics.

JAPAN

Azusa Ebisuya (PhD). Associate Professor at the Faculty of Business Administration, Hosei University, Japan. She teaches organizational management, global business, and international human resource management. Her research endeavors are focused on international virtual-team management, emotional intelligence, and cross-cultural communication.

Gayan Prasad Hettiarachchi (PhD). Visiting Research Fellow at the Graduate School of Engineering Science, Osaka University, Japan. He is also the Head of Research at OpenDNA Inc., Japan. His research interests are focused on advanced analytics and decision sciences for guiding basic R&D, enterprise resource planning, and corporate strategy.

Tomoki Sekiguchi (PhD). Professor at the Graduate School of Management, Kyoto University, Japan. He received his doctoral degree from the University of Washington, United States. His research interests include employee behaviors, person-environment fit, hiring decision-making, cross-cultural organizational behavior, and international human resource management.

LITHUANIA

Raimonda Alonderienė (PhD). Professor at ISM University of Management and Economics, Lithuania, and Director of People and Organizational Development at Devbridge, Cognizant Softvision company. She is a lecturer and supervisor in the Master of Management program and a supervisor in Innovation Management and International Marketing and Management Master of Science programs. Her research interests include HRM, lifelong learning, self-directed learning, learning communities, generational differences in organizations, leadership, and project management.

Ilona Bučiūnienė (PhD). Professor and the Dean of the Doctoral School at ISM University of Management and Economics, Lithuania. She teaches Social Research Methodology and is a supervisor in the Doctoral Program in Management and in Innovation Management and Global Leadership Master of Science programs. Her research areas are sustainable HRM and employee well-being, diversity management, and HRM in the context of emerging technologies.

Lilija Vilkancienė (MPhil). Senior Lecturer at ISM University of Management and Economics, Lithuania. She teaches Academic Writing and Presentation Skills courses for Management and Marketing, Economics and Politics, and Finance program students at bachelor level. Her research interests include content and language integrated learning (CLIL) methodology, and teacher competencies and implementation in both secondary and tertiary education.

MEXICO

Jacobo Ramirez (PhD). Associate Professor in Latin American Business Development at the Department of Management, Society, and Communication (MSC), Copenhagen Business School (CBS). His research focuses on people management in contexts of security risk and on how businesses can help mitigate the impact of climate change.

Laura Zapata-Cantú (PhD). Associate Dean of Academic Affairs and Associate Professor in the Strategy and Management Department in the School of Business at Tecnologico de Monterrey, Mexico. Her research focuses on business strategy, how IT impacts human resource management, transfer of knowledge, and new ways of working.

POLAND

Michael Gaylord (PhD). Visiting Professor at GPMI Research Institute, BA Waterloo, MA University of Warsaw. His research focuses on business, the economy, and sustainability issues.

Peter Odrakiewicz (PhD). Scientific Director at GPMI Research Institute, Graduate Faculty Professor at Gniezno College Milenium, Visiting Professor at EU Erasmus exchanges and Visiting Professor at the University of La Verne.

Radosław Skrobacki (PhD). Adjunct Professor at Gniezno College Milenium and Research Head of the Market Research Department at GSW Milenium.

ROMANIA

Kinga Kerekes (PhD). Associate Professor at the Faculty of Economics and Business Administration, Babeș-Bolyai University, in Cluj-Napoca, Romania. She teaches subjects related to human resource management and project management at both bachelor and master levels. Her research interests cover the study of companies' HRM practices and of labor market trends.

RUSSIA

Anna Di Nardo (MBA, PhD). Associate Professor and Director of Programmes of the Master of Science at Burgundy School of Business in France. She teaches in the areas of organizational behavior and cross-cultural management. Her research is focused on governance, leadership, and ethics.

SAUDI ARABIA

Hadeel Mohammed Alkhalaf (PhD). Assistant Professor at Buraydah Private Colleges, Saudi Arabia. She teaches several modules of HRM at the College of Humanities and Administrative Sciences. Her research focuses primarily on HRM practices in SMEs and the influence of context on people management in general.

SINGAPORE

Audrey Chia (PhD). Associate Professor at the NUS Business School, with a concurrent joint appointment at the Yong Loo Lin School of Medicine, National University of Singapore (NUS), and she also directs NUS Business School's Leadership Development Programme. Her research applies leadership, change, and innovation as theoretical foundations to address health, environmental, and social challenges.

SLOVAKIA

Imre Antalík (PhD). Associate Professor in the Department of Economics and Vice-Dean of the Faculty of Economics and Informatics at J Selye University. His main research area is the competitiveness of SMEs and the factor flows in the border regions.

Zsuzsanna Szeiner (PhD). Assistant Professor and Head of the Department of Economics at J Selye University's Faculty of Economics and Informatics. Her research focuses on identifying and comprehending critical components of employee engagement and retention, as well as the analysis of employment strategies and other human-centered issues of today's organizations.

SOUTH KOREA

Huh-Jung Hahn (PhD). Associate Professor in the Business Administration Department at Winona State University in the United States. She teaches Human Resource Management, Training and Coaching, Organizational Development, and Leadership Development.

Sewon Kim (PhD). Associate Professor of Management at the State University of New York (SUNY) Empire State College, where he teaches various organizational behavior/human resources courses. His research interests center around coaching, strategic talent management, organizational effectiveness, and global management and leadership.

Joonghak Lee (PhD). Assistant Professor in the College of Business at Gachon University, South Korea. His research interests are in people analytics, international human resource management, and diversity and inclusion.

SWITZERLAND

Nikolett Nagy (MSc). Associate Director Talent Scouting at Novartis in Switzerland and a graduating student of MAS Human Capital Management at ZHAW, School of Management and Law, in Switzerland.

Nicoline Scheidegger (PhD). Researcher at the School of Management and Law of the Zurich University of Applied Sciences in Switzerland. She is a lecturer for Leadership and Strategy in the Bachelor and Consecutive Master's Program and Head of the Leadership Program in the Postgraduate Master's Program.

Jennifer L. Sparr (PhD). Senior Researcher and Lecturer at the Center for Leadership in the Future of Work, University of Zurich, Switzerland. Her research and teaching are focused on paradox and leadership, organizational change, and innovation.

THAILAND

Chaturong Napathorn (PhD). Associate Professor at Thammasat Business School, Thammasat University in Thailand. His research interests include strategic human resource management, international human resource management, and employee relations.

UNITED ARAB EMIRATES

Scott L. Martin (PhD). Associate Professor in the Department of Management at Zayed University, Abu Dhabi, UAE. His research focuses on how employees can be more proactive in identifying problems and opportunities at work.

UNITED STATES

Wendy J. Casper (PhD). Peggy E. Swanson Endowed Chair and Distinguished University Professor of Management at the University of Texas at Arlington. She also serves as Associate Dean for Research for the College of Business. Wendy studies the work-nonwork interface, DEI, and employee well-being.

Shelia A. Hyde (PhD). Assistant Professor of Management at Texas Woman's University. She teaches Human Resource Management courses in the undergraduate business and MBA programs. Her research interests include work and nonwork role issues such as balance and enrichment, remote work, neurodiversity, and gender issues at work.

Marla L. White is a PhD candidate at the University of Texas at Arlington. In Fall 2023, she will join the Pamplin College of Business at Virginia Tech as an Assistant Professor. Her research interests include leadership, intersectionality, discrimination, and diversity management.

Foreword

The Global HRM Series has for over two decades been leading the way in advancing our understanding of global human resource management. Edited and authored by leading, high-profile researchers in the field of human resource management (HRM), this series of books offers students and reflective practitioners accessible, coordinated, and comprehensive textbooks on global HRM. Individually and collectively, these books cover the core areas of the field, providing an invaluable resource for scholars in HRM globally. Taking an expert look at an increasingly important area of global business, this well-established series has become the benchmark for serious textbooks on global HRM.

The series is organized into two distinct strands: The first reflects key issues in managing global HRM, including HRM in multinational enterprises (MNEs), global leadership, global compensation, global talent management, global careers, managing human resources in cross-border alliances, managing global legal systems, the structure of a global HR function, and global labor relations. The second strand of the series provides a comparative perspective on HRM, such as managing human resources in various regions across the globe as well as an institutional perspective on HRM. Forthcoming volumes engage with key contemporary issues such as equity, diversity, and inclusion in the global context and the use of HR analytics globally.

This *Third Edition of Global Human Resource Management Casebook*, edited by Liza Castro Christiansen, Michal Biron, Pawan Budhwar, and Brian Harney, is unique in the global HRM field in that it is a collection of HRM cases that not only span the globe but also span the global HRM issues and global comparative perspectives of the book series. The breadth of countries covered in the *Casebook* is impressive, with cases from 31 countries. These cases are written by a combination of leading international scholars and leading emerging scholars in the field of HRM. The cases provide insight into the management of human resources in developed and emerging economies and in companies ranging from small and medium-sized enterprises to large MNEs. As with all the books in the series, the cases utilize the most recent and classic research and are grounded in what companies around the world are doing today.

This *Third Edition of the Global Human Resource Management Casebook* has been revised in important ways. Several cases have been updated and refreshed. The edition also includes several new cases broadening the scope of countries covered. The teaching aids have been further developed to assist faculty in utilizing the cases in classroom settings. These teaching resources are available online for qualified instructors.

As well as the *Third Edition of the Global Human Resource Management Casebook*, several other books in the Global HRM Series adopt a comparative approach to understanding HRM.

The comparative HRM textbooks describe HRM topics found at the country level in selected countries, particularly within regions, such as the Middle East, Europe, Central and Eastern Europe, Africa, North America, and Latin America. Thus, the comparative textbooks in the Global HRM Series can be used quite effectively in conjunction with the *Third Edition of the Global Human Resource Management Casebook*.

We are proud of the diversity of authors from all around the world who have worked to produce the numerous books included in the Global HRM Series. The scholarly perspectives and the practical company examples cited in these books are exceptionally diverse. Many Global HRM authors are pioneers in their areas of expertise and all are deeply knowledgeable about the topics they address. We are very grateful to all these authors and appreciate their efforts on behalf of the Routledge Global HRM Series.

The publisher and editors also have played major roles in making this series possible. Routledge has provided its global production, marketing, and reputation to make this series accessible to faculty, students, and practitioners throughout the world. In addition, Routledge has provided its own highly qualified professionals to make this series a reality. In particular, we express our deep appreciation for the work of our Series Editor, Alexandra McGregor. Her encouragement, expertise, and support have been invaluable to us as editors of the Global HRM Series as well as to authors of specific books. For everything Alex and her predecessors at Routledge have done, we thank them all. We also acknowledge the insights of reviewers who assist with evaluating the proposals for volumes and provide suggestions for improvement. Together we are all very excited about the Routledge Global HRM Series and hope you find an opportunity to use the *Third Edition of the Global Human Resource Management Casebook,* as well as all the other Global HRM books.

David G. Collings, Trinity College Dublin, Ireland
Elaine Farndale, Penn State University, United States
Fang Lee Cooke, Monash University, Australia
August 2023

Preface

The last edition of the *Global HRM Casebook* was published in 2017. Since then, the COVID-19 pandemic has massively changed the world, having serious implications for the Human Resource Management (HRM) function globally. The Third Edition of this Casebook is intended to highlight the evolving work practices and processes, and the diversity of emphasis of HRM and practices being developed to manage human resources in different national and international contexts across industry sectors. It offers useful insights and learning about HRM policies and practices from case studies of real organizations operating in varied circumstances. Acknowledging the context-specific nature of HRM, this book highlights the prevalence of a variety of HRM practices in diverse national and international settings along with the unique combination of factors and variables contributing to the practice of same. Some of the case studies build on the earlier version published in the last edition of the book and reveal longitudinally how things have evolved in those companies over the last 7–8 years. The Casebook then offers rich material based on up-to-date research evidence and emerging trends in the field of HRM, which should be useful to support teaching of International HRM as a specific field of study. Additionally, the diverse variety of topics covered in the cases in this volume should be appealing to students pursuing related courses.

An overview of the cases covered in this volume reveals a combination of similarity across a range of challenges experienced by the HRM function in the case organizations as well as unique issues. For example, there is core HRM focus on attracting talent (see cases from Canada, Denmark, Japan, and Lithuania), HRM response to COVID-19 (e.g., in cases from Chile, India, Switzerland, and the UAE), the role of HRM in dealing with culture and values (see cases from Chile, Mexico, South Korea, and Switzerland), diversity and inclusion (in cases from Botswana, Finland, India, Singapore, Thailand, and the USA), developing relevant HRM systems (e.g., evident in cases from Germany, Italy, Saudi Arabia, and the UAE), pursuing international HRM (see cases from Mexico and Slovakia), influence of institutional context on HRM policies and practices (in cases from Cyprus, Germany, Russia, Saudi Arabia, and Slovakia), HRM in MNCs (in cases from Finland, Hungary and Mexico), rewards (see cases from Israel and Poland), skills and talent development (e.g., in cases from Austria, Denmark, France and Slovakia), approaches to HRM in small and family businesses (see cases from Greece, Israel, Japan and Singapore), HRM and sustainability/CSR (in cases from Columbia and Italy), and work life balance and turnover challenges in modern day organizations (see cases from Japan and South Korea, and Columbia and Romania, respectively). These bode well with the recent writings in the field and the linkages of the highlighted topics with both individual and organizational performance.

TABLE 0.1 Cases and topics

	Country	Case	Industry	Topics
1	Australia	Australian Universities	Education	• Casual Workers • COVID-19 Response • Institutional Context • Locality/Region • Sustainability/CSR
2	Austria	McDonalds	Hospitality	• Career Progression • Culture and Values • Employer Branding • International HRM • Institutional Context • MNC • Skills/Talent Development
3	Botswana	University of Botswana	Education	• Attracting Talent • Diversity and Inclusion • Institutional Context
4	Canada	La Vie en Rose	Retail	• Attracting Talent • International HRM • MNC • Productivity
5	Chile	SKY Airlines	Transport	• COVID-19 Response • Culture and Values • HRM System
6	Columbia	Valor Insurance Company	Financial Services	• HRM System • Sustainability/CSR • Turnover
7	Cyprus	Zenon University	Education	• Career Progression • Culture and Values • Diversity and Inclusion • Institutional Context • Skills/Talent Development
8	Denmark	Grundfos	Manufacturing	• Attracting Talent • Digital Transformation • Skills/Talent Development
9	Finland	Petrocom	Consulting; Energy	• Diversity and Inclusion • Employee Experience • International HRM • MNC
10	France	NEWMOTOR	Transport	• Digital Transformation • MNC • Skills/Talent Development
11	Germany	Alliance of Opportunities	Cross-industry	• Digital Transformation • HRM System • Institutional Context • Skills/Talent Development

(Continued)

TABLE 0.1 Continued

	Country	Case	Industry	Topics
12	Greece	GrandTechExpert	IT	• HRM System • Small/Family/Growing Firm
13	Hungary	The Tungsram Group (GE Lighting)	Manufacturing	• International HRM • Institutional Context • MNC
14	Iceland	Marel	Manufacturing	• HRM System • Merger & Acquisition • MNC
15	India	ICICI Bank	Financial Services	• COVID-19 Response • Diversity and Inclusion
16	Israel	FoodCo	Manufacturing	• Culture and Values • Job Design • Productivity • Rewards
17	Italy	Romano Lana	Manufacturing	• Culture and Values • HRM System • Small/Family/Growing Firm • Sustainability/CSR
18	Japan	Pasona Group Inc.	Consulting	• Attracting Talent • COVID-19 Response • Culture and Values • Employee Experience • Locality/Region • Work Life Balance
19	Lithuania	Devbridge	IT	• Attracting Talent • Employer Branding • Small/Family/Growing Firm
20	Mexico	Global Care	Healthcare	• Culture and Values • HRM System • International HRM • MNC
21	Poland	XYZ	Hospitality; Retail	• Employee Experience • HRM System • Rewards • Small/Family/Growing Firm
22	Romania	Fomco Group	Energy; Manufacturing; Transport	• Culture and Values • Institutional Context • Locality/Region • Small/Family/Growing Firm • Turnover

(Continued)

TABLE 0.1 Continued

	Country	Case	Industry	Topics
23	Russia	Okskaya Shipyard	Manufacturing	• Attracting Talent • Casual Workers • Culture and Values • International HRM • Institutional Context • Productivity
24	Saudi Arabia	Al-Habib Medical Group	Healthcare	• Culture and Values • Digital Transformation • HRM System • Institutional Context
25	Singapore	On Cheong Jewelry	Manufacturing	• Diversity and Inclusion • Skills/Talent Development • Small/Family/Growing Firm • Sustainability/CSR
26	Slovakia	Hälg Textil AG	Manufacturing	• Culture and Values • International HRM • Institutional Context • Productivity
27	South Korea	Company A	Cross-industry	• Attracting Talent • Culture and Values • Employee Experience • Productivity • Skills/Talent Development
28	Switzerland	Novartis	Pharma	• COVID-19 Response • Culture and Values • Institutional Context • Remote working • Skills/Talent Development • Work Life Balance
29	Thailand	Somen	Manufacturing	• Diversity and Inclusion • HRM System • Institutional Context
30	UAE	United Bank	Financial Services	• COVID-19 Response • Culture and Values • HRM System • Skills/Talent Development
31	USA	MSW Technology	Manufacturing	• Diversity and Inclusion • Employee Experience • Institutional Context

Our overall analysis of the case studies also reveals national differences evident in the covered set of 31 cases from around the world, providing a good comparative picture of the scene. A combination of international factors (e.g., the COVID-19 pandemic), national factors (such as institutional and cultural) and variables (such as international experience of the case companies, competition, exposure to risk, etc.) are influencing HRM systems of the case companies differently. In this Third Edition of the Casebook, the editors encouraged the case authors to include such information in addition to case questions and teaching notes. This edition includes a range of new country cases, as well as cases from the first edition, which have been updated.

A variety of industry sectors (such as manufacturing, education, financial services, transport, amongst others) are covered in the case studies. Expectedly, a range of key actors/stakeholders (such as employees, employers, managers, government, society, unions, and customers) are highlighted to play a key role linked to HRM in the case companies. The growing strategic nature of the HRM function and, in particular, during the COVID-19 pandemic to deal with multiple competing stakeholders' interests comes across clearly from some of the case studies. This is in line with the emerging research evidence and proposals from professional bodies, such as the Chartered Institute of Personal Development in the UK and Society for HRM in the USA. Several emerging themes salient to the post-pandemic era are also emerging from a few case studies. These include an increased emphasis on casual work, remote working, employee experience, aspects of job design, and career progression. Some highlight the key role played by the HRM function in dealing with the challenges thrown by the COVID-19 pandemic and emerging patterns of work processes. We hope that the cases presented in the volume contribute to a global understanding of the HRM profession and its potential to make a significant positive difference in organizations in the global context.

Acknowledgments

This edition of the *Global HRM Casebook*, like the two earlier editions of the *Casebook*, was initiated by and accomplished through a novel collaboration among members of the Human Resources Division of the Academy of Management: the HR Division Ambassadors Program. The Ambassadors Program was established in 2008, with the aim of achieving three main goals. First, to involve the worldwide membership of the HR Division through contributions by representative scholars (the Ambassadors) from each country in which the Division has members. Second, to promote the activities of the HR Division and the AOM more broadly to its international membership. Third, to make practical contributions to the field of HRM through collaborative research projects.

This *Casebook* is the result of the first such project. Other projects produced over the years include, for example, Professional Development Workshops at the AOM's Annual Meeting, the HR Division International Conference (HRIC; Beijing, China, 2014; Sydney, Australia, 2016; Dublin, Ireland, 2019; Sun City, South Africa 2023), and a Special Issue in The *International Journal of Human Resource Management* ("A Global Perspective on Diversity and Inclusion in Work Organizations").

The Ambassadors Program was the brainchild of John Hollenbeck (Michigan State University), Past Chair of the HR Division. The program falls under the remit of the Division's International Committee, which was then chaired by Steve Werner (University of Houston) who facilitated the implementation of the program. The editors of the third edition of this book, Liza Castro Christiansen, Michal Biron, Pawan Budhwar, and Brian Harney, have served the HR Division in different capacities. However, the editors reserve real acknowledgment for the contributors to the *Casebook*, without whom this innovative project would not have been completed.

PART I

Western Europe

CHAPTER 1

Austria

Talent Development at McDonald's Austria: A Compromise between Local Demands and Global Standards

Wolfgang Mayrhofer, Katharina Pernkopf, and Astrid Reichel

CASE SYNOPSIS

We follow the successful establishment of a private center for apprentice training in Austria and its discontinuation after four years. We show how influential actors in a subsidiary of a large transnational organization used the interplay between strong global standards for talent development and local demands for a highly regulated vocational training system in the context of a competitive labor market to establish a private vocational training center. The case also discusses how this very need – to balance global standards and local demands – later resulted in the discontinuation of the training center.

LEARNING OUTCOMES

1. Gain insights into the challenges of attracting and developing talent for manual jobs.
2. Understand corporate and HRM strategy.
3. Understand the relevance of global HRM standards and local demands for globally operating companies.

DOI: 10.4324/9781003307099-2

4. Understand how to balance global standards and local responsiveness.
5. Understand how single actors can make a difference even in a tightly regulated context.

KEYWORDS

Transnational organization, global standards, local demands, vocational training, franchise, Austria

> We are committed to leveraging our scale to provide training and education programs to build a path forward for people that supports their goals, no matter where they are in their lives.
>
> (McDonald's Corporate, 2021a)

McDonald's is the world's market leader in system gastronomy. It takes advantage of being a transnational organization by combining global and local elements across the countries in which it operates. The company has successfully positioned itself as the biggest system-caterer on the planet by aligning it with the zeitgeist. With respect to HRM, McDonald's uses its international network of specialists to discuss problems, enable mutual learning, and find globally informed but locally adjusted solutions. According to its mission statement, McDonald's invests in talents, creates career paths starting from the grill, and sets up internal training centers accordingly. Global standards set by the global headquarters in Chicago guide these activities, which creates inevitable tensions with local demands such as legal rules and cultural values. McDonald's is set up as a franchise organization with national subsidiaries acting as service centers for the hand-picked franchisees in the respective country.

ORGANIZATIONAL SETTING

McDonald's Cooperation

McDonald's operates in nearly 39,200 locations around the globe, serving almost 70 million customers in 119 countries a day. About 93% of restaurants are franchised to independent local owners under contractual arrangements with the company, which employs two million people worldwide (Annualreports.com, 2020).

According to Forbes, McDonald's ranks tenth on the world's most valuable brands list (Swant, 2019). Very standardized delivery of products and related services that are continuously optimized, combined with professionalization through advanced training, are crucial for the ongoing McDonald's success story. Since the days when McDonald's used to be the uncontested number one family restaurant in the USA, a number of legal cases and social and food movements in the last decades have fostered the perception of McDonald's as a place to buy low-cost food and as a low-end employer (see also a video at www.youtube.com/watch?v=f-pvvkfvFkI).

McDonald's constantly strives to change this image, with an emphasis on serving quality products and being a good, people-development-focused employer (*Business Insider*, 2015).

McDonald's Austria

McDonald's was the first fast-food chain to enter Austria in 1977. The first restaurant was opened in the city center of Vienna and kicked off a cultural revolution in the land of *Wiener Schnitzel*. First skeptically viewed by locals and critically commented on by the media as an unnecessary competitor to Vienna's well-known sausage stands ("*Würstelstand*") that served the still beloved Austrian version of fast food, McDonald's – with its unfamiliar business model of the franchise system – was fast in positioning itself as a good quality fast-food provider adhering to Austria's high food quality standards. McDonald's Austria (termed "*Mäci*" or "*Schachtelwirt*" ("box pub") by the locals) achieved a market share of 72% in the system-catering industry in 2020, showing the highest concentration of McDonald's restaurants per inhabitant in Europe (Karner, 2020). McDonald's in Austria is also a major employer. Forty-three Austrian franchisees run 95% of the 199 restaurants, which together employ over 9,600 people from 92 nations (McDonald's Austria, 2021).

BACKGROUND TO THE CASE

Basic Country Information

Austria is a well-developed country in the heart of Europe. In 2019, it had a GDP of approximately 397.5 billion euros (Wirtschaftskammer Österreich, 2021), ranking under the top 30 of the world and fifth in the European Union (Statistics Austria, 2021a). Its economy consists of a large service sector, a sound industrial sector with "hidden champions" prominent on the world market such as Doppelmayr (ropeway engineering), Frequentis (control center solutions), or Jungbunzlauer (biotech), and a small, but highly developed agricultural sector (1.2% of GDP). Austria is a welfare state, ranking fourth among OECD countries for social spending per capita (OECD, 2021). Austria's population amounts to 8,932,664 (Statistics Austria, 2021b). About 1.8 million people are located in Austria's capital, Vienna, which ranked as the most livable city worldwide for ten years in a row (Mercer, 2019).

Austrian Employment Legislation, Employee Relations, and Labor Market Dynamics

Generally, harmony is a highly valued principle in Austria. Austrians are committed to promoting corporate success while paying attention to people's welfare. Reaching a compromise is important in political decision-making, reflected most prominently in the system of Social Partnership, a voluntary system of negotiations between parties representing opposite interests, e.g., trade unions and employer's associations. Establishing and maintaining fair and protective working conditions is central in the extensive legal regulations for dependent labor and the primary task of Social Partnership between employer and employee associations (OEGB, 2021), a system that locally and globally operating organizations like McDonald's cannot ignore. The

Austrian labor market is characterized by low unemployment rates and large numbers of non-Austrian citizens (17.1%) and people born outside of Austria (20%) (Statistics Austria, 2021b). These numbers, far beyond comparable figures for classic immigration countries such as the USA (10.6%; OECD, 2021), are due to Austria's long tradition of hosting migrants and refugees from nearby countries (Turkey, former Yugoslavia, Slovakia, Czech Republic, Germany) plus the 2015 influx of refugees from the Middle East (Statistics Austria, 2021b). Immigrants have always been an important group for McDonald's, which not only integrated them into the labor market but also promoted them to leadership roles (Eurofond, 2009).

The Apprenticeship System in Austria

After compulsory education (nine years), Austrian students can enter apprenticeship training which takes place at two different sites: At the company and at the part-time vocational school ("*Berufsschule*"). Thus, it is referred to as a "dual vocational training system". On-the-job training constitutes the major part of an apprenticeship, and – because apprentices are company employees – the company provides them with full social insurance as required by law. Apprentices may only be trained in legally recognized apprenticeship trades, e.g., catering specialist, chef, system catering, or restaurant specialist in the food industry. Companies that train apprentices are obliged to provide them with the skills and knowledge specified in the occupational profile to comply with the country's standards. Part-time vocational schools aim to provide theoretical basics related to the respective occupation, to complement on-the-job training, and to deepen apprentices' general knowledge.

Currently, about 40% of all Austrian teenagers enter the apprenticeship system upon completion of their compulsory education. After finishing their apprenticeship (usually after three years), about 40% of these young people, now known as "journeymen" ("*Gesellen*"), continue to work for the company where they had been trained.

Apprenticeship training has lost some of its attractiveness due to a general trend toward tertiary education, the lack of flexibility in educational pathways, low-income levels, and the concentration of apprentices in only a few occupations. Many companies are therefore confronted with difficulties finding talented, vocationally trained people. At the same time, Austrian companies show decreasing interest in providing training opportunities. Reform measures have already been taken in collaboration with all parties, including financial support for companies that train apprentices, removal of bureaucratic impediments, and more information about less popular and non-gender-specific occupations (Austrian Press Agency OTS, 2019). Vocational training in Austria – like the majority of all schools and universities – is publicly funded and organized. Currently, eight private vocational schools exist in Austria (Wirth, 2017).

MCDONALD'S AS A TRANSNATIONAL COMPANY

Handling Global Standards and Local Demands

McDonald's has had an impact on Austria and its food service industry, but Austria has also had some influence on McDonald's on a global scale. Andreas Hacker, former managing director of McDonald's Austria, was crucially involved in the process of introducing the concept of McCafé into the chain. Moreover, he was the first non-American on the Board of Directors at the US American headquarters. Several years ago, Austria also managed to soften the strict rules of the company and added beer to its menu, as the absence of beer had been identified as one reason why especially male customers avoided the fast-food chain (Hell & Martinek, 2012). These examples hint toward McDonald's transnational strategy. The product or the brand is very much interrelated with the labor process, and McDonald's allows competent country HR managers to act in locally responsive ways as long as global standards such as product quality are ensured.

As outlined above, McDonald's is an important employer for the country. Criticism directed toward working conditions was successfully fended off by introducing the first collective wage agreement in 2011, which is regularly adjusted. The apprenticeship salary exceeds the common rate in Austria and is considerably higher than in other similar programs. In light of its success in the country and its investments in training, McDonald's is seen as a stable company that provides transparent and accessible career opportunities. Indeed, the company received the "Investors in People" award, an international accreditation awarded by the Austrian Federation of Industry, the Federal Ministry of Economics and Labor, and the European Social Fund. McDonald's Austria constantly develops its (employer) brand and accordingly updates its website at www.mcdonalds.at/, social media, and in-store communication, not only with information on products but also on McDonald's as an employer.

Talent Development between Global Standards and Local Demands

Referring to the words of Hamburger University founder Ray Kroc, the company purposefully invests in people: "If we are going to go anywhere, we've got to have talent. And, I'm going to put my money in talent" (Steward, 2021: 329). In 1961, McDonald's first major internal training center was established, the Hamburger University in Illinois, USA. Training at Hamburger University covers topics in restaurant operations procedures, service, quality, and cleanliness. It has turned into the company's global center of excellence. McDonald's operations' training and leadership development has spread out from there. So far nine international campuses around the globe have opened their doors (McDonald's Corporate, 2021b). These centers have the purpose of training people working for McDonald's. As a rule, they do not serve the public interest by educating system-catering experts. However, credits can be transferred to other bachelor study programs. As of 2015, Hamburger University has had more than 275,000 graduates (Walters, 2015).

Austria sends the more advanced talents to the Hamburger University campus in Munich. Basic talent development has always taken place locally. McDonald's commitment to employee development translates into vertical and horizontal career opportunities in the restaurants and the service center (the Austrian subsidiary's central office). Ambitious employees can work their way up even if they are unskilled workers or come from different jobs. This very inclusive approach adds, however, to high staff fluctuation rates in McDonald's restaurants. The service center wants to encourage apprenticeships to increase the workforce's skill levels, to provide well-structured opportunities for (young) people's education, and to increase employees' commitment.

Setting Up and Closing a Private Vocational School in Austria

Vocational training in system catering is seen as an education for the restaurant managers of the future. During most of this three-year program, apprentices spend time on company-related training in the restaurant they work for. Since the franchisees are not obliged to train the apprentices, the cooperation of franchisees is needed for (increasing) the share of certified system caterers among McDonald's Austria employees. In Austria, vocational training is organized as a dual system, and so apprentices have to leave the restaurant for some periods of the year and go to a vocational school ("*Berufsschule*") where they are assigned to learn together with cooks, waiters, and people from other trades. Around 2,000 beneficial aspects of a more tailor-made program for McDonald's' apprentices were discussed, and the idea of a private vocational school was born during a meeting in a typical Austrian wine tavern ("*Heuriger*"). Driven by a local HR manager and a board member, the Austrian service center of McDonald's wanted to provide more education than strictly necessary, for example, language courses and further training in culture and ethics. Yet, it took McDonald's Austria several years to finally open this so-called "Academy for System Catering" in February 2014.

The Academy for System Catering was framed as an "elite training center" by limiting the maximum number of apprentices per year to 50. A strong identification with the products was indispensable for establishing a meaningful win-win situation between employer and employee. The school was financed by the franchisees, who trained the apprentices practically in the restaurants and sent them to the Academy for System Catering. For some years, the model worked as intended. Each year, enough students (30–50) were sent to the school to cover the costs for teachers, rooms, teaching material, and administration. After a few years, however, numbers started to decline. All students who started with the Academy could properly finish their education, but in 2018, the Academy was shut down. Apprenticeship training again returned to the standard model in Austria – doing practical training at their workplace and attending a public vocational school together with apprentices from other employers. Given the overall good quality of public education in Austria, McDonald's Austria still strongly believes in vocational training as an ideal preparation for a restaurant management career. Employer branding activities advertise careers with vocational training ("*Karriere mit Lehre*") to create a pool of trained system caterers for restaurant management. For building McDonald's-specific skills, the training in the restaurants, countrywide courses, and apprentice events complement the training of the public vocational training schools.

How Talent Development between Global Standards and Local Demands Had an Impact on the History of a Private Vocational Training School in Austria

McDonald's is organized as a transnational corporation. The company's headquarters is located in the USA, and subsidiaries are spread over 100 countries, with thousands of franchisees operating the restaurants. McDonald's pursues an active HRM strategy (Rosenzweig, 2006) that governs the relationship between the headquarters and the service centers in the host countries. There are global standards primarily for job design. The processes ensuring the reliable and predictable quality of McDonald's products worldwide are highly regulated (McDonald's Corporate, 2021c). A commitment to talent that is able to produce the quality food and restaurant feeling aimed for and its development is a very strong corporate value. The corporate strategy for attracting and retaining this talent is an inclusive and developmental one that fosters internal careers in which people live the American dream of making their way up from rags to riches through hard work and ambition (McDonald's Corporate, 2021a). When it comes to deriving country strategies from this global strategy, local responsiveness is high at McDonald's. Subsidiaries have the freedom to find ways to recruit, retain, and develop talent that fits the respective country's context.

The Academy for System Catering was a very good example of a local response to a global challenge of finding and retaining talent while using the local opportunities offered within the Austrian vocational training system. McDonald's-specific training aimed to ensure McDonald's quality standards and increase employee commitment. An HR manager who had been given time and resources to focus on apprentices was the main driving force behind the establishment of the Academy for System Catering. He had the support of a board member who also believed that a locally rooted, tailor-made education program would be successful. When setting up the school, the Austrian country management had to meet competing demands. The global headquarters had its concept of developing in-house talent, Austrian politics had its understanding of quality vocational training, and potential apprentices had their individual educational expectations. In addition, franchisees were those to ultimately decide if they would train apprentices and send them to the Academy for System Catering.

The HR manager's personal career path at McDonald's was key for getting enough franchisees on board and training apprentices as well as sending them to the Academy. His path represents an ideal-typical way of a very successful career within the McDonald's family that exploited all the opportunities the company offered him. He went from cooking hamburgers and serving people in a restaurant to managing a restaurant. After changing to the McDonald's service center, he was sent to newly established restaurants to train the people there. This career path provided him with a large network of franchisees and great credibility among them. Thus, when he advertised the Academy for System Catering, franchisees were willing to send their people there. The McDonald's idea of working your way up seemed to have been very helpful for establishing the private vocational school.

However, it also played an important role when it was closed again in 2018. The HR manager who was the face of the Academy left McDonald's in an amicable separation driven by pull, not push, factors. So did the board member who supported the project. The specific position concentrating on apprentices was not filled again, and vocational training became just an additional task for the new HR manager covering many other areas. In this situation, the various career paths of McDonald's constituted a competition for the Academy of System Catering and reduced the interest in sending young people to this private vocational school. Being a certified system-caterer is not a pre-condition for working at McDonald's. People can start as unskilled workers or with different backgrounds, get training in the restaurants, and move up even to the board of directors. It seems that this alternative was a key factor that led franchisees to report that they did not have enough people who wanted to start an apprenticeship and a management career at McDonald's.

CASE STUDY QUESTIONS FOR DISCUSSION

1. In your opinion, why did McDonald's' Austrian service center decide to run a private vocational school?

2. Given what you know about the Austrian cultural and legal environment regarding vocational training,
   (i) What are the benefits of running a private as opposed to a public vocational school?
   (ii) Do the career opportunities McDonald's offers fit with the Austrian country context?
3. Which corporate, which international, and which HRM strategies do McDonald's headquarters follow?
4. What can other subsidiaries around the world and the global headquarters learn from the Austrian case?

REFERENCES

Annualreports.com. 2020. *Annual Report.* McDonald's Cooperation. https://corporate.mcdonalds.com/corpmcd/investors/financial-information.html.

Austrian Press Agency OTS. 2019. *Lehrlings-Reform darf keine Türschildreform werden.* https://www.ots.at/presseaussendung/OTS_20190508_OTS0044/lehrlings-reform-darf-keine-tuerschildreform-werden.

Business Insider. 2015. *Inside McDonald's Hamburger University.* http://www.businessinsider.com/mcdonalds-hamburger-university-2333?IR=T.

Eurofond. 2009. *Denmark: The Occupational Promotion of Migrant Workers.* http://www.eurofound.europa.eu/observatories/eurwork/comparative-information/national-contributions/denmark/denmark-the-occupational-promotion-of-migrant-workers.

Hell, D., & Martinek, T. 2012. McDonald's Aufstieg zum Staatsburger. Trend. http://www.trend.at/wirtschaft/business/mcdonald-s-aufstieg-staatsburger-336632.

Karner, A. 2020. Wir sind nicht der Kiosk ums Eck. Trend. https://www.trend.at/wirtschaft/mcdonald-chef-piza-wir-kiosk-eck-11486421.

McDonald's Austria. 2021. *Das Unternehmen McDonalds in Österreich.* https://www.mcdonalds.at/ueber-uns.

Mcdonald's Corporate. 2021a. *Jobs, Inclusion & Empowerment.* https://corporate.mcdonalds.com/corpmcd/our-purpose-and-impact/jobs-inclusion-and-empowerment.html.

Mcdonald's Corporate. 2021b. *Skills and Education.* https://corporate.mcdonalds.com/corpmcd/our-purpose-and-impact/jobs-inclusion-and-empowerment/skills-and-education.html.

Mcdonald's Corporate. 2021c. *Food Quality & Sourcing.* https://corporate.mcdonalds.com/corpmcd/our-purpose-and-impact.html.

Mercer. 2019. *Vienna Tops Mercer's 21st Quality of Living Ranking.* https://www.mercer.com/newsroom/2019-quality-of-living-survey.html.

OECD. 2021. *Social Spending.* https://doi.org/10.1787/7497563b-en.

OEGB. 2021. *Austrian Trade Union Federation: ÖGB.* https://www.oegb.at/der-oegb/austrian-trade-union-federation.

Rosenzweig, P.M. 2006. The dual logics behind international human resource management: Pressures for global integration and local responsiveness. In G.K. Stahl & I. Bjorkmann (Eds.), *Handbook of Research in International Human Resource Management*: 36–47. Cheltenham: Edward Elgar.

Statistics Austria. 2021a. *National Accounts.* https://www.statistik.at/web_en/statistics/Economy/national_accounts/index.html.

Statistics Austria. 2021b. *Population by Demographic Characteristics.* https://www.statistik.at/web_en/statistics/PeopleSociety/population/population_change_by_demographic_characteristics/population_with_foreign_background/index.html.

Steward, J. 2021. Developing employees and managers. In G. Reese & P. Smith (Eds.), *Strategic Human Resource Management*: 327–360. London: SAGE.

Swant, M. 2019. The World's most valuable brands list. *Forbes.* https://www.forbes.com/the-worlds-most-valuable-brands/#73297f95119c.

Walters, N. 2015. McDonald's Hamburger University can be harder to get into than Harvard and is even cooler than you'd imagine. *Business Insider.* https://www.businessinsider.com/mcdonalds-hamburger-university-2333.

Wirth, T. 2017. Eine private Schule soll alles können. *Die Presse.* https://www.diepresse.com/5323025/eine-private-schule-soll-alles-konnen.

Wirtschaftskammer Österreich. 2021. *WKO Statistik. Wirtschaftslage und Prognose.* https://wko.at/statistik/prognose/bip.pdf.

CHAPTER 2

France

NEWMOTOR: An HR Policy to Develop New Skills at a French Company in the Aeronautics Industry

Thierry Colin, Benoît Grasser, Ewan Oiry, and Fabien Meier

CASE SYNOPSIS

NEWMOTOR[1] is part of a French international group that is one of the leaders in the aeronautics industry. Their plant was created from scratch, in a rural area, with no industrial tradition. Public authorities offer financial support to develop employment in this region.

NEWMOTOR produces very complex composite material parts for "aircraft engines of the future" that consume less fuel, are lighter, and are much quieter. In a very short period, NEWMOTOR had to master an innovative 4.0 industrial process and rapidly increase production volumes to be able to satisfy a full order book. The skills required could not be totally defined a priori because the use of composite materials moved away from the traditional working methods in aeronautics. In addition, the extremely strict quality standards in the aeronautic industry made the challenge even greater. This case presents the human resource management issues raised by such an industrial challenge, especially the building of an HRM system in order to allow the development and transmission of new skills and the recruitment of 200 new employees within a few months.

KEYWORDS

Industry 4.0, aeronautic, competencies, tutoring, recruitment, France

DOI: 10.4324/9781003307099-3

LEARNING OUTCOMES

1. Examine the transfer of production skills of operators from one site to another in an innovative context.
2. Explore massive recruitment when the required skills do not exist in the local labor market.
3. Design an internal skills transfer system through tutoring.
4. Maintain the efficiency of the skills transfer system beyond the launch phase.

THE NATIONAL AND ORGANIZATIONAL CONTEXT, HRM PROBLEMS, AND PROPOSALS TO CONSIDER IN ORDER TO RESOLVE THE HRM PROBLEMS

The French national context is difficult to analyze from an international perspective. Its economic dynamics and labor market present numerous specific features that, from an external point of view, may appear surprising or even paradoxical.

At an international level, the French labor market is often considered highly conflictual and dogged by numerous strikes.

The French national context is quite different from other European countries such as the German and Scandinavian setups, where negotiation between social partners tends to be much more effective. The unionization rate in France is among the lowest in the world (10.3%), and French trade unionism is divided among numerous organizations, none of which really dominates. Faced with weak, divided unions, management generally sees collective bargaining as a constraint, often imposed by law. The high level of conflict should therefore be analyzed as a consequence of the weakness of collective bargaining and not as an indicator of the power of the trade unions. This general observation is even more relevant when it comes to the issue of work organization, in which French trade unions are particularly uninvolved. From an HR point of view, the consequence is that the organization of work, particularly in industry, is considered to be the prerogative of engineers.

At the same time, and this is what may sometimes appear paradoxical, France is also characterized by very high labor productivity, a fact that is less well known. Although this high capacity also has its downsides (such as burnout and occupational disease), it ensures that France is truly competitive internationally in terms of costs, particularly for the production of complex and innovative goods and services.

This very intense labor productivity is made possible, among other things, by a highly skilled workforce capable of piloting the many automated machines (both industrial and service-producing) that enable the development of innovative products and services. Equally paradoxically, this highly skilled workforce means that the more manual professions have been downgraded for years and have had difficulty recruiting the necessary personnel – even fairly skilled staff, such as maintenance technicians.

Among these paradoxes, contradictions, and heterogeneities, the role of local territories should also be emphasized. In fact, beyond the Paris region, which continues to concentrate most of the head offices of large companies, and several large specialized geographical centers – such as aeronautics in Toulouse and innovation in the Rhône-Alpes region – some French territories face severe employment difficulties involving progressive desertion. Once again, the analysis is complex in this case because, among these territories in difficulty, some are historically and structurally sparsely populated while others, on the contrary, are quite densely populated yet have a workforce undermined by the disappearance of old industries and struggling to acquire the skills needed to enter the innovative industries being developed. The territory presented in this case is one of these areas: While historically, the local skills required were in mining and the steel industry, the current demand is for skills to design and build the cars of the future.

NEWMOTOR is a subsidiary of AERO, which is a group operating in the aeronautics, defense, and space sectors. The company specializes in the design and production of engines for civil and military aircraft and spacecraft but also manufactures a range of other technological products, mostly related to aeronautics. With more than 75,000 employees in more than 15 different countries, AERO relies in particular on high technology, its excellent mastery of industrial processes, and highly qualified personnel. Having always given high priority to performance and safety issues, AERO is now facing a huge challenge in terms of respect for the environment; it is implementing numerous innovations aimed at making it possible to fly "low-carbon" aircraft and reduce the carbon footprint of its activities.

To meet this target, NEWMOTOR was created in the mid-2000s. Its mission was to manufacture composite material parts for new-generation aircraft engines. Composite materials are inherently lighter than metal and they also allow the production of parts with more complex shapes and better performance. These two advantages combined make it possible to manufacture new-generation engines, which are more fuel efficient.

This choice was relevant from a technological point of view but raised a very important challenge in terms of HRM, in particular, developing brand-new skills and recruiting a large number of operators. The manufacturing processes used were highly innovative: Everything had to be built in respect of both work organization and the necessary skills. The AERO group could rely on feedback from an initial factory that had started producing the same type of parts in North America. However, when NEWMOTOR was launched, the American experience was recent and the site itself was still learning how to increase the reliability and productivity of its production processes.

In addition, NEWMOTOR faced specific challenges related to its rural location. As part of its support policy for areas experiencing economic difficulties, the French state and local authorities provided substantial public aid for the creation of NEWMOTOR, in return for the creation of nearly 200 jobs.

NEWMOTOR was therefore set up in an environment characterized by low population density, and the available workforce did not reflect any particular industrial tradition, especially in the aeronautical field. Initially created with just over 20 employees, NEWMOTOR started with a very full order book and had to recruit more than 200 new workers over a period of two years, mainly production operators.

NEWMOTOR's HR department was small (one HR director and two assistants) but could count on the support of the HR Director of the AERO group, who was very experienced, especially in competencies development.

NEWMOTOR's HR team, for its part, had to deal with the group's organizational culture, which put a strong focus on engineers and in some ways constituted the historical DNA of AERO. Moreover, the specific context of aeronautics imposes strict requirements in terms of quality and reliability: Human lives are at stake, and there is no question of taking risks with safety! As a result, there is a strong attachment to formalism and process control, and it is not always easy for HR managers to share their concerns for the more subjective human side, whether individual or collective.

The small HR team at NEWMOTOR was therefore faced with four challenges:

1. It had to design a system enabling it to draw on the experience of the American "sister" factory, bearing in mind that the learning curve was incomplete and that the cultures were not identical.
2. It had to devise a recruitment process enabling it to attract, identify, and select nearly 200 new production operators.
3. It then had to devise a system for disseminating the necessary competencies internally and validating them, in line with the strict requirements of process reliability.
4. Last but not least, it had to think about making the various solutions it had found sustainable beyond the launch phase.

FIRST CHALLENGE: DRAW ON THE EXPERIENCE OF THE SISTER FACTORY WITHOUT COPYING IT

Only a few months separated the creation of NEWMOTOR from that of its sister factory in North America. These few months were nevertheless enough to generate valuable lessons, and AERO naturally wanted to make NEWMOTOR benefit from this experience. In addition to this learning effect, a second objective was the search for a convergence between the two sites, in order to rationalize the processes at the group level and better control the quality of the products.

From an HRM point of view, the question was how to organize this transmission of competencies between operators at two sites separated by an ocean.

Several measures were taken in order to achieve it. NEWMOTOR managers regularly visited the sister plant to familiarize themselves with the new products and the target organization. More unusually, the new production operators recruited in the French plant all spent several (up to five) two-week training periods at the American plant. On their return, this core group of production operators trained at the North American plant was then tasked with passing on their competencies to newcomers at the French site.

The two HR departments also decided to regularly compare a set of agreed social management indicators: Absenteeism rate, turnover, qualification level, and progress of the recruitment plan. They also opted to deal in greater depth with targeted issues, such as the monitoring of psychosocial risks and the training plan.

These HR teams also wanted to improve the organization of work at both sites. The AERO group and its two plants were well aware that they were in a phase of exploring new technologies and that what one plant learned could be useful to the other. It was therefore not simply a question of the French factory copying the American factory. On the contrary, it involved ensuring that any good practices identified at either one of the two sites could be identified and transferred to the other site. A project was therefore created combining the HR teams of both sites, with the aim of ensuring convergence and cross-site learning in terms of organization.

However, another parameter to be taken into consideration disrupted this desire for convergence: The French and American operators and managers did not share the same culture and did not operate in the same way. For example, the American operators were very attached to having very precise work instructions to follow and did not tend to question them, even though they were not always convinced of their relevance. Conversely, it appeared that French production operators only agreed to strictly follow work instructions if they were personally convinced of their effectiveness, and they clearly expressed their disagreements when this was not the case. The intention here is not to over-generalize, but in this case, these contrasting trends were indeed observed and confirmed by the managers of both sites. This discrepancy, which was rather unsettling at first, ultimately helped to enrich the overall approach at both sites. The American operators' need for precise work instructions reinforced the French engineers' discourse on the need for formalism and respect for procedures. At the same time, the French operators' need for understanding and involvement allowed the content of the work instructions and their use to evolve, to the benefit of continuous improvement on both sites.

SECOND CHALLENGE: RECRUITING OVER 200 PRODUCTION OPERATORS IN AN UNFAVORABLE CONTEXT

When it was set up, NEWMOTOR had just over 20 employees and an order book that would ensure production for the next five years. It was therefore necessary to recruit intensely (more than 200 workers in less than two years) to ensure the growth of production.

However, given the initial choice of location, the local recruitment pool was essentially made up of jobseekers with no professional experience in aeronautics or in working with composite materials. The objective was therefore to identify candidates likely to be trained quickly in these new professions and to design a program enabling them to acquire the necessary competencies.

Such a large volume of personnel recruitment was a real challenge, all the more so as NEWMOTOR is subject to very high industrial demands: The parts produced have a direct impact on the safety of passengers and flights, which requires compliance with the strictest standards, such as the European quality assurance standard for the aeronautics and space market EN9100. It was therefore essential that future NEWMOTOR employees would be able to meet the very high industrial requirements, even though they were not specialists in the tasks concerned.

In production, recruitment concerns several skilled professionals, such as mechanics, quality controllers, non-destructive testing operators, gluers, and painters. The gluer's job, for example, consists of applying a number of coatings by hand and gluing additional protections that allow the parts to be more resistant, in particular to fire, and to penetrate the air better. The job requires a great deal of dexterity (cutting, fitting, and applying coatings), theoretical knowledge (understanding the specific characteristics of composite materials, etc.), and the ability to strictly follow procedures set out in work instructions.

To meet this challenge, the company implemented actions to broaden and qualify the recruitment base, train candidates, and recruit personnel.

When NEWMOTOR was set up, it implemented a proactive policy of mass recruitment of jobseekers. It established partnerships with the town where it was located, the region, local temporary employment agencies, and the national employment agency (called "Pôle Emploi" in France). NEWMOTOR also worked with technical schools, engineering schools, and professional training organizations. These partnerships aimed to select, train, and recruit jobseekers with very heterogeneous profiles.

A special unit was set up to select jobseekers. Selection was based on an interview and an assessment of manual and reasoning competencies (through a half-day test). At this stage, information was also provided on the training that would be offered and the employment opportunities. At the end of this phase, the successful candidates followed a four-and-a-half-month training course on composite materials, the industrial world, and information technology. The training focused on learning a skill specific to NEWMOTOR (gluing, inspection, three-dimensional control, or machining). During this training, the candidates were able to learn key procedures, processes, and techniques thanks to access to all the industrial equipment present in the factory.

The actual recruitment operations took place at the end of this training program, which meant that not all of the trainees were recruited. NEWMOTOR's HR team carried out a very thorough study of each of the positions to be filled, systematically and very closely involving the operational managers concerned.

The selection process consisted of several stages, from a pre-interview by telephone to a simultaneous interview with the future line manager, including validation of the contractual elements by both parties.

All in all, this system worked very well. Butchers, for example, were integrated into the plant and were able to work in jobs with high industrial demands! More than 200 production operators were ultimately recruited over a period of three years, enabling NEWMOTOR to satisfy its customers, both in terms of quantity and quality.

THIRD CHALLENGE: FACILITATING THE INTERNAL TRANSMISSION OF COMPETENCIES THROUGH A TUTORING SYSTEM

In order to accelerate the transmission of skills and ensure that they had been mastered, NEWMOTOR moved toward an ambitious tutoring program aimed at having newcomers trained by more experienced employees.

Tutoring has deep roots. In France, it dates back to a system called "companionship", which was the dominant method of training craftsmen during the Middle Ages. In this relationship, the apprentice is put in a real work situation, guided by a journeyman, a tradesman who has himself learned to master the various techniques associated with his profession and produced a "masterpiece".

Inspired by this traditional method, NEWMOTOR formalized a specific tutoring system. Each newcomer is allocated a tutor chosen from among the experienced operators. Access to autonomy then takes place through a course in three successive stages (see Figure 2.1):

FIGURE 2.1 Formalized tutoring system

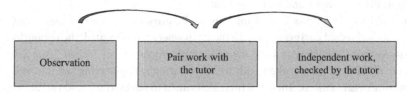

Observation	Pair work with the tutor	Independent work, checked by the tutor

1. The first stage is an observation one where the new employee has to be content with observing the work to be carried out with a trained employee.

2. The second stage involves joint work; the trainer and the trainee work on the same object, at the same time.

3. In the third and final stage, the trainee is alone at the workstation.

The whole process is formalized, including the system itself and the validation of each stage by the quality department. Note that the tutors oversee the entire operations, to make surethat production objectives are met.

Beyond the function of passing on skills, tutoring acts as an integration process for newcomers. Strong links connect tutors and trainees, and the latter thus become part of a working community.

FOURTH CHALLENGE: MAKING THE SYSTEM SUSTAINABLE THROUGH MANAGEMENT TOOLS

All of the measures and systems described above enabled NEWMOTOR to overcome its main HR challenges, i.e., recruiting more than 200 production operators, without a suitable job pool, and training them in new trades in a context of seeking maximum control over the quality and reliability of processes. The orders could be met with the required level of quality. It is therefore a clear success from this point of view.

In the future, recruitment will not be so massive. However, as in any company, there will still be recruitments to replace departures and adapt to possible increases in production. The problem of transferring skills will therefore remain crucial, as new employees will have to be trained to the same high standards.

The HR team that designed the system was small, as we have seen, and its members were destined to pursue their own careers, either within the AERO group or elsewhere. However, control of the skills transfer system was based on the largely tacit expertise of this team. There was therefore a clear risk of losing control of the skills transfer process.

A second risk may arise. A large part of the motivation of the first tutors was based on their impression of being the pioneers of an adventure and of contributing to the development of a technological innovation that is intrinsically very stimulating and symbolically very rewarding. There is indeed a real cause for pride in participating in the progress of aeronautics and in the manufacture of new-generation engines! However, once the launch phase was over, there was a risk that a degree of apathy would set in and that production imperatives would take precedence over the need to pass on skills.

Lastly, it became apparent that the problem of transferring skills was not limited to the start-up phase and did not only concern newcomers. On the one hand, it was necessary to ensure that the skills acquired during the integration and initial training phase remained operational over time, and on the other hand, it had to be taken into account that any operator, even an experienced one, could need periods of upgrading or support to change jobs.

Aware that these three types of problems could compromise the effectiveness of the transmission of skills and therefore the sustainability of industrial excellence, the HR team therefore considered possible solutions.

With regard to the first problem, the HR team decided to formalize the various systems it had designed and implemented as best it could. All of the HR tools, and in particular those relating to tutoring, were therefore written in the form of procedures so that they could be easily passed on to future HR staff. However, by proceeding in this way, they encountered a major difficulty that they had initially underestimated: The tutoring system was not only based on mechanically reproducible standard sequences but also on many subjective assessments and on a large number of informal exchanges between the HR staff, the tutors, the production teams and the workshop managers.

The second problem, that of tutor fatigue and demotivation, was tackled from several complementary angles.

Firstly, in order to avoid excessive contradictions between the rationale of production and the rationale of learning, it was proposed that the first stages of learning should be "protected" by creating "school spaces" based on simulated work situations.

A second line of work consisted in positioning the tutors' roles very clearly in relation to their hierarchy and in relation to the other production operators. This initially involved using symbolic means, such as wearing distinctive T-shirts and badges, or promoting them in internal communication. This was followed by the drafting of a tutoring charter that explicitly recognized and defined the function of a tutor.

The third and final area of work consisted of drawing up a skills reference framework for tutors. This is structured around three blocks of skills: One relates to mastery of technical content, the second to pedagogical mastery (oral and written communication, understanding of others, persuasive skills, etc.), and the last to behavioral skills (self-control, sense of innovation, aptitude for teamwork, etc.).

The last problem identified, i.e., not limiting the effort of transmitting competencies to newcomers and the integration period, also appeared to the members of the HR team as vital for the company. The transmission of skills is no longer done only with clearly identified actors at a given time and in a limited space but can potentially concern all production operators (and their managers) over different periods. It was therefore decided to set up situated training content, based on videos and written instructions, made available to operators at all key posts.

Through the design of all of these tools, the HR department was seeking to ensure that the transmission of skills would be sustainable and to secure the level of mastery. But it also intended to convince the production department managers that industrial excellence is not just a question of technical mastery but that it also depends on a subtle balance between mastery of processes and human dynamics. In this world of engineers focused on measurement and reproducibility, the HR department managers felt that they must continue their efforts to be understood.

CASE STUDY QUESTIONS FOR DISCUSSION

1. Identify the different HR tools mobilized in the management of the staggered launch of the two production sites. In your opinion, what are the operational implications of the tools used? Have cultural differences been sufficiently considered?
2. Analyze the recruitment process designed by NEWMOTOR's HR team. What are its advantages and disadvantages?
3. In your opinion, what are the advantages and disadvantages of using tutoring in the specific case of NEWMOTOR?
4. How could you help NEWMOTOR's HR team convince its top management that it is necessary to maintain efforts in terms of skills transmission from experienced workers to the new recruits?

NOTES

1 This name is being used to preserve the anonymity of the firm.

BIBLIOGRAPHY

D'Iribarne, P. 2009. National cultures and organizations in search of a theory: An interpretative approach. *International Journal of Cross Cultural Management, 9*(3), 309–321.
Rouleau, L., & Balogun, J. 2011. Middle managers, strategic sensemaking, and discursive competence. *Journal of Management Studies, 48*(5), 953–983.
Sandberg, J., & Tsoukas, H. 2020. Sensemaking reconsidered: Towards a broader understanding through phenomenology. *Organization Theory, 1*(1), 1–34.

Supplementary Resources

Resource 1: The leap engine in video (https://www.youtube.com/watch?v=X2G6cQ63Z8c)
Resource 2: A new aerospace composites plant, in Rochester (https://www.youtube.com/watch?v=Nwc8rEdyxzI)
Resource 3: A study on global aviation human resource management (https://www.researchgate.net/publication/235259833_Global_aviation_human_resource_management_contemporary_recruitment_and_selection_and_diversity_and_equal_opportunity_practices)

CHAPTER 3

Germany

Talent Development in Complex and Dynamic Environments: New Approaches in the Context of the German Business System

Marion Festing

CASE SYNOPSIS

This case, on the one hand, provides important information about the German business context and human resource management (HRM) in Germany, while on the other hand, it addresses the important challenges facing companies responding to the structural changes in an increasingly dynamic and complex economic environment, with a specific focus on talent development. While the need to provide appropriate learning opportunities and leverage the human capital of a company prevails in all countries, the German context has led to the emergence of particular solutions, such as an intense discussion about a legal framework on part-time education, particular learning initiatives and platforms initiated by companies such as Bosch or Continental together with other stakeholders, and the emergence of talent-sharing as a talent development tool in the context of interorganizational networks, applied, for example, by Lufthansa.

KEYWORDS

Talent development, talent-sharing, learning, skills, business system, Germany

DOI: 10.4324/9781003307099-4

LEARNING OUTCOMES

1. Learn about the particularities of the German business system and how they influence HRM in Germany.
2. Understand how changes in the business environment (e.g., digitalization) influence the requirements for employees' skills and what this means for talent development.
3. Understand how the particularities of the German business system shape particular solutions for talent development at the state level and in the context of other stakeholders.
4. Understand how the particularities of the German business system shape particular solutions for talent development in the context of interorganizational networks.

COUNTRY BACKGROUND: GERMANY

The Federal Republic of Germany is the largest national economy in the European Union (EU). At the end of 2021, it had 83.2 million inhabitants and a competitive labor market characterized by a strong demand for qualified labor. In November 2021, 45.3 million people were in employment, while the unemployment rate was 3.2% at the same time. Only Poland, the Czech Republic, and the Netherlands had lower unemployment rates in the EU. After the second year of the COVID-19 pandemic, in 2021, growth rates stood at 2.7%, and, mainly due to the increase in energy prices, inflation was 5.3%.

The backbone of the German economy is the small and medium-sized enterprise (SME) sector and the so-called "Mittelstand", including many hidden champions and family businesses, all of which represent more than 90% of German enterprises and over 50% of economic production. The most important sectors in the country's economy include medicine and healthcare, transport and logistics (including, for example, automotive), chemicals and pharmaceuticals, technology and innovation, energy, and financial services. With a gross domestic product (GDP) of 3,563 billion US dollars (2021), Germany is the world's fourth-largest economy.

Germany is home to a steadily growing number of around 420 higher education establishments, including universities, fostering academic excellence. Together with the so-called "dual vocational training system" (explained below), this leads to a relatively high level of education for a large part of society. With respect to gender equality, there are strong initiatives. For example, in 2015 and in 2021, the legal basis for introducing quotas on supervisory and executive boards was established. This was especially important because the percentage of female members on executive boards had decreased during the COVID-19 crisis. However, the (unadjusted) gender pay gap still sits at 19%, and the number of females in top management is low. Consequently, there is a great deal of room for improvement in this regard. At the same time, Germany – especially in cities like Berlin or Cologne – is a place where start-ups, creativity, and entrepreneurship are of major importance.

Like many industrialized countries, Germany is characterized by important demographic changes caused by decreasing birth rates and increasing life expectancy, and it is suggested that in-migration from abroad might slow down the process of demographic aging in the population living in the country. Furthermore, migration and the integration of relatively high numbers of refugees, who settled in the country in 2015, and in the context of the Ukraine war in 2022, will be central socio-political issues for the foreseeable future.

THE HRM ENVIRONMENT IN GERMANY

Human resource management (HRM) in Germany can only be understood in connection with the unique institutional heritage specific to the country and by considering historical developments and the socio-cultural environment. In this context, it is important to highlight three major features of the German business system and their implications for HRM.

First, due to their ownership structure, most German companies have a *long-term orientation* and are not under the same pressure to achieve the short-term business success indicators that are common in many companies whose shares are traded on the stock market (for an overview see Festing, 2012). For an understanding of the long-term dimension in the German HRM model, it is important to know that labor is often interpreted rather as a fixed production factor (acknowledging, despite this wording, the people dimension inherent in labor). This may be the result of the fact that the complex labor law does not allow a "hire and fire" policy, i.e., labor contracts cannot be terminated easily. Therefore, investment in human resources, for example by developing talents in various training programs, is a key success factor in the German economy and is expected to provide a high return on investment.

This notion is in line with the second major feature of the German business system, namely, its *strong developmental orientation*. One such example is the initial dual vocational training arrangement, which combines simultaneous theoretical learning in professional schools with on-the-job learning in firms. Each year, two-thirds of school pupils in Germany are trained within this system, and this vocational qualification is highly accepted in corporations as well as in society. The well-known German "Facharbeiter" (skilled worker) is one result of this system – these are individuals who are well-trained professionals in their field and are seen as one of the backbones of the German economy. Developmental orientation is further displayed in many single HRM practices, such as long-term-oriented training schemes and career planning, or from a long-term perspective in rewards, as depicted in Table 3.1. However, dynamics in the business environment are currently challenging this traditional way of approaching HRM and calling for more agility (for an overview of employee agility, see Salmen & Festing, 2021).

The third key principle of the German economy, which is highly important for HRM, is the social market economy model. Among others, it emphasizes a *cooperative approach between employers and employees* at various levels of the firm, region, industry, and state. Cooperation between management and employees is based on the understanding that consensus and collectivism in employment relations are important in German society. Collective bargaining and co-determination at the regional, industry, company, and plant levels are supported by regulations at the state level, including the principle of non-interference of the state in the bargaining process between employers and employees (Tarifautonomie), the latter of which addresses, for instance, working hours, wage levels, and salaries, as well as the pay mix. The regulation of industrial and employment relations extends to the individual and work contracts level, stipulating the rights

TABLE 3.1 Selected features of the German national business system and HRM issues and practices

Selected HRM-relevant features of the German economy	Selected HRM issues and practices in Germany
Long-termism	Turning labor into a more fixed production factor encourages investment in human capital
Management-employee cooperation Co-determination Collective bargaining	• Works councils have strong information, participation, and decision-making rights with respect to all HRM practices, thus restricting management discretion • Works councils safeguard employment relations, including employment security, by making employee dismissal difficult • The co-determination system ensures communication and the integration of labor issues in strategic planning (via a labor director on the board and works councils) • Collective bargaining ensures a collective orientation • Leads to comparably low wage differentials between various groups of employees
Developmental orientation	Developing and retaining talents is of major importance: Employee development: • Initial dual vocational training system • Other educational schemes Employee retention: • Staff development through training on various jobs • Long-term career planning, with technical competence and functional expertise as core values based on performance appraisals and high investment in training and career development measures, including team effectiveness • Lon-term-oriented rewards, with an emphasis on individual rewards and profit-sharing

Source: Adapted from Festing, (2012: 47).

of the employed. The various levels of management-employee cooperation based on legislation and regulation, promulgated by the German state, are depicted in Table 3.1.

In the past, the institutional environment in Germany was perceived as having a rather negative impact on HRM, due to the perceived rigidity of the encompassing industrial relations system, which was supposed to prevent managers from using innovative HR techniques. However, it is often argued that the constraints imposed by the rigid industrial relations system are offset by important positive effects: Competitive advantages result from this system of employment relations, mainly in the areas of training and associated highly valuable human capital, communication, and employment stability.

There have been several major *challenges to the traditional German institutional context*, including market changes relevant to the reunification of East and West Germany and the completion of the EU's internal market. Nonetheless, neither initiative has led to major changes in the principles of the German institutional environment, including the industrial relations system. On the contrary, this system has proven to have especially positive effects in times of crisis. For example, in the course of the financial crisis in 2008/2009, cooperatively organized short-time working schemes and strong investments in training prevented high unemployment and strengthened the workforce. During the COVID-19 pandemic, short-term work was used even more intensively, with the highest number of companies ever doing so in Germany reaching nearly 345,000 in 2021. This helped those industries that were strongly affected by COVID-19, such as the hospitality industry. In peak times in 2020, more than 60% of employees were supported with short-term work schemes and respective pay in order to prevent unemployment.

This case study will focus on the effects that these pillars of the German business system have on HR development, which is challenged by a more dynamic and complex business environment.

THE HRM DEVELOPMENT CHALLENGE: COPING WITH THE SKILL DEMANDS OF A DYNAMIC AND COMPLEX WORK ENVIRONMENT

In a McKinsey (2021) study, it was predicted that by 2030, around 6.5 million Germans will need to either substantially update their skills or completely change their job, including appropriate training. While some industries may be more concerned than others, this trend applies across industries and companies. Some jobs will disappear and new jobs will be developed, and in some areas there will be a need to solve the challenge of a severe skilled labor shortage. The COVID-19 crisis has accelerated some of these trends by initiating much stronger digitalization in business models that goes beyond online commerce and by requiring respective employee skills (Allianz der Chancen, 2022).

As one of the responses to these needs, in Germany, an "Alliance of Opportunities" has been founded. This is a cross-sector initiative of currently 26 companies and institutions that has set itself the goal of counteracting the effects on employees of structural change in the world of work in the sense of a community of responsibility. The companies involved cover more than 1 million employees in Germany and more than 3 million worldwide. The alliance states that all actors within the labor market need to work together to successfully reach the overall goal of transformation, including the state, chambers of commerce, companies, employer associations, unions, works councils, and, of course, the individual employee (Allianz der Chancen, 2022). As indicated above, this cooperative approach is typical for the German social partnership system, as it is characterized by a strong consensus orientation.

SOLUTIONS: DEVELOPING SKILLS FOR A DYNAMIC AND COMPLEX WORK ENVIRONMENT

The following three ways of coping with skills demands stemming from a dynamic and complex work environment will be described. They include a) discussions about required legal frameworks for part-time education, b) learning initiatives initiated by companies and other stakeholders, and c) talent development on the company level, applying the innovative practice of talent-sharing in interorganizational networks.

PERSPECTIVES ON A LEGAL FRAMEWORK FOR PART-TIME EDUCATION (BILDUNGSTEILZEIT)

Companies need to invest in the continuing education of their employees, especially in these times of enormous structural change. While many of them have already invested in learning platforms and support lifelong learning, there is also a call for the state to create a legal and organizational infrastructure that supports individuals and firms alike in this matter. As a response to structural change, the German Federal Ministry of Labor has suggested a *National Continuing Education Strategy* that should support continuing education. The aim is to ensure the employability of employees in these times of extensive change by offering them a chance to update their knowledge, to learn a completely new profession, and thus to invest in fundamental retraining. While the state can set the framework, many actors have a role in ensuring the functioning of this initiative, i.e., companies, social partners, the Federal Employment Agency, training providers, politicians, chambers of commerce, associations, and the employees themselves: "They all form a community of responsibility, united by a common goal: to create sustainable bridges to new employment opportunities, also from within working life" (Bohle, 2021).

One of the suggestions that emerged in the context of the National Continuing Education Strategy is a part-time education framework, an approach that already exists in one of the countries neighboring Germany, namely, Austria. This would include, for example, that during the training period, the employee would reduce his or her working time to 50% but would receive 80% of his or her usual pay. This additional payment of 30% could be enabled by further contributions made by the employer and the state. These regulations could apply on a voluntary basis for those employees whose current tasks or jobs are threatened by digitization or structural change, and they would be offered the chance to participate in well-defined training sessions that could be rewarded by a certificate granted by the state. For example, an IT system tester whose job is eliminated by automation could work as a software engineer, or a university administrator could become a teacher. The part-time education scheme would have many advantages for employees, the state, and the economy by ensuring the employability of the individual, preventing high unemployment costs, and providing well-trained talent. However, there are also critical voices emphasizing the rigidity of such a system and the possibility that it would be exploited opportunistically.

LEARNING INITIATIVES AND PLATFORMS INITIATED BY COMPANIES TOGETHER WITH OTHER STAKEHOLDERS

One example of a learning initiative initiated on a firm level is the German company Bosch, which has created the initiative the *Bosch Learning Company*. The goal is to make continuing education an integral part of the business strategy. As Volkmar Denner (Chairman, Board of Management, Robert Bosch GmbH) states, "We need to increase and expand our expertise and skills. It is the only way that we will be able to help shape the fundamental change in which we find ourselves and use it for Bosch" (Bosch, 2017a, p. 4).

Bosch offers a variety of educational formats, ranging from classical on-the-job training and in-person training in classrooms through to digital content and self-organized learning. At the same time, the company asks employees to engage themselves in their own development. For example, in order to foster self-organized learning, the initiative "Working out loud" includes a certain number of associates organizing virtual weekly meetings in a defined group over a period of several months. Thus, they exchange and deepen their knowledge on a topic that they have chosen themselves. The number of these learning cycles is growing rapidly. Initiatives like these reveal the dynamics that can emerge from digital learning. According to Bosch, "The crucial factor is 'learning agility', the ability to generate knowledge quickly and efficiently across divisional and national boundaries and then to share it" (Bosch statement, 2017b, translated by the author). This is in line with the academic discussion about learning agility, defining it as the "ability [of an individual] to come up to speed quickly in one's understanding of a situation and move across ideas flexibly in service of learning both within and across experiences" (DeRue et al., 2012, pp. 262–263), thus highlighting speed and agility in learning processes.

Overall, elements for digital learning include community-based learning, virtual classrooms, open online content, gamification, video learning, and the SuccessFactors app, all of which can be found on the company's learning portal. These platforms foster digital transformation, enable time- and location-independent learning, and promote informal and self-directed education (Bosch, 2017a). In summary, the Bosch Learning Company focuses very much on the individual's initiative, responsibility, and peer learning, and strongly supports these processes with an appropriate infrastructure provided by the firm.

Another example is the *Continental Institute of Technology and Transformation* (CITT), founded by the company German Continental. The major goal is to support transformation in the automotive industry. It offers training in the areas of Industry 4.0, new drive concepts, and digitalization. In the first phase, the focus should be on the group of unskilled and semi-skilled workers, in order to provide them with training certified by the Chamber of Commerce. As explained by Chief Human Resources Officer Ariane Reinhart, "In the course of electrification and digitalization, simple jobs are increasingly being replaced by complex tasks that require training" (Haufe, 2019, translation by the author). Since the changes affect the entire industry, she emphasizes that policymakers, social partners, and companies need to pull together. However, she also stresses the self-responsibility of the individual worker for their development and for ensuring their responsibility, pointing out that CITT can only provide a framework with an advisory board that facilitates links between important stakeholders and provides a communication platform.

The transformation of the German economy and the country's associated continuing education strategy are subsidized by the Federal Employment Agency (BA). While the company Continental did not disclose the amount of financial support provided by the government, the overall rules are well documented; for example, for companies with more than 2,500 employees, the Federal Employment Agency pays up to 25% of wages during the training period. Across all industries and federal states, spending on continuing education amounted to around 543 million euros in 2020.

TALENT-SHARING: LEARNING IN INTERORGANIZATIONAL NETWORKS

Talent-sharing is a human resource development practice that has recently been introduced as another way of developing talent as a response to the increasingly dynamic business environment. In addition, it has been identified as an important measure in the German "Alliance of Opportunities" (Allianz der Chancen, 2022), calling for the creation of a better infrastructure to facilitate interorganizational talent exchange (Allianz der Chancen, 2022). Usually, talent-sharing requires a fixed time period of one week to longer durations, the definition of a specific learning and development goal (e.g., related to new technologies, management techniques, or cultures), and a plan for transferring the new knowledge to the home organization. It serves the development purposes of the individual, as well as of the organization, and should foster innovation and renewal as a response to the dynamic work environment. Companies engaging in talent-sharing include some of the largest listed on the German Stock Exchange, e.g., Lufthansa and Daimler.

Success factors for talent-sharing can be found on the organizational level as well as in the talent him- or herself. From an *organizational perspective*, the success of talent-sharing depends on the one hand on the design of the program established by the human resource or talent managers of an organization. They must provide information and procedures to select the right persons for such a program and establish processes that initiate and reward the knowledge-sharing process within/after the talent-sharing period, thus ensuring career progress for the individuals and organizational learning processes. The design of the program includes, for example, a clear definition of learning objectives, respective reviews, establishing forums for talent exchange, and room for implementing newly generated ideas.

Furthermore, line managers play an important role when it comes to the integration of the newly gained insights. Here, their openness to the new measure, as well as their interest in the new knowledge, play an important part. Instead of thinking about unproductive working time, they need to appreciate talent-sharing as a precious way of developing new skills.

According to a study by Salmen and Festing (2022), talents are likely to benefit from talent-sharing if they have an open mindset as well as a specific motivation and respective abilities. Further details on such a talent profile are depicted in Table 3.2.

CASE STUDY QUESTIONS FOR DISCUSSION

1. Characterize the basic features of HRM in Germany in relation to the German business system.

2. Discuss the impact of structural change in the business environment on the employability and skills of the workforce.

3. Describe the advantages and disadvantages of a legal framework for part-time education in Germany.

4. Outline how companies can foster self-organized and peer learning. How does this approach differ from traditional learning approaches? What are the advantages and the disadvantages?

TABLE 3.2 Talents' characteristics facilitating talent-sharing

Characteristics	Specific elements
Motivation	• **Willingness to learn** • **Willingness to contribute to the host organization** • **High intrinsic motivation** • **Highly ambitions to reach talent-sharing goals**
Ability	• **Capacity for reflection** • **Capacity to structure oneself** • **Analytical competencies** • **Existing technical expertise** • **Networking skills (e.g., including making small-talk)** • **High level of comprehension** • **Communication skills**
Open mindset	• **Openness to new topics, people, and curiosity** • **Tolerance toward uncertainty** • **Impartiality** • **Gratitude** • **Respectfulness** • **High self-esteem** • **No exaggerated expectations** • **Initiative**

Source: Salmen and Festing (2002: 19)

5. Outline the principle of talent-sharing. What are the success factors of a talent-sharing program, and what are the potential risks? Please build two groups. One group represents talent managers who are in favor of introducing talent-sharing, while the other represents managers who are critical of talent-sharing. First, develop your arguments for or against talent-sharing. Then, engage in a discussion with the other group, with the goal of reaching an agreement on how a successful talent-sharing program could be implemented. Please present the cornerstones of your agreement at the end of the session.

REFERENCES

Allianz der Chancen. 2022. Initiative für eine neue Arbeitswelt. Retrieved 21 February 2022 from https://allianz-der-chancen.de/

Bohle, B. 2021. Von Arbeit in Arbeit – Die Bildungsteilzeit als eine Antwort auf den Digitalen Strukturwandel. Retrieved 21 February 2022 from https://www.linkedin.com/pulse/von-arbeit-die-bildungsteilzeit-als-eine-antwort-auf-den-birgit-bohle

Bosch. 2017a. Bosch Corporate Learning 2025 Moocathon: Tag 1: Der digitale Wandel verändert die Rolle des Weiterbildens. Retrieved 21 February 2022 from https://media.cogneon.de/index.php/s/d6lCr9f7ML6zBRR

Bosch. 2017b. Denner's View: "Wer nicht lernt, bleibt analog." Retrieved 22 February 2022 from www.bosch.com/de/stories/denners-view-digitales-lernen/

DeRue, D. S., Ashford, S. J., & Myers, C. G. 2012. Learning Agility: In Search of Conceptual Clarity and Theoretical Grounding. *Industrial and Organizational Psychology*, 5(3): 258–279.

Festing, M. 2012. Strategic Human Resource Management in Germany: Evidence of Convergence to the U.S. Model, the European Model, or a Distinctive National Model? *Academy of Management Perspectives*, 26(2): 37–54.

Haufe. 2019. Continental gründet Institut für Weiterbildung. Retrieved 22 February 2022 from https://www.haufe.de/personal/hr-management/continental-gruendet-institut -fuer-weiterbildung_80_493990.html

McKinsey. 2021. Germany 2030: Creative Renewal. Retrieved 22 February 2022 from https:// www.mckinsey.com/featured-insights/europe/germany-2030-creative-renewal

Salmen, K., & Festing, M. 2021. Paving the Way for Progress in Employee Agility Research: A Systematic Literature Review and Framework. *The International Journal of Human Resource Management*, online publication. https://doi.org/10.1080/09585192.2021.1943491

Salmen, K., & Festing, M. 2022. 'Talent Sharing' as a Response to a Dynamic Environment: Implications for Learning and Development. Paper presented at the Academy of Management Meeting, Seattle.

Important statistics have been drawn from:
https://de.statista.com
https://www.destatis.de

Supplementary Resources

Federal Ministry of Labour and Social Affairs, Germany. This English-language version of the official internet site of the ministry provides concise and up-to-date information on labour market policies and programmes as well as labour regulations in Germany. It also contains a number of publications on employment, industrial relations and social security, including short-time work: http://www.bmas.de/EN/Home/home.html (accessed on November 30, 2022).

Insights About the Discussion on the Future of Work and Skills: Post Covid19: https://www .mckinsey.com/industries/public-and-social-sector/our-insights/defining-the-skills -citizens-will-need-in-the-future-world-of-work (accessed on November 30, 2022).

McKinsey. 2021. *Germany 2030: Creative Renewal: Full Report in German*: https://www .mckinsey.com/~/media/mckinsey/locations/europe%20and%20middle%20east/ deutschland/publikationen/2021-06-23%20deutschland%202030%20artikel/mckinsey _report_deutschland_2030_kreative_erneuerung_2021.pdf (accessed on November 30, 2022).

CHAPTER 4

Switzerland

Flexible Work Aligned with Organizational Culture: Choice with Responsibility at Novartis

Nikolett Nagy, Nicoline Scheidegger, and Jennifer L. Sparr

CASE SYNOPSIS

Novartis is a biotechnology and pharmaceutical company based in Basel, Switzerland, with more than 100,000 employees worldwide. The case is about the "Choice with Responsibility" (CwR) work model as part of Novartis' P&O (People and Organization) strategy and culture development program. CwR was launched during the COVID-19 pandemic to leverage best practices from the pandemic's acceleration of remote work to proactively co-create the future of working at Novartis. Thus, it provides a rich case for understanding flexible work as part of a strategic culture change, to illustrate the implications of flexible work for leadership, team-based work, and employee life domains, and to reflect the bright and dark sides of flexible work – within and beyond the pandemic. The case triggers a discussion around the concepts of choice, responsibility, and trust in flexible work.

KEYWORDS

Flexible work, organizational culture development, responsibility, new leadership, Switzerland

DOI: 10.4324/9781003307099-5

INTRODUCTION

Novartis is one of the ten biggest pharma companies worldwide and among the ten biggest companies in Switzerland. The company's headquarters and R&D are based in Switzerland, while production and sales locations can be found all over the world. In the highly competitive global pharma market, Novartis has recognized the core role of its human capital for its competitive advantage. In 2018, well before the COVID-19 pandemic, the company started an extensive culture change program that put a focus on "unleashing the power of people". During the COVID-19 pandemic, Novartis initiated "Choice with Responsibility" (CwR) to leverage best practices from the pandemic's acceleration of remote work to proactively co-create the future of working at Novartis. In this case, we present CwR at Novartis as a rich and timely example of an organization's transition toward more flexible working conditions, and we highlight important implications. Please note that the case study mirrors a snapshot from the end of 2021 when Novartis launched and experimented with new working models within the ongoing pandemic.

NATIONAL AND ORGANIZATIONAL SETTING

About Switzerland

Switzerland is a landlocked, mountainous country in central Europe with a population of 8.7 million inhabitants. In Switzerland, three-quarters of all companies operate in the tertiary sector (i.e., services). Small- and medium-sized enterprises (i.e., companies with less than 250 employees) make up more than 99% of the market-based companies and provide two-thirds of the workplaces in Switzerland. The other almost 33% of employees work in large companies, with only around 19% in companies with more than 1,000 employees, such as Novartis (Swiss Federal Statistical Office, 2021). In 2022, Switzerland was ranked as the most innovative country in the world for the 12th year in a row (WIPO, 2022).

NOVARTIS – A GLOBAL COMPANY WITH SWISS ROOTS

General information about Novartis. Novartis is a biotechnology and pharmaceutical company based in Basel, Switzerland, with sales of USD 48.7 billion (2020) and 106,000 full-time employees worldwide with 11,900 working in Switzerland. Novartis was created in 1996 through a merger of Ciba-Geigy and Sandoz. The company and its predecessor companies trace roots back more than 250 years, with a rich history of developing innovative products, sold in approximately 155 countries around the world. Today, Novartis is a globally active company.

Novartis' culture transformation and People and Organization (P&O) strategy. Novartis used to be a traditional company in many ways. Structures and culture were hierarchical, with decisions made at the top and limited room for employee flexibility and autonomy. In 2018, the newly appointed CEO Vas Narasimhan initiated a process to transform the company's culture. This strategic decision was based on the belief that to fulfill Novartis' purpose of "reimagining medicine to improve and extend people's lives", it is essential to "unleash the power of Novartis' people". For Novartis, this means transforming the company's hierarchical culture to a culture where people can fully apply their talent, creativity, and energy to their work.

The culture transformation journey started with an analysis of the current culture. An employee survey in May 2018 showed that employees enjoy coming to work and are proud of the company, but it also revealed concerns about competitive behaviors and the desire for a more collaborative style of working. Based on the insights about innovative cultures (i.e., the concept of "UNBOSS" by Kolind and Botter, 2012), Novartis started to build a culture around three core values: "Inspired, Curious, Unbossed". The desired culture is described as when "leaders set clear goals, serve their teams, and remove obstacles rather than controlling and micromanaging employees" (Novartis, 2018: 23). In our case, we focus on "Choice with Responsibility" (CwR), which is a key piece of Novartis' journey toward a more flexible working model and an important initiative within the culture transformation.

BACKGROUND ON FLEXIBLE WORK IN SWITZERLAND

Forms of Flexible Work: Definition and Model

Flexible work arrangements are any policies that grant workers greater control and flexibility over when and/or where work is conducted. The three most basic options are flexible place, flexible time, and reduced time. Flexible place refers to where the work is conducted, also referred to as telecommuting (flexplace, work from home, virtual work). Flexible time refers to when the work is conducted and includes flexible hours and compressed workweeks. It generally consists of a set of "core hours" during which employees are expected to be at the workplace but provides decisions latitude regarding the time employees leave and arrive from work. Reduced time includes part-time and seasonal work or job sharing (Baltes et al., 1999).

Flexible work arrangements have emerged in response to societal developments, including technological changes and greater global competition. Information and communication technologies allow work to be performed at any time from almost anywhere. These changes not only affect individuals but also organizations that are challenged to change the way they are organized and work.

In order to estimate the dissemination of mobile and flexible work in companies, the FlexWork phase model was developed by the Swiss WorkSmart Initiative[1] (Weichbrodt, Tanner, Josef, & Schulze, 2014/2015). The model consists of five ascending phases of flexible work in organizations and focuses on the following four dimensions:

- Infrastructure/architecture (e.g., fixed vs. flexible workstations).
- Technology (e.g., stationary desktop computers, mobile devices, or cloud solutions).
- Work model (e.g., working from home only as an exception vs. broad acceptance of mobile-flexible working in the corporate culture).
- Organizational structure (e.g., steep hierarchies vs. shift toward network model).

The model can be used for a quick assessment of workplace flexibility in the organization. Phase 1 describes the traditional work model that is location-based and oriented around fixed working hours. In phase 5, the company is location-independent and virtual (Weichbrodt, Bruggmann, & Folie, 2020; see teaching notes for an overview of the model).

FLEXIBLE WORK IN SWITZERLAND AND THE COVID-19 PANDEMIC

Flexible work development in Switzerland. Until the early 1980s, working hours in Switzerland were regarded as a largely rigid parameter that left no room either for companies or employees to adapt (Thom, Blum, & Zaugg, 2002). Since then, more and more organizations have been introducing flexibility into their employees' working hours. However, mobile work was still not widespread.

Implications of the COVID-19 pandemic on flexible work in Switzerland. When COVID-19 started to spread around the world in early 2020, the global trend of work flexibilization was abruptly and massively accelerated (Kniffin et al., 2021). In Switzerland, employers were required by law to allow their most vulnerable employees to fulfill their work obligations from home as of March 13, 2020. To meet the requirements of social distancing, private and public organizations sent all or part of their workforce to work from home. In Switzerland, the share of employees who work at least partly from home was 54% (Deloitte, 2021).

The pandemic has eased off while we write this case, and we observe now both a much greater demand on the side of employees and a much greater openness toward flexible work on the side of Swiss organizations than before the pandemic. A study by Hänggi et al. (2021) supports this observation by showing that the mentioning of remote working options in job advertisements – previously only a topic in the job interview – has increased considerably.

Against this background, we now present the case of "Choice with Responsibility" at Novartis as an example of a Swiss company that addressed flexible work with strategic intent within the COVID-19 pandemic.

DETAILS OF HRM PROBLEMS/ISSUES CORE TO THE CASE STUDY

Choice with Responsibility at Novartis

"Choice with Responsibility" (CwR) is part of the ongoing cultural transformation process at Novartis and represents its journey toward the future of working. Figure 4.1 shows the timeline of the CwR initiative. CwR was implemented in July 2020, in response to the COVID-19 pandemic. Thus, CwR was part of Novartis's response to an unprecedented crisis, where virtually overnight everybody – whether working in the office, field, lab, or manufacturing plant – had to think differently about how, where, and when to work. However, also independent of the pandemic, CwR is an important part of the cultural transformation toward an "Inspired, Curious, Unbossed" workforce. In that sense, the initiative focused on exploring flexible work in 2021, planning for the evolution of future working models in 2022, and the shift into post-pandemic working models in 2023.

For Novartis, *choice* means that individuals and teams collaboratively redesign how they work, which includes defining flexibility in terms of when and where to work, with the goal to foster outstanding collaboration, impact, performance, and well-being. *Responsibility* means aligning individual preferences with team and manager expectations and preferred ways of working for consistent, impactful collaboration.

FIGURE 4.1 Timeline of "Choice with Responsibility"

CwR timeline

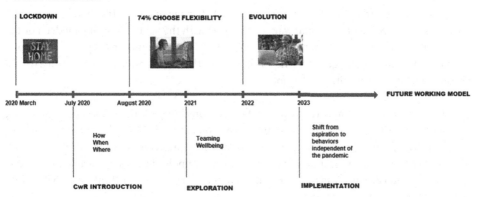

Novartis describes CwR as a "team aligned, associate[2]-inspired and manager enabled" initiative. *Team aligned* means agreeing with the team on how and when the employee will collaborate and get things done, whether remotely, on site, or in a mix. Thus, teammates are required to develop an open dialogue, flexibility, and trust to ensure effective collaboration to excel both as individuals and team in both performance and well-being.

Associate-inspired means that employees lead the way to how, where, and when they work (within national or state borders) to create the greatest impact in their role and to support a healthy work-life balance. The individual choice comes with individual responsibility to align the individual choices with the team, and to keep the manager informed about activities and availability.

Managers enable employees and teams as they explore and adopt new ways of working, which supports both individual needs and collective impact. Managers are expected to trust employees to make an impact in their roles wherever they work. Ideally, the team will find the best solution, but where the team is unable to decide, the leader will need to make a call as to the best way forward.

Furthermore, Novartis offers support and resources for employees and teams to work flexibly, enabling productivity as well as health, safety, and well-being. Millions have been invested to help employees to equip themselves to work comfortably from home.

ADVANTAGES AND CHALLENGES OF CWR

In terms of culture transition, CwR, soon after the implementation, showed positive effects. Virtual working has democratized meetings, making it easier for everyone to feel seen and heard and allowing more people to speak up and participate. When everyone is in the same little box on the screen in virtual meetings, this can give space to shine to those employees who are shier than others and typically have less presence in a face-to-face conversation. Employees have had the privilege of learning more about each other and deepening their relationships through these virtual windows into each other's worlds, learning about their homes, families, and pets. It has fascinated many to see how productive virtual work can be, how hybrid and flexible ways of working develop, and how much people value having more flexible time with families.

In an employee survey conducted in August 2020 after the first COVID-19 wave, 74% of the employees indicated that they would want to continue with the flexible working model. For this case, we interviewed Novartis' employees to illustrate their viewpoints on CwR. The senior project manager in talent management, who has been with the organization for more than a decade describes her experience with CwR as follows:

> First of all, it encourages employees to take responsibility for their work, thus increasing accountability and sense of belonging to the company. The initiative promotes satisfaction, by affording freedom and self-determination. With reduced commuting, we are able to save time, not to mention reduce environmental pollution. We were able to get rid of our second car since I mainly work from home. Furthermore, I think that CwR is long overdue in today's technological age.

This resonates well with what colleagues from talent acquisition experience: "In talent acquisition it is a huge plus. The possibility of CwR also makes our company much more attractive for highly talented future employees – this is what talents ask from me each time I speak to them".

While the idea is very welcomed by many, obstacles and challenges are there. According to one of the senior leaders,

> Flexibility is great, but it was challenging to inspire your team during the pandemic, when everyone is exhausted. We tend to work more hours and it is sometimes difficult to maintain boundaries between work and private time/space, and you are also unable to have informal and spontaneous exchanges with your colleagues.

This statement makes clear that flexible work – not only in a pandemic – comes with challenges. It crystallizes how easy it is to fall into endless, back-to-back virtual meetings and how hard it is to stay connected – no longer bumping into one another and having spontaneous and creative conversations at the water cooler, coffee station, or lunch. Work-life boundaries erode quickly. Personal experiences have shown how levels of anxiety and feelings of isolation have been increasing and how work can narrow and become very task oriented.

Another challenge is the differences between groups of employees. While remote work is possible for some groups, others need to be on site to perform their tasks. As there is a great diversity of roles across Novartis, which will not allow all the same degree of flexibility, the company is still exploring how it is possible to offer more choice, inspiring workspaces, and well-being support across the organization in the ongoing CwR journey. To identify future ways of flexible working for employees working on site, such as for operators and lab technicians, experiments are underway and include reinventing/creating new shift models and also increasing part-time workers as part of shift work (job sharing in production/lab and in shift work). The company aims to offer half-days after work completion, during which employees can devote themselves to other topics (e.g., learning/training/recreation or leaving early). In addition, employees get one day (per month/quarter) for training/learning and re-energizing, and they have the possibility to do training from home.

PROPOSALS TO RESOLVE THE ISSUES

There is no single way to do Choice with Responsibility "correctly"; it is a learning process, and all the employees need to experiment to find out how they can make the biggest impact in their teams. Novartis continues to support the implementation of CwR within the teams. In so-called "How conversations", each team is asked to discuss how to best collaborate in the future, guided by questions like: "How are we individually and collectively looking after our experience and well-being?" and "How are we going to manage our work and maximize impact?".

It is not yet known where exactly this new way is heading or leading, but Novartis chooses to trust the employees' feedback via online employee engagement surveys for guiding the efforts. Novartis holds on to the idea that all the decisions about whether and how often employees need to be physically present at a site/office should be made by the individual employees in alignment with the team, based on the work that needs to be done, the impact that is expected and the ways of working, which are the best to achieve this. As of today, there will be no global rules for the number of days to be at the office. Offices are vital hubs of innovation, collaboration, and team building, and many employees are expected to choose to work there frequently.

The case of Novartis shows that now is the time to think about flexible work models. The advantages and challenges illustrated in the case are shared by many other companies in Switzerland and worldwide. The shift to remote work during the pandemic increased the sense of inclusion among workers because everyone was in the same virtual space. The transition to hybrid forms of work will bring new challenges for learning how to collaborate in these settings (Microsoft, 2021). Gaps between high-skill and low-skill workers will probably grow wider due to the alternative work arrangements, which are possible or not possible (Spreitzer, Cameron, & Garrett, 2017). The Novartis way of focusing on culture and employee autonomy with responsibility, management, and organizational support is supported by recent HRM research-based recommendations to create sustainable flexible work environments (Waples & Baskin, 2021). These efforts are worthwhile because flexible work promises a competitive advantage in terms of attracting and retaining talent to organizations (Onken-Menke, Nüesch, & Kröll, 2018). Furthermore, when implemented carefully, flexible work promises positive outcomes not only for performance but also for employee health (Shifrin & Michel, 2021), thus allowing for more sustainability in organizations.

CASE STUDY QUESTIONS FOR DISCUSSION

1. Benefits and downsides of the culture change: In your opinion, why did Novartis start to change its corporate culture?
    (i)   What are the intended goals and benefits of "Choice with Responsibility"?
    (ii) What could be potential downsides (e.g., "always at work culture")? How can Novartis make sure to harness the benefits and to minimize the downsides?
2. National and international fit of the working model:
        Given what you learned about Switzerland, how well does "Choice with Responsibility" fit Novartis' employees in Switzerland? What could be cultural challenges? Novartis is

an international company with locations around the world. Do you think that "Choice with Responsibility" works in all regions? Where do you expect a good fit, where not, and why?

3. Perspectives of different employee groups:

Consider the following statement of a senior manager of internal communications at Novartis (Glueck, 2021): "One of the things I appreciate most about Choice with Responsibility: Personally, I never have the feeling that Novartis regards CwR as a generous gesture by the company towards its employees, but that there is sincere interest in a partnership of equals behind it". What do you think about this statement? Do you think that all employees would agree with this statement (consider different functions at Novartis, e.g., R&D, production)? Why/why not?

4. Choice, responsibility, and trust:

Novartis won the German Human Resource Management Prize 2021 with its work model "CwR" in the category "leadership" (Novartis, 2021). The jury was convinced that this model helped to implement the new leadership culture of "unbossed" with elements like participation, freedom from hierarchy, and focus on strengths and talents. In an "unbossed" workplace, how can Novartis make sure that employees do the right thing?

5. Flexible work as a competitive advantage:

Discuss the implications of the "CwR" model for

(i) HR marketing (e.g., employer branding, employee retention; see e.g., Barnes, 2021)

(ii) Competence management (e.g., competence model, competence development)

(iii) Performance management (e.g., goal setting, reward structures)

Do you agree with Novartis that flexible work is a competitive advantage?

NOTES

1 Initiative launched by a consortium of large Swiss companies to initiate and accompany the adoption and realization of flexible forms of work in Switzerland: https://work-smart-initiative.ch/de/.
2 Novartis refers to all employees as associates.

REFERENCES

Baltes, B. B., Briggs, T. E., Huff, J. W., & Wright, J. A. 1999. Flexible and Compressed Workweek Schedules: A Meta-analysis of Their Effects on Work-related Criteria. *Journal of Applied Psychology*, 88: 1005–1018.

Barnes, A. 2021. *Novartis CEO Says Remote Work Hybrid Should Mean Access to New Talent Pools*. BioSpace. https://www.biospace.com/article/novartis-ceo-says-remote-work-hybrid-should-mean-access-to-new-talent-pools/. Retrieved 2021-12-03.

Deloitte. 2021. *Home-Office Umfrage 2021 [Home Office Survey 2021].* https://www2.deloitte .com/content/dam/Deloitte/ch/Documents/about-deloitte/deloitte-ch-umfrageergebnisse -home-Office.pdf. Retrieved 2021-12-03.

Glueck, T. 2021. *"Choice with Responsibility": Unleashing Potential and Reinforcing Our Values & Behaviors.* LinkedIn. https://www.linkedin.com/pulse/choice-responsibility-unleashing -potential-our-values-tobias-glueck/. Retrieved 2021-12-03.

Hänggi, R., Kriegel, M., Zumkehr, M., Bachler, M., Scheidegger, N., Hannich, F., Heierli, R., & Oswald, C. 2021. *JobCloud Market Insights: Corona Spezial 2020. Eine verhaltensbasierte Studie des Scheizer Stellenmarktes in Zusammenarbeit zwischen der JobCloud AG und ZHAW [JobCloud Market Insights: Corona Special 2020. A Behavioral Study of the Swiss Job Market in Collaboration Between JobCloud AG and ZHAW.].* Zurich: JobCloud AG.

Kniffin, K. M., Anseel, F., Ashford, S. J., Bamberger, P., Bhave, D. P., Creary, S. J., Flynn, F. J., Greer, L. L., Narayanan, J., Antonakis, J., Bakker, A., Bapuji, H., Choi, V. K., Demerouti, E., Gelfand, M. J., & Johns, G. 2021. COVID-19 and the Workplace: Implications, Issues, and Insights for Future Research and Action. *American Psychologist,* 76: 63–77.

Kolind, L., & Bøtter, J. 2012. *Unbossed.* Aarhus: Jyllands-Postens Forlag.

Microsoft. 2021. The Next Great Disruption Is Hybrid Work: Are We Ready? *2021 Work Trend Index: Annual Report.* https://ms-worklab.azureedge.net/files/reports/hybridWork/pdf /2021_Microsoft_WTI_Report_March.pdf. Retrieved 2021-12-03.

Novartis. 2018. Unleash the Power of Our People. *Novartis Annual Review 2018*: 22–24. https:// www.novartis.com/sites/novartis_com/files/novartis-annual-review-2018-en.pdf.

Novartis. 2021. *Novartis: Employer of Choice.* https://www.novartis.de/karriere/darum-novartis /novartis-employer-choice. Retrieved 2021-12-03.

Onken-Menke, G., Nüesch, S., & Kröll, C. 2018. Are You Attracted? Do You Remain? Meta-Analytic Evidence on Flexible Work Practices. *Business Research,* 11: 239–277.

Shifrin, N. V., & Michel, J. S. 2021. Flexible Work Arrangements and Employee Health: A Meta-analytic Review. *Work & Stress,* https://doi.org/10.1080/02678373.2021.1936287.

Spreitzer, G. M., Cameron, L., & Garrett, L. (2017). Alternative Work Arrangements. Two Images of the New World of Work. *Annual Review of Organizational Psychology and Organizational Behavior,* 4: 473–499.

Swiss Federal Statistical Office. 2021. *Kleine und mittlere Unternehmen [Small and Medium Sized Entrepreses].* https://www.bfs.admin.ch/bfs/de/home/statistiken/industrie -dienstleistungen/unternehmen-beschaeftigte/wirtschaftsstruktur-unternehmen/kmu .html. Retrieved 2021-12-01.

Thom, N., Blum, A., & Zaugg, R. 2002. Arbeitszeitmanagement: Zur Verbreitung und Implementierung von flexiblen Arbeitszeitsystemen in schweizerischen Unternehmen und Institutionen [Working Time Management: On the Diffusion and Implementation of Flexible Working Time Systems in Swiss Companies and Institutions.]. *Die Betriebswirtschaft [The Business Administration],* 62: 488–511.

Waples, E., & Brock Baskin, M. E. 2021. Not Your Parent's Organization? Human Resource Development Practices for Sustainable Flex Work Environments. *Advances in Developing Human Resources,* 23: 153–170.

Weichbrodt, J., Bruggmann, A., & Folie, A. 2020. *FlexWork Survey 2020: Befragung von Erwerbstätigen und Unternehmen in der Schweiz zur Verbreitung mobil-flexibler Arbeit*

[FlexWork Survey 2020: Survey of Employees and Companies in Switzerland on the Prevalence of Mobile-Flexible Work.]. Olten: FHNW School of Applied Psychology. https://irf.fhnw.ch /handle/11654/31702. Retrieved 2021-12-03.

Weichbrodt, J., Tanner, A., Josef, B., & Schulze, H. 2014/2015. Die Entwicklung von Arbeitsflexibilität in Organisationen anhand des Flex-Work-Phasenmodell [The Development of Work Flexibility in Organizations Based on the Flex-work Phase Model]. *Wirtschaftspsychologie [Business Psychology]*, 4/1: 11–22.

WIPO. 2022. *Global Innovation Index 2022*. Retrieved from: https://www.wipo.int/global_ innovation_index/en/2022/.

PART II

Scandinavia

CHAPTER 5

Denmark

Toward a More Inclusive Approach to Developing Talent

Liza Castro Christiansen

CASE SYNOPSIS[1]

For the Danish multinational pump manufacturer, Grundfos, the pursuit to remain number one in all their markets goes hand in hand with becoming number one in recruiting and developing talent. Their Strategy 2025 of being customer-driven focuses on selecting and recruiting new talent and developing these new hires while simultaneously affording opportunities for development to existing employees. The requirement to re-align strategic objectives with external and internal pools of human resources resulted in a re-focusing of the Global Graduate Program to attract younger recruits, in addition to devising custom-made development schemes catering to the individual needs of leaders and current staff. This case highlights how Grundfos has evolved its exclusive talent program from one for the few to extended inclusive people development initiatives for the broader employee population.

LEARNING OUTCOMES

1. Understand why and how a global company prioritizes inclusive people development over exclusive talent management.
2. Learn about trending international recruitment processes and training for new graduates through technology.

DOI: 10.4324/9781003307099-7

3. Understand how people development is used to retain talent.
4. Appreciate the evolving role of human resource management (HRM) from strategic partnership to the strategic leadership of people and processes.

KEYWORDS

People development, talent management, recruitment and retention, graduate program, Denmark

INTRODUCTION

During the period from 2009 to 2016, Grundfos had a strong focus on innovation and on building innovative capabilities in the company through a talent engine that was to produce not only leaders but also innovators and specialists. Grundfos needed to build a stronger talent pipeline for leadership as well as for people who were not only innovative but also highly specialized. Efforts were dedicated to building a talent management program that was forward-looking, comprehensive, and integrated. Both the processes of developing the program and the phases in developing talent took time such that as of 2016, only 380 leaders, innovators, and specialists had completed the talent program. Grundfos needed a faster and more effective way to identify and recruit relevant human resources who could harness the growing market potential (Castro Christiansen, 2012; 2018).

HISTORICAL BACKGROUND AND ORGANIZATIONAL SETTING

Grundfos was established in 1945 by Poul Due Jensen under the name Bjerringbro Pressestøberi og Maskinfabrik: Bjerringbro Press Foundry and Machine Factory (Bjerringbro is the town where the headquarters are located), and in 1967, the firm changed its name to Grundfos. Grundfos has production, sales, and service facilities in the world's most important pump markets, and they plan to continue to increase their presence in new markets. With 84 facilities in 59 countries, there are differing needs for high-quality pumps and consultancy services. Grundfos customizes its solutions to meet local requirements and gives maximum freedom to local operations while at the same time harvesting efficiency gains from global alignment. By focusing on regional production facilities and a local set-up, Grundfos can demonstrate respect for local values, culture, social conditions, and ways of doing business. This multinational company highlights the importance of centralization with an appropriate degree of decentralization that benefits both their subsidiaries, the markets they serve, and the company's long-term objectives, the most important of which is to be the number one producer of pumps in terms of excellence in every country where they operate: "If we cannot be No. 1 – or No. 2 – in any country, we would rather pull out". This ambition spreads throughout everything Grundfos does, including the recruitment and development of local and regional talents who manage their presence and operations in all their markets.

HUMAN RESOURCE MANAGEMENT IN DENMARK[2]

The practice of HRM in Denmark is derived from its institutional roots. The Danish HRM model can be described as collaborative with a distinctly more developmental or humanistic approach, often based on the value of the employees and their employment relationship with the firm. Despite this collaborative emphasis, as characterized by efforts to create and communicate a culture of partnership between employer and employee as well as among employees, it is easy for employers to fire and hire employees, a concept that has become known as "flexicurity" (the combination of two English words "flexibility" and "security"). The term "flexicurity" describes a labor market policy that enhances national competitiveness by providing employers the flexibility to hire and fire and by providing stability and security to employees. The Danish model functions as a form of unwritten contract between the government and labor market partners, the Danish Employers' Association, and the Danish Confederation of Trade Unions. It works only with the acceptance of these three parties. Flexicurity, an integrated strategy for enhancing flexibility and security in the labor market, attempts to reconcile employers' need for a flexible workforce with workers' need for security.

The economic landscape in Denmark is predominantly made up of many small- to medium-sized organizations. There are far fewer very large organizations in Denmark than in other major industrial nations in Europe. Danish companies have tended to specialize, and Denmark is famous not for mass-market products but for production, which stresses creativity in design and excellence in the quality of the finished goods.

In most Danish organizations, the majority of the administrative functions are outsourced or executed by IT systems, and the HRM department still constitutes only a very small percentage of the total organization. Line management holds the strongest responsibility of all HRM areas (e.g., compensation and benefits, recruitment, and training), so they are held more accountable for their HR/people management practices than HR managers are. Larger organizations tend to have their own HRM departments, which enjoy a strong partnership with top management. This is evident in the growing responsibility of global HR partners, as is also the case with Grundfos. This development stems from the attention that organizations continue to give to the alignment of HR strategy and business strategy (Andersen & Minbaeva, 2013; Castro Christiansen & Higgs, 2008a; 2009), the need to constantly re-align the HR ecosystem to achieve the required fit (Snell & Morris, 2021), and the cultivation of HRM competencies, not only among HRM executives but also among business managers. It also indicates a deeper understanding and greater need and appreciation for the role of HRM (Castro Christiansen & Higgs, 2008b; McCracken, O'Kane, Brown, & McCrory, 2017).

In a similar vein, HRM practices, e.g., skills development and training, are planned with a view toward realizing the longer-term needs of the organization. Although the top tier receives priority in exclusive talent management (Iles, Chuai, & Preece, 2010; Bonneton, 2019), all employees receive development and training possibilities as part of the yearly employee performance dialogue, bending more toward inclusive talent management (Iles et al., 2010; Bonneton & Festing, 2020). Danish organizations are still quite conservative about formalizing career development schemes in terms of career plans, high-flying programs, and development centers, in which case, career development through job-related learning and collaboration with managers and colleagues is practiced more. Grundfos is among the very few Danish multinational organizations that have gone their own way in designing career development opportunities in the form of a talent program.

TALENT MANAGEMENT IN DENMARK

Denmark is basically a knowledge society and a very innovative society, with an extensive technologically advanced population. Danish companies constantly find innovative ways of developing in the markets where they compete, and with this comes an innovative way of developing people. It is perhaps one of the reasons why some of the tech giants have established subsidiaries in Denmark: Facebook in Esbjerg, Apple in Viborg, and Google in both Aarhus and Copenhagen. Denmark was also among the first countries that easily adapted to the challenges of the COVID-19 pandemic, where companies resumed operations and collaborated with customers and partners through virtual means. The questions that challenged Danish organizations at the outset of the pandemic were: "How should we change the way we work?" and "How should we make ourselves more self-sufficient?".

Talent management, or rather, people development in Denmark, has emerged as one of the cornerstones of the HRM strategy. Talent management in Danish companies is a more integrated component of training and development that actually starts on day one of employment and continues through to the yearly employee performance dialogue, a privilege that each employee is entitled to and one important obligation and commitment that organizations have toward their employees, with outcomes leading to designing the employee's further development in order for them to perform even better in their current and forthcoming responsibilities. While talent management might be for a few, people development is for everyone a trend that has caught the attention of more recent research (Meyers, Collings, & Paauwe, 2015; Bonneton & Festing, 2020). The guiding rule for Danish organizations is to continue creating and harnessing value and to communicate their employee value proposition not only to the employees they already have but also to those whom they want to recruit. Candidates want to work for a company not only because of the products or services that it sells but because of the opportunities that the company will give them to grow professionally and personally. Companies are aware that the more they put into people development, the more the competition will also put into it, and this explains why people development is key for Danish companies.

BACKGROUND TO THE CASE

One of the means through which Grundfos tried to meet future challenges was the establishment of their "Talent Engine" concept, a massive step beyond the HRM activity that had been traditionally in place. Talented people at Grundfos were trained and developed in individually designed programs within the Talent Engine on one of three routes: Leaders, innovators, and specialists. The talent program was confined to a nominated few, and from 2009 until January 2016, the Talent Engine produced an average of 50 to 60 talents every year, resulting in a pool of 380 in 2016 out of an employee population of 17,000 (Castro Christiansen, 2018). The "production" of the needed talents not only took a long time, but it also proved to be very costly. Considering the market potential emerging in its various sites, a change in the approach to talent management was necessary.

The intake of new talents for the old Talent Engine was put on hold in late 2015, the last cohort of talents was produced in 2016, and a new program was introduced in 2017 with a focus on the following:

Cost efficiency. People development should be cost-effective, and it should be for the benefit of the broader population. It should emphasize the ability to acquire new skills in a fast and agile way, and it should help accelerate the development of a bigger pool of capabilities.

Succession pipeline. Pipelines for leadership positions should be ensured by identifying the right people and instilling in them leadership behaviors that blend courage, visionary thinking, and the ability to plan and prioritize accordingly.

Tools development. Easy online tutorials, training modules, templates, and questionnaires for the leaders and for the talents in different geographical areas, rather than running programs from the headquarters, must be developed. Cutting-edge learning technology and a wide range of courses and digital learning opportunities should give employees immediate access to learning and development, so they can learn while in the flow of work – wherever and whenever – they need it.

HRM-supported talent development teams. Multiple career possibilities should be offered, and all employees can navigate in many different career directions across the 59 countries in which Grundfos is represented. These will be provided and supported by HR but driven by regional/local leadership.

A NEW TURNING POINT

One positive outcome of the previous talent program was the leaders' acceptance (and everyone's, for that matter) of the specific Danish cultural phenomenon called "*janteloven*" ("Do not think that you are better than others"), which is essentially the Danish philosophy of egalitarianism. At Grundfos, open communication has helped alleviate the detrimental effects of "*jantelov*". Understanding that talent development could be a shortcut to achieving business results, and not a block, has made it easier for changes to be made in the current talent management process.

Based on the key lessons learned from the previous talent program, and with equal emphasis given to increasing the pipeline for newly recruited talents from outside the organization and to further developing those who are already in the organization, the HRM capability has been restructured together with a more decentralized and distributed model for training. A large proportion of the HRM budget is spent on recruiting the right resources for entry-level positions and on growth and training activities that reach more people and can develop more competencies in the organization.

THE WAY FORWARD

To be number one means to put in the necessary resources to be the best pump manufacturer in the world. It also means to be number one in people development and to have only the people who are the best at what they do.

Recovering from the pandemic, the new Strategy 2025 restructures Grundfos from being a sales-oriented company to a customer-driven company with simpler and quicker decision-making on the implementation of the three-pronged people development program consisting of the Leadership Program for leaders, the Graduate Program for new recruits, and the Power Up Grundfos (P-U-G) for everyone. The repositioning of the Leadership Program and the P-U-G also has the double purpose of strengthening the employee retention strategy.

THE LEADERSHIP PROGRAM

There are two different layers within leadership: Managers who lead managers, and managers who lead people who are not managers, so there are different opportunities to develop as a leader. Leaders are sent to a course within three months of taking up a leadership position, and to a follow-up course to brush up on how they work with people at least once every second year, a must within the new organizational restructuring where most leaders manage people who do not sit physically in the same offices in Denmark, the United States, India, or China, or in any of the 59 countries, and who have different needs and different time zones. As part of the employee motivation scheme, employees assess their managers once a year; managers are given a score on how they are doing, and if they fall under a certain limit, they will need to undergo additional leadership training. This collaborative exercise helps leaders to be updated on the new ways that they must lead. It is crucial that everybody is on board even though they can be up to 4,000 kilometers away from each other.

THE GLOBAL GRADUATE PROGRAM

The Global Graduate Program is a two-year development journey offered to around 25 hand-picked graduates with a strong drive, curiosity, intellectual strength, global mindset, and passion to contribute to global change. It runs in Denmark, India, China, and the United States. It consists of four projects in four different departments. These projects constitute the building blocks of the program, and they are the means to accelerate competence growth. Each of the four projects lasts around six months, and at least one project should be in one of the 59 departments.

Development during all four projects is supported by the following:

- A dedicated mentor, who will ensure organizational understanding and guidance on career progression.
- An assigned buddy throughout the graduate journey.
- A structured and individualized personal development plan.
- A program manager, who will provide support throughout the program.
- Challenging projects that will take the graduates out of their comfort zone.

One notable change that occurred at Grundfos was delayering, such that smaller departments with six people or fewer were merged into bigger departments. In the old Talent Engine, the key priority was getting as big as possible (from 17,000 to 75,000 employees), but management realized that Grundfos could be as big without employing more people because they were on their way to going fully digital. Everything they have been doing since 2017 has become more digital and data-driven.

Work has since involved automation processes and machine learning, artificial intelligence, and virtual reality.[3] For instance, virtual reality glasses are used for recruitment. Lead Talent Specialist and Global Graduate Programme Head at Grundfos, Birgitte Dam, has not seen or met the applicants to their Graduate Program whom she interviewed during the last four years. Grundfos ships out VR glasses to the whole world, for example, to Austria, Australia, the United States, China, Singapore, Norway, Sweden, Germany, and all other places where there are potential recruits.

> We met in this virtual space where we could engage in team exercises. We also have a platform where I could take them on tours within Grundfos virtually, so we were in Grundfos' premises, but they were actually in their own living rooms.

POWER UP GRUNDFOS

Power Up Grundfos (P-U-G) is a key organizational talent development initiative that enables internal talent pools and employees to take on different or greater responsibilities. They undergo a rigorous developmental experience over the course of 15 to 18 months by being exposed to a stretch project ensuring personal insights, and formal and informal learning. There is a full mentorship program leading to a broadening of perspectives, both personally and professionally. External suppliers, such as consultancies, are contracted as appropriate.

PEOPLE DEVELOPMENT

Overall, people development at Grundfos is now more inclusive. They consider their human resources not only as having potential but also talent, and they want talent development to be for everybody. One of the key deliverables in 2022–2023 is to ensure that a) all human resources feel that they have talent, just in different layers and at different levels; and b) that there are processes through which they can continuously develop. Through digitalization, people development is scalable and made available to all without sounding like mass production because people develop within their chosen routes (see, for example, Khoreva, Vaiman, Bondarouk & Salojärvi, 2019). People development, in its individual form, is for everyone, depending on their personal and professional needs, and programs are individually designed with the dual objective of growing these human resources and keeping them in the company. These customized programs also form part of Strategy 2025 to push the agenda toward implementing diversity, equity, and inclusion.

NEW LEARNINGS

Five years since the start of the new people development program at Grundfos, Birgitte Dam has a couple of key learnings to share: The first is to recognize that there is no "plug and play" in people development. Concepts can be developed, but they do not fit all and everybody, especially when talking globally. The second is not to underestimate the importance of communication, especially that of early communication, and acknowledge that one can never communicate too much when it comes to people, processes, and changes.

Very clear and precise dialogue should be ensured because the worst experience is to give people poor information that is open to multiple interpretations. Ensuring consistency of communication is key to successful people management, especially on a global scale. This is essential for those HRM people who execute and facilitate the training (Sparrow, Scullion, & Farndale, 2011). Town hall meetings for Grundfos' full HRM organization of 600 people with all the global HR functions are held every second month.

CHALLENGES

The people development program in getting leaders more skilled at leadership and in getting existing talents more specialized in their respective fields is generally stable, but recruiting younger talents for the Graduate Program has had some challenges: A few have said "no" when offered the job.

Even if the applicants undergo the most extensive recruitment process and succeed through the different steps, tests, interviews, and assessment centers for four months, one or two out of the 25 accepted each year still decide to do something else. They have decided that they want to be a specialist instead of a graduate or a "generalist" even if their engagement with Grundfos would open in specialisms later. This is a trend that Grundfos has seen all over the world.

> We ask people to be open minded and flexible. If they already have a career path set in their mind, then our graduate program is not for them because in our program, we will ask them to further explore different options. But what we have experienced is that they are sure of what they want to do, and it is so important for them to set their path now than later,

according to Birgitte Dam.

When asked how she deals with the few applicants who have said "no", Birgitte Dam explained,

> We want people to equally choose Grundfos as we have chosen them because in this way, we can truly screen and filter the most relevant candidates. If they say "no" after a year, then we have not only wasted a lot of efforts, but an important post for a more suitable graduate. It is better to be honest with each other's time from the beginning.

THE FUTURE

One of the main priorities that Grundfos has is how to attract the right entry-level talents.

How can we acquire and secure the right talents in-house?

How can we constantly make ourselves relevant to the people with the potential to bring value to Grundfos' business?

CASE STUDY QUESTIONS FOR DISCUSSION

1. Compare and contrast exclusive talent management with inclusive people development. Can you think of any other organizations, apart from Grundfos, that execute one or the other? Or both? What may be the reason for their choice?

2. What are the responsibilities and roles of HRM specialists at Grundfos?

3. According to the case and learnings from the previous Talent Engine, what are the factors that contribute to an effective people development strategy?

4. Imagine yourself as a potential entry-level applicant to Grundfos' Graduate Program. What would you recommend that Grundfos should do to make itself more relevant to you and to people who share the same ambition of becoming a specialist from the start?

NOTES

1   The author would like to thank Birgitte Dam, Lead Talent Specialist and Global Graduate Programme Head at Grundfos, for the series of interviews that she provided in developing and writing this case.

2   The author would like to thank Kim Staack Nielsen, CEO of Dansk HR (The Danish HR Association), for providing the background on human resource management and talent management in Denmark.

3   In the manufacturing plants in Denmark, Hungary, and France, training blue collar workers has become a faster and more effective process. The workers get virtual reality glasses and they are given a machine, which they learn to operate through the VR glasses with remote controls in their hands. If they do something wrong, the VR glasses will vibrate. Everything is done systematically, so the six-week learning process to handle the machinery is narrowed down to six working days.

REFERENCES

Andersen, T.J. & Minbaeva, D. 2013. The role of human resource management in strategy making. *Human Resource Management*, 52(5): 809–827.

Bonneton, D. 2019. *Exclusive talent management practices: Reconciling organizational and boundaryless careers?* Paper presented at the annual meeting of the Academy of Management, Boston.

Bonneton, D. & Festing, M. 2020. *Balancing exclusive and inclusive talent management in a multinational company in symposium: Studying the tensions between 'exclusive' and 'inclusive' talent management.* Paper presented at the annual meeting of the Academy of Management, Vancouver.

Castro Christiansen, L. & Higgs, M. 2008a. How the alignment of business strategy and HR strategy can impact performance. *Journal of General Management*, 33(4): 13–33.

Castro Christiansen, L. & Higgs, M. 2008b. *Do HR competencies enable organisations to perform more effectively? An empirical study of HR competencies and organisational performance in Danish companies.* Paper presented at the annual meeting of the British Academy of Management, Leeds.

Castro Christiansen, L. & Higgs, M. 2009. *HR strategy and business strategy alignment: Operationalizing the dynamics of fit.* Paper presented at the annual meeting of the Academy of Management, Chicago.

Castro Christiansen, L. 2012. Grundfos invests in talent. In Hayton, J., Biron, M., Castro Christiansen, L. & Kuvaas, B. (Eds.), *The global human resource management casebook, first edition* (pp. 61–71). New York and London: Routledge.

Castro Christiansen, L. 2018. Redesigning talent assets: Grundfos revisits their talent engine. In Castro Christiansen, L., Biron, M., Farndale, E. & Kuvaas, B. (Eds.), *The global human resource management casebook, second edition* (pp. 55–63). New York and London: Routledge.

Iles, P., Chuai, X. & Preece, D. 2010. Talent management and HRM in multinational companies in Beijing: Definitions, differences and drivers. *Journal of World Business*, 45: 179–189.

Khoreva, V., Vaiman, V., Bondarouk, T. & Salojärvi, S. 2019. *Exploring the influence of digitalization and global talent management.* Paper presented at the annual meeting of the Academy of Management, Boston.

McCracken, M., O'Kane, P., Brown, T.C. & McCrory, M. 2017. Human resource business partner lifecycle model: Exploring how the relationship between HRBPs and their line manager partners evolves. *Human Resource Management Journal*, 27(1): 58–74.

Meyers, M.C., Collings, D.G. & Paauwe, J. 2015. *Talent management: Towards balance in theory and research.* Paper presented at the annual meeting of the Academy of Management, Vancouver.

Snell, S.A. & Morris, S.S. 2021. Time for realignment: The HR ecosystem. *Academy of Management Perspectives*, 35(2): 219–236.

Sparrow, P., Scullion, H. & Farndale E. 2011. Global talent management: New roles for the corporate HR function? In H. Scullion & D. Collings (Eds.), *Global talent management* (pp. 39–55). London: Routledge.

CHAPTER 6

Finland

Look Who's Talking: Implementing Corporate Diversity and Inclusiveness Practices in Finland

Adam Smale

CASE SYNOPSIS

This case introduces students to international HRM issues surrounding the implementation of a diversity and inclusiveness program, developed at corporate headquarters in the United States, in one of the multinational's foreign subsidiaries located in Finland. Taking the subsidiary perspective through the eyes of local HR manager, Maria, the case describes how Petrocom has gone about implementing its "Global Organization" vision that included the roll-out of its new "Global Workforce Diversity Management and Inclusiveness Initiative". The case follows the challenges the initiative has faced as a US, corporate-centric approach to diversity management that has been confronted with specific features of local Finnish culture. The case focuses on how the main protagonist, Maria, responds to critical questions about the local need for these practices, the approach to implementation, and who should be teaching whom about diversity and inclusiveness.

KEYWORDS

Multinational corporation, diversity and inclusiveness, foreign subsidiary, transfer of HRM practices, Finland

DOI: 10.4324/9781003307099-8

LOCAL HRM GETS THE CALL FROM CORPORATE

Maria, the HR manager of Petrocom[1] Finland, had been both excited and anxious when news came through from corporate headquarters that Finland had been selected as one of the first to implement the new "Global Workforce Diversity Management and Inclusiveness Initiative" (hereafter D&I Initiative). The mission of the D&I Initiative was to support the integration of employees who may differ in terms of both visible (e.g., gender, race, and age) and invisible characteristics (e.g., sexual orientation, values, beliefs, income, and education). Maria had known that it was going to mean a lot of work and that getting local buy-in for a corporate initiative of this kind would be a huge challenge. Although she knew that there had been few cases of harassment or discrimination, she felt that Finland and the people at Petrocom Finland had limited experience in confronting certain areas of workforce diversity management in comparison with their European counterparts. Maria just hoped that her personal convictions about the business case for diversity management would be shared by others.

IMPLEMENTING THE GLOBAL D&I INITIATIVE IN PETROCOM FINLAND

Petrocom Group, a well-known US energy multinational, operates in nearly 100 countries and employs more than 100,000 people. In the early 2000s, the Petrocom Group initiated a significant restructuring. The restructuring included the launch of its "Global Organization", which for HRM strategy meant, among other things, greater standardization of its policies, practices, and processes. Based on the successful model of managing workforce diversity in Petrocom's US home-country operations, Petrocom developed a five-year implementation plan, which sought to integrate the principles of diversity and inclusiveness into key business and HRM practices throughout their worldwide operations. In doing so, Petrocom HQ aimed to attract and retain key global talent, to increase productivity through improved employee engagement, and to strengthen its reputation within the global community.

Representing one of the smallest of their foreign operations, Petrocom Finland employed 1,700 people across 400 service outlets when the D&I Initiative began. Since "Diversity and Inclusiveness" was adopted as one of Petrocom's formal "Global Standards", it was clear from the beginning that there was to be little scope for deviations in implementation, which was evident in the kick-off memo from the Global Head of the D&I Initiative:

> Naturally, there will be some legal limitations to its application that will be considered, but otherwise we assume that the D&I Standard is translated directly and that there are no local modifications. This is necessary to create a truly global D&I Standard for Petrocom and to ensure the implementation of one of our key business principles.

During implementation, the D&I Initiative was perceived as an external and largely US, Anglo-Saxon intervention concerned only with the narrower issues of gender, nationality, and the staffing of senior country positions with host-country nationals (i.e., not expatriates).

FINLAND: HIGHLY RANKED, INCLUSIVE, AND OPENING ITS DOORS

Finland is an advanced industrial economy located in Northern Europe and has a population of 5.5 million. After gaining independence in 1917, and having still been a largely agrarian economy in the 1950s, it has rapidly developed into a prosperous knowledge economy (Evans, Smale & Björkman, 2018). Today, Finland is leading or near the top of many international comparisons in terms of growth and development in the economic, technological, and social spheres. For instance, Finland is ranked seventh on the Global Talent Competitiveness Index 2021 out of 134 countries, which captures a country's ability to attract, develop, and retain valuable human capital (Lanvin & Monteiro, 2021). According to the World Economic Forum's Global Competitiveness Report (2020),[2] Finland is ranked first for public governance, education, and skills for the markets of tomorrow, and incentives for long-term investments in stability and inclusion.

The success of the Finnish economy has been driven by the combination of economic efficiency and growth, a peaceful labor market, an egalitarian distribution of income, and social cohesion, all backed up by a generous social security system. The Finnish economy remains heavily manufacturing-based, led by engineering and high-technology firms. However, the 2008 financial crisis coupled with the rapid decline of Nokia – Finland's national champion – has led to some key restructuring and austerity measures. Hope for the future is increasingly being placed on digital skills and innovative start-ups, epitomized by gaming companies such as Supercell (creators of Clash of Clans).

Managing Workforce Diversity in Finland

From a legal perspective, the cornerstone of Finnish legislation relating to workforce diversity is the 1999 revised Constitution, according to which everyone is equal before the law. In addition, there are several acts and codes that prevent discrimination in work communities based on any visible or invisible aspects of diversity (e.g., the Penal Code; the Employment Contracts

Act (55/2001); the Act on Equality between Women and Men (609/1986, 2005); and the Equality Act (21/2004)).

From a cultural perspective, one of the hallmarks of modern-day Finnish society is strong egalitarian values and inclusion. This is reflected in different aspects of Finnish society, not least the focus on achieving social mobility and equal opportunity. Finland again performs well here, ranked number three in the Global Social Mobility Index (2020)[3] and number two in the Global Gender Gap Index (2021).[4]

However, Finland could also be characterized as somewhat bipolar. On the one hand, Finland is representative of a Nordic welfare state that has integrated equality legislation with a distinctively inclusive political ideology, which has served to promote with good effect certain aspects of diversity such as gender equality. Finland was the first country to give women equal political rights, and there is evidence of its positive long-term effect on working life, despite some persistent pay inequalities. On the other hand, progress in the acceptance and inclusion of ethnic, cultural, and sexual minorities has been much slower. While cultural openness to different sexual orientations has changed considerably from being somewhat of a taboo subject in Finnish society to more of an open subject of discussion, many immigrants in Finland still report discrimination in society, job markets, and the workplace.

One possible explanation for this is Finland's relative cultural, racial, religious, and linguistic homogeneity, and thus historical lack of exposure to certain minority groups. However, in line with similar developments in other countries, this composition is in flux due to increased labor mobility. The contracting labor market has become particularly topical in Finland, as the aging population is placing increasing pressure on the country's ability to attract skilled migrants. Multiculturalism remains relatively low. Based on 2020 figures, the proportion of the population with a non-national background is 8%, which is one of the lowest percentages among the EU countries.

ENTHUSIASM GLOBALLY RECEIVES MIXED REACTION LOCALLY

The implementation of the D&I Initiative (see Table 6.1 for the range of tools used) did not encounter any significant legal obstacles in Finland, as Petrocom Finland was cautious from the outset not to violate any local laws and to allow legally-obliged modifications. This was also reflected in the responses of local union representatives (who are typically quite influential in the highly unionized Finnish business environment), who remained relatively silent throughout the implementation process, despite some short-lived defensive reactions at the beginning when discussions turned to the employment of immigrants (e.g., the effect of low-cost labor on employee wage levels and rights). Instead, the biggest challenges were associated with the level of priority given to diversity management and how to introduce the issue of diversity sensitively into the workplace.

Getting Priorities Straight

From the outset, people within Petrocom Finland disagreed about the level of priority that should be given to diversity management issues. These arguments were based on whether diversity management represents a critical business issue, its relevance in a workplace setting, and its

TABLE 6.1 Diversity management implementation tools used in Petrocom Finland

Through people	Through information systems	Through formalization	Through decision-making (centralization)
• Local "Diversity Coordinators" • Benchmarking among diversity coordinators • Diversity training • Managerial-level and regionally standardized "Diversity Auditors" • Development and appraisal discussions at a managerial level • Local voluntary workshop sessions	• Corporate internet • Stakeholder communication • Diversity publications and roadmap • Company intranet • Self-evaluation tools • Survey findings • E-learning material • Diversity "games"/quizzes • Annual corporate, regional, and local diversity plans	• D&I standard (mission and values) • D&I Policy Framework • D&I integration into existing organizational policies (e.g., Harassment & Discrimination) • "Barometer"-style survey on the working environment • D&I-focused survey • Leadership self-appraisals and 360° appraisals • Diversity criteria on organizational and individual balanced scorecards • Diversity criteria added to reward and bonus schemes • Signing of Annual Diversity Assurance Statements	• Diversity Council (corporate level) • Diversity Steering Group (corporate level) • Regional HQ • Local "Diversity Coordinators"

Source: Adapted from Sippola and Smale (2007)

relevance, given Finland's and the Finnish unit's demographics. The newly appointed Finnish diversity coordinator believed the D&I Initiative was an important business issue and had come at the right time due to increasing diversity challenges.

> Our local unit faces more and more challenges related to personnel. Not only have these groups now become a very important target for recruitment in Finland, but we also have to understand that such a variety of individuals can't be managed in the same way, so we need to adapt. I think we need to pay more attention to these groups, and consider the special needs of women, ethnic minorities and other groups that face obstacles to inclusion.

Petrocom Finland's CEO was more diplomatic but still believed that diversity management issues were premature. However, several employees in the Finnish unit described the D&I Initiative as an overreaction and "like using a sledgehammer to crack a nut", as one disgruntled employee explains:

> We have been told that diversity is just about anything that distinguishes individuals from each other, like religion, culture and ethnicity, language and so on. But I still think that here in my work it is a question of males and females being equal. We haven't got any immigrants, for example. In my work, everybody speaks Finnish and some English. Religion isn't visible here, why would it be? It is work, after all. I guess the guys at headquarters have a point generally, and I understand that the main issues are important at that level. A small office in Finland doesn't count for much there and thus it has to go with the flow, regardless of the local importance of these matters. Suddenly we have all kinds of promotional events and trainings going on. I'll be retired before those things become important here.

Maria faced constant challenges about how to strike the right balance between raising awareness, and educating and supporting individuals to focus on the unfamiliar aspects of work and behaviors presented by the principles of D&I, and on the other hand, bringing the level of attention to a level that didn't overshadow key business issues since employees started to view it with skepticism and as a passing fad. At times, she herself questioned what the company's role as a local subsidiary was supposed to be:

> We are not here to change society. That's not our prime reason for being in Finland. We are here to do business. But we have to do it as a good Finnish company, as a good Finnish citizen, so that everyone who works for Petrocom can be proud of what we are doing. But I don't feel that our task is to be the one who comes and breaks the walls down.

Cultural Sensitivities

At a relatively early stage in the implementation, it became apparent that the magnitude of cultural adjustments in communication required to openly discuss diversity meant that the Finnish subsidiary considered itself insufficiently prepared to embrace everything that was being suggested by HQ. For example, the suggested use of affinity groups (i.e., groups formed around shared characteristics such as women in leadership, or career experiences of LGBT employees) was regarded as inappropriate and not adopted by the Finnish subsidiary. It was argued that they represented a culture-specific tool reflecting Anglo-Saxon assumptions that everybody is ready and willing to "open up" and discuss personal issues with others in a group.

For employees, the introduction of sensitive and personal issues in discussions of D&I made typically reserved Finnish people feel noticeably uncomfortable. Middle managers started to voice concerns about whether these types of discussions would require them to "reveal who we really are" to their colleagues. The questioning of people's values regarding diversity and inequality was also shown to be a painful experience for some. Maria recalls a landmark team meeting a year into the implementation process in which they discussed issues of inequality and were asked to share personal experiences:

> The atmosphere was unique. The subjects of discussion were unique. The inner dynamics of that team were discussed openly. It had people crying. And that was certainly a first for that department!

The perceived Anglo-Saxon approach of discussing diversity-related issues in the open in order to raise awareness and provide evidence of "progress" did not sit comfortably with the much more modest, reserved, and private nature of the Finns. Although Maria suspected possible traces of denial in people's attitudes to diversity, even fairly open-minded employees voiced their preferences to keep such personal matters separate from the workplace and were opposed to confronting them in intimate, face-to-face settings. Maria tried to explain this is an informal email to corporate HQ:

> It may just be the Finnish way. People feel uncomfortable when, for example, sexual ori-entation is brought up as a topic of discussion, and then you are given the instruction to change your mindset, your behavior, to be more open towards this. I think most people think that the best way to approach diversity is to be pragmatic – just focus on the work at hand. To do that, you have to cooperate and get along with everybody.

FIVE YEARS ON: LESSONS LEARNED, AND WHAT NEXT?

Having rolled out the D&I Initiative to all its international operations, Petrocom HQ felt that important societal issues remained unaddressed and that they needed a way to build in perfor-mance measures that were based on the employee perspective, not just ticking boxes once poli-cies and practices were in place. The D&I Initiative was therefore expanded to include two new elements in addition to Diversity and Inclusiveness: Equity, and Belonging. While Equity was about supporting those with less privileged backgrounds to grow, develop, and pursue their full potential, Belonging was to become a new corporation-wide metric to assess employees' feelings of safety, acceptance, and being valued.

While putting the final touches on her feedback report about the new expansion for the corporate D&I Board, Maria shuddered slightly at the prospect of having to sell yet another "Made in America" set of HRM policies and practices to the managers of the Finnish unit. Reflecting back on how she had felt when she first heard about Finland's inclusion in the global D&I Initiative, she was right to have felt excited and anxious since the D&I Initiative had proven to be rewarding yet very challenging. Maria knew that Petrocom Finland had started off in a strong position in certain areas such as gender diversity and that Finland could teach the rest of Petrocom a thing or two about inclusion and equity. Progress had been made in recruiting racial minorities and supporting their integration in the workplace. However, Maria intuitively knew that the expanded D&I Initiative would need to be more effective in influencing people's attitudes concerning the more invisible aspects of diversity such as individuals' beliefs and sexual orientation. It will also take on extra significance in light of the rapid growth in the number of skilled immigrants they are planning on hiring to replace many of the Finnish employees entering retirement.

Maria still felt Petrocom Finland was at a crossroads. With many corporate expectations met, were Finnish society and the employees at Petrocom Finland ready for this latest expansion and further progress in these difficult areas, and what was the best way to do it? Maria still believed she could make a positive impact, but where should the line be drawn?

CASE STUDY QUESTIONS FOR DISCUSSION

1. Given what you have understood about the Finnish context regarding the HRM practice of workforce diversity management, together with the perceptions of employees at Petrocom Finland about the importance of workforce diversity issues:

    (i) How would you present the business case for diversity and inclusiveness in the Finnish subsidiary without coming across as over-sensationalizing the issue?

    (ii) How might Finland's standing and recent demographic changes in Finland help or hinder you in the above?

2. How would you best seek to reconcile Petrocom Finland's desire for a more locally-driven approach to the HRM practice of diversity management versus Petrocom Group's "Global Organization" vision, strategy, and global D&I standard?

3. "I don't feel that our task is to be the one who comes and breaks the walls down". Where do (i) Petrocom's, (ii) Petrocom Finland's, and (iii) Maria's responsibilities begin and end in terms of HRM practices being used as a means to shape Finnish employees' attitudes and behaviors about diversity and inclusiveness?

NOTES

1 For confidentiality purposes, a pseudonym is used, and certain details concerning the organization's titles and activities have been altered.
2 World Competitiveness Report. 2020. How Countries are Performing on the Road to Recovery, World Economic Forum. www3.weforum.org/docs/WEF_TheGlobalCompetitivenessReport2020.pdf.
3 Global Social Mobility Index. 2020. World Economic Forum, available at: www.weforum.org/reports/global-social-mobility-index-2020-why-economies-benefit-from-fixing-inequality.
4 Global Gender Gap Index. 2021. World Economic Forum, available at: www.weforum.org/reports/global-gender-gap-report-2021.

REFERENCES

Evans, P., Smale, A., & Björkman, I. 2018. Macro talent management in Finland: Contributing to a rapidly evolving knowledge economy. In V. Vaiman, P. Sparrow, R. Schuler, & D.G. Collings (Eds.), *Macro Talent Management: A Global Perspective on Managing Talent in Developed Markets* (pp. 170–189). Routledge.

Lanvin, B., & Monteiro, F. 2021. *The Global Talent Competitive Index: Talent Competitiveness in Time of COVID.* INSEAD.

Sippola, A., & Smale, A. 2007. The global integration of diversity management: A longitudinal case study. *International Journal of Human Resource Management, 18*(11): 1895–1916.

Supplementary Resources

The case is partly based on fieldwork and findings published in: Sippola, A. & Smale, A. (2007). The global integration of diversity management: A longitudinal case study. *International Journal of Human Resource Management, 18*(11), 1895–1916.

Further Reading

Lauring, J. 2013. International diversity management: Global ideals and local responses. *British Journal of Management, 24*(2), 211–224. *[For a comprehensive and data-based overview of Finnish culture and leadership].*

Lindell, M., & Sigfrids, C. 2007. Culture and leadership in Finland. In J. S. Chhokar, F. C. Brodbeck, & R. J. House (Eds.), *Culture and Leadership Across the World: The GLOBE Book of In-Depth Studies of 25 Societies* (pp. 109–140). Psychology Press. https://doi.org/10.4324/9780203936665

Extra Resources

Global Talent Competitive Index (GTCI): A ranking of countries around the world based on how they grow, attract and retain talent, available at: https://www.insead.edu/faculty-research/research/gtci

Nordic Business Diversity Index. 2021. *Diversity of Senior Leadership in Nordic Listed Companies,* available at: https://www.3bility.fi/wp-content/uploads/NordicBusinessDiversityIndex_2021.pdf

Statistics Finland: 'Finland in figures' is an information package about Finland and Finns. Finland in figures provides key up-to-date data on population, housing, education, enterprises and culture in the form of statistics and graphics. Visit: https://www.stat.fi/tup/suoluk/index_en.html

CHAPTER 7

Iceland

The Integration of HRM Practices in a Global Company: Acquisitions at Marel, Iceland

Ingi Runar Edvardsson and Ivo Rothkrantz

CASE SYNOPSIS[1]

Marel is a highly successful company that has been growing fast over the last few years, mainly through strategic mergers and acquisitions (M&As) with other companies but also through organic growth. For the period 2017–2026, Marel has set a target of a 12% average annual increase in revenues, through both organic growth and acquisitions. Marel was founded in Iceland in 1983 and is a global market leader in the manufacturing of equipment, software, spare parts, and service for the food processing industry. The company is highly innovative and spends 6% of annual revenues on R&D. The company has around 7,000 employees worldwide and operates on six continents. The aim of this case is to analyze the challenge that the M&As of Marel with other successful companies in the food production industry have on the integration and coordination of human resource management policy and practices.

KEYWORDS

Human resource management, integration, national legislation, food production industry, Iceland

DOI: 10.4324/9781003307099-9

LEARNING OUTCOMES

1. Acquire knowledge and understanding of the coordination and integration processes of human resource management (HRM) in global companies.
2. Develop analytical skills to examine mergers and acquisitions in a global company.
3. Develop interpersonal skills to communicate effectively with other team members on potential solutions to HRM problems.
4. Enhance decision-making skills to provide solutions to complex HRM situations.
5. Formulate strategies and recommendations for action on HRM issues.

INTRODUCTION

Marel is a highly successful private global market leader in the manufacturing of advanced equipment, software, spare parts, and services for the food processing industry. Marel's headquarters are in Gardabaer, Iceland. The company traces its roots as far back as the 1930s and operates across 30 countries, including Iceland, Australia, Brazil, Denmark, France, Germany, Norway, the Netherlands, the United Kingdom, the United States, and China. The company is proud of its multinational heritage.

Marel was established in Iceland in 1983 and has grown rapidly based on a dynamic organizational culture and a simple hierarchy. Marel has increased its sales and revenues through the merger and acquisition of a number of rival companies since 1997. The aim of Marel is to fully harness the potential synergies from the integration of the companies and to present one common "face" to the customer.

The industrial relations systems of Iceland and the other countries that Marel operates in, as well as the national cultures, are different in many ways, making the integration of the human resource management (HRM) practices and organizational cultures of the company a considerable challenge. This case will analyze the mergers and acquisitions, and their impact on HRM issues, the organizational culture, and other important aspects related to the daily operations of Marel. The case will attempt to answer the following questions: How is the integration process planned after companies have been merged with Marel? How do the differences in labor legislation and national cultures affect the HRM function in the enlarged Marel company? How are the recruitment process, training of personnel, decision-making, and incentive schemes planned in the global company?

HISTORICAL BACKGROUND OF MAREL[2]

Marel was formally established in Reykjavik, Iceland, on March 17, 1983, by a group of 22 companies, mainly Icelandic fish processors. The history of Marel goes back even further to 1977 when two engineers at the University of Iceland began to explore the possibility of developing and manufacturing onboard scales intended to improve weighing accuracy and efficiency in the fish processing industry.[3] In the beginning, the company employed fewer than ten employees. Most came from one of the founding companies, Framleiðni hf, and from the Faculty of Science at the University of Iceland. In 1987, the number of employees had risen to around 50 but subsequently decreased to 30 and stayed that way until 1990 when Marel began to recruit again (Jon Thor Ólafsson, interview in 2010).

Early on, it was recognized that the Icelandic fish industry would not suffice as the primary market for the company's products. Management, therefore, looked to Norway, mainly because the processing procedures there were like those employed in the Icelandic market. In 1983, the first Marel scale was sold to Norway through an agent, and in 1985 a sales office in Canada was established. At the same time, a new product was launched – a marine scale that made onboard processing more accurate. The company also added Russia to the list of countries it sold to. Until 1992, the marine scale and graders were the main sources of income for Marel, but the company was close to stagnating in terms of growth. In 1992, Marel began selling flow lines to the fish industry, which revolutionized the handling of fish products.

In the late 1980s, Marel began to transfer knowledge accumulated in the fish industry to the poultry industry with the development of a concept similar to the fish industry flow lines. The research and development required for this transfer of knowledge took a few years, and in 1995 the company was ready to establish a subsidiary in the United States, which, at the time, was the largest market for poultry in the world. In 1996, the company took another major step when it began to sell equipment to the red meat industry.

Today, Marel's main product categories include weighing, grading, batching, portioning, inspection, processing lines, and integrated software solutions. Marel services customers looking to escalate their level of automation, food quality, and traceability. At present, Marel is focused on innovations related to automation, robotics, and digital solutions.

Since 2006, Marel has followed a two-phased growth strategy designed to establish the company as the market leader. The goal was to first increase turnover through organic growth and strategic mergers and acquisitions. Economies of scale were considered necessary in order to be able to provide customers with the service they need and to be able to follow them into emerging markets in Eastern Europe, South America, and Asia. Economies of scale and increased market share were achieved through strategic mergers and acquisitions.

With support from shareholders, Marel completely transformed the landscape in the industry, and the company's market share has grown from 4% to 15% since 2006 (Marel, *Advance with Marel*). The revenues of Marel have risen from 200 million euros in 2006 to 1,361 million euros in 2021 (Table 7.1).

LABOR MARKETS AND REGULATION

There are some notable differences between the HRM practices of Iceland and other countries. First, the union density in Iceland is far higher than in other countries. In 2018, 90.7% of employees in Iceland were union members, compared to 16.5% in the Netherlands, 16.6% in Germany, 67.5% in Denmark, and 49.9% in Norway. Likewise, the bargaining coverage (the number of workers that the unions negotiate for) is highest in Iceland, at 90%, while it is lowest in Germany, at 54% (OECD Labor Force Statistics, 2022). Second, employee involvement is much more widespread in many European firms that have work councils present (Dietz, Hoogendoorn, Kabst, &

TABLE 7.1 Historical development of Marel

Mergers and acquisitions	Number of employees
1997 Carnitech A/S, Denmark	250
2006 AEW Delford, UK	3500
2006 Scanvaegt, Denmark	
2008 Stork Food Systems, the Netherlands	
2016 MPS, the Netherlands	
2017 Sulmaq, Brazil	
2018 MAJA, Germany	
2019 Cedar Creek, Australia	
2019 Curio, Iceland	
2020 TREIF, Germany	
2020 PMJ, the Netherlands	
2021 Stranda Prolog, Norway	
2021 Valka, Iceland	7000+

Schmelter, 2004). Such employee involvement is absent in Iceland (Edvardsson, 1992). Third, the labor legislation in Iceland is far less restrictive than in many other countries. On a comparable scale ranging from 0–6, the "strictness of employment protection" in Iceland was 2.88 in 2018, compared to 3.19 in the Netherlands, 3.63 in Germany, 2.88 in Demark, and 2.50 in Norway. The "strictness of employment protection" measures the procedures and costs involved in dismissing individuals or groups of workers and the procedures involved in hiring workers on fixed-term or temporary work agency contracts[4] (OECD Labor Force Statistics, 2022).

Iceland has been a member of the European Economic Area since 1994. Many aspects of HRM are affected by the Social Chapter of the Maastricht Treaty, such as working hours, working conditions, consultation, equal opportunity, social security, dismissals, employee representation, etc. (European Union).

The labor markets in Iceland and many European countries function in many respects quite well. The employment rate, or the percentage of people between the ages 15–64 who are employed, was 86.8% in Iceland in 2018, which is close to the high end of the spectrum in an international context. Similarly, the unemployment rate was quite low in Iceland in 2018, at 3.7%, compared to 5.0% in Demark, 3.4% in Germany, 3.8% in the Netherlands, and 3.8% in Norway. Part-time employment is far higher in the Netherlands than in Iceland, 36% compared to 16%, while the percentage of self-employed is similar (12.4% compared to 13.7%) (Statistics Iceland, 2022).

NATIONAL HRM PRACTICES

In general, HRM practices in Icelandic firms are similar to firms in Denmark, the Netherlands, and the United States, according to the 2018 Cranet survey (see Table 7.2). The table reveals that the majority of firms in the survey have a written HRM policy, and HRM managers sit on the board of management and are involved in the development of corporate strategy. The only difference is that HRM managers in the United States are more involved in the development of corporate strategy than in the other countries.

THE OPERATIONAL CONTEXT AT MAREL

When Marel in Iceland was established in 1983, a divisional structure was put in place. Later, the strategic decision was made to follow the market and to base the new structure on the four industry segments that the company specializes in – fish, meat, poultry, and retail – and food service solutions. The new structure is based on the model of a matrix organization where a board of management has the highest authority.

The board of directors constitutes seven members, three women and four men, that have a long experience in international business. The executive team consists of nine directors, five women and four men, under the leadership of Chief Executive Officer, Arni Oddur Thordarson (Marel, Management).

TABLE 7.2 HRM practices in firms in Denmark, Iceland, the Netherlands, and the United States in 2018

	United States	Denmark	Netherlands	Iceland
Written HR policy	64	72	64	83
HRM managers on the main board of management	69	71	71	68
HRM managers involved in the development of corporate strategy				
From the outset	88	56	-	76
Performance-related pay				
Management	54	56	60	66
Professional/technical	58	37	44	59
Manual	48	26	34	47

Source: Arney Einarsdóttir, Katrín Ólafsdóttir, and Ásta Bjarnadóttir, 2018. Figures in the table are %.

THE HRM CONTEXT AT MAREL AND MERGED COMPANIES

From the beginning, the CEO and managing directors of Marel in Iceland took care of all HRM issues related to their respective divisions. In early 1999, one of the directors took on the role of HRM manager, but within a few months, Marel recruited an HRM manager from outside the organization. It was then that Marel first introduced a formal HRM strategy, appraisal interviews, and formal recruitment procedures (Jakobsdottir, interview in 2010). It can be said that until 1999, Marel's approach to HRM was less developed, mostly concerning recruitment and termination of employment, salary processing, and vacation scheduling. At present, Marel has a sizable and global HRM function led by the Vice President of People and Culture, who is ultimately responsible for the HRM policies. Teams with representatives from the respective functions (Marel + acquired organization) are responsible for integrations, and they determine the HRM integration plan and speed. Many of the HRM policies define or reinforce Marel's culture and are, therefore, non-negotiable, while others reflect national legislation and culture, and are less urgent to align in the integration process. In Marel, there is, thus, both central and integrated HRM policy, as well as local policies adhering to regional demands.

Managers at Marel have vast experience in merging with other companies in the food production industry. An "Integration Playbook" has been drafted, which highlights the overall integration approach and key items to consider in an integration project. It provides guidance, but is not a full recipe, because no integration is the same. A big part is determined prior to acquisition in the integration strategy (part of the M&A process), but a lot is also clarified in the integration planning phase and then tweaked during execution. For HRM, there is a distinction in HRM "technical" integration of the function and the organizational alignment and design, which is supported by HRM but driven by the business and often steered by the integration team and steering committee.

HUMAN RESOURCES

The employees of Marel have been steadily growing in number since 1990, especially following the acquisitions since 2006. Today, Marel employs approximately 7,000 employees worldwide, growing from 3,500 employees in 2009. The majority of employees are currently located in Europe. The job profiles in Marel are engineers in innovation, field service engineers and customer service coordinators dealing with services, account managers in sales, project managers, various skilled factory employees like welders, CNC operators, assembly technicians, and support functions (HRM/finance/IT). To complement the offerings of equipment, service, spare parts, and software, there is a fast-growing group of software engineers and UX (user experience) designers.

HRM POLICY

Marel is committed to building and maintaining a diverse and inclusive culture, where all people feel valued and engaged, and are treated with respect, dignity, and fairness. Marel is committed to its values, which are *Unity*, *Innovation*, and *Excellence*. The company encourages equality of opportunity, values diversity in all its forms, and fosters a culture of inclusion. Bullying, discrimination, and harassment are not tolerated, and Marel ensures adherence to its diversity and inclusion commitments, as stated in the company's policy on diversity and inclusion (https://marel.com/media/41wmsszp/marel-global-diversity-inclusion-policy.pdf).

ORGANIZATIONAL CULTURE

From the beginning, Marel was defined as an entrepreneurial organization. This is reflected in different aspects of its organizational culture, such as risk-taking. A lot of time and capital is spent on research and development without knowing the return on investment (ROI). The acquisitions of companies that are equal or even larger in size can also be an indication of risk-taking.

The entrepreneurial nature is also reflected in another aspect of the organization's culture, namely in the devotion to innovation that has made Marel a global leader in its field. The structure implemented in the manufacturing process in 1997 was very innovative; it was based on dividing manufacturing into individual production cells. This structure is still in place at the company headquarters in Gardabaer, Iceland. Still another relevant feature of Marel's culture is the growth strategy presented in 2006 and the merger and acquisitions that followed, after careful analysis of about 130 companies. Finally, autonomy is highly encouraged at Marel, and managers have the freedom to take independent decisions. This feature is especially encouraged among teams developing new solutions in cooperation with customers (Ólafsson & Hermannsdóttir, 2009).

THE PRACTICAL HRM DILEMMA IN A NEW MERGED COMPANY

International companies face many challenges, such as hiring managers in newly merged companies, designing pay structures, training schemes, performance management, and so on.

The scale of a big company makes it possible to hire experts in specific areas that support the entire organization, making specialists available across the globe. The geographical distance, as well as size, makes the need for standards bigger, but also more difficult to implement or change. Regarding HRM, this means that global policies need to be designed in a way that they are specific enough to achieve their purpose while leaving enough flexibility to adjust to local situations like legislation or local customs.

At Marel, the recruitment of managers and other employees is the responsibility of the global recruiting team that supports the more strategic roles, while regional recruiters are responsible for recruiting the local workforce, mainly in local manufacturing, sales, and service. The global HRM information system at Marel is of great importance in the hiring process, making the legal entity easier to tackle. At the beginning of mergers with other companies, the compensation and benefit standards, as well as recruitment, are not yet aligned, which is then addressed as part of the integration process itself.

Training programs are in place, which range from onboarding into the company, to technical knowledge of machines and software, to skills development, like presentation, leadership, and project management skills. There is also individual coaching. In the integration process, the focus is on cross-training the sales/service and innovation teams on the products and solutions provided by Marel and the acquired company. At the same time, the new employees learn about Marel's history, ways of working, culture, and policies through a Connection journey. This Connection journey is a set of interactive gatherings that help to teach and implement Marel standards as well as formal training, while also allowing employees to get to know each other and the organization. The program has generic components for all employees and splits out into more specific groups for specific topics (e.g., all managers or sales process respectively). In some cases, language courses, primarily in English, are provided to enable a wider group to interact with global colleagues in the official company language. Some acquisitions have operated so locally that the English skills are limited to a small group of management.

Marel's philosophy is that competitive, fair, and responsible rewards combined with good working conditions and good career development possibilities are a good long-term strategy to make Marel competitive in hiring and maintaining outstanding employees (Marel internal document). In the 30+ countries that Marel operates in, all are unique in terms of local market conditions and cultures. Marel's goal is to implement a globally consistent, competitive, and transparent framework for rewarding employees, while allowing local variations due to local market practices. Employees should be paid equitably for the same job with a base salary framework aligned to the local general market. Individual performance is measured by individual targets related to sustainable growth in the job and development of competencies, which links to annual salary increases. Performance-based incentives (bonuses) maintain the close linkage between performance and reward by compensating for the achievement of company and individual targets. Marel aims to have a global bonus framework with the flexibility to adapt regionally or locally, depending on regional and local market practices.

A lot of the work in Marel is done in teams, which can be with a local team in a specific discipline, but also cross-functional, cross-border, and/or in collaboration with customers and partners. Integrations are also done as a team effort with workstream teams for the specific integration topics that consist of specialists and/or leaders from both companies who jointly design, plan, and execute the integration program. They are guided by design principles that have been set up in the integration strategy (prior to acquisition). Awareness of cultural differences is stressed in the integration of teams. One manager at Marel noted:

> People are usually curious and excited about getting started and finding out more about the "other side". Recent acquisitions have also been with family-owned businesses, which puts a whole new dimension on top of the country-specific differences. The family business culture is usually very strongly oriented at an owner or group of family members that drive the business. When this is integrated into a more corporate organization, the employees need to get used to making more independent decisions, instead of having everything run up to the owner(s) for a final decision. It gives a lot stronger sense of empowerment, but at the same time the group is less compact because reporting lines are no longer limited to one main location, but now extend into the wider Marel organization, that is, when the integration project is completed. In integrations it is also important to create a relative level playing field: both companies are often successful, be it with a different scale and expertise. Unintentionally the acquiring company can come across as arrogant and "we know best", where often the strength is in combining know-how, portfolio,

customer groups and geographies. This requires strong change management in the work stream teams as well as in the overall integration project management.

Knowledge transfer can pose a challenge in international knowledge organizations like Marel. At Marel, various formal and informal ways are used to transfer knowledge within the company, such as codifying documents that are stored centrally with regards to, for example, ways of working and operating procedures; some parts are standard governance structures used on all parts of the organization but with different individuals for each unit (e.g. innovation processes). Collaborative ICT platforms (e.g., Teams and intranet) are in place to share tacit knowledge and to collaborate. There are also formal training programs in place. In integrations, a selection of these systems is on the priority list to facilitate (cross-border) collaboration and sometimes bridge language barriers.

With modern IT tools, collaboration has become easier, and a video conference can be set up with just a click of a button. Information can be easily shared, but misinterpretation can also occur. Strong value is put on meeting in person to build business relationships with people and react to non-verbal communication more directly. During the COVID-19 pandemic, this has become very apparent: The integration project can run, but as soon as the people are able to meet, an increase in progress and mutual understanding takes place because of the direct interaction.

With a clear goal to grow revenues from 5% to 7% on average through acquisitions by 2026 (see Marel website), Marel will continue to acquire and integrate businesses into the organization. With the practical experience of the integration team and the rest of the organization, more integration activities can be facilitated using technology, but every acquisition is different, so the focus on employees and culture will remain one of the main success factors of integration.

CASE STUDY QUESTIONS FOR DISCUSSION

1. What are the main developments presented in the case regarding HRM in a global company?
2. What challenges and opportunities do continuous M&As with other companies impose on recruitment in Marel?
3. What challenges and opportunities does running a business on six continents impose for training and development within Marel?
4. What challenges and opportunities do M&As with other companies have on performance management systems at Marel?
5. How does the organizational culture within Marel affect HRM policy and practice?

NOTES

1 The author has permission from Marel to publish this case. The case was written with Ivo Rothkrantz from Marel.
2 All references in this section, unless otherwise stated, are based on Marel's website: www.marel.com.

3 All references in this section, if not otherwise stated, are based on Marel's web site: www.marel.com.

4 To explain the scale, for instance, individual dismissals of workers with regular contracts yields the score 0 if the dismissal period is 0–2 days, 1 if the days are fewer than 10, 2 if the days are 11–18, 3 if days are 17–26, 4 for 27–35 days, 5 for 36–45 days, and finally 6 if the dismissal days are more than 45.

REFERENCES

Dietz, B., Hoogendoorn, J., Kabst, R., & Schmelter, A. 2004. The Netherlands and Germany: Flexibility or rigidity? In C. Brewster, W. Mayrhofer & Morely, M. (Eds.), *Human Resource Management in Europe: Evidence of Convergence?*, 73–94. Amsterdam: Elsiver.

Einardóttir, A., Ólafsdóttir, K. & Bjarnadóttir, A. 2018. *Mannauðsstjórnun á Íslandi (Human Resource Management in Iceland)*. Reykjavik: Háskóli Íslands, Viðskiptafræðideild.

Edvardsson, I. R. 1992. *Printing in Action: General Printing in Iceland and Sweden*. Lund: Lund University Press.

European Union. n.d. *Facts About the 'Social Chapter'*. Downloaded on January 27th 2022 from https://ec.europa.eu/commission/presscorner/detail/en/MEMO_97_13

Marel. 2010b. *Advance with Marel*. Iceland, Gardabaer: Author. Unpublished material.

Marel. n.d. *Management*. Marel. Downloaded on January 27th 2022 from http://www.marel.com/company/Management/

OECD Labour Force Statistics. 2022. *OECD. StatExtracts (2022). OECD. StatExtracts.* Downloaded on January 27th 2022 from http://stats.oecd.org/Index.aspx?DataSetCode=MEILABOUR

Ólafsson, S. & Hermannsdóttir, A. 2009. Vaxtarsaga Marel. Downloaded on April 20th 2010 from http://www3.hi.is/Apps/WebObjects/HI.woa/swdocument/1014597/marel_loka.pdf, 2009.

Statistics Iceland. 2022. Labour market statistics in OECD countries 2022. Downloaded on January 27th 2020 from http://www.hagstofa.is/lisalib/getfile.aspx?itemid=11612.

Central and Eastern Europe

CHAPTER 8

Hungary

An American Transnational MNC in Hungary: Past, Present, and Future of HRM Evolution

József Poór, Katalin Szabó, Katalin Balog, Zsolt Barna, and Tamás Hámori

CASE SYNOPSIS

First, we present the key socio-economic characteristics of the Hungarian economy and labor market. Next, we review the place and role of FDI (foreign direct investment) in the Hungarian economy. The first acquisition and European investment of General Electric (GE) was Tungsram in Hungary in 1990. It was a challenge for both parties: Tungsram's organization, production, and stock capacity and portfolio had to be coordinated with the interests of the company. In the following, we review the three most important development stages of GE's Hungarian subsidiary (1990–2003; 2004–2017; and 2017 until the present). Here we refer to the most significant development tasks and present the HRM tasks related to the indicated periods. The COVID-19 pandemic reached Hungary in mid-March 2020. Hungarian subsidiaries of large international companies also suffered significant losses in the supply chain and had customer problems. During the second and third waves of COVID-19, GE in Hungary launched more serious developments (e.g., healthcare) which are presented briefly in the case.

KEYWORDS

General Electric (GE), multinational corporation (MNC), life cycle, HRM, Hungary

DOI: 10.4324/9781003307099-11

INTRODUCTION

The late Jack Welch,[1] head of General Electric (GE), who was known as "Neutron Jack", decided in 1989 that GE would acquire Tungsram, a company in the Hungarian economy with a history of more than 100 years (Holusha, 1989). In the uncertain transitional situation, the leader of GE, who was constantly transforming the company, might not have expected that the company he had acquired, GE Tungsram, would continue to operate successfully in Hungary after more than three decades. This is the path the company is continuing to follow in the changed market conditions. Global corporate executives also took notice of the changes in world politics, the end of the Cold War, and the transformation of a bipolar world. This process, accelerating in the mid-1980s, faced these multinational firms with a new situation, which allowed them to enter the then-unified Eastern European market (Wolf & Poór, 1992). This provided an option for wider access to the markets of transition countries and developing countries, where, in many places, countries of The Council for Mutual Economic Assistance (Comecon; the trade organization of former socialist countries) that were part of the disintegrating communist bloc (e.g., Bulgaria, Czechoslovakia, German Democratic Republic/GDR, Hungary, Romania, Poland, and the Soviet Union) were the dominant players. This was the case for General Electric's Jack Welch, who took steps to enter the Hungarian market by acquiring an established company with a strong market history.

The Socio-Economic Situation of Hungary

General Situation

Before the sudden political changes in 1989, eight countries existed in the region. The political and administrative map of the region has undergone drastic changes. Besides the Eurasian region of the former Soviet Union, there are now 15 countries, with more than 200 million people. Before the political changes, the whole region had been culturally treated very similarly by the Western world. These nations belonged to the communist bloc. Within the new borders, we must recognize a rich diverse historic and cultural environment.

The transition has been overshadowed by high inflation and a drastic decrease in output performance. In the meantime, the increasing number of countries in the region, including Hungary, have managed to change this trend. During the economic challenges of the previous decade, most of the countries within the region had begun to grow. Despite economic growth and the low inflation rate of many Central and Eastern European (CEE) countries including Hungary, large GDP differences remain between the highly developed OECD and CEE countries.

Foreign Capital in Hungary

In Central and Eastern Europe, FDI was not significant until the change of regime in 1989. In Hungary, the first joint venture was established in 1972 by the German company Siemens. In recent years, despite temporary declines, the amount of inward FDI has increased significantly. In the period from 1990 to 2018, Eastern Europe, excluding Russia, received more than USD 1,167 billion in FDI. In Hungary, the figure for the same period was USD 100 billion (EUR 80 billion). This FDI inflow has contributed greatly to the export-oriented economic development of the region to Hungary's integration into global economic processes (Jirasavetakul-Rahman, 2018).

In the developed countries of the Western world, the share of foreign firms employing people is 5% to 6%, except for the smaller countries like Ireland (50%) and New Zealand (25%). In Eastern Europe, in three of the Visegrad countries – Slovakia, Hungary, and the Czech Republic – the share of foreign firms employing people is 30%, 22%, and 16%, respectively, and in other countries in the region, it is 6% to 8%.

Following the change of regime in Hungary, a high number of large Western companies set up joint ventures and then subsidiaries in the country. Two distinctive routes of capital investment in Hungary can be identified. Firms following the so-called gradual, evolutionary path have had long-standing relationships with Eastern European firms, typically going back to the period before the regime change, and subsequently, when the legal environment allowed, they acquired majority or wholly owned subsidiaries by buying up the ownership package of their partner(s). Companies following the revolutionary path[2] have been spreading worldwide since the second half of the 1990s.

FDI in the European Union, including Hungary and other countries in Central and Eastern Europe, is growing. Foreign presence is particularly significant in the manufacturing sector in Hungary. In 2016, foreign-controlled enterprises accounted for a quarter of the value added of total business in EU member states. The highest share of foreign-controlled enterprises (51%) contributed to the value of the business sector in Hungary.

National and Business Culture

According to Hofstede and Hofstede (2005), among different groups of nationally based organizational cultures, Hungary belongs to the well-oiled machine that mainly includes countries with German culture and language. Organizations in these countries are characterized by strong planning, regulated operational processes, and bureaucracy at all levels, and Hungary is included because it is characterized by a German cultural influence. Hungarian managers are less leader-type decision-makers and thus have the characteristics of this type of thinking.

The Labor Market

The Hungarian labor market has undergone major changes over the last 30 years. In 2019, the year before the outbreak of the COVID-19 pandemic, the unemployment rate at the national level fell to 3.5%. Many industries experienced very large labor shortages. Current labor market data show that the COVID-19 outbreak has not eliminated labor shortages in the Hungarian economy.

GE IN HUNGARY

1990–2003

General Electric

Thomas A. Edison, the inventor of the incandescent lamp, founded the company in 1878. General Electric's greatness is also demonstrated by the fact that it is the only company to have been included in the basket of stocks used to calculate the Dow Jones Industrial Average from its inception until 2018.

General Electric Lighting (hereafter GEL), the lighting division, which was the second largest manufacturer in the world, continued to be one of GE's core businesses. GE Lighting – because of its product portfolio – offered fewer opportunities for spectacular growth than those for Edison's General Electric in the last century. In the market for conventional incandescent lamps, it was only possible to compete at low margins, and the development of new, innovative light sources required huge investments and high levels of constant R&D expenditure. GEL's 1989 sales of USD 2.3 billion accounted for 5% of GE's total sales of USD 44 billion. GEL was the market leader in the United States, and not many people at that time thought that this position could be threatened by any other competitor. This excellent market position was overshadowed by just one unfortunate fact: Most of GEL's revenues came from the US market. The weakest point of the GEL business was a market share of only 2% in Europe, a market with an annual turnover of USD 2.5 billion, which was insignificant compared to Philips and Osram (the two big competitors).

GE had three alternatives for international expansion in 1989:

- An alliance with a major European manufacturer (strategic alliance).
- An acquisition.
- Greenfield investment (tax incentives directly linked to the activity and the role of the employer to promote investment).

Tungsram

Tungsram, founded in 1896, was the third oldest light source manufacturer in the world after GE and Philips. Innovation played an important role in the acquisition, as most of its products were traditionally sold abroad. This market position was eroded during the socialist period, but at the end of the 1980s, it still ranked third among European light source manufacturers, accounting for 8% of the European market.

Acquisition

In 1987, the Hungarian government asked the international consultancy firm Arthur D Little (hereafter ADL) to evaluate Tungsram. In brief, ADL stated that the way to revitalize Tungsram was to obtain capital, new production technology, and modern management procedures with the help of a strategic investor. This strategic investor in 1989 (on the eve of the regime change) became GE, which on January 1, 1990, bought 50% plus one share of the shares in the light source manufacturer Tungsram for USD 150 million. Between 1990 and 2002, it invested USD 1 billion in Tungsram and thus acquired all the shares in the company.

Rationalization

Following the takeover, in the early 1990s, GE Tungsram's 20,000 employees were reduced to 9,000 and had a less bureaucratic administration. To improve innovation, half of GEL's R&D activities were relocated to Hungary.

GE's traditional organizational culture, which has been developed and anchored over a long period of time, ensures that employees adopt a uniform attitude. This corporate culture is based on American cultural norms (such as optimism and self-confidence) and on the style and actions of GE's managers (previously, mainly Jack Welch's best practices, such as mass layoffs and the rapid sale of underperforming units). Initially (from 1990 to 1991), GE was cautious about changing the culture it had inherited from Tungsram (learning from previous unpleasant experiences in France), but in 1992 it decided to move faster, appointing a new American manager to lead Tungsram. GE sought to reduce the cultural opposition through intensive professional and language training and by moving employees between divisions.

As a traditional company, Tungsram was functional and hierarchical. There was very little communication between departments. Decisions were made only by top management. GE reduced the organizational levels from 15 to 4, and in this flat organization, most jobs with full responsibility and accountability were challenging and imposed high expectations on the job holders. The customer focus helped employees understand the need for change and the constant search for better solutions. The culture change was mainly driven by integration at the European level, the creation of cross-functional and cross-country teams, posting abroad, training, courses, and the introduction of and familiarization with GE policies and practices. After the acquisition, foreign employees in senior management positions were the main drivers of change. The good selection of ex-pats, which was based on skills, cultural sensitivity, and people management, ensured the smooth transition and the success of the first step toward the integration into GE. There were two other groups of people who had major roles in the transition. The first group was the new generation of managers including the graduates from GE entry-level programs, which were not only for local graduates but also for ex-pats. The second group, which was the winner of the changes, included professionals and skilled workers, who gained much more responsibility and independence because of delayering. Finally, the most important driver of the changes was growing cross-functional and cross-country teamwork where the Hungarian team members had the opportunity to experience the GE culture in practice. The expansion of employment opportunities for people living in various areas, especially in former industrial districts, is a priority issue and a task for current economic policy.

Growth and Headcount Increase

During the 1990s, the growth of light source production slowed down in the United States, and in global markets, low-cost Chinese firms strengthened. GE's response was to close several

FIGURE 8.1 Staff numbers at Tungsram Hungary (1990–2018)

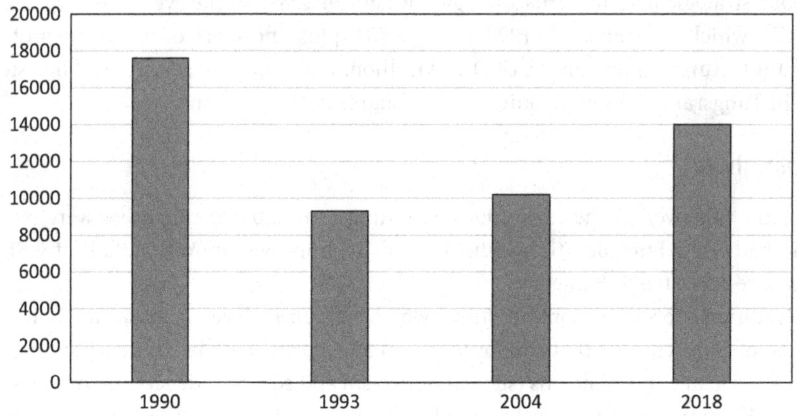

Source: Authors' own research

plants in the United States and Western Europe and to move production to lower-cost production sites (Mexico, Hungary). In February 2002, GE Tungsram became the new European, Middle East, and African (EMA) headquarters for GEL.

Figure 8.1 shows that the total number of employees at Tungsram was reduced from 17,600 to 9,200 by the end of 1993, taking into account the appropriate staffing and employment levels. There was then a slow increase again to 10,200, thanks to significantly increased productivity and profitability. The composition of employment also changed. With the elimination of the administrative staff, the share of salaried employees fell from 20% to 10%. (Note: Downsizing, acquisitions, restructuring, and optimization continued in the second half of the 2010s, and by 2018 the number of employees reached 14,000. This number does not include subcontractors who have been outsourced since then.)

2004–2017

Reorganization

On July 10, 2004, GE announced that the long-touted outsourcing would also affect the European, Middle Eastern, and African divisions of the consumer and industrial departments of GE Hungary zrt. (zrt.: private limited liability company) based in Budapest. The outsourcing would bring the division under the ownership of its shareholders. The move would affect two-thirds of the company's 15,000 employees in Hungary. It would mean selling or becoming independent of the division's three well-established organizations, which produced household appliances, lighting, and industrial products. The reduction in the number of divisions from six to four was driven by the need to streamline operations and increase efficiency. According to Jeff Immelt, CEO of GE, this move would allow the company, which produced almost everything from light bulbs to nuclear power plants, to better focus on its divisions that produce high-margin products (e.g., water purification equipment, locomotives).

The Wall Street Journal of July 27–28, 2008, published a surprising piece of news. Jeffrey Immelt, the CEO, quoted elsewhere in the book, announced that the company's various divisions would be combined into four global businesses: Technology Infrastructure, Energy Infrastructure, GE Capital (banking), and NBC Universal Entertainment. The businesses in the other areas would either be outsourced or sold. This would include the household, credit card, lighting, and industrial businesses. Would the fate of GE Tungsram Hungary depend to a large extent on this restructuring and divestments?

Due to the global credit crisis of 2008–2009, GE Capital lost a third of its profits in the third quarter, which contributed to a 22% drop in profits for the group.

HRM Challenges

It was a big challenge for HRM regarding how to implement the restructuring, as it significantly affected domestic factories and jobs. The number of semi-skilled worker-type jobs decreased in Hungary, as technological development required a different type of skilled labor. On the one hand, manufacturing was being downsized, and on the other hand, skilled workers were being hired – a dichotomy that really drove this occupational challenge.

The changeover strategy also meant a new HRM strategy. The first step was a change of leadership at the senior management level to the position of Global HR Director for GE Lighting. The new leadership was tasked with eliminating more than 2,000 jobs over two years, 2010–2012. (In 2010, GE Lighting employed 7,500 people in Hungary, compared to 17,000 globally.) The group's redundancies were carefully managed, with union cooperation and additional benefits offered to employees, building on the existing collective agreement. In the area of severance payments, they made an exemplary effort to remunerate their employees, and on the other side, they offered outplacement services to Hungarian employees, special tailor-made job placement plans, and assistance in retraining and further training and in becoming self-employed. Government and local employment organizations were also involved.

At the same time, a shortage of professionals in Hungary who could meet the new challenges increased the difficulty. On the other side, hundreds of engineers could have been recruited, but – worldwide, where technology centers operate – there were not enough of them. The main obstacle to recruitment was related to engineers, as there were not enough well- and specially trained ones, especially in the area of light-emitting diodes (LEDs), not only in Hungary but also in Europe. One of the reasons for this is that training was not adapted to this innovation in time, and a specialized training program was not yet a focus of domestic education. As a solution, universities in Hungary, the United States, Canada, and China were contacted to ensure that higher education facilities were offering the required levels of specialized training before recruitment. GE established very good cooperation with the Budapest University of Technology, and they are currently working together on research and development projects. In the future, curriculum adaptation to market needs is necessary. Nowadays, it is mainly young and enthusiastic engineers who, having had general training, spend years in practice specializing.

2017–Present

Latest Rationalization

The economic crisis of recent years also had an impact on GE. There have been layoffs in many areas and some factories have closed, and since the peak of 333,000 employees in 2015, more than 100,000 people have been laid off. The fact that GE is present in almost all sectors of the economy and on all continents has played a major role in ensuring that the overall impact of the crisis, which has affected the whole world and all industries, has been less pronounced overall than for companies operating in only one sector of the economy.

GE's worldwide activities are divided into four main businesses:

1. Power.
2. Aviation.
3. Healthcare.
4. Renewable energy.

Buy-Out of Lighting Division

General Electric sold its "light" and car lamp businesses in 2018, and in February of that year, GE Hungary CEO Jörg Bauer announced plans to buy those businesses in Europe, the Middle East, Africa, and Turkey. The company would now operate under the name Tungsram Group. Tungsram continued to make acquisitions and in 2018 took over 22 subsidiaries in 23 countries. It regularly launched new business units and developed them. GE's subsidiary GE Lighting was acquired by Savant System Inc. in 2020. Today, GE Lighting continues to operate as a Savant Company, retaining its original name.

The Tungsram Group (GE Lighting) of Europe, the Middle East, and Africa is headquartered in Budapest, as is the global technology center of the lighting business, where a team of around 160 engineers works on the development of the lighting of the future. GE Lighting has seven factories in Europe, six of which are in Hungary – in Budapest, Győr, Hajdúböszörmény, Kisvárda, Nagykanizsa, and Zalaegerszeg. The division's product portfolio currently includes architectural lighting, hotel lighting, commercial lighting, indoor lighting, outdoor lighting, and automotive lighting.

Currently, the following technologies are used: LED, HID (high-intensity discharge lamps), LFL (fluorescent lamps), CFL (compact fluorescent lamps), halogen lamps, and incandescent lamps.

The company has a focus on innovative smart products and services. Today, Tungsram has repositioned itself as a premium European lighting brand in the global market. Most of the development, design, and manufacturing have remained in Hungary. In addition to lighting technology, it is also present in the fields of smart solutions, indoor plant cultivation, and component manufacturing.

GE in Europe

GE has been present in 22 countries in Europe for nearly 130 years, in all five of its main businesses. In total, the company employs 92,000 people in the region. In nearly

900 locations, it achieved an annual revenue of €19 billion. GE has important businesses in several key sectors, including aviation, power generation, healthcare, and additives. GE is a key player in driving growth and competitiveness on the continent. The company continued to expand in Europe from 2016–2020. Sixty percent of GE's total major acquisitions, €18 billion, have been made in the European market. Alstom was the largest acquisition in GE's history. In recent years, GE acquired Germany's Arcam and Concept Laser (for €549 million) and LM Wind Power (for €1.65 billion). GE has been operating successfully in Hungary since the end of 1989 and as Tungsram Group since 2016. GE is currently the largest US employer and investor and one of the largest exporters in Hungary, with more than 2,000 key suppliers.

The Impact of COVID-19

The day-to-day changing COVID-19 situation brought very serious difficulties along with a shrinking market. The market changes and the diversified activities set new expectations for the HRM field. A shortage of skilled workers, the need to restructure production, and escalating wages are all major challenges for the HRM field, as is the need to ensure job security and to provide an adequate social safety net. The slowdown in automotive production and the postponement of lighting projects have hit the company hard.

The pandemic has, however, brought a boom in the healthcare business, with several new products being considered healthcare-related: One of the most important is the UV Sanitizer, a device that disinfects objects with ultraviolet light. This is a metal box the size of a microwave or small refrigerator in which everyday objects, appliances, and medical equipment can be disinfected without chemicals.

The market launch is still in progress, but there is already worldwide interest in the product, which is why the company is counting on its success. Tungsram was one of the first companies to use this technology in 1934 in the field of manufacturing lamps with different charges, and the solution is now enjoying a renaissance due to the epidemic.

The other product is a face shield based on a Hungarian development, which is already in production and is being sought for market potential.

The increasingly successful components business, which was created to tie up capacity no longer used in the lighting market, with its outstanding know-how in metal, plastics, ceramics, and glass (all needed for the traditional light bulb), has already found new markets. Other HRM solutions to retain staff in the pandemic situation included the introduction of reduced working hours for three months, albeit with no pay increases and no cafeteria on site, and no redundancies due to the pandemic.

CASE STUDY QUESTIONS FOR DISCUSSION

1. What were the most important business challenges and critical HRM problems after the establishment of GE Hungary (1990–2003; 2004–2017; and 2017 until the present)?
2. What steps has the company taken considering the new market situation and COVID-19?
3. What challenges does GE have to face in the HRM field today?

NOTES

1 Jack Welch (1935–2020). When he retired from GE, he received a severance payment of USD 417 million, the largest such payment in business history.
2 We distinguish two basic ways of internationalization in our case study. One is the slow, gradual so-called evolutionary development. This path was followed by many Western international companies in Eastern Europe in the 1990s. Several, so-called even before the regime change, FMCGs (Food and Fast Moving Companies) maintained good relations with companies from several countries in the region within the framework of license and franchise contracts. The other is the so-called revolutionary development. The latter was followed, for example, by some Western European and American multi-nationals, when they "bought in" immediately after the opening of Central Europe after the fall of the Berlin Wall (e.g. Volkswagen/Škoda, General Electric/Tungsram), i.e. they acquired the majority or sole ownership of companies operating here.

SOURCES

Aráoz, F. C. 2020. Jack Welch's Approach to Leadership. *Harvard Business Review*, March 3. https://hbr.org/2020/03/jack-welchs-approach-to-leadership (Accessed: 4 August, 2021).

GE HRM Project. https://www.slideshare.net/mathananto/ge-hrm-project (Accessed: 25 December, 2021).

GE Hungary. 2020. http://www.ge.com/hu/hu/company/factsheet_hu.html. (Accessed: 6 February, 2020).

Glader, P. 2008. GE Will Cut Costs, Jobs, Immelt Says. *Wall Street Journal*. https://www.wsj .com/ articles/SB122488325347467925 (Accessed: 14 February, 2021).

Hakikit, E. 2015. HR Transformation in GE: 4 Competencies for Success. https://www.insidehr .com.au/hr-transformation-in-ge/ (Accessed: 25 December, 2021).

Hofstede, G. & Hofstede, J. G. 2005. *Cultures and Organizations: Software of the Mind*. McGraw-Hill.

Holusha, J. 1989. Venture Planned by G.E. in Hungary. *New York Times*, November 16. https://www.nytimes.com/1989/11/16/business/venture-planned-by-ge-in-hungary.html (Accessed: 4 August, 2021).

Immelt, R. J., Gulati, R., & Prokesch, S. 2017. Inside GE's Transformation. *Harvard Business Review*, September–October, 41–55.

Jirasavetakul, L. B. F., & Rahman, J. 2018. *Foreign Direct Investment in New Member States of the EU and Western Balkans: Taking Stock and Assessing Prospects*. International Monetary Fund.

Marer, P. 2002. Company Culture. GE Tungsram 1989–2002 (In Hungarian). http://unipub.lib .uni-corvinus.hu/4642/1/VT_2003n7_8p50.pdf (Accessed: 16 February, 2021).

Poór J. D., Engle, D. A., Blstaková, J., & Joniaková, J. 2017. *Internationalisation of Human Resource Management: Focus on Central and Eastern Europe*. Nova Science Publishers.

Wolfe, J., & Poór, J. 1992. Socio-economic Note Hungary 1990 and Csepel Mechanical Tools Factory. In Wheeler, T. L. & Hunger, D. J. (eds.) *Strategic Management and Business Policy*, Addison-Wesley Publishing Co., pp. 1014–1061.

CHAPTER 9

Lithuania

Devbridge Lithuania: The War for IT Talents

Ilona Bučiūnienė, Lilija Vilkancienė,
and Raimonda Alonderienė

CASE SYNOPSIS

The case explores the situation of a fast-growing private Lithuanian capital information technology (IT) company, specializing in digital transformation and custom software development. Established in the United States by a team of Lithuanians, Devbridge has successfully expanded internationally creating branches in Lithuania, Canada, the UK, and Poland, and has developed digital products for some of the world's largest brands. However, during the last few years, Devbridge, and especially its Lithuanian branch, has been facing challenges to attract new IT professionals. Moreover, the COVID-19 pandemic exacerbated this situation due to increased competition for IT talent. This case addresses employer branding covering talent attraction and retention in the IT industry.

KEYWORDS

Talent management, employer branding, information technology industry, war for talents, Lithuania

DOI: 10.4324/9781003307099-12

LEARNING OUTCOMES

1. Understand the essence of talent management and the role of HRM in talent management.
2. Understand the role of employer branding in talent management.
3. Reveal typical HRM challenges in talent attraction, motivation, and retention.
4. Explore the context of the information technology industry as well as the challenges and opportunities of a globally operating company, which has a branch in a small country.

INTRODUCTION

In April 2021, Viktoras Gurgždys, Devbridge Vice President for Engineering invited Raimonda Alonderienė, the Director of People & Organizational Development, to address the critical industry challenge of how to prevent local IT talent drain, limiting the firm's ambition for further growth. During the firm's 13-year history, Devbridge has earned a solid reputation as an "extraordinary custom software" developer that delivers measurable results for its clients and their customers four times faster than the industry average, resulting in annual double-digit growth rates (revenue has grown by 30–40%). However, the firm's ability to realize new opportunities is increasingly tempered by the shortage of qualified/accessible/core talent, meaning that new clients and projects are put on hold. In 2021 alone, the company hired over 160 employees in Lithuania, but order books suggest there is room for about 100 more. The COVID-19 pandemic fueled demand for digital products that also lifted competition for IT professionals in the labor market to levels hardly ever seen before, making the war for IT talents ever more salient.

LITHUANIA: COUNTRY BACKGROUND

Lithuania is an Eastern European country with a coastline at the Baltic Sea in the west, whose history goes back to settlements founded many thousands of years ago. The Lithuanian language, belonging to the Indo-European family, is one of the oldest languages in the world. Lithuania as a state was established in the 13th century and remained strong and independent until the end of the 18th century when it was occupied by the Russian Empire. Independent between the two world wars, Lithuania was annexed by Russia and incorporated into the Soviet Union in 1940. In 1990, Lithuania declared the restoration of independence, the first of the Soviet Union republics, starting the collapse of the Soviet system.

After regaining independence, Lithuania has developed rapidly; it has restructured its economy for eventual integration into Western European institutions. In 2004, the country became a member of NATO and a member state of the European Union (EU) and in 2015 joined the Eurozone.

In 2021, Lithuania was among the top five countries in the world by postsecondary (tertiary) education. It is the largest and most populous (2.8 million habitants[1]) of the three Baltic states.

Lithuania is well known for its life sciences sector (the fastest growing in the EU) and the food sector (milk, meat, and grain processing compose the major share of the total value created by Lithuanian producers). Laser technology is a key industry for Lithuania, allowing the country to make its mark internationally. In recent years, the development of alternative energy in Lithuania has been rapidly accelerating. The country's government is focused on promoting the growth of the renewable (hydro, wind, biomass, and solar) energy sector, with the ambitious goal of reaching 45% RES share by 2030.[2]

Lithuania is number one globally in terms of access to public Wi-Fi, number three by digital skills availability, and number three in the EU for 4G LTE coverage.[3] The educated workforce and development of IT technologies have attracted investments, especially in the information and communication technology (ICT) sector,[4] and Lithuania has become a center of excellence in ICT solutions, software development, fintech, and worldwide renowned start-ups. This sector employs around 27,000 people, comprising 2.8% of total employment. The Lithuanian ICT industry is well known for its quality and well-developed infrastructure, the pool of ambitious young talents, and promising tech companies.

COMPANY BACKGROUND

Devbridge was established in 2008 by five Lithuanians who left the country after the restoration of Lithuanian independence in 1990, to pursue their "American Dream". After liberation, the freedom to explore opportunities in other countries motivated many people to go and find these opportunities for themselves, as the citizens of Soviet countries were not allowed to travel outside the borders of the Soviet Union and lived in isolation from the rest of the world. The founders, only one of whom had a computer science background, opened their first office in Illinois, United States, and successfully developed the company. In 2011, Devbridge opened its first Lithuanian office and established an engineering department. In December of 2021, Devbridge was acquired by Cognizant Softvision, to continue scaling their product design and development services. The company has more than 600 employees in Lithuania, Poland, the United States, the UK, and Canada. The Lithuanian branch employs more than 500 people, mostly IT specialists distributed by the breakdown of IT specialist categories typical for IT companies: 20% of them are juniors, i.e., beginners, about 40% are regular or mid-level professionals, and about 40% are seniors, i.e., those who are experts. Divisions abroad are responsible for establishing and keeping customer relations, attracting new customers, and project initiation. Devbridge works in global cross-functional project teams: When contact is made with a client, a project team from Chicago and from Lithuania is formed to develop the project.

EMPLOYER BRANDING

Devbridge is trying hard to brand itself as an attractive employer to win IT talent, as the labor market for IT professionals is overstretched, demand significantly exceeds supply, and the competition for IT professionals is fierce. There are only about 7,000 potential IT specialists for Devbridge in the Lithuanian labor market. Moreover, new IT companies are still coming to

Lithuania. They are attracted by the quality of the Lithuanian IT workforce, i.e., IT professionals in Lithuania have a high level of competence. Thus, IT specialists are in high demand in the job market and receive a fairly large flow of job offers. For example, an IT professional receives on average of six or seven emails a week from different companies with job offers.

In the process of talent attraction, the employer image is of vital importance: It is essential for the candidates that the company is known, has a good reputation, and is positively referred to by its current employees. Devbridge works with big, well-known global companies that have extremely large project diversity, scope, and complexity, which in turn attracts IT professionals. Moreover, the present stage of Devbridge development provides flexibility and broad personal development prospects for IT professionals: Devbridge is no longer a start-up company. At the same time, it is not a large corporation with rigid formalized processes and hierarchies. It has been in the market long enough, it is growing rapidly, and it is big enough already; it employs IT experts and has a reputation as a reliable, solid employer.

Devbridge seeks to employ IT talents with high potential, who could become valued team members, work successfully, and enjoy being part of the team. For Devbridge, a talent is some-one who creates value for the organization, in any division or project. Devbridge business phi-losophy is based on the principle that the greater the talent that works for the company, the easier it is to attract new talents in the future. Devbridge seeks to stand out from other IT com-panies by professionalism and by striving for excellence. Big international projects, teamwork, and transparency are the main elements attracting IT specialists to Devbridge.

Devbridge is known in the labor market for the teamwork, professionalism, and competence of its employees. The opportunity to work with colleagues from whom they will be able to learn and with whom they will be able to share knowledge is important for potential IT professionals.

Transparency is another feature distinguishing Devbridge in the ICT labor market. Devbridge managers recognize that current and prospective employees value trust, openness, and transparency. As the market in which the company operates is relatively small, people know each other and rumors run fast, the true situation becomes known very quickly. Thus, from the very beginning, Devbridge has shared with its employees all relevant information, such as finan-cial performance, revenue and profit, and new and lost clients. Employees know their own and others' position levels and remuneration ranges, and are informed in advance about expected end-of-year bonuses.

Devbridge has gained a good employer reputation: It has received international and national best workplaces and best companies to work for nominations. In 2022, the company won the title of the most desirable employer in Lithuania.

TALENT TURNOVER

Despite the big effort of talent retention, annual turnover at the Devbridge Lithuanian branch is about 12%. It is lower than the average of 17% in the IT industry. Devbridge recognizes that IT professionals do not want to stay with one company for their entire career, instead seeking to change and grow. Moreover, opportunities are easily available because competitors regu-larly headhunt IT professionals. To be competitive in the labor market, Devbridge monitors the level of salaries and raises them on a regular basis once or twice a year. Salaries paid by

Devbridge are higher than the average in the IT industry in Lithuania; they reach the 75th percentile. The turnover of young employees is higher than that of senior, as young people have high expectations and perceive many attractive opportunities and distractions. They stay in the same company for two years, decide that they already know everything, and move on. Senior employees are more stable. This does not mean that their ambitions are lower: They just have more established life circumstances, including a family. Senior IT professionals typically go to other companies to work as managers of IT departments or as managers of smaller IT companies.

Thus, Devbridge regularly monitors the situation in the labor market and puts a lot of effort to attract and retain IT talents.

TALENT ATTRACTION

In their search for talent, Devbridge seeks to ensure that a person who joins the company brings not only the knowledge the company needs, but also matches its culture. According to a talent acquisition manager,

> We want them to come, to have an ambition to do more, to be better, to grow, to be curious, and not to be indifferent, not to come and sit somehow safely. We [the company] are moving forward in terms of growth, both quantitatively and qualitatively. That's what we expect from the candidates.

Since the demand exceeds supply in the IT specialists' labor market, Devbridge takes an individual approach to attracting potential candidates. For example, it may be important for one candidate to work with the latest technology or in smaller or larger teams or projects; another might seek higher rewards or international experience, and so on. Therefore, the goal of talent recruitment is to find out what the needs of each candidate are and whether the company can meet them.

Such an individual approach to headhunting is effective because it is widely believed by recruiters that the main tool in headhunting – offering a higher salary to candidates to lure them from another company – is not effective. It can also be detrimental to the company itself, as it might conflict with compensation fairness and demotivate existing employees. Thus, the salary offered to new employees is in line with the current Devbridge employees' salaries for similar competencies.

Attracting candidates to different positions and the sources of search are fundamentally different. To attract junior candidates and develop their professional competencies, Devbridge founded the in-house Sourcery Academy providing free courses for IT beginners. On average, 25–40% of the most talented graduates of the Sourcery Academy stay at the company. Devbridge works closely with universities to be visible, to strengthen its branding among potential candidates, and to shape the company's image. Devbridge professionals give guest lectures and presentations at study fairs, and teach IT at universities.

Attracting candidates for regular and senior positions is different from junior positions, as for these positions, employees are recruited proactively. The company places its job advertisements on various portals and on its web page. However, these advertisements are no longer effective for candidates for regular and senior IT positions, as there are no available candidates for these positions in the labor market. Therefore, Devbridge, like other ICT companies, proactively look for and personally contact potential candidates, to try and have them join the company. Online platforms and social networking are important sources of search for candidates for regular and senior positions. LinkedIn, as well as several other specialized platforms such as Stack Overflow and GitHub, are the most useful platforms.

Devbridge treats potential candidates gently and in a non-binding way: "Come to just talk, come to get acquainted, we will tell you how we live, what we do". Non-binding communication is especially important for employees in regular and senior positions because they are often satisfied with their current job and are less reluctant to transition. This situation reflects the prevailing IT talent headhunting trends in Lithuania, as, according to recruitment experts (Januzyte R., 2021), only 20% of candidates go to the first job interview with the intention of changing their job, when in the past it was 80–90%.

Devbridge develops and uses an internal candidate database, accumulated by communicating with potential candidates (with their consent) and keeping in touch with them on a regular basis. Lithuania is a small country, so there are not many new candidates, and Devbridge is able to keep in touch with IT professionals by coming back regularly and inquiring if something has changed and if they would consider moving to Devbridge. The company has a referral program that encourages employees to recommend their friends and acquaintances to work at Devbridge.

TALENT DEVELOPMENT AND RETENTION

IT Talent Development

The opportunity to learn both as an IT professional and as a leader is an important motivator for IT professionals. Understanding the importance of professional development is key to an employer's attractiveness. Devbridge provides possibilities for all its employees to grow not only as IT professionals but also as leaders pursuing both professional and leadership career paths.

Devbridge has a clear career development system. A career path in the company is planned for new employees. Personal development begins from onboarding when newcomers are assigned to two mentors, an experienced co-worker, and a line manager, who help newcomers to quickly integrate and network.

The company fosters IT talent professional development by providing different training and encouraging them to share knowledge in regular *knowledge-sharing sessions*, during which employees make presentations on their chosen topic, the ones they have expert knowledge about. Every employee is given *a self-learning day* once a month, during which they decide what they want to learn and where to advance their knowledge. On that day, an employee stays away from work and immerses themselves in learning. The company has a database of books and professional literature, and each employee has access to courses and the latest books, both online and physical, and can deepen their knowledge at any time. Special training budgets are dedicated to teams to fund external training and lectures, to travel to conferences, and so on, and team members decide at their own discretion how to use this budget.

Line managers play an important role in IT talent development. Several times a month, each employee has one-on-one meetings with their line manager and talks about themselves, the job, and the team: How they are doing, what is not going well, and what can be done better. These regular meetings are also important for IT talent retention, as they help to monitor employee satisfaction with their job, co-workers, career, and other job-related aspects as well as to proactively take actions to prevent any employee intentions to leave the company.

HRM Deployment and Leadership Development

The company has a specific HRM architecture where the HRM department is a strategic partner and has a consultant role, and the majority of HRM practices, such as newcomers' orientation, mentoring, motivation, and helping to define training needs and career paths are deployed and performed by line managers. Devbridge uses the entire system for this purpose, developing managers mainly from within.

The company has an internal leadership academy that uses both external and internal training. The training program covers interpersonal psychology (topics such as understanding yourself and working with yourself as a leader) and working with a team and with clients. Recently, the company launched a new initiative – New Team Leaders' Community – where new team leaders meet regularly to address issues that are relevant to them. In this way, new leaders share knowledge and learn from each other.

Devbridge also gives all employees the opportunity to test their leadership skills by being lecturers or mentors to young people at the Sourcery Academy and thus gain leadership skills. They can later become project leads and test themselves, as well as take their first leadership steps. They are assisted in this process by their line managers. The example and support of line managers is an important element of organizational culture: Employees see and learn from their leader, share the leadership challenges in one-on-one sessions, and thus grow.

Strengthening Team Spirit and Organizational Culture

Devbridge considers the working environment as an important element of teamwork, which is why employees' workplaces are in a common space. There are teamwork rooms and some special places for the employees to relax (for example, table football, etc.). The company provides free tea, coffee, snacks, cookies, and free Friday lunches, and "pampers" employees in other ways. The COVID-19 pandemic has taught people to work remotely; however, Devbridge sees a lot of potential in employees staying close to one another and encourages employees to work from the office. Management considers that remote meetings do not substitute in-person communication: Working from the office and being close to each other, having "live" project meetings and discussions, and informal communication over a cup of coffee in the kitchen, developing team spirit and strengthening organizational culture, and at the same time engaging employees in sharing knowledge and learning from each other.

Devbridge organizes whole organization events twice a year, and budgets of several hundred thousand are allocated so that Devbridge employees from all around the globe may fly and stay together for a few days. A traditional summer camp includes competitions, entertainment, fun, sleeping in tents, and a range of different activities to promote better understanding and commitment to the company.

FUTURE CONSIDERATIONS

In 2022, Devbridge growth plans became even more ambitious – to hire over 200 IT professionals. However, its growth has been hampered by a shortage of IT professionals in Lithuania. According to Raimonda, Devbridge Lithuania is already stuck: It knows (and has contacted) all potential employees. "There are people we have been talking to for four or more years. Sometimes it works, sometimes it doesn't". Devbridge realizes that they are collecting "crumbs", and the company cannot grow as much as it would like. The limitations of the Lithuanian IT labor market are evidenced by a Swedish IT company, which employed only 150 people instead of the intended 1,000 in 2021 (Grinkevičius, 2021).

Seeing a shortage of IT professionals in Lithuania, Devbridge established a division in Poland at the end of 2020. The company expects a larger number of potential IT employees in Poland.

In Poland, it is easier to attract IT professionals because, unlike in Lithuania, candidates apply for new positions themselves, even when the recruitment is carried out by an unknown company. Poles are also impressed by Devbridge's large global projects and higher-than-market salary levels. Devbridge started hiring in Poland for senior and regular positions, and these employees were first integrated into Lithuanian teams (where they worked for up to six months) so that they could embrace the company culture and then were assigned as managers in the Polish branch. This is how the first Polish managers were developed. Thirty employees had been employed in Poland by the end of 2021.

Devbridge executives understand that to continue to grow by 30% annually, new talent needs to be found. But from where? How could their integration be sped up? Devbridge managers are really concerned about where to look for and how to attract new talent.

CASE STUDY QUESTIONS FOR DISCUSSION

1. What are the HRM theoretical approaches in talent identification and talent management? What is talent management?
2. Who are considered talents in Devbridge? Which theoretical talent management approach best reflects the approach at Devbridge Lithuania?
3. What is employer branding? What is the role of employer branding in talent management?
4. What job elements are important for IT talents? What are the key selling points of the employer brand of Devbridge in attracting and retaining talent? What opportunities and challenges, related to the specifics of a global and a Lithuanian country context, does Devbridge face in talent management?
5. Where should the company look for, and how should it attract new talents beyond its current approaches? How should it seek to retain talents?

NOTES

1 Oficialios statistikos portalas. 2021. https://osp.stat.gov.lt/gyventojai1.
2 IEA (international Energy Agency) Lithuania. 2021. Energy Policy Review. p. 12 https://iea.blob .core.windows.net/assets/4d014034-0f94-409d-bb8193e17a81d77/Lithuania_2021_Energy_Policy _Review.pdf.
3 www.enterpriselithuania.com/en/business-sectors/ict/.
4 https://en.wikipedia.org/wiki/Economy_of_Lithuania.

REFERENCES

Grinkevičius P. 2021. November 10. Švedų įmonė antrus metus Kaune nori samdyti 1000 darbuotojų, rado 150. *Verslo Žinios*. Švedų įmonė antrus metus Kaune nori samdyti 1.000 darbuotojų, rado 150 - Verslo žinios (vz.lt).

Januzyte, R. 2021. December 1. Įdarbibimas: Talent medžioklė baigia išstumti įprastas atrankas. *Verslo Žinios*. Įdarbinimas: talentų medžioklė baigia išstumti įprastas atrankas - Verslo žinios (vz.lt).

Oficialios statistikos portalas. 2021. *Lietuvos gyventojai (2021 leidimas)*. Gyventojų skaičius ir sudėtis - Oficialiosios statistikos portalas.

Supplementary Resources

Collings, D. G. & Mellahi K. 2009. Strategic talent management: A review and research agenda. *Human Resource Management Review* 19(4): 304–313.

Edwards, M. R. 2017. Employer branding and talent management. In Collings D. G., Mellahi K. & Cascio W. F. (Eds.) *The Oxford Handbook of Talent Management*. Oxford University Press: 233–248.

Hausknecht, J. P. 2017. Talent and turnover. In Collings D. G., Mellahi K. & Cascio W. F. (Eds.) *The Oxford Handbook of Talent Management*. Oxford University Press: 361–374.

Lewis, R. E. & Heckman R. J. 2006. Talent management: A critical review. *Human Resource Management Review* 16(2): 139–154.

CHAPTER 10

Poland

Informal Employee Motivation, Rewards, and Flexible Management in a Dynamic SME Environment in Poland

Peter Odrakiewicz, Radosław Skrobacki,
and Michael Gaylord

CASE SYNOPSIS

This case study considers the human resource management (HRM) challenges and changes, especially those related to reward management, facing "XYZ" company, a Polish small to medium-sized enterprise (SME). "XYZ" is a 20-plus-year-old family-run company that specializes in advertising and production of company signs, from small to large welded constructions, business trade fair expo preparation, event management, and printing services located in Poland. The study examines how "XYZ" implements policies designed to improve innovation, staff cohesion, and entrepreneurship through its system of rewards, in the context of a challenging and evolving HRM dynamic in Poland. As it faces various constraints imposed by these changes, the company tried using various HRM approaches, while also considering the country's rapidly shifting employer–employee atmosphere, legal and institutional changes, and sociocultural developments.

KEYWORDS

Performance-based rewards, motivation, SME flexibility, informal management style(s), Poland

DOI: 10.4324/9781003307099-13

LEARNING OUTCOMES

1. Learn about HRM development in Poland in recent years.
2. Become familiar with HRM challenges in Poland, especially in small and medium-sized enterprises.
3. Understand motivational tools used in a reward system in a Polish SME.

ORGANIZATIONAL SETTING

"XYZ" is a family-owned company located in Poznan, Poland, part of the country's small and medium-sized enterprises (SME) sector. The company specializes in the advertising, marketing, production, and service of products, and works mostly with customers in western Poland with limited orders from Germany and growing business from other companies operating in Europe. According to sources from the EU Commission Small Business Act (SBA) fact sheet about Poland's "non-financial business economy", SMEs accounted for slightly more than half of overall value added in 2018, which was a share of 52.9%. Between 2014 and 2018, overall SME value added increased by 26.3%, while in large firms the rise was 23.2%. Overall SME value added was expected to rise between 2018 and 2020, exceeding the growth projected for large firms. By the end of 2020, it was predicted that SMEs would generate about 98,700 jobs (European Commission, 2019). Poland's SBA profile remains below the EU average in skills and innovation and in the single market and internationalization, directly affecting the competitiveness of Polish SMEs. Poland scores on par with the EU average inresponsive administration and entrepreneurship. It has above-average scores for the environment, state aid, public procurement, and access to finance. Since 2008, most progress has been observed in the single market, access to finance, state aid, public procurement, and responsive administration (The Government of Poland, 2016).

Poland correctly identifies its pressing development gaps in areas such as skills, innovation, and internationalization, and addresses them with new and existing policy measures, although the scale and effectiveness of these measures are not always sufficient. Such policies are especially important, as they help to ensure the long-term competitiveness of Polish SMEs. There is a significant focus on improving the legislative framework (covered by the areas of responsive administration and entrepreneurship) through deregulation, more favorable administration, and the digitization of services. Still, SMEs would welcome a more coherent interpretation of laws by public administration and more predictable changes in the regulatory framework, with a better implementation of the "SME test". Other areas, such as the environment, are less prominent in Poland's SME agenda. Shortening the time it takes to resolve insolvency, reducing its cost and providing support for previously insolvent – but honest – entrepreneurs, and recognizing the role of SMEs in green transformation could help to address those areas (OECD, 2021).

The Small Business Act for Europe (SBA) is the EU's flagship policy initiative to support SMEs. It comprises a set of policy measures organized around ten principles, ranging from entrepreneurship and "responsive administration" to internationalization. To improve the governance of the SBA, the 2011 review of it called for better monitoring (European Commission, 2019).

SOCIOECONOMIC BACKGROUND AND LABOR ORGANIZATIONS IN POLAND

The Republic of Poland is in central Europe, sharing borders with seven other European countries. Poland is a member of the European Union, NATO, the United Nations, the World Trade Organization, and the Organization for Economic Cooperation and Development.

Poland's economic history exemplifies a transition from a centrally planned economy, under communism, to a primarily capitalistic market economy today. The relatively quick introduction of new labor law (in 1990) allowed the private sector to develop rapidly, and privatization – although at times faced with public criticism – in virtually all sectors has been robust and ongoing since that time, especially in technical fields such as IT, pharmaceuticals, and vehicle manufacturing. According to many experts, joining the EU greatly facilitated private sector development in Poland and, with less regulatory burden and expense, greatly increased exports to neighboring EU economies (Adekoya, 2014). The country continues to aim toward entering the single European currency (the euro). However, public opinion is widely divided as to the timing of adopting the euro as the country's currency.

SIGNIFICANT CHANGES IN BUSINESS OPERATIONS FOR SMES IN POLAND

One of the important features of the evolution of the business environment in Poland affecting human resource management (HRM) has been the attempt to lessen any negative impact of administrative and reporting tasks for SMEs. Tax and HRM-related obligations have been reorganized. Many SMEs, such as the firm examined in this case, have very small HRM departments, having one or two specialists only. Many times, the owner is the only HRM person and relies on the help of their administrative office specialist. HRM is, for small and medium-sized enterprises, a very important process, encompassing all facets of company operations. It is vital to a company's success. Many SME micro-family firms manage HRM processes – such as gathering HR monthly data, making sure all required state health and social insurances are paid, and implementing health and safety training measures – through their owners, which is the case in the company that is the subject of this study, although some small companies choose to entirely outsource them.

An additional noteworthy development has been the popularity of using business-to-business contracts as a replacement for hiring full-time employees. This way, many SMEs aim to avoid the high administrative costs associated with lengthy reporting requirements and full-time employment contracts. For instance, some companies hire employees for a fixed period or a limited number of hours each month, sometimes specifying only the tasks to be carried out. This allows employees to be insured by the employer through the state insurance agency, which covers health-related needs, such as medical visits. At the same time, it encourages their present or former employees to start their own micro SMEs and continue cooperating based on business-to-business (B-to-B) contracts. With B-to-B contracts, the contractor is responsible for paying their own insurance, which in Poland is a big part of the income payable each month, regardless of the number of B-to-B orders gained. Some SMEs, consisting of one person in Poland, are formed only so that the professional can become self-employed, find better job prospects, and provide for one's own daily needs; unfortunately, due to complicated tax, HRM-health and safety reporting requirements, social security and obligatory health insurance payments, one can easily go out of business or be forced to unregister their micro-one-person business to avoid paying insurance. Unless this system is improved, the further growth of some SMEs will be limited, and many may go out of business entirely. Sometimes, both HRM features for SMEs in Poland (i.e., workers are employed on full-time employment contracts and the company also hires independent service providers) exist simultaneously, when in fact all should be full-time employees. B-to-B contracts are over-utilized by many SMEs in Poland to avoid the expensive – but obligatory – insurance premiums, social security, health, unemployment insurance, and excessive reporting. This can cause hesitation when considering hiring full-time employees – the preference many times is given to B-to-B relationships, when, in fact, an employer–employee relationship exists and is enforced, with set working hours and direct supervision. In such cases, the employee is not awarded an employment contract and may be steered into a B-to-B relationship. This raises ethical concerns, contradicts labor law, can invite a rigid company structure, and threatens to hurt the competitiveness of many SMEs, as they have less innovative potential in comparison to similar micro SMEs in other EU countries.

THE IMPACT OF CHANGING STANDARDS OF INCOME

On January 1, 2021, changes to labor law in Poland meant that the minimum wage increased to PLN 2,800 (about USD 730) per month (Currency Converter, 2021). Average monthly gross wages in Poland between 1995 and 2020 increased by nearly 37%, reaching PLN 5167 (USD 1345, according to Currency Converter) in 2020, according to the Central Statistics Office. Issuing holiday pay to employees is now compulsory even for companies with less than 50 employees. These developments have put more pressure on companies to meet rising expectations regarding salaries and benefits on the part of prospective and existing employees, and thus have increased overhead costs for many SMEs. For the business organization featured in this study, although the owners applaud the increased standard of living in Poland, they believe that the necessity of fulfilling the same legal responsibilities as large corporations has put them at a slight disadvantage, consequently motivating them to find alternative and creative ways to maintain existing employees and cultivate healthy and mutually beneficial relationships with new ones.

TYPES OF EMPLOYMENT CONTRACTS AND THEIR IMPACT ON SOCIETY

Health insurance contributions are obligatory for all types of employee–employer relationships, although there are various types of contracts from which to choose. Permanent contracts, because they stipulate that both employees and employers have important binding responsibilities to one another, are perceived as being more secure and more conducive to relationship-building and are the favorable type of contact for an employee – but are the least popular among employers because they must pay the maximum social and health benefits.

Other types of agreements are as follows: A contract stating employment for a specific period (agreed to by both parties), where the expiration date is agreed upon, a contract for specific work, in which the employee undertakes to perform a specified task for the owner and no health insurance payments are required (thereby lowering employment costs for the employer), and the encouragement of various flexible work arrangements outside of official labor law, mainly to avoid high labor costs. The ultimate result of this has been that many new job seekers prefer to be self-employed. Many SMEs are entering into such employment relationships with their present or former employees, who are now re-established as own-company owners. For employers, such B-to-B contracts limit the costs of servicing the employee but can result in a lack of coverage for illness, disability, and insufficient retirement funds. This means that the benefit to the company is mainly the reduction of administrative costs related to the service of a full-time employee. Secondly, provisions in the labor code have been eliminated, resulting in much more relationship flexibility. Although this may sound sensible, it can have negative consequences for employees – for example, it is easier to fire them, and, being underinsured, employees risk having inadequate retirement pensions. These factors, it would appear, could result in a negative impact on the functioning of the labor market and on society.

THE ETHNOGRAPHIC STUDY OF HRM AT "XYZ" COMPANY

Company Profile

"XYZ" is a small family-owned company with a turnover not exceeding €2 million annually, cooperating with up to ten employees. Its head office and its service office are both in the city of Poznan. Most employees live close to the company's headquarters. The company is recognized locally as one of the leading suppliers of advertising signs, store renovation specialists, and marketing event organizers. The owners have high-quality relations with the local community, as the firm supports local charities. The structure of the company is divided into three departments: 1. Administrative and General Management, Accountancy, and IT; 2. Sales and Service, and 3. Production, Warehousing, and Service Specialization, including drivers of service vehicles.

TYPES OF CONTRACTS OFFERED AND MANAGEMENT STYLE

In many ways, contract-wise, the company fits the current profile of a burgeoning micro-enterprise in Poland: It employs a small number of workers and associates, and it offers B-to-B contracts for some employees. However, it also offers full-time permanent employment contracts for established employees. The owners believe that maintaining a willingness to adjust contract types allows them to accommodate the needs of their diverse demographic. For instance, it recognizes the value that the company's older workers place on illness, disability, and retirement funds being sufficiently covered.

Typically, upon beginning a new position, the employee has a three-month trial contract. This three-month period is a time for the employer to decide whether the person chosen is appropriate, for the employee to decide whether the job is a good fit, and to determine if they are comfortable with the firm's work environment. Within this period, this firm covers its employees' social and health insurance costs. If the employer is satisfied with the employee's performance after this three-month period, the employee is offered a temporary contract for a specified period, usually for one year. This one-year period, the owners feel, is a time for the employee to develop their skills and talent, discover what motivates them, and produce results that, ideally, benefit the entire team. Within this period, "XYZ" covers its employees' social and health insurance.

Because the owners believe that flexibility will help build a healthy employer–employee relationship, if this one-year contract goes well the employee may be offered a B-to-B contract or, alternatively, a permanent employment contract – the latter being more likely if the employee has met or has exceeded all work-related requirements. This permanent contract is very profitable for the employee. Within this period, "XYZ" pays for its employees' social and health insurance. For seasonal workers, they use either a contract for a specific work agreement, usually without an extended benefits package, offered to employees who host events during international fairs, and to students who wish to work during their holidays, or a contract of mandate, for those employees whose job duties are very tangible, for example, the translation of products catalogs, building a new warehouse, etc.

Additionally, "XYZ" employs extra workers for short time periods when the company is facing a large amount of "additional work". As far as HRM is concerned, the two owners fulfill many duties, such as the selection of new employees, contracts, pay, and benefits. The owners bilaterally make decisions concerning employee motivation, training and development, and salaries. However, because they aim to inculcate transparency, they encourage senior employees to participate in some other responsibilities that may have been, in the past, reserved for upper management, such as conducting interviews, securing new clients, and determining hours of work.

RESOURCE CHALLENGES AND CONSTRAINTS

Currently, working conditions in Poland favor employees. In other words, due to the large number of jobs available and the relatively small labor pool, employers are pressed to find workers to fill positions available. As a result, facing a high potential for employee turnover, the owners of "XYZ" are under high pressure to constantly increase salaries to keep workers and associates motivated. This puts a high burden on the company's financial performance and operations.

In addition, non-wage labor costs have grown during the past decades in Poland. Although some administrative tasks, such as the processing of invoices, can be done in-house, due to the complexity and length of time associated with fulfilling the work-related health insurance requirements of the country's labor code and meeting pension contributions, it has been necessary to outsource many other tasks, such as health and safety inspections. This has increased the business overhead costs.

SYSTEM FOR MOTIVATING EMPLOYEES

"XYZ" uses various types of motivators: Base salary, plus a premium based on performance, performance-based extra rewards, and non-monetary rewards, such as time off and offering used company goods for sale to employees at a discounted price. Other rewards derive from the flexibility that the owners offer employees. For instance, in the event of a crisis, employees can contact the owners at any time and arrange to complete their work at an alternative time (later) while they deal with their crisis. It is believed that maintaining such a friendly atmosphere builds rapport and motivates employees to continue to work for the firm.

Employees are paid a base salary each month, regardless of their performance. However, performance-based motivation is given to employees that reflects the value of their contributions to the company's performance. Employees who make greater contributions are given higher pay than those who contribute less time and effort. Rather than increasing the person's base salary at the end of the year, employees may receive 10% to 15% of their net sales, in conjunction with demonstrated performance during that performance period (at the beginning of each month). This kind of reward system is very likely to be used when performance can be objectively assessed in terms of the number of units of output or similar measures, rather than via a subjective assessment by a superior. Service and production workers follow similar reward schemes related to their performance.

"XYZ" uses monetary and non-monetary rewards for each of its employees. As alluded to above, all employees receive equal non-monetary rewards; however, monetary rewards are based on individual performance during the year. These are given to employees at either the midway point of the year or at the year's end. For those who show outstanding performance, the company provides further special training. Sometimes situations require an extra performance effort because the job must be completed in a short period. Therefore, teams may need to work very hard to achieve goals. It is made clear that cooperation is highly valued in the company, and the owners are conscious of the importance of praising their employees when teamwork produces successful outcomes. A monetary bonus may also be given if the employee lands a new contract. However, this practice is not always encouraged, as the ownership has found that it can lead to all employees wanting the same bonus, hence reducing collaboration and increasing over-competition. By encouraging team unity, focusing on rapid goal achievement, and issuing timely – but moderate – monetary bonuses for exemplary work, the employees are expected to be further motivated to accept future job assignments and continue working at the company.

Furthermore, in recent years, the top management of "XYZ" has attempted to cultivate independence among their staff. They have observed that this effectively motivates employees, allowing them to set their own goals, make decisions, and solve problems based on their own initiative. The resulting sense of accomplishment regarding having set one's own goals and achieved them, the feeling of task mastery, and having the autonomy to direct their own work, enhances creativity within the company and builds up energy levels.

"XYZ"'s owners know that, in addition to motivation, setting the correct style and tone of communication is very important to their organization's prosperity. They seek to maximize staff rapport and interpersonal contact so they try to build professional yet friendly relationships with all employees. The owners and most employees refer to each other by their first names, which is unusual in Poland. They recognize staff excellence and loyalty informally by conveying warmth and ensuring that all contributors are complimented and treated as equally as possible. The company organizes bi-weekly whole-company, in-person meetings, which usually begin with a short informal training session for employees. This is consistent with the face-to-face interactions that the company has continually encouraged. Having such an intimate environment, they believe, will further advance success – both in the short term and down the road.

It can be observed that both monetary and non-monetary rewards increase employees' motivation and reduce turnover. At the same time, the owners recognize that being flexible with the timing and issuance of these rewards – not to mention remaining flexible regarding the types of contracts offered to employees – is necessary to reflect the changing work styles and trends in Poland, as well as to accommodate the evolving socioeconomic dynamics in the country. These dynamics, it appears, cannot be ignored: Heading into the future, the Polish government may very well discourage B-to-B contracts, hence companies must be prepared to choose among which employee–employer HRM relationships will best meet the changing demographic needs. Keeping in mind the desire to provide health and welfare stability in a rapidly aging society, there is an increase in the more traditional full-time employee contracts. The owners of "XYZ" contend that they are prepared for such a scenario.

CASE STUDY QUESTIONS FOR DISCUSSION

1. Why is it important to motivate employees? How should employers motivate their employees?

2. Unlike the old reward system, the new strategies implemented at "XYZ" include quantitative and qualitative components. In what ways do the implemented strategies encourage employees' motivation toward work and teamwork?

3. Consider what effect the introduction of the euro as a currency in Poland would have in the future of "XYZ" operations.

REFERENCES

Adekoy, R. (2014, May 1). How the EU transformed Poland. *The Guardian*. How the EU transformed Poland | Remi Adekoya | The Guardian.

Currency Converter. (2021, August 30). *Check Live Foreign Currency Rates*. https://www.xe.com/currencyconverter/

European Commission. (2019, September 9). *SBA Fact Sheet*, page 9. file:///C:/Users/Downloads/Poland%20-%20SBA%20Fact%20Sheet%202019.pdf

Government of Poland. (2016, September 5). *Latest Statistical News*. https://stat.gov.pl/en/latest-statistical-news/communications-and-announcements/list-of-communiques-and-announcements/average-monthly-gross-wage-and-salary-in-enterprise-sector-in-june-2021,11,91.html

OECD Library. (2021, September 6). *Poland 2020*. https://www.oecd-ilibrary.org/sites/0e32d909-en/index.html?itemId=/content/publication/0e32d909-en.

Supplementary Resources

The authors suggest reading from websites that further detail labor laws in Poland and employer obligations, such as the information found in these sites:
https://www.gov.pl/web/family/basic-information-on-labour-law
https://www.gov.pl/web/family/obligations-of-the-employee
https://www.gov.pl/web/family/obligations-of-the-employer
https://www.hg.org/legal-articles/employment-law-in-poland-37567
https://www.lawyerspoland.eu/employment-law-in-poland

CHAPTER 11

Romania

Dealing with Employee Turnover at Fomco Group, a Successful Family Business from Romania

Kinga Kerekes

CASE SYNOPSIS

Fomco Group[1] is a family business that was established in 2002 in Romania. Over time, the company has developed into a group of six firms, which are active in different fields. The case begins with a presentation of the Romanian context, followed by a short description of the company and its HRM procedures. The case focuses on the main challenge faced by the HRM department recently, which is the high turnover among newcomers, exploring key causes, as well as the solutions adopted by the company.

KEYWORDS

Employee turnover, employee retention, recruitment and selection, employee integration, Romania

LEARNING OUTCOMES

1. Understand the challenges of employee (especially newcomers) retention.
2. Understand the challenges that the free movement of labor within the European Union (EU) member states presents for Romanian companies.

DOI: 10.4324/9781003307099-14

3. Recognize the importance of testing personality traits and job fit during the selection procedure to avoid high employee turnover.
4. Understand that workplace integration is a common task of line managers and HRM personnel, and it is crucial for employee retention.

BACKGROUND INFORMATION OF ROMANIA

Population Demographics and Education

Romania is one of the largest countries in Central and Eastern Europe (CEE), with a territory of 238,391 km² and 19.2 million inhabitants in 2021. The share of women is 51.1%, and around 53.6% of the population lives in the urban area. The population is aging and shrinking, due to a decline in fertility and high emigration of young adults (National Institute of Statistics, 2021a; Romania Insider, 2020). Overall life expectancy at birth in 2019 was 75.6 years, more than five years below the European Union (EU) average (Eurostat, 2021).

The educational level of the population is rather low; in 2020 only 18.7% of 25- to 64-year-olds had completed tertiary education (the EU average was 32.8%), and the percentage of young people (aged 15 to 34) neither in education nor in employment or training (NEET) was 17.8% in 2020, among the highest in the EU (Eurostat, 2021).

Economy and Business Environment

The country has changed dramatically in the last three decades from political, social, and economic viewpoints. Following the fall of the communist regime in December 1989, democratic institutions were installed, and the transition began from a state-controlled economy toward a capitalist free-market economy. In the first ten years of transition, the economy of Romania shrank, and over 3.5 million jobs were lost. After 2000, a period of economic growth began, but the global economic and financial crisis from 2008 impacted Romania severely. The country's economic growth relaunched in 2011 and has been since one of the highest in the EU.

The World Bank classified Romania as an upper-middle-income country, with a total GDP of USD 249 billion and a GDP (gross domestic product) per capita of USD 12,968.8 in 2020. Due to the coronavirus pandemic, Romania's economy contracted by 3.9% in 2020, but in 2021 a growth of 7.3% was expected (World Bank, 2021). Despite the favorable developments, Romania remained one of the least developed countries of the EU: GDP per capita in purchasing power standards (PPS) did not reach three-quarters of the EU average (71.7% in 2020), and 23.4% of the total population is considered to be at risk of poverty[2] (Eurostat, 2021).

The *Global Competitiveness Index* for Romania in 2019 was set at 51 out of 141 economies, with a score of 64.4 (on a scale from 1 to 100). Romania achieved the highest score (90 points) for macroeconomic stability, and the best rank (32nd) for ICT adoption, while the lowest score (42 points) was awarded for innovation capability, and the lowest rank (86th) for the financial system (World Economic Forum, 2019).

Small and medium-sized enterprises[3] (SMEs) represented 99.7% of Romanian companies in 2019, accounted for 69.6% of the total turnover,[4] and employed 71.7% of the total workforce (National Institute of Statistics, 2021a).

Labor Market

Over half of the Romanian private businesses (52%) declared in 2019 that shortage of skilled employees (especially technicians, support staff, or sales experts) had caused them financial losses. Entrepreneurs estimated their total loss due to labor shortage to be 3.7% of Romania's GDP (PwC Romania, 2019).

The main factors that have contributed to the labor shortage in Romania are the free movement of labor within the EU, combined with the continuous decline in the working-age population, skills mismatch, and unattractive wages (Kerekes & Molnar, 2017).

In 2020, the employment rate of the 20 to 64-year-old population was 70.8%, increasing since 2010 (64.8%), but below the EU average of 72.4%, while the unemployment rate of 15 to 74-year-olds was 5.0%, significantly lower than the EU average of 7.0% (Eurostat, 2021).

Romania offers less attractive jobs with much lower wages than the more developed EU member states. The annual net average earnings of a single person without children in 2020 in Romania amounted to USD 9703[5] (35.4% being the EU average), while labor productivity per hour worked in Romania was 74.7% of the EU average (Eurostat, 2021). The higher the position one occupies, the closer the person's wage is to that found in Western countries.

Income disparities are among the highest in the EU, mainly driven by the large gap between the capital region of Bucharest and the rest of the country (COM, 2021). Wages differ among the economic sectors, the highest monthly earnings were recorded in computer programming, consultancy, and related activities (2015 US$ in October 2021), while the lowest was in accommodation and food service activities (447 US$). Employment income is taxed at a flat rate of 10% and is subject to social and health contributions (National Institute of Statistics, 2021b).

Romanian CEOs surveyed in 2021 were overall optimistic about increasing their headcounts, however, 82% of them mentioned the availability of key skills among the top threats to growth prospects (PwC Romania, 2021).

Characteristics of the Labor Market in Mureș County, the Region of the Case Study Company

Mureș County is situated in the central part of Romania. Its center is Târgu Mureș, a city with around 145 thousand inhabitants, where the most important administrative, economic, educational, and healthcare activities are concentrated. Companies from the city and its neighboring settlements employ workers from all over the county. As distances within the county are rather short and housing prices in the city are quite high, daily commuting to work is a preferred option for those who live in the countryside. Therefore, the county can be considered one single labor market.

In the past 20 years, the population of Mureș County decreased continuously (from 608,776 in 2002 to 585,494 in 2021), with the working-age population[6] (20–64-year-olds) representing 61% to 63% of the total. The number of employees was around 130,000, and the number of registered unemployed varied between 6000–6500, both being heavily impacted by the global financial crisis from 2008–2009 and the COVID-19 pandemic. Monthly earnings in Mureş County are 4–13% lower than the national averages (National Institute of Statistics, 2021a).

HRM Practices and Challenges

HRM practices in Romania are strongly influenced by employment legislation, which is based on the Romanian Constitution and Labor Code, on EU and international law and standards, and several other laws and government decrees. Legal provisions on hiring practices are limited, public institutions and companies have to organize contests to select employees, while for private companies these are not mandatory. The employer has to conclude an individual employment contract and register it in an electronic database before the beginning of the employment relationship. As a rule, the individual employment contract is open-ended, and only limited cases provided by the Labor Code may be concluded for a fixed term. Employees have certain minimum rights granted by the law, such as the minimum wage, paid annual leave (20 working days) and public holidays, maximum legal working time (48 hours a week), overtime compensation, health and safety measures, and non-discriminatory practices (Volonciu, 2021).

As a general practice, HRM professionals can be found in companies with over 70 to 100 employees. Line managers make the final decision regarding most of the interventions in the key functions of HRM, based usually on consultation with the HRM department. External service providers are most often used for training and development, but also for recruitment and selection (Kerekes & Zaharie, 2017).

The head of the HRM department is part of the top management team in 76% of the companies. The highest share of HRM professionals is involved in recruitment, employee relations, staff administration, learning and development, and onboarding. The typical HRM professional is a woman with tertiary education, who completed non-formal training in HRM and spent most of her career in HRM-related activities but did not join any professional organization (HR Club, 2020).

The most important challenges for the HRM function in 2019–2020 were recruitment, retention, and lack of competencies (HR Club, 2020; Valoria, 2020). Due to the economic uncertainties caused by the COVID-19 pandemic, staff turnover in Romanian companies decreased in 2020 to an average rate of 17.2% from 23.1% in 2019 (PwC Romania, 2020).

HISTORY AND ACTIVITY OF FOMCO GROUP

Fomco Wood Ltd. was founded in Cristeşti (Mureş County) by Bernát Nyulas in 2002, together with his wife, Judit. Taking advantage of a business opportunity offered by a foreign partner, the company started selling speed limiters and tachographs in Romania. Initially, there was not much interest in the product, but in 2003, it became mandatory for trucks with a larger load capacity to install tachographs, so the demand suddenly increased.

Over time, competitors appeared, and the company diversified its activities to further develop. In 2005; the company began producing doors and windows, and in 2010 its portfolio was expanded with the sale, installation, and operation of GPS tracking systems. Recognizing the potential of renewable energy production, a solar park was set up in 2012, and the company started selling and installing solar systems for others. One of the most significant steps of diversification was the real estate investment launched in 2017, which aimed to build an entire residential area.

The coordination and control of such a complex activity became increasingly challenging for the owners, so in 2017 they decided to make the operation of the company more transparent. A management consultant was also involved in the change process. The first step was to divide the company into separate units for each type of activity (wood manufacture, trade, solar systems, real estate investment, truck services, GPS systems, and business services). Currently, Fomco Group incorporates seven companies, which act as independent economic entities.

The goal of Fomco Group is to continuously grow while ensuring its employees' and their families' satisfaction. Its core values are performance, efficiency, organization, results orientation, teamwork, and respect for the customer. The company believes that honesty, openness, mutual trust, and respect are keys to a successful and lasting business relationship.

HUMAN RESOURCE MANAGEMENT PRACTICES AT FOMCO GROUP

Fomco Wood Ltd. started as a family business and operated with three employees. With the increase in the volume and diversity of activities, the workforce had to increase, and by the end of 2021, the total headcount of the companies within Fomco Group had reached 153.

Until 2008, the company did not have a separate HRM function, and HRM-related tasks were performed by the owners and accountants. Then, on the proposal of a consultant, Judit (the co-owner of the company and member of the management board), completed a training course and then took over the HRM tasks (except payroll, which was still carried out by the accounting department).

In 2010, the company subscribed to a foreign-developed recruitment and selection software suitable for handling job announcements and testing (personality and productivity test), and Judit was trained to use this software. As the software performed well and fulfilled the expectations of the managers, it has been used by the company to recruit and select new employees ever since. Due to the growth of the company, another HRM professional was hired in 2013.

Since 2019, HRM activities have been carried out by Fomco Business Management Ltd., founded in 2018 to provide business services (business development, innovation, legal, accounting, financial, marketing, sales, personnel, controlling, and auditing) to all the companies belonging to Fomco Group. The HRM department currently operates with five qualified employees, headed by Judit.

Attracting and retaining practices are crucial for keeping employee turnover low, and the responsibility for their success is shared among the HRM department and managers. The main workforce planning, recruitment, selection, integration, and compensation procedures applied at Fomco Group are the following:

- The annual plan of the company defines the headcount and the composition of the workforce needed to achieve the strategic objectives. Managers, in consultation with the HRM department, determine the required number of employees and decide upon workforce expansion or reduction.

- Recruitment and selection tasks are carried out independently by the HRM department. The recruitment methods used are varied: Job advertisements posted on the company's website, job placement portals, social media, and in the local press, job fairs, and direct applications. Headhunting agencies are only involved in the recruitment of highly qualified positions (managers and professionals). Workers are also recruited directly from educational institutions or through personal recommendations.
- During the selection process, several methods are used, such as interviews, psychological and ability tests, and reference reviews. The most important tools are the performance and personality tests, which are carried out and evaluated with the help of special software.
- The company pays much attention to the workplace integration of employees, and therefore recruitment and development decisions are made by the HRM department in consultation with line managers. In addition to internal and external training, other methods, such as coaching, mentoring, career advice, involvement in projects, or other tailor-made methods, are also used for staff development.
- Decisions related to pay and benefits are taken by the managers. Wages are determined on the basis of job classification, but there may be individual or team/department-level differences. In addition to the classification wage, employees receive a performance bonus with an individual, team/department, and enterprise component. Benefits include private pension schemes and transport costs to the workplace.

CAUSES OF HIGH EMPLOYEE TURNOVER AND MEASURES UNDERTAKEN TO REDUCE IT

Between 2020–2021, all companies within the group aimed at growth, and the average headcount of 115 in 2020 was planned to increase to 150 in 2021. Managers have been constantly pressuring the HRM department to hire new employees as quickly as possible.

To meet these increasing demands from managers, at the beginning of 2021, another qualified HRM professional was hired, who was entrusted with the recruitment and selection of new employees. Shortly after the recruitment of the new HRM professional, Judit, the head of the department, fell ill, so she was unable to familiarize her new colleague with the HRM processes and methods used by the company and with the use of the selection software. Therefore, although the new HRM professional was qualified and experienced, she was not properly prepared for the complex tasks that awaited her at Fomco Group.

Recruitment was successful, many people applied for the advertised jobs, partly because several local companies ceased or reduced their activities due to the economic impact of the COVID-19 pandemic, leaving many without jobs.

Due to the large number of applicants, the selection process took longer than expected, but the managers urged the hiring of new staff, so the HRM department tried to speed up the process under pressure. As HRM staff were completely busy recruiting and selecting, there was not enough time for workplace integration, training, and follow-up, thus a part of the newcomers failed to meet the high expectations of the company. Some of the underperforming employees quickly resigned on their own accord, and others were laid off.

In the autumn of 2021, Judit faced the fact that 11 of the 40 newly hired employees had left during the year, and the retention rate for newcomers decreased to 71% and 72% in 2020 and

2021, respectively, from the usual nearly 80% (see Table 11.1). The situation needed urgent remedy, as the labor demand within the group had been constantly growing and the HRM department would have to achieve a significant increase in headcount (about 40 people) in 2022, as well.

In the absence of proper onboarding, the new HRM professional was not familiar with the selection process and the software used by the company. She, therefore, carried out the selection using other, less effective methods, such as CV screening and traditional job interviews. In addition, due to the coronavirus pandemic, many people in Mureș County were left without work and applied for the advertised jobs, without having either the required qualifications or the proper motivation to work for the company. Filtering out these candidates took much time and effort. Furthermore, the number of newly recruited employees was high (four to five per month). Integrating, training, and mentoring these newcomers imposed a heavy burden on managers in addition to their everyday activities. Finally, as the epidemic subsided and with the partial lifting of restrictions, the possibility of working abroad reopened, so several newcomers resigned and went to work in Western Europe in search of better earnings (for example, some of the truck service employees got employed as truck drivers).

To reduce employee turnover, the HRM department has elaborated in detail the selection and integration process (see Figure 11.1).

TABLE 11.1 Evolution of headcount at Fomco Group in the period 2019–2021

Indicators	2019	2020	2021
Average headcount	122	115	145
New hire	39	48	40
Exit within 3 months	4	7	4
Exit between 3–6 months	2	6	1
Exit between 6–12 months	3	1	6
Exit over 12 months	0	0	7
Total exit	9	14	18
Exit rate	7%	12%	12%
Fluctuation rate (total exit + new hire)/average headcount	39%	54%	40%
New hire exit rate exit within 12 months/new hire	23%	29%	28%
New hire retention rate new hire retained after 12 months/new hire	77%	71%	72%

Source: Fomco Group

FIGURE 11.1 The process of recruitment, selection, and integration at Fomco Group

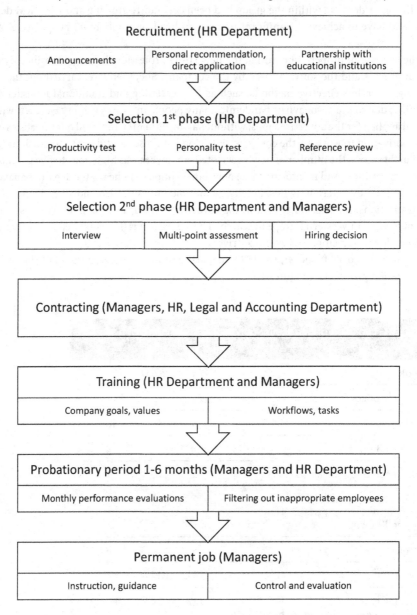

Source: Author's own edition

Productivity tests must be carried out by all applicants, followed by personality tests, reference verification, and face-to-face interviews. This procedure ensures that decisions about the applications are based on a multi-point assessment.

During workplace integration, all new employees have to attend training, where they learn about the company's values, the workflows, and the tasks to be performed.

In the first six months after being hired, new employees are evaluated monthly by their superiors, with the help of the HRM department, so that employees who are not performing well can be quickly filtered out, and those root causes of poor performance, which are independent of employees, can also be identified and eliminated.

The newly developed process was put into practice at the end of 2021. The two-phased selection proved to be effective, as only professionally suitable and motivated applicants are being employed. Judit hopes that the careful selection, combined with the onboarding training and close supervision will improve new hire retention.

CASE STUDY QUESTIONS FOR DISCUSSION

1. What are the main differences between labor market conditions in Romania and your own home country? How do these conditions influence HRM practices?
2. Compare wages in Romania to wages in your home country.
3. How did the HRM function evolve within Fomco Group since its establishment?
4. Which were the causes of high employee turnover at Fomco Group?
5. How did the HRM department react to high employee turnover? Which other measures could Fomco Group introduce in order to improve employee retention?

NOTES

1 www.fomcogroup.ro/
2 The risk-of-poverty threshold is set at 60% of the national median income.
3 SMEs are defined by the European Commission as having less than 250 persons employed, and an annual turnover of up to EUR 50 million, or a balance sheet total of no more than EUR 43 million.
4 Income resulted from sales of goods and commodities, execution of works and provision of services, excluding rebate, commissions, and other discounts for the customers. Data on turnover do not include VAT.
5 1 EUR = 1.1422 US$ (European Central Bank reference exchange rate for 2020, retrieved 18 December 2021, from https://sdw.ecb.europa.eu/quickview.do?SERIES_KEY=120.EXR.A.USD.EUR.SP00.A).
6 Legal working ages have been changed in the studied period from 16–57 years to 16–61 years for women and from 16–62 years to 16–65 years for men.

REFERENCES

COM 2021. *Country Report Romania 2020*. Retrieved 19 December 2021, from https://eur-lex.europa.eu/legal-content/EN/TXT/PDF/?uri=CELEX:52020SC0522&from=EN

Eurostat 2021. *Database*. Retrieved 20 December 2021, from https://ec.europa.eu/eurostat/web/main/data/database

HR Club 2020. *Starea funcţiunii de HR în România (State of the HR Function in Romania, in Romanian Language)*. Retrieved 19 December 2021, from https://hr-club.ro/ro/system/files/Raport_Starea_Functiunii_de_HR_in_RO_2020.pdf

Kerekes, K., & Molnar, I. 2017. Causes and effects of the mismatch between demand and supply on the Romanian labor market. *Forum on Economics and Business*, 20 (133), 34–58.

Kerekes, K., & Zaharie, M. A. 2017. Romania. In: Poór, J., Engle, A. D., & Brewster, C. (eds.) *HRM in Transition-practices of MNC-Subsidiaries in Central and Eastern Europe Russia and Kazakhstan (2015–2016)*, Komarno: J. Selye University, pp. 171–192.

National Institute of Statistics 2021a. *Tempo Online Database*. Retrieved 20 December 2021, from http://statistici.insse.ro:8077/tempo-online/#/pages/tables/insse-table

National Institute of Statistics 2021b. *Monthly Average Earning*. Retrieved 20 December 2021, from https://insse.ro/cms/en/content/monthly-average-earning-78

PwC Romania 2019. *Central and Eastern Europe Private Business Survey 2019*. Retrieved 19 December 2021, from https://www.pwc.com/gx/en/entrepreneurial-and-private -companies/emea-private-business-survey/cee-epbs-report.pdf

PwC Romania 2020. *HR Barometer: Romanians Opted for Job Security in 2020. Staff Turnover in Romanian Companies Decreased to 17.2%*. Retrieved 19 December 2021, from https:// www.pwc.ro/en/press-room/press-releases-2021/hr-barometer--romanians-opted-for-job -security-in-2020--staff-tu.html

PwC Romania 2021. *PwC Global CEO Survey 2021: Key Findings for Romania*. Retrieved 19 December 2021, from https://www.pwc.ro/en/publications/PwC_Romania_CEO -Survey_2021_ENG.pdf

Romania Insider 2020. *Half of Young Romanians Want to Leave the Country, Sociologists Say*. Retrieved 19 December 2021, from https://www.romania-insider.com/young-romanians -leave-sociologists

Valoria 2020. *Tendințe și provocări în HR (HR Tendencies and Challenges, in Romanian Language)*. Retrieved 19 December 2021, from https://valoria.ro/wp-content/uploads/2020 /12/Tendinte-si-provocari-in-HR-2020_ALL_RO.pdf

Volonciu, M. 2021. *Employment Law Overview 2021–2022. Romania*. Retrieved 25 July 2022, from https://knowledge.leglobal.org/wp-content/uploads/sites/2/LEG_MEMO_Romania _25.01.21_compressed.pdf

World Bank 2021. *The World Bank in Romania*. Retrieved 18 December 2021, from https://www .worldbank.org/en/country/romania

World Economic Forum 2019. *The Global Competitiveness Report 2019*. Retrieved 18 December 2021, from https://www3.weforum.org/docs/WEF_TheGlobalCompetitivenessReport2019 .pdf

CHAPTER 12

Russia

Okskaya Shipyard: Employee Retention

Anna Di Nardo

CASE SYNOPSIS

This case illustrates an organization's response to a radical change in the external environment caused by a major political and economic shock. In 2021, the Russian labor market saw substantial growth. As a result, 76% of employers reported serious shortages of qualified specialists, affecting almost all key sectors (Tradesman International, 2022). Given the traditionally low labor mobility in Russia, the changes were reactive in nature, forcing organizations to adopt new business strategies and adjust their HRM policies and practices. Given the financial and market restrictions imposed by the external change, the management team at Okskaya Shipyard (OSV), a Russian company located in the Nizhny Novgorod region, focused on HRM practices that improved performance and helped the firm to maximize its efficiency. These practices included the provision of training for workers, broader job definitions, and meticulous personnel-selection and personnel-retention processes.

LEARNING OUTCOMES

1. Understand how the process of massive transformation at the operational level and related HRM practices fit into the broader context of the external environment.
2. Recognize the link between HRM practices and strategic decisions and their implementation.

DOI: 10.4324/9781003307099-15

3. Recognize how a culture of innovation and productivity improvements relates to the absence of a centralized HRM function and an employee retention strategy.
4. Understand the need for contingent workers and their impact on operations.

KEYWORDS

Culture of innovation, contingent workforce, employee retention, change management, Russia

INTRODUCTION

Since the beginning of the market reforms in 1991, Russia has transformed from a planned economy to a market-oriented economy. As of 2021, it had the fifth-largest economy in Europe, the eleventh-largest in the world (by nominal gross domestic product (GDP)), and the sixth-largest by purchasing power parity (PPP). Russia's vast geography is an important determinant of its economic activity, and the country has the world's largest natural gas reserves, second-largest coal reserves, and eighth-largest oil reserves, as well as the largest oil-shale reserves in Europe.

In 2019, the oil and gas sector accounted for 40% of Russia's federal budget revenues and up to 60% of its exports. In the same year, the value of natural resources accounted for 60% of the country's GDP. Russia has one of the lowest external debts of the major economies, although its inequality in household income and wealth remains comparatively high. Since the Russian invasion of Ukraine in 2022, the country has been subject to sanctions and boycotts by the Western world and its allies, a move described as an "all-out economic and financial war", intended to isolate the Russian economy from the global financial system. The European Bank for Reconstruction and Development has estimated that the damage done by the sanctions has triggered "the greatest supply shock since at least the early 1970s" and would retract Russia's economy by 10% in 2022. Since early 2022, Russia has ceased publishing many of its official economic statistics (https://en.wikipedia.org/wiki/Economy_of_Russia).

Russia has a labor force of approximately 70 million people, making it the world's sixth largest. Two of the most distinctive features of the Russian labor market are the rapid expansion of university-level education and the gradual disappearance of the low-educated labor force. The proportion of tertiary education holders (including university and college) exceeded 70% in 2015. However, given the existing job structure and a large proportion of low-skilled jobs, this has led to a growing problem of overeducation, with the uneducated labor force having all but disappeared. Workers with nine or fewer years of schooling comprise less than 4% of all employees, and the majority are close to retirement or of retirement age. Workers with secondary and lower levels of education also face declining employment opportunities, partially due to a mismatch between their skillsets and the requirements of modern manufacturing practices, as well as old age (Gimpelson, 2019).

High employment and low unemployment rates in the presence of low-wage floors and near-unconstrained wage flexibility are associated with an array of low-paid jobs. Rather than providing more generous unemployment protection, the Russian labor market relies on keeping workers in low-paid employment, with low pay substituting for open unemployment.

THE LABOR MARKET IN THE NIZHNY NOVGOROD REGION

The Nizhny Novgorod region is one of Russia's largest industrial centers, among the top ten in terms of the volume of manufactured products shipped by processing enterprises. The region has unique scientific and technical potential and a powerful educational base. According to independent experts, the Nizhny Novgorod region ranks third in the Russian Federation for scientific and technological development (after Moscow and St. Petersburg). There are 96 organizations in the region engaged in scientific research and development. The region has also successfully attracted foreign investors, who have brought advanced working practices and offer attractive working conditions.

Given the high demand for qualified workers, especially in manufacturing, competition for workers is high. To handle the labor shortage, OSV relies on contractors as contingent workers. Depending on the type of vessel, up to 50% of the workforce is supplied by these contractors. At the same time, OSV's management has developed a policy of employee retention, seeking to decrease the organization's dependence on costly contractors and to introduce more efficient production methods.

OSV AND THE RUSSIAN SHIPBUILDING INDUSTRY

The far-reaching land and maritime borders of Russia, the largest country in the world, require its sea and river fleet to be deployed in different regions, each characterized by diverse geographical and climate conditions. As such, Russia has a large fleet, which it must constantly strengthen and modernize. Historically, shipyards in the USSR have focused primarily on the construction of naval and specialty ships, such as icebreakers. This was reflected in the technological specifics of the shipyards, which centered on the long-term construction of large, complex ships, rather than relatively simple ones. Historically, the largest Russian shipyards combined the construction of military and civil vessels, which allowed them to manage the cyclical nature of the business, to some extent. For example, JSC United Shipbuilding Corporation, ranked among the top 100 largest military companies in the world in 2017, derived 89% of its revenue from military sales. At the same time, many civil vessels, designed for various purposes, were ordered in socialist countries.

Several factors have hindered the development of Russian shipbuilding enterprises and prevented them from improving production and financial performance:

- Shortages of skilled engineering workers and managerial staff, resulting in low productivity.
- Absence of an effective management model for the industry and individual companies.
- Lack of capital investments, resulting in a long-lasting stagnation of production and a lack of innovation.
- Outdated technological and engineering solutions.
- High tax and customs burdens, which coincide with inefficient and corrupt authorities.

- Low quality and unstable supply of domestic components and products, the degradation of domestic enterprises that produce components and equipment, leading to a need for large purchases of equipment abroad.
- Budget cuts due to the Crimea annexation and, as a direct consequence, the imposed economic sanctions (https://infoline.spb.ru/upload/iblock/72c/72c32a4f8bbec992ac00a69 0589d9568.pdf).

OSV has occupied a rather unique place in the Russian shipbuilding industry. Established in 1912, it has mainly worked in civil shipbuilding, specializing in the construction of medium-sized vessels (e.g., cargo ships, tankers, tugs, and special and fishing vessels) and pontoon bridges. Located in Navashino in the Nizhny Novgorod region (population 14,583), along the Oka River, OSV was a so-called "city-forming enterprise".

The concept of a city-forming enterprise originated in the Soviet Union. At times, settlements known as "mono-towns" would emerge due to the presence of a large factory, industrial complex, or facility strategically located in a territory. A considerable proportion of the inhabitants of the mono-town would work at this facility, and the economy and welfare of the citizens would often depend on the city-forming enterprise. In the USSR, labor mobility was restricted by various laws. However, in modern Russia, the major barriers for people who want to move from one area to another are economic – unaffordable housing, high-interest rates, low wages, etc. The management of the city-forming enterprises bears responsibility for the economic and social well-being of the local populations. Moreover, the rhythm of city life is closely related to the enterprise and its technological cycle. One example of this connection is the open public celebration of the launches of new vessels. In the past, the shipyards, which are usually closed to the public, have opened their doors to the cities' populations.

Despite its exposure to many unfavorable macroeconomic factors, OSV generally enjoyed relatively healthy financial and operational performance until 2014.

RADICAL CHANGE

The usual routine was broken in 2014 when the shipyard was severely affected by a sequence of political and economic events that resulted in the devaluation of the Russian currency and a drastic increase in the central bank's interest rate. The State Transport Leasing Company, the major Russian leasing operator, increased the extent to which it leased vessels and stopped the production of new vessels, as they had become unaffordable for its clients. By the beginning of 2015, OSV had lost RUB 1.8 billion and accumulated RUB 3 billion in debt. On a global level, shipbuilding is accustomed to the challenges associated with increasing competition. However, what happened to Russian shipbuilding in 2014 went far beyond the usual market dynamics. Western sanctions imposed on Russia in 2014 as a result of the annexation of Crimea had the most severe impact on the shipbuilding industry.

MANAGERIAL TEAM

In 2015, OSV's managerial team was led by an experienced executive director, Vladimir Kulikov. Kulikov was brought to the shipyard in 2009 with the mission of saving the enterprise, which was on the edge of bankruptcy. His initial six-month contract turned into seven years. A classic "red director",[1] who had started his career in the industry as a welder, he climbed the ladder to production director before becoming an executive director with 25 years of experience in the industry. His motto was "Trust, but verify".

When Kulikov joined OSV in 2009, he brought with him two senior managers and 70 qualified workers. Together, they formed the basis for a new organizational culture. He immediately ceased the use of the "selector" – a practice that was common during Soviet times and had been inherited by many market-driven enterprises. The "selector" was a weekly morning meeting in the form of a conference call, involving the use of a device that divided the audience into those who had two-way communication (i.e., could listen and speak; as a rule, this was the person running the conference call) and those who had one-way communication (i.e., could only listen). Kulikov insisted that all participants in the weekly meetings should instead gather in his office and go over the orders on which the shipyard was currently working. His aims were to instill a perception of ownership, to encourage proactive activities among the managers, and to increase the dialogue among the managers of various shop floors. For the first few weeks, the managers were resistant to asking questions when the orders and technical documentation were read. However, they gradually began asking questions. According to Kulikov, this was a breakthrough.

Another routine introduced by Kulikov was daily visits to the shipyard's various shop floors. These visits lasted for one hour and provided a framework for direct communication among the shipyard's top management, shop-floor management, and workers.

In the five years after Kulikov's appointment, the shipyard earned a solid market reputation. It was viewed as a rare shipyard in Russia, able to deliver on budget and on time. One reason for the shipyard's success was its organizational culture, which created close ties among the shop-floor managers and workers. Each shipyard shop floor functioned as an independent unit and employed from 10 to 60 people. As such, each shop floor resembled a small business. All administrative aspects related to people management (e.g., time-tracking, annual and sick leave, payroll) were delegated to the HRM specialists. There were no HRM managers to handle formal HRM policies and practices. Moreover, the shop-floor managers held full responsibility for workers' performance, as well as traditional HRM practices such as performance appraisals, training, and development. OSV used tariff-based wage systems for its workers.

THE TARIFF-BASED WAGE SYSTEM

The tariff-based wage system is the most common compensation system in Russia, used by both government agencies and commercial organizations. The system is based on a ranking of employees' salaries that depends on their qualifications, length of service, acquired skills, development, and conditions, and on the nature of their work. The model is applied in government agencies, while private companies have their own tariffs, which are approved by the relevant trade unions.

There are two types of tariff systems: Piece-rate and time-based. The piece-rate wage system is used by organizations that provide services, perform work, or produce goods. The profit depends directly on the speed of the employees' work, so it is beneficial to pay not per unit of time, but per unit of production. The payment formula is simple: An employee is paid for the work they accomplish. The quantity of the product is multiplied by the unit price (i.e., the per-piece rate). This wage system encourages employees to continually improve their performance and quality of work. The time-based form of remuneration is used by enterprises with no need or opportunity to calculate the workload in normative hours. The tasks of these employees do not include the production of goods or services. Therefore, it is optimal to pay wages for their time and not for the amount of work they complete. Almost all administrative and economic personnel are renumerated using this system. Remuneration is based on the qualifications of the employee and the actual hours worked in the accounting period.

OSV uses both types of tariff-based systems. In 2014, it had 560 workers employed on the basis of time-based tariffs and 738 employed on piece-based tariffs.

NEW CHALLENGES

In the spring of 2015, Denis Samsikov was appointed executive director of OSV, with the task of evaluating the financial performance of the enterprise and, if necessary, closing it. The KPIs were far from promising. The once-successful shipyard was struggling. The production output had decreased threefold, with debts now totaling RUB 2.6 billion, overshadowing the RUB 2.3 billion in revenues.

While closing the shipyard seemed to be the most obvious choice, Samsikov had two major concerns: The loss of RUB 4.8 billion and the reputation of the shipyard's major shareholder, Volga Shipping Company. In addition, Samsikov was impressed by the quality of the management team. It was obvious that the shipyard had become a hostage to the macroeconomic situation in Russia. Furthermore, Samsikov felt that the technological processes were functioning well, the organizational culture was strong, and the work ethics could provide a strong foundation for a potential turnaround. What was really needed, he thought, was the managerial flexibility that would allow the shipyard to survive the current crisis and last until the markets adjusted. After two days of tense discussions, Kulikov and Samsikov, supported by a rather skeptical CFO Svetlana Vikulova, decided to give the shipyard a chance, given that it would pay off all debt without external financing within three years.

MARKETING, CUTTING COSTS, AND IMPROVING PRODUCTIVITY

The management team decided to adopt a strategy based on a new market approach that involved reducing expenses and improving productivity while maintaining the shipyard's high-quality standards and its reputation for on-time delivery. The shipbuilding industry imposes strict timeframes on shipyards, and failures to deliver vessels on time are associated with severe fines and potential cancellations of orders. With this in mind, OSV's management focused on reliability and its ability to deliver on time through speedy production processes. On-time deliveries have a significant impact on customer satisfaction and, thus, on an organization's market reputation. The speed of production processes, usually measured as the time between the reception of inputs and the delivery of the product to the customer, reflects whether shipyards can rapidly respond to customer demands (Bayo-Moriones, & Merino-Díaz de Cerio, 2002).

From a market perspective, the rescue began with a radical shift in the business-model paradigm. Most shipyards' plans are based on their expected margins (up to 30%). Samsikov decided that OSV did not have this luxury and that the only solution would be to take all orders for all possible vessels, as long as those orders were at least somewhat profitable. Vikulova calculated that OSV's break-even point was at 30% capacity (1.2 million normative hours per year), and this was set as the shipyard's target (see Table 12.1).

The next step was to reduce operational expenses and improve productivity. Most costs are determined by the market (e.g., costs of materials, equipment, and accessories, as well as other direct costs for project documentation, financial guarantees, insurance, etc.). The only costs controlled by the shipyard are personnel expenses, which generally account for 25% of the total cost of a ship (see Table 12.2). The management team therefore immediately laid off numerous employees and cut the payroll and bonuses, while retaining the core of the workforce in order to deliver the existing orders. Despite its expectation that these measures would be unpopular, OSV's management counted on the workers' loyalty and commitment, owing to its understanding that the market would most likely bounce back in two to three years. Any HRM changes also had to take the labor market in the Nizhny Novgorod region into consideration.

OSV struggled for almost a year, and the actions undertaken by the management had a negative impact on the morale of its employees. The first step taken by management was to restore the trust-based relations that had been lost. A crucial element in building trust was direct and transparent communication between senior and middle managers and shop-floor workers. The managers believed that, without trust, there would be no way to overcome the crisis. Senior managers showed their commitment to the rescue plan and made themselves available to discuss all related issues. Line managers were also encouraged to spend more time with their employees.

An important part of these trust-building activities was a program to improve working conditions in the shops and the shipyard. For instance, workers' locker rooms were improved, as were roofs and windows in the shops, canteens, and other utilities. These changes offered a powerful signal that management cared about the workers and their well-being. In addition, programs such as cultural events for the employees and their families were designed to restore the traditional value system rooted in "family values" and to promote feelings of belonging.

TRAINING AND DEVELOPMENT

Finding and retaining qualified employees have always been an issue in shipbuilding (Tradesman International, 2022). Marine labor is a difficult and demanding profession, requiring a diverse skill set and deep knowledge. The best shipyard workers possess a deep love of honest craftsmanship and a maritime heritage on which they pride themselves. Reliability and experience are key. So, how does one find these perfect craftsmen, despite the traditionally cyclical nature of the industry?

OSV also faces challenges with retention. Being located in a manufacturing-intense region, it had to compete with its direct competitors and with other industries for workers. As the shipyard's management wanted to improve productivity, it decided to provide workers with training and development (T&D) opportunities. The initiative addressed the training and educational needs of the hourly staff in the following areas:

TABLE 12.1 Consolidated statement of operations, Okskaya Shipyard, 2014–2021, RUB million

No.		2014	2015	2016	2017	2018	2019	2020	2021
1	Number of ships built, N	2	5	5	5	7	9	10	8
1.1	Ministry of Defense orders	0	0	0	2	0	0	1	0
2	Workload, normative hours, million	2.2	1.2	1.7	1.2	2.3	3.5	3.9	4.0
2.1	Ministry of Defense	58.329	94.551	36.5533	423.674	328.175	372.147	156.469	357.809
3	Net product sales	1.697	2.303	3.841	4.595	2.801	9.067	9.215	9.369
3.1	Ministry of Defense	211	220	960	2.088	930	880	1.348	691
4	Operating income	654	565	933	1.214	1.123	3.380	2.235	1.859
4.1	Ministry of Defense	32	33	285	697	292	277	469	181
5	Operating expenses	1.350	2.177	3.662	4.291	2.383	6.761	8.148	8.676
5.1	Overheads	570	525	689	678	925	1.050	1.183	1.181
5.2	Wages	474	434	548	529	695	857	939	972
5.3	Contractors	398	127	200	97	510	987	1.346	1.473
6	Net income	−492	−498	116	−36	244	1.880	859	0
7	EBITDA	203	6	184	163	433	2.255	1.095	
8	Borrowed funds	2.605	2.364	2.517	1.268	933	0	0	
9	Capital expenses	11	10	20	40	71	79	74	66
10	Financial effect of operational-efficiency program			23	43	437	457	35	20

Source: Okskaya Shipyard data, 2022

1) Motivation for change and commitment.

2) Technical knowledge.

3) Acquisition of second qualifications.

4) Quality-improvement techniques.

5) Safety improvements.

Based on their T&D profile, workers were trained either in certified training centers or in the shops by instructors who were, generally, experienced OSV employees.

The T&D program marked the start of a bottom-up operational-efficiency program. Promoting lead production principles, OSV's management decided not to create dedicated subdivisions or staff units that would be charged with planning and executing programs focused on lean manufacturing, operational efficiency, and similar objectives. Instead, measures and initiatives were developed to improve efficiency, with minimal organizational formalities and a transparent incentive system. Over a period of six years from the introduction of these HRM

TABLE 12.2 Cost structure of building a ship

No.	Cost item	Cost per vessel (RUB, millions)	% of total cost
1	Materials	189	21.3
2	Equipment and accessories	339	38.2
3	Transport and supply costs	3	0.3
4	**Total material costs**	**531**	**59.9**
Total workload (normative hours): 403,541			
6	Payroll costs	53	6.0
7	Contractors	152	17.1
8	Services of other agents	20	2.2
9	**Personnel expenses, total**	**225**	**25.4**
10	**Other direct costs**	**26**	**3.0**
11	**Direct costs, total**	**783**	**88.1**
12	Overheads	**105**	11.9
13	**Total costs**	**888**	**100.0**

Source: Okskaya Shipyard data, 2022

initiatives, the management team received more than 200 proposals for improving operational efficiency and paid out more than RUB 5 million in incentives. The accumulated financial effects of the proposals submitted by workers amounted to savings of RUB 1 billion over the six-year period.

TECHNOLOGICAL MODERNIZATION

To improve productivity, the shipyard upgraded technological solutions in various ways:

- Transitioning to metal processing based on modern computerized plasma installations (a measure that increased the productivity of metal processing and the metal-processing capacity by 50%, to 25,000 tons per year).
- Unifying welding equipment – a critical factor for quality management.
- Modernizing the foundry shop.

To cut operating expenses, management also implemented an energy-efficiency program and modernized the shops' lighting and heating systems.

Following the modernization program, OSV became a modern shipbuilding organization that ensured high quality and competitive construction costs. The enterprise could build any kind of vessel and was limited only by the dimensions of the inland waterway. The advantages were advanced operational efficiency, strict adherence to contractual conditions, a flexible pricing policy, proven procurement procedures, and low overhead costs.

CASE STUDY QUESTIONS FOR DISCUSSION

1) What immediate HRM actions would you take to address the crisis and keep the shipyard afloat?

2) The case addresses some major challenges for HRM in manufacturing (the workforce shortage, recruitment challenges, retention and attrition, and low employee engagement). How did OSV's management address these challenges? How would you address them?

3) Should OSV introduce HRM positions to cope with future challenges? What would be the advantages and disadvantages, as compared to the current model?

NOTE

1 "Red directors" are a term in Soviet, post-Soviet, and Russian economics and politics, currently denoting the managers from the Soviet industrial and managerial elite, directors of enterprises who took leading positions in the Soviet era and remained in them after Russia's transition to a market economy. The new managers, who replaced the red directors and who had often had a Western business

education, largely adopted the management style of their predecessors. Some of the red directors "survived" the market conditions and continue to be part of the economic elite to this day.

REFERENCES

Bayo-Moriones, A. & Merino-Díaz de Cerio, J. 2002. Human resource management, strategy and operational performance in the Spanish manufacturing industry. *M@n@gement*, 5, 175–199. https://doi.org/10.3917/mana.053.0175

Gimpelson, V. 2019. The labor market in Russia, 2000–2017. Retrieved September 19, 2022, from https://wol.iza.org/articles/the-labor-market-in-russia/long

https://en.wikipedia.org/wiki/Economy_of_Russia

Tradesmen International. 2022. Finding qualified shipyard workers: Is it possible? Retrieved September 19, 2022, from https://www.tradesmeninternational.com/news-events/finding -qualified-shipyard-workers-is-it-possible/

CHAPTER 13

Slovakia

International Human Resource Management within the European Textile Industry

Zsuzsanna Szeiner and Imre Antalík

CASE SYNOPSIS

In this case study, we present the case of a Swiss-owned textile company. The company has been operating for 40 years, and during this time it has gained a market-leading position in the market of workwear manufacturers in Switzerland. In the early 2000s, it implemented a greenfield investment in the Central and Eastern European region. We describe the situation and characteristics of the textile industry, as well as the company's challenges in a foreign environment. We present the role played by the company's human resources base in product quality and competitiveness, and the mechanisms through which the company manages its human resources in the international environment, especially during a period of labor shortages. Finally, the future expectations of the company will be discussed.

KEYWORDS

Labor retention, textile industry, workwear manufacturer, Slovakia

DOI: 10.4324/9781003307099-16

LEARNING OUTCOMES

1. Learn about HRM challenges in the textile industry.
2. Understand how an international company applies principles and practices from its home base to new and complex environments.
3. Understand how a local company's HRM practices are adapted to those of its international owners and management.

INTRODUCTION

Hälg Textil AG is a Swiss-owned family business operating in the textile industry for 40 years. The company was founded by Doris and Roman Hälg in Ticino (Switzerland) in 1983. Hälg Textil AG is now one of the biggest manufacturers of industrially cleanable workwear in Switzerland. At its two manufacturing plants, 150 employees design and sew the company's high-quality textile products. The unique value proposition of this company is the excellent service of individual customer needs, the availability of small series orders, short delivery times, reliable quality, and additional consultancy services. The company strives to operate on a sustainable basis and therefore uses state-of-the-art manufacturing technologies and quality raw materials. In the early 2000s, the management decided to expand in the Central and Eastern European region in order to optimize operational costs and to take full advantage of the available opportunities. The management considered a number of criteria when choosing the location for the new manufacturing plant, then decided to expand in southwestern Slovakia. The main priority was to be able to maintain a high standard of production. There were several arguments in favor of choosing southwestern Slovakia, such as geographical proximity, cultural similarity, disciplined and reliable workforce, expected low wage costs, and a predictable political and business environment; all of these were strengthened by the country's accession to the EU in 2004. Currently, 99% of the production and promotion is carried out by Jobtex s.r.o. (Llc.), the Central Eastern European plant of the company.

THE EUROPEAN TEXTILE AND CLOTHING INDUSTRY

The beginnings of the European textile industry can be traced back to the 13th century (Turnau, 1988). Today, it is a developed industry with sales of $147 billion (EU-27) that relies heavily on exports. The EU is the second largest exporter of clothing products (WTO, 2021) (See Figure 13.1).

Although EU-based companies earn USD 33 billion in sales from clothing exports, imports are more than twice as much, USD 72 billion. The main export markets of the European textile and clothing industry are Switzerland and Great Britain. The largest amount of textile and clothing imports come to the EU from China, Bangladesh, and Turkey. According to Eurostat

FIGURE 13.1 Top 15 clothing exporters of the world (Bn EUR)

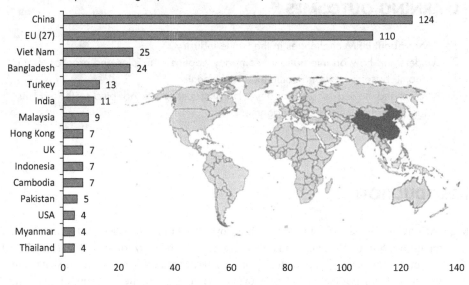

Source: Authors' own compilation based on Euratex, 2022

data, currently 143,000 textile and clothing manufacturing companies operate throughout the European Union. Sixty-three percent of them are engaged in clothing production, and the remaining 33% are in textile production. The sub-sector of technical textiles is one of the most dynamically growing fields. Increasing demand for technical textiles is based on their application in various industries such as healthcare, construction, automotive, and agriculture. (Euratex, 2022). Industrial textiles account for 14% of the EU's textile and clothing exports and 17% of the total production of the T&C sector. The turnover of workwear production accounts for 2% within the industry. Workwear exports represent 1% of the total industry exports (Eurostat, 2022).

Of the companies operating in the sector, 99.8% are micro, small, or medium-sized enterprises, with 88.8% being micro-enterprises employing fewer than ten people.

According to Eurostat statistics, the European textile and clothing industry employs 1.3 million people (with 750,000 in clothing production) currently, 70% of whom are women. At the beginning of the 2000s, the textile industry was employing close to 3.3 million people in the European Union. Although there are fewer individuals working in the sector overall, the value added per employee is improving. In the European textile and apparel industry, employee productivity improved from 20.8% to 30.2% between 2009 and 2018, according to data from EURATEX (2020) (see Figure 13.2).

One of the most significant challenges of the European T&C industry is the aging of the profession. The proportion of employees over 50 years of age has increased by 2% per year over the past ten years. Their proportion was 25% in 2011 and 40% in 2021 (see Figure 13.3).

The COVID-19 crisis presented unexpected challenges to the already stagnant European textile industry: In 2020, clothing production fell by 9.7% and textile production by 9.2% (Eurostat, 2022). With the disappearance of trade-restrictive measures, industrial production was on a

FIGURE 13.2 Employment in the T&C industry 2009–2021, by segment, EU-27

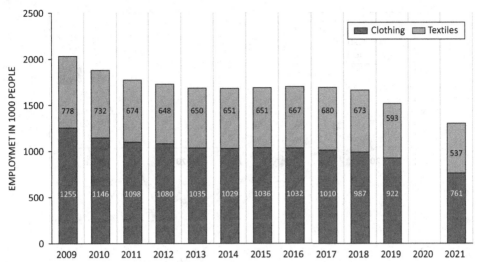

Source: Authors' own compilation based on Statista, 2022

FIGURE 13.3 Proportion of workers over 50 in T&C between 2011 and 2021

Source: Authors' own compilation based on Euratex, 2022

growth path in 2021. The subsequent period presented new challenges for the industry (see Figure 13.4).

The European sanctions policy caused a steep rise in energy prices, which is seriously affecting the textile sector. The European energy crisis put certain, particularly vulnerable, segments of the T&C industry in an extremely disadvantaged position. The production of man-made, synthetic, and cellulose-based fibers is particularly energy-intensive. The disappearance of European fiber products would have immediate consequences for the textile industry and society as a whole. The activity of textile dyeing and finishing is also relatively energy-intensive. These activities are essential in the textile value chain in order to give textile products added value through color and special functions (e.g., medical applications). The global competitiveness of the European textile industry is hindered by high energy prices, the solution of which

FIGURE 13.4 Industry turnover 2004–2021, annual change in percent

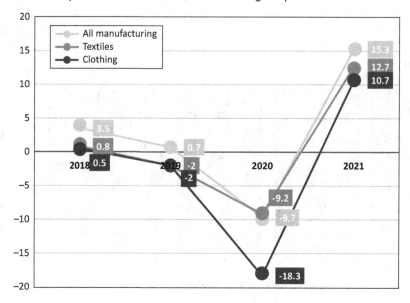

Source: Authors' own compilation based on Euratex, 2022

requires decisions to be made at the EU level, such as the reviewing of the price mechanism of the electricity market or the regulation of gas prices.

SWISS WORKWEAR MANUFACTURING IN SLOVAKIA – ADVANTAGES AND CHALLENGES

Hälg AG, the Swiss workwear manufacturer, entered the Slovak market in 2004, when its owner, Roman Hälg, set up a Slovakia-based Llc. The availability of skilled and disciplined labor was the highest priority for Hälg AG, which operates in a typically labor-intensive industry. The company's competitive advantage had been built on high-quality products and short delivery times. Southwestern Slovakia provided adequate localization advantages for the Swiss company. Several textile companies existed in Western Slovakia even before the regime change. The associated vocational training had also been maintained for decades. The average unemployment rate was 13% at the time in Slovakia (with 10% in the western part of the country). Cultural differences were not significant since both societies are characterized by Christian traditions and a very similar work ethic. Qualified labor was available, with labor costs nearly 70% lower than in Switzerland. The geographical distance (1000 km by road) is not significant. Since Slovakia accessed the EU, both countries had been members of the European Economic Area, so foreign trade barriers had also disappeared. Today, Western Slovakia is a lot more characterized by labor shortages. With more industries lacking a suitably qualified workforce, businesses in these sectors have to face ever-increasing competition for the workforce. Jobs in the textile industry are becoming less attractive, and fewer young people choose sewing as a learned profession.

There is fierce competition in the textile industry. The biggest challenge is the pressure from Asian (China, India, Bangladesh) and South American competitors, but Africa is also increasing its presence in the global market. In Europe, there are competitors in the Balkans. Swiss corporate culture has strict requirements for production that are reflected not only in the high-quality standards of products but in terms of human rights and environmental demands as well. The company does not compete with its prices. It provides shorter delivery times (it can take up to 12 to 16 weeks for Asian manufacturers) and reliable, stable, and flexible services. They meet these conditions better than their competitors in Asia, South America, and the Balkans.

Although the company was able to increase its sales turnover year after year until the period before the COVID-19 crisis, the owner does not plan to expand the production plant, which he justifies by the fact that it is difficult to maintain the employee base. There are no good prospects for its significant expansion. During the COVID-19 period, production fell by almost 10%, but this decline did not last long. In 2022, new challenges appeared in the form of accelerated inflation and rising energy prices in the EU.

HRM CHALLENGES IN THE EUROPEAN T&C INDUSTRY

The key players in every process of the production activity are the company's human resources.

In the case of the textile industry, the technology does not become obsolete too quickly. The company's machine park, which consists of 15-year-old or newer sewing machines, is considered to be up-to-date and modern. In the industry under discussion, the role of human labor is what is really important. Human work matters to a much greater extent than technology. It is important to note that sewing machines only work for an average of 14 seconds each minute. The rest of the time is spent loading and unloading the material, which requires human labor. What is more, sewing is only the end of the entire work process. This is preceded by a creative workflow: Design and tailoring.

Nevertheless, the labor force has been undervalued, as prices have fallen due to fierce competition in the textile industry in recent years. Wages are difficult to raise or even to maintain in such circumstances. Maintaining the human resource base is becoming increasingly challenging for the company. Fewer and fewer young people choose tailoring and sewing today. The sector is characterized by an aging workforce, partly due to the lack of vocational training and the lack of motivation for young people to work in the textile industry. Many international companies have settled in the region in the last 20 to 30 years. Automotive, electronics, wholesale, and retail chains are able to pay higher wages and provide more benefits to employees.

For the time being, the textile enterprise can maintain its employee base, and thus production, but the management is aware of the fact that, following the current trend, they will be able to employ significantly fewer workers in the coming years. In order to solve this increasingly pressing issue, several alternative solutions have been considered by the management.

It was suggested that they recruit workers from countries outside the EU, such as Ukraine or Serbia. As a further alternative, the possibility of employing prisoners was explored. These options were rejected due to high risk factors. The management examined the possibility of outsourcing some activities and decided that embroidery could be done much more efficiently this way. The question of robotization was also raised. Clothing production, on the other hand, can only be mechanized to a limited extent: Even in the case of production with robots, human labor would be required, and service is only available overseas.

So far, no long-term solution has been found for the problem expected in the future. At the same time, it seems that the company's retention policy has been successful for now.

The incentive system has been developed based on the needs and expectations of the employees. Some 90% of the plant's workforce is female. The key expectations are job security and predictable employment relationship, a friendly, supportive atmosphere, and good personal relations. This is exactly what the company offers them. The work schedule is in one shift, taking into account the household chores and responsibilities of women. The personal development of the employees has been promoted in the form of language courses. The company also provides hot meals at the workplace. The management attaches great importance to team-building programs and events that reward the employees and strengthen their commitment to the company. A family atmosphere prevails within the company. The Swiss and Slovak teams also meet in person every year, and they are in daily contact with each other through electronic telecommunication devices. Vacant positions are often filled from within the company by retraining or promotion.

Recent events have negatively affected the company's purchasing of raw materials. Examples include the border closures ordered due to the COVID-19 pandemic and the ongoing Ukrainian–Russian conflict. The management focuses on its well-established systems and long-term business relationships, as well as its employees. In the current uncertain situation, the management has been trying to maintain the status quo. It has no growth or other expansive plans.

CASE STUDY QUESTIONS FOR DISCUSSION

1. What are the current HRM challenges in the textile industry?
2. How does Hälg Textil AG apply the principles and practices from its home base to the local company in Slovakia?
3. How does Jobtex s.r.o. (Llc.) adapt HRM practices to those of its international owners and management in Switzerland and at the same time meet local labor needs?

ACKNOWLEDGMENTS

The authors gratefully acknowledge the contribution of the Scientific Grant Agency of the Slovak Republic under Grant No. 1/0688/21.

REFERENCES

EURATEX. 2020. Facts & key figures of the European textile and clothing industry. [Web page]. Retrieved from: https://euratex.eu/wp-content/uploads/EURATEX-Facts-Key-Figures-2020-LQ.pdf

EURATEX. 2022. Facts & key figures 2022 of the European textile and clothing industry. [Web page]. Retrieved from: https://euratex.eu/wp-content/uploads/EURATEX_FactsKey _Figures_2022rev-1.pdf

EUROSTAT. 2022. Prodcom: Statistics by products: Overview. [Web page]. Retrieved from: https://ec.europa.eu/eurostat/portal/page/portal/statistics/search_database

STATISTA. 2022. Employment in the textile and clothing manufacturing industry in the European Union from 2009 to 2021, by segment. [Web page]. Retrieved from: https://www .statista.com/statistics/417725/eu-european-union-textile-clothing-industry-employment -by-segment/

Turnau, I. 1988. The organization of the European textile industry from the thirteenth to the Eighteenth Century. *Journal of European Economic History*, 17(3): 583.

WTO. 2021. World trade statistical review 2021 - Top 10 exporters and importers of clothing, 2020. Retrieved from: https://www.wto.org/english/res_e/statis_e/wts2021_e/wts2021_e .pdf

PART IV

Mediterranean, Middle East, and Africa

CHAPTER 14

Botswana

Diversity Management in an Institution of Higher Education in Botswana

Dorothy Mpabanga

CASE SYNOPSIS

This case study explores HRM policies and practices that are designed to manage international employees at the University of Botswana.[1] The case provides an assessment of employment laws and their impact on diversity management policies and practices in a university setting. The university relies mainly on employment laws, as it does not have a specific diversity management strategy. The university should develop an HRM strategy to manage its diverse workforce and facilitate ways to communicate with all stakeholders.

KEYWORDS

International employees, human resource management, employment laws, diversity practices, higher education, Botswana

LEARNING OUTCOMES

1. Assess HRM policies and practices designed to manage international employees in the context of an institution of higher education in a developing country.

DOI: 10.4324/9781003307099-18

2. Understand changes and improvements made in HRM policies to accommodate diversity management practices within the existing employment laws.
3. Evaluate these initiatives and try to recommend other relevant ones from the existing diversity management literature.

BACKGROUND TO THE CASE

The department of human resource management (HRM) in the case study is responsible for the recruitment, selection, induction, and placement of local and international staff and ensures that it attracts and retains the best employees from within and outside the country. This includes ensuring that international workers are taken care of from the recruitment stage up to their arrival in Botswana so that they can adapt smoothly to the local environment. The University of Botswana has an international education and partnerships office, which works closely with the HRM department to support international visiting faculty and students. The university has developed HRM policies that supplement national laws and regulations. Bonolo,[2] the HRM manager, is tasked with the recruitment of foreign staff. Thuto[3] is a manager in the International Office.

ORGANIZATIONAL SETTING

The University of Botswana was established in 1982, and it was the first institution of higher education in the country. In 2013, it had 18,716 students (University of Botswana, 2013/14), 56% of whom are female. The figures later declined to 13,686, mainly because the tertiary education sponsorship model by the government shifted in focus to science, technology, engineering, and mathematics (STEM) fields of study (Republic of Botswana, 2012; University of Botswana, 2018/19). The university has nine faculties and offers programs in business, education, humanities, engineering and technology, medicine, social sciences, health, and natural sciences (University of Botswana, 2018/19).

A strategic plan was developed in 2008, which focused on providing relevant and high-quality programs, intensifying research performance, improving student experience, and enhancing HRM for excellence in delivery (University of Botswana, 2008). The plan was revised in 2019, and new strategic objectives were developed in 2020 that entail producing quality graduates, promoting research and innovation, increasing societal engagement and impact, facilitating sustainable management of finances, improving the quality of service, operational efficiency and effectiveness, and building employee capabilities (University of Botswana, 2022).

The university had approximately 2,417 employees, of which 62% were administrative staff and 38% academic staff. Of the latter, 72% were local and 28% were non-citizen staff (University of Botswana, 2012/13). The students comprise national and international students from different countries; for example, 2.1% of students come from the Southern African region while 2.6% are from the rest of the world (University of Botswana, 2012/13). The number of international students declined slightly from 4.8% in 2012/13 to 4% in 2018/19 (University of Botswana, 2018/19), potentially due to the university's lack of close monitoring and implementation of the internationalization policy to diversify the student population and the competition from local and regional universities.

The university uses the general conditions of service policy to administer and manage employees, as prescribed by provisions of Section II of the university's Act and Statutes (University of Botswana, 2013/14). The general conditions of service are mostly in line with the Botswana constitution and the employment act.

The Constitution of Botswana includes clauses on diversity management, stating that there should be no discrimination against employees on the basis of marital status, gender, religion, race, ethnicity, and political beliefs (Republic of Botswana, 1966).

NATIONAL SETTING: BOTSWANA

Botswana is a landlocked country situated in the southern part of Africa. It shares borders with South Africa, Namibia, Zimbabwe, and Zambia. The country is vast but has a small population of about 2.4 million people, the majority of which are under the age of 25 years old (Statistics Botswana, 2022). The country gained independence from the British colonial government in 1966 and is one of the longest-surviving democracies in Africa (Molomo, 1998).

Botswana has enjoyed a stable political and economic environment and experienced one of the highest growth rates in the 1980s after the discovery of diamonds in the 1970s (Salkin et al., 1997). This led to the country accumulating foreign reserves of approximately USD 4.9 billion in 2020, which were down to USD 4.8 in 2021 after the battle against the COVID-19 pandemic of 2020 (Bank of Botswana, 2021). Economic growth has slowed down in recent times, as compared to the 1980s and 1990s; the economy grew by 3.5% in 2019 and contracted by 7.9% in 2020/21 (Bank of Botswana, 2020). Despite the relative political and economic stability, the country continues to have some challenges, of which the most pressing are high unemployment rates of approximately 35%, particularly among the youth, high levels of poverty, particularly among female-headed households, high rates of HIV/AIDs infections, and high levels of inequality (Bank of Botswana, 2021).

MANAGING A DIVERSE WORKFORCE IN BOTSWANA

Managing international workers differs from managing domestic or local workers. HRM functions are similar, but HRM issues are more complex and HRM managers generally have to deal with and handle more issues affecting international employees (Carbery & Cross, 2013: 209). Dessler (2017) asserts that organizations recruit internationally if they cannot find locals with the required qualifications. However, governments can regulate such processes by providing legal requirements. For example, in the United States, the Department of Labor requires that organizations should recruit locally before filing foreign labor certification requests (Dessler, 2017: 602). This is similar to the Employment Act in Botswana, which stipulates that recruitment must commence locally before recruiting outside the country.

Carbery and Cross (2013) observed complex issues associated with managing foreign workers because they entail more activities in addition to normal HRM domestic functions, including international relocation, developing procedures that accommodate a diverse group of international staff, and more involvement in their lives, such as extending support and assistance with housing, visa applications, healthcare, and family circumstances. As the cost of using expatriates is usually greater than using local workers, organizations should develop policies that would minimize early expatriate returns (Dessler, 2017).

THE EMPLOYMENT ACT CAP 47:01 OF 1982

The Employment Act, developed in 1982, is significant in Botswana's labor relations, as it facilitates and guides the development of employment policies by organizations, including incorporating diversity management policies and programs. The Act was reviewed in 2008 and 2010 to include females, people with disabilities, children, and those of a different sexual orientation (Republic of Botswana, 2008; 2010). Since the revisions of the employment act in 2008 and 2010, organizations in Botswana are encouraged to employ diverse workers. For example, the number of people with disabilities and women working in the construction, mining, military, and security sectors has increased.

Organizations are also developing and enhancing their diversity and inclusion HRM policies to protect employees from abuse, bullying, and harassment. This may also be a result of increasing media coverage of issues affecting individuals from disadvantaged populations. The Ministry of Employment, Labour Productivity and Skills Development enforces the employment act, and promotes workplace health and safety, productivity, and work ethic (Republic of Botswana, 2022).

EMPLOYMENT OF NON-CITIZENS ACT, CAP 47:02

The Employment of Non-Citizens Act regulates and guides the employment of international workers through the Department of Labour and Social Security (Republic of Botswana, 2022). The Act prescribes that recruitment should start by first sourcing within the country before recruiting external human resources and that local staff possessing the required qualifications and experience should be given priority over foreign nationals. Organizations are required to report the composition of their workforce and skills development to the Department of Labour and Social Security on an annual basis. Non-complying organizations are liable to a fine. The act also outlines conditions of service, such as salaries and benefits paid to international workers. As shown in Table 14.1 below, international workers' salaries are higher than those of local staff to attract and retain them. Despite the higher salaries offered to expatriate staff, the university has been losing faculty to universities in the region, such as South Africa and Namibia, as they offer more competitive salaries.

TABLE 14.1 Employees' average monthly wage earnings by citizenship

Origin	2017	2018	2019	2020	2021
All citizens	6,270	7,407	5,380	5,853	6,219
All non-citizens	16,039	17,379	20,374	13,355	9,299

Exchange rate: USD 1=Pula 12.24 (www.oanda.com)

Source: Bank of Botswana, 2021, page S-29.

IMPLEMENTATION OF DIVERSITY MANAGEMENT POLICIES AT THE UNIVERSITY OF BOTSWANA

The university does not have a specific diversity management policy to manage international staff other than implementing what the laws require regarding the employment of non-citizens. This has led to a decline in the number of international staff and students at the university. Furthermore, the change in the tertiary education policy to focus on STEM courses and the competition the university faces from local and regional universities has impacted the diverse population of international staff and students. The university hence uses HRM policies and a practice contained in the conditions of service. Thus, the university lacks a diversity management strategy that would enhance the diversity of staff and student population, and the programs offered. The advent of COVID-19 and its restrictions on the movement of people have contributed to the further decline in the number of international staff and students.

MANAGING INTERNATIONAL STAFF AND STUDENTS

According to Bonolo, the university recruits international staff using laws and regulations as contained in the Employment of Non-Citizens Act and the Immigration Act of 2011. She indicated that the university used to be exempt from applying for work and residence permits. However, this waiver was canceled in 2010 when all international staff entering the country had to apply for residence and work permits before entering the country. In addition, the Employment Act requires that the recruitment process starts by sourcing staff locally. If the university cannot identify suitable candidates locally, it is then allowed to recruit outside the country. Recruitment of local professors is a challenge for the university due to the limited number of locals with doctorate degrees and required years of experience in teaching and research. Another challenge is that most professors retire at the age of 65 years, rendering the recruitment of younger professors with the same qualifications but limited experience problematic.

Once the candidate has agreed to take up employment with the university, the HRM department commences the process of applying for work and residence permits on behalf of the staff member. When permission to work and reside in Botswana has been granted by the immigration and labor departments, the HRM department sends these documents to the international staff member to commence their journey to Botswana. The HRM department is required by law to facilitate travel to Botswana, assist with logistical arrangements such as finding accommodation and other amenities, and conduct orientation once they have arrived in the country.

DIVERSITY MANAGEMENT PRACTICES AND CHALLENGES AT THE UNIVERSITY

The university engages in various diversity management practices like annual events, (a welcome dinner for all first-year students, a cultural week for students and staff to experience diverse cultures, cultural visits for international students), orientation for new students, and induction for academic staff. These practices are carried out as extra-curricular activities designed to help staff and students to settle in the country more easily.

The university does not have an explicit diversity management strategy for staff and students, other than following employment of non-citizens' law. The declining number of international staff and students may be partly due to the lack of close monitoring of the internationalization policy. Losing non-citizen staff to competitors was also due to the delays in the processing of residence and work permits. The COVID-19 pandemic that restricted international travel compounded the situation.

SOME CHANGES IN HRM POLICIES

Bonolo had previously raised the issue of the lengthy process of application and approval of work and residence permits for international staff, which contributed to the university losing expatriate staff to other local and regional institutions of higher education. However, the situation has improved since 2018, as the processing of applications has been reduced from 90 to between 7 and 30 days for a visa, 14 days for a work permit, and 30 days for a residence permit (Republic of Botswana, 2022). Furthermore, according to Thuto, the problem of having to deal with multiple immigration officers when submitting applications prior to 2018 no longer exists.

IMPROVING DIVERSITY MANAGEMENT

Well aware of the challenges it is facing in recruiting international faculty and students, the university has been taking several initiatives to improve its diversity practices within the confines of the law:

1. **Establishing a point of contact.** The university has improved the website to be more interactive and provides online information regarding university structures and systems, faculties and departments, programs of study, and an online application process (University of Botswana, 2018; 2021). This is to facilitate the transition of international students into the country. This initiative could further be improved by establishing points of contact in each faculty to promote diversity at faculty and departmental levels. The university's Student Representative Council could be used to promote diversity among the student population, together with the Living and Learning Communities (LLC) program. The LLC is a student-led program, which organizes different annual activities like cultural festivals, leadership training, sports, fashion shows, environmental issues, and community engagement (University of Botswana, 2018/2019) for students in residential blocks. In addition, the university could establish points of contact through student social clubs and societies, which are established to help students acclimatize and enrich their campus life experience through drama, dance, politics, economics, and culture-oriented clubs (University of Botswana, 2018/2019).

2. **Developing innovations in processing residence and work permits.** To further speed up the processing of visa, work, and residence permits, the government introduced the online visa application in March 2022 through the digitization initiative, which should alleviate delays (Republic of Botswana, 2021). The advent of COVID-19

and adherence to its protocols has enhanced the use of electronic means of communication (Republic of Botswana, 2020; Bank of Botswana, 2020).

Thuto indicated that the university's new website has improved access to information and communication with stakeholders, including international staff and students. Communication has also improved through email, Twitter, YouTube, Facebook, and WhatsApp (University of Botswana, 2022). Hence, international students can apply for admission, accommodation, register and pay online, and obtain information through social media. In addition, he said the above social media encourage students to use technology before departure from their home country and after arrival in Botswana to access information regarding welfare issues, including orientation and immigration requirements.

3. **Reviewing labor laws to enhance internationalization.** The university has developed a new strategy that aims to enhance the diversification of the research, teaching, and learning environment through increased stakeholder engagement and the recruitment and retaining of international staff and students. The government is working in consultation with employers and workers' representatives to review labor laws mainly to enhance and align them to international labor standards (Republic of Botswana, 2021).

4. **Intensifying consultations with and between stakeholders.** Thuto reflects on how consultations with the university's departments have improved in an effort to facilitate the transition of international students and staff into the country and the university. For example, the International Office works closely with academic and support departments to attend to issues of international student welfare, programs offered, registration, accommodation, psychosocial support services, and immigration issues. In this regard, the International Office plays a significant role in coordinating and facilitating the provision of diverse services to international staff and visiting scholars.

5. **Engaging the union representatives in immigration and labor matters.** The government collaborates with employers in the public and private sectors and workers' associations to improve labor relations in the country (Republic of Botswana, 2021). The university could educate and train union members on labor laws and diversity management issues to provide them with a better understanding of the laws and what is possible to achieve within the law, and at the same time enhance the university's relations with the authorities.

6. **Acknowledging diversity**. The university has a new strategic foundation, which strives to promote and diversify the teaching and learning environment through a stronger focus on research innovation and collaborative teaching, the internalization of curricula, and the global accreditation of programs especially science, technology, and engineering programs (University of Botswana, 2022).

The university has a department of culture, sports, and recreation, which is aimed at enhancing students' experience in these areas and driving the university's strategy toward personal and social development. Other departments including student clubs and societies are involved in promoting diversity through career planning and counseling, disability support, languages, voluntary work, and cultural visits (University of Botswana, 2022).

7. **One-stop service to assist international students and staff.** The International Office is responsible for implementing the internationalization initiative of the university. Thuto not only provides diverse services to international students and staff (e.g., information about registration, campus accommodation, health, immigration, culture, recreational, and other psychosocial support services) but also works closely with other departments, monitors the implementation of the diversity management strategic initiatives, and reports annually on progress and challenges, and on how equal access and inclusion in teaching, research, and learning develops (University of Botswana, 2018/19, 2022).

8. **Developing, monitoring, and evaluating diversity management strategy and policies.** The university has assigned an HRM officer who is responsible for dealing with staff welfare issues, in particular, handling the immigration matters such as applications for residence and work permits. Thuto focuses on student welfare issues including immigration while Bonolo concentrates on facilitating work and residence permits for staff. The two officers implement international staff and student welfare issues by working closely with other university departments to report progress and problems faced.

The reporting of achievements and challenges in diversity management by the university are published in an annual report. Furthermore, the annual report presents trends of the university's engagement at the national and international levels, reports statistics of staff and student exchange, and describes progress made in teaching and innovation. Challenges are reported in the annual report, including financial constraints faced by the university as a result of the declining number of students due to the reduction in public funding and fierce competition from local and regional universities (University of Botswana, 2018/2019).

As a way to address the above problems and enhance diversity management, the university has introduced new policies and has revised some HRM policies to enhance staff management including the Staff Training and Development policy developed in 2000 and revised in 2021, the Sexual Harassment Policy of 2018, tolerance and learning to appreciate diversity and differences, adjusting to university life, coping with physical abuse and stress, depression, conflict resolution (2018), and anger management (2017) (University of Botswana, 2022). To enhance diversity management, the university needs to develop an explicit HRM strategy, which includes diversity management. The university should revise the existing conditions of service, as they are outdated. The university must regularly monitor and evaluate the new strategy to attract and retain diverse staff and students.

CASE STUDY QUESTIONS FOR DISCUSSION

1. What are the core functions of the university's HRM department?
2. The university does not have a formal strategy for diversity management and it has to comply with the current employment laws. But it has introduced a number of initiatives (policies and practices) in order to recruit and manage international employees. How do these initiatives in the context of an institute of higher education in a developing country compare to current best practices?
3. Evaluate these initiatives and recommend other relevant ones from the broader diversity management literature.

NOTES

1 The author is grateful to the University of Botswana for granting permission to publish this case. The views expressed in this case study are those of the participants/respondents and are not the views and/or opinions of the University of Botswana.
2 Fictitious name: Translates to "politeness" in Setswana.
3 Fictitious name: Translates to "education" in Setswana.

REFERENCES

Bank of Botswana. 2020. *Annual Report*. Gaborone. http://www.bob.bw accessed 20 January 2022.

Bank of Botswana. 2021. *Annual Report*, Gaborone. http://www.bob.bw accessed 29 November 2022.

Carbery, R., & Cross, C. 2013. *Human Resource Management: A Concise Introduction*. Palgrave Macmillan. London.

Dessler, G. 2017. *Human Resource Management*, Pearson, Boston.

Molomo, M. G. 1998. The role and responsibilities of members of parliament in facilitating good governance and democracy. In Edge, W. A. & Lekorwe, M. H. (eds.) *Botswana Politics and Society*, J. L. Schaik, Pretoria.

Republic of Botswana. 1966, 2002. *Botswana Constitution*, Government Printer.

Republic of Botswana. 1982, 2003, 2008, 2010. *Employment Act, CAP 47:01*, Government Printer, Gaborone.

Republic of Botswana. 2003b, 2010, 2016. *Trade Disputes Act*, Government Printer.

Republic of Botswana, Employment of Non-Citizens Act, CAP 47:02, The Immigration Act of 2011, Republic of Botswana, The Manpower Development, Training and Localization Policy, Government Printer.

Salkin, J., Mpabanga, D. Selwe, J., & Wright, M. (eds.) 1997. *Aspects of the Botswana Economy; Selected Papers*, Lentswe la Lesedi, Gaborone.

Statistics Botswana. 2022. *Botswana Projections: Census Preliminary Results*. http://www.gov .statsbots.org.bw accessed 25 July 2022.

University of Botswana. 2008. *Strategy for Excellence: 2016 and Beyond*, University of Botswana, Gaborone.

University of Botswana. 2012/13. *Annual Report*, University of Botswana, Gaborone. http:// www.ub.bw accessed 15 November 2015.

University of Botswana. 2013/14. *Annual Report*, University of Botswana, Gaborone. http:// www.ub.bw accessed 29 March 2016.

University of Botswana. 2018/19. *Annual Report*. University of Botswana, Gaborone. http://www .ub.bw accessed 15 January 2022.

University of Botswana. 2022. *Creating a Future for the Knowledge Generation, The Strategy for 2020–2029*. University of Botswana, Gaborone. http://www.ub.bw accessed 17 January 2022.

CHAPTER 15

Cyprus

People Management in Academia: Anna-Maria Harilaou's[1] HRM Concerns

Eleni Stavrou and Nicoleta Nicolaou Pissarides

CASE SYNOPSIS

The case concerns people management issues of academic staff at the law department of the University of Zenon, a public higher education institution located in Cyprus. It outlines the promotion and career process as well as the context in which such process takes place, including the organizational, institutional, and cultural factors involved. The example provided in the case is about a female academic and the challenges she faced in her career within a masculine, high-power distance culture with limited adoption of requisite HRM practices and in a country that faces political division. While she prevails in the end, managing to rise through the ranks and become a professor, she is perplexed by the lack of professionalism and effective human resource management (HRM) at her university. In this respect, she wants to find ways to improve her organization's culture by contributing toward the adoption of suitable HRM practices that will be systematic and fair.

KEYWORDS

HRM, academia, tenure, culture, Cyprus

DOI: 10.4324/9781003307099-19

LEARNING OUTCOMES

1. Understand human resource planning in an academic setting.
2. Understand how key figures in organizations can impact HRM processes.
3. Analyze mentoring and career planning opportunities for academics.
4. Analyze and connect national culture with HRM in an international setting.
5. Identify HRM practices that can facilitate the promotion of female academics.
6. Identify a set of competencies for tenured faculty.

After 24 years in the law department at Zenon University, Anna-Maria Harilaou, once the departmental chair, thinks back at the challenges and opportunities encountered over the years and is contemplating how to improve her department's culture and HRM practice.

THE UNIVERSITY

Zenon University is a state university in Cyprus. It was founded in 1987 in Larnaca – a small city in Cyprus – and it is one of the three state and six private universities currently in place. It has nine schools, 302 academic staff, and 227 teaching staff in total (Table 15.1).

Cypriots are very proud of this university. It takes its name after Zenon (deriving from Zeus – the head of the ancient Greek Olympian Gods), a Cypriot philosopher and founder of Stoicism who identifies with the city. To be hired as a member of the academic staff at the university, one needs to hold a Ph.D. degree from an accredited university. Academic positions (lecturer, assistant professor, associate professor, professor) are offered based on university regulations and one's qualifications. The first two ranks are on tenure-track contracts while the last two are permanent (tenured) positions (see Figure 15.1).

TABLE 15.1 Academic and teaching staff at Zenon University

	Male	Female	Total
Professor	80	10	**90**
Associate Professor	71	39	**110**
Assistant Professor	48	28	**76**
Lecturer	20	6	**26**
Special Teaching Staff	21	35	**56**
Special Scientists (Teaching Staff)	88	83	**171**
	328	**201**	**529**

FIGURE 15.1 Hierarchy of academic positions at Zenon University

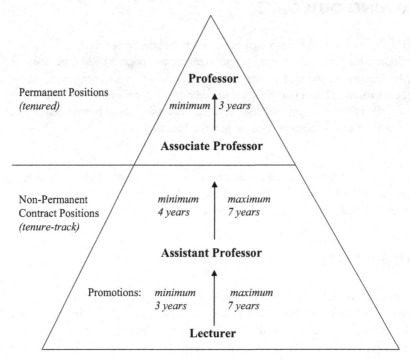

Official university regulations indicate three broad evaluation areas, in no order of importance: Research, teaching, and service to the university/community. Other than these, most schools within the university do not have well-specified criteria, e.g., number or type of publications, quality of teaching, or level of service. In practice, only research and, specifically, publications in highly ranked journals count for promotion in the law department, as demonstrated below.

A TIMELINE OF EVENTS

The law department offers undergraduate and graduate programs in various areas of law and is part of the School of Social Sciences. It consists of 12 colleagues, all relatively young (age range 35–58) and mostly males (9/12). Due to this very small number, and to meet high teaching needs, the department hires external teaching staff on a per-course basis.

Anna-Maria completed her studies in very competitive universities in the United States on earned scholarships. She joined Zenon University as visiting faculty in 1997, and a year later was hired as an assistant professor. She has been very active in teaching and supervising students at both the undergraduate and graduate levels. In addition, she has been the main person in charge of maintaining the department's undergraduate and graduate programs in business law. Meanwhile, she has been an active researcher, working on intricate research questions and creating a solid publication record over the years.

She was unsuccessfully evaluated for tenure at first in 2006. The committee's report noted that, while she met (even exceeded) all other criteria, she did not have the highly regarded publications the department wanted (those considered top publications in the United States), but rather she had more specialized, very good, publications. It was clear from the report that nothing else mattered than the specific top publications. A similar situation took place with one of her male colleagues in the department, Peter, who specialized in European law. A third colleague, John, did receive tenure because he did have two of the desirable top publications.

For the first time, it was revealed explicitly that only specific "top" publications count for tenure. It all started toward the end of 2004 when the then chair of the department took the liberty to create a list of 16 journals that, based on his own search, were deemed of a high enough standard for each major field of law. Three of those in each major field were marked as "top" journals. It was a trend then; journal rankings were first introduced to business schools (Sangster, 2015) and were used in career-defining decisions (Tourish & Wilmott, 2015). Even though other colleagues disagreed with this idea, some even in writing, he and two other colleagues managed to pass it through the department council with the explicit note that this list is only indicative.

Nevertheless, the list was used as a condition in the tenure interviews of Anna-Maria, Peter, and John, about a year later. Soon after tenure was refused to Anna-Maria and Peter, and after much discussion, the list was formally discarded. Those in favor of keeping the list rationalized that "at least now colleagues know what is expected of them even without the list there". The terms of the psychological contract were established (Rousseau, 1998).

Three years passed, and Anna-Maria's tenure process, and Peter's soon after, first began. They knew this was their last chance. Anna-Maria spoke with tenured colleagues in the department who seemed positive. Some even clarified an unofficial "gentlemen's agreement"[2] that had been quite widespread through the grapevine over the previous three years: "High flyers" who have (two of) the revered "top" journal publications will be granted tenure the first time; hard workers with solid academic record and a portfolio of respectable publications will be granted tenure the second time; those without a portfolio of solid publications will be weeded out. This was added to the new psychological contract (Rousseau, 1998) between "the department leadership" and tenure-track faculty.

Peter was successful the second time around. Unfortunately, even though Anna-Maria had a solid record, she was not recommended for tenure, to the surprise of everyone in the department (except the committee members). Colleagues lost their trust in the "system", not knowing what and who to believe anymore. Even the new departmental psychological contract was breached.

This perceived violation of the psychological contract created unprecedented friction, high insecurity, and dissatisfaction among colleagues in the department. Both overt and covert conflict was characteristic of daily interactions while many discussions took place in small groups behind closed doors: Transparency, collaboration, and free academic spirit had all been buried under the fear of separation, punishment, and reprimand (Harvey, 1988). All this upheaval succeeded in leading the School Promotion and Tenure Committee's majority vote (five to three) in favor of Anna-Maria receiving tenure. In a similar manner, colleagues in the senate two months later voted (21 to 2) in her favor. Finally, Anna-Maria had made tenure!

The story does not end here. Between 2016 and 2019, two other colleagues faced challenges in their evaluation process. It seems that the department had not been very consistent with its decisions, creating procedural injustice. These colleagues did not succeed the first time, but they did the second. However, these ups and downs caused, once more, serious ripple effects in departmental cohesiveness. It was not until 2021 that things started to calm down again. By this time, Anna-Maria had become a professor. She was also able to become more actively involved in school and university committees.

THE LARGER CONTEXT

The Republic of Cyprus, established in 1960, with a population of around 1 million, is a small island country in the southern-eastern Mediterranean basin that has experienced much political conflict over its 8,000-year history, in part, due to the Turkish invasion in 1974 and subsequent occupation of a large part of the island.

Cyprus shares much in common with the other southern EU countries, such as its institutional environment, its cultural values, and the role of people management (Papalexandris and Stavrou-Costea, 2004). Cyprus provides high employment protection and moderate social protection for particular occupational groups such as civil servants but provides little social safety for the long-term unemployed, newcomers to the labor market, workers in the underground economy, or immigrants. Much of the child or elderly care is expected from the female family members without pay. Despite efforts at the EU level, the male bread-winner model persists even though women may be just as educated and qualified, if not more, than their male counterparts (Stavrou & Papalexandris, 2016).

Cultural issues of very high uncertainty avoidance (Cyprus UAI score 115) promote a system of high formalization and hierarchy, while the high-power distance (Cyprus PDI score 75) promotes a gap between the powerful and the not: Those with high positions of power want to keep the power to themselves rather than share it with the rest; those with low power accept it. In the Cypriot culture, even though shifting toward individualism is still more collective (IDV score 42), people tend not to want to deviate from group norms. In-groups and out-groups are standard, and, in combination with high power distance, the in-group is favored by the powerful. There are few women in high-power positions in Cyprus, including tenured women at Zenon University when compared to their male counterparts (39 associate professors and 10 professors among 302 tenured faculty, see Exhibit 1), reinforcing the Cypriot masculine culture (MAS score 58). Cypriot culture is also more long-term oriented (LTO score 59), valuing traditions, lifetime employment, and looking to future well-being rather than immediate results (Stavrou & Eisenberg, 2006). In turn, performance orientation takes second place. While all other values are in line with Anna-Maria's departmental culture, this last cultural value seems to be in contrast. *Or was the performance orientation toward specific top-tier journals merely an excuse to suppress a different underlying issue?*

Within the above context, people management at Zenon University and among Cypriot organizations at large is not strategic. It is often handled by people who have no knowledge of or expertise in HRM. The orientation of HRM in Cyprus has remained stagnant in past practices and traditions. To illustrate, the most common hiring practice is still the interview, usually nonstructured. Quite often, "who" you know is a more important criterion than "what" you know. While Cypriot organizations pride themselves in the emphasis they place on staff training and development, serious questions are raised as to the monitoring and effectiveness of such efforts or their connection to training needs. Training needs analyses are not common. While most large organizations have performance management systems, many, mostly in the public sector, are linked directly to promotions, resulting in everyone being rated as excellent. Such practices are an indication that managing people has a long way to go before becoming a change agent or even being taken seriously in Cyprus.

Finally, in contrast to most of southern Europe, the academic tradition in Cyprus is absent. The average Cypriot cannot distinguish between the role and work of an academic and that of a high-school teacher. The concept of "research" and "academic publications" is quite unknown. Nevertheless, academics and academic institutions are highly regarded.

PEOPLE MANAGEMENT AND ACADEMIA

People management practices are rarely discussed in the context of academic institutions Yet academics need to be trained and developed (i.e., through seminars, conferences, workshops), to have transparent, (relatively) clear evaluation criteria and career paths, and to be appraised fairly for their performance. In academic institutions with a long academic tradition, such issues have been addressed somehow, tested throughout the years, and even somewhat resolved: This process usually evolves within a cultural and institutional context over a long period of time.

Applying the traditional HRM practices in academia involves recognizing and openly discussing a number of dilemmas: (1) Transparency vs. autonomy, (2) equality vs. homogeneity, (3) accountability vs. academic freedom, and (4) HRM managers vs. academics being in charge of the hiring and promotion process (van de Brink, Thunissen, & Fruytier, 2013). The more transparent (and thus, more accountable) the processes become, the more they are deemed time-consuming and disruptive to academic freedom. In turn, key performance indicators are often dismissed, and academics prefer to stick to their collegial system. The committees involved, and the one in Anna-Maria's case is no exception, are of the perception that increasing the transparency and formalization of procedures will end in "rigid" decision-making mechanisms. As a result, administrative HRM departments in universities are involved mainly in paper-pushing activities, lacking the power to ensure that hiring and promotion committees manage procedures requisitely. Academic professors tend to think they are the best qualified to identify a candidate's merits and that no HRM professional is needed to advise on job profiles, evaluation criteria, performance appraisals, recruitment, and selection processes (e.g., structuring interviews, chairing the interviewing panel, compiling the report, and helping focus on other qualities in the academics than those purely research-related, etc.). Furthermore, academics high up in their field's scientific hierarchy exercise considerable power over the standards that govern their fields (van de Brink, Thunissen, & Fruytier, 2013) and often are positively biased toward people very similar to themselves, demonstrating an underlying tendency for "cloning" (Essed, 2004). Hence, homogeneity in gender, age, and religion strongly influence decisions in academia. The status quo is not to be disrupted; equality is *not* a priority! *Or is it?*

In the Cypriot context, these issues have not been resolved; they have not even been addressed. Before even getting to these intricate dilemmas, more basic matters need immediate attention. These include, but are not limited to, strategic goals at university, school, and department levels derived from the university's vision and mission; measurable criteria for achieving them; incentives and rewards; and implications if not achieved. Partly due to a lack of experience running such institutions on the island, thus the lack of such context diachronically, and partly due to the Cypriot culture in which Cypriot academics are no exception, academic institutions lag behind in establishing requisite management systems for their administrative, much less for their academic staff.

Academic institutions worldwide are nowadays being pressured into proving that academic research has an economic, societal, and/or cultural impact (Gruber, 2014), in addition to the academic impact as disputably measured by citation counts and journal rankings (Sangster, 2015). This puts even more pressure on all academic institutions in establishing measurable performance impact indicators.

In the law department at Zenon University, given its structure, culture, and short history, professors hold the ultimate power. They are the gatekeepers and the mindguards of the department. And quite often, they disagree with each other. The rest of the faculty have been expected to agree with and follow their decisions: As a result, often they need to choose with whom to side. Many departmental decisions have been overturned based on who was present or absent. As younger colleagues have moved to higher ranks, this culture is slowly starting to change. But it is not uncommon for the lower levels of faculty to still experience, in silence, aggressive overt disagreements among professors, or even to be the recipients of such aggression.

Within this masculine, high-power distance context, little mentoring takes place from "senior" to "junior" colleagues. Training and development are left almost entirely to those in power: Colleagues may attend conferences and seminars at their own discretion, but at the end of the day, as Anna-Maria realized the hard way, only publications in "top" academic journals count. So, academic colleagues are advised to "spend their time wisely". This one-dimensional criterion, according to Anna-Maria, would have been perhaps acceptable in a large university abroad, where academic institutions abound, research support is open-handed, graduate programs thrive, colleagues have shared interests, and resources are indeed available. Or, if this criterion was communicated explicitly upon hiring a colleague, then expectations, fair or not, would have been clear from the start.

But before these expectations are communicated, shouldn't department colleagues first collectively make a strategic decision about the content of these expectations? It is clear that research ranks first on the priority list. Is academic impact the absolute goal in the Cypriot context? If yes, should it continue to count for 100%, or will teaching and service also bear any weight? If so, how much weight? And after answering these questions, a whole set of other questions will need to be addressed so that the department will have a well-thought-out strategic HRM plan that will lead them to success.

CONCLUSION

Anna-Maria is still contemplating how her department should build constructively on university regulations to approach this whole issue of hiring, developing, evaluating, and rewarding academic colleagues fairly and strategically. She cannot stop wondering what the value of teaching, service, and research should be in a country like Cyprus: Should context matter, or does only one best academic model exist? And if the latter, which one is it? If context does matter, from where should she begin? Should the measures applied be strict or allow for academic freedom? Would the incorporation of guidelines and transparent procedures increase bureaucracy? How will equality flourish when excluding dissimilar people is the norm? Should she disrupt the status quo and promote more equitable and transparent processes? Should journal rankings be used as a performance indicator? Should she also try to incorporate indicators to assess the economic, societal, or cultural impact of research in her department? And if so, which ones? Should HRM procedures involve a professional HRM adviser at all stages, or do the academic professors know better? All these questions were spinning in Anna-Maria's mind as she was contemplating how to approach the matter in a strategic and fair way for her department.

CASE STUDY QUESTIONS FOR DISCUSSION

1. What are the main people management issues of this study? How are these related to the resource-based view of the firm?

2. How does the Cypriot context affect these issues at Zenon University? (Further reading about Cyprus or the southern European context may be needed). How do these issues relate with an institutional and cultural lens?

3. What are the constraints and opportunities, from a people management perspective, for Anna-Maria moving forward?

4. If you were a management consultant, what do you think needs to be done differently in relation to hiring, development, and evaluation of academics at Zenon?

    (i) Provide a specific plan of action and its implications.

    (ii) How are your recommendations influenced by your cultural background?

5. Draft a list of generic competencies that would be important for an associate professor and professor within a context similar to that of Zenon University.

NOTES

1 To preserve the privacy of the organization discussed, all names, dates, and other identifying information have been modified.
2 Male gender in the wording is purposeful.

REFERENCES

Essed, P. 2004. Cloning amongst professors: Normativities and imagined homogeneities. *NORA: Nordic Journal of Feminist and Gender Research*, 12(2): 113–122.

Gruber, T. 2014. Academic sell-out: How an obsession with metrics and rankings is damaging academia. *Journal of Marketing for Higher Education*, 24(2): 165–177.

Harvey, J.B. 1988. *The Abilene Paradox and Other Meditations on Management*. Lexington: Lexington Books.

Papalexandris, N. and Stavrou-Costea, E. 2004. Human resource management in the Southeastern Mediterranean corner of Europe: The case of Italy, Greece and Cyprus. Chapter 10 in Brewster, Mayrhofer and Morley (eds) *Convergence and Divergence in European HRM*, Burlington, MA: Elsevier Butterworth-Heinemann, 189–230.

Rousseau, D.M. 1998. The psychological contract at work. *Journal of Organizational Behavior*, 19: 665–671.

Sangster A. 2015. You cannot judge a book by its cover: The problems with journal rankings. *Accounting Education*, 24(3): 175–186.

Stavrou, E. and Eisenberg, J. 2006. Mapping Cyprus' cultural dimensions: Comparing Hofstede and Schwartz's values frameworks. In 18th International Congress of the International Association of Cross-Cultural Psychology (IACCP, Greece, July 2006).

Stavrou, E. and Papalexandris, N. 2016. Chapter 4 in *International Human Resource Management: Contemporary HR Issues in Europe* (3rd edition), edited by M. Dickmann, C. Brewster, and P. Sparrow, Routledge/Taylor & Francis Group.

Tourish, D. and Willmott, H. 2015. In defiance of folly: Journal rankings, mindless measures and the ABS guide. *Critical Perspectives on Accounting*, 26(1): 37–46.

Van den Brink, M., Fruytier, B. and Thunnissen, M. 2013. Talent management in academia: Performance systems and HRM policies. *Human Resource Management Journal*, 23(2): 180–195.

CHAPTER 16

Greece

What Can HRM Do for Me? HRM as a Business Development Function in a Technology SME

Maria Vakola

CASE SYNOPSIS

A technological SME private company called "GrandTechExpert" (GTE)[1] was founded in Greece in 2000. GTE managed to survive the economic crisis of 2007–2008, but its owner and general director was struggling to take it forward. The owner did not welcome the idea of having an HRM professional onboard because he could not see the value. His paternalistic leadership style created internal problems. Talented employees were complaining that they were being treated like children by the owner, and there was a high turnover rate of temporary employees. A serious health issue kept the owner away and when he came back, he decided to bring HR on board. The newly hired HRM professional initiated systematic recruitment, selection, performance, and training processes. These processes contributed to the solution of several internal problems and at the same time contributed to an increased number of returning customers.

KEYWORDS

Human resource management, business development, paternalistic leadership style, SME, Greece

DOI: 10.4324/9781003307099-20

LEARNING OUTCOMES

1. To understand the reasons and tensions that explain HRM exclusion from business functions.
2. To realize business outcomes before and after HRM adoption.
3. To identify HRM functions when it is created.
4. To understand the obstacles for an HRM professional in an SME context.
5. To understand the role of HRM as a business development partner.

ORGANIZATIONAL AND NATIONAL CONTEXT

The company was founded in 2000 by Stavros D. who quit his career in sales at a big technology company and decided to invest all his money into his own company. His company "GrandTechExpert" (GTE) managed to survive despite the economic crisis of the last ten years, and it now has 35 permanent employees and 140 temp employees who are hired to support the services and projects that the company sells to its customers.

Stavros thinks that GTE has the potential to thrive, but he feels that he is not supported by his team and people. Two years ago, he hired a high-potential candidate not really for his skills and knowledge but for his network and connections with business and high-profile people. Stavros was very disappointed to see that the new employee was a toxic person who created many problems for his team, and as a result, he lost some talented employees who had worked for many years for his company. Stavros also feels very tired and exhausted, and he gets irritated often, especially in meetings. He wonders why the salespeople are on the payroll since he brings 70% of new clients. One visit to his office and one can understand the climate in this company. The phones are ringing all the time, and all the decisions, important or trivial, need to go through him.

He does not welcome the idea of creating an HR department because of the extra cost which cannot be justified by the size of the company. The sales director has made multiple requests for a dedicated person in HR and tried to convince him to hire one. He describes many times a situation where temporary people are hired but have not shown up or leave without notice or are not a good match with key job requirements. The sales director explains to Stavros that HR can justify the extra cost because it will not be an internal function but a business development one which can support the sales team to create value.

The company is located in Greece. 94.6% of Greek businesses (680,038) are micro-enterprises employing less than ten people, 4.8% (34,701) are small enterprises, 0.5% (3,819) are medium-sized enterprises, and 0.1% (522) are large enterprises. In 2021, SMEs in Greece achieved strong growth in value added of 20.5%, after a decline of 14.9% in 2020 (European Commission, 2022).

ORGANIZATIONAL CLIMATE AND STRUCTURE

GTE is a small but very respectable company in the field, and it is known as reliable and trustworthy. The company has recently moved offices, and it is now situated in more modern premises in a neighborhood that is considered a technological hub, as many technological companies rent spaces there. Despite the modern premises, the layout keeps the offices divided into three different floors, and there aren't any common spaces or open offices. Out of the 35 employees, only four are women, who hold assistant and reception positions, and there is only one woman who is responsible for writing proposals for public bidding. Stavros's personal assistant deals with the CVs and joins him in the interviews for hiring. There are instances where hiring can be very stressful because temporary staff needs to be sent to their customers urgently to implement their services. They also need to cover for dropouts, which is a frequent occurrence. Stavros's personal assistant often complains that she does not have either the skills or the time to continuously work on hiring temporary staff/employees.

There are many instances of talented people complaining that they feel they are being treated like children by Stavros. Everything needs to go through him and his office. They say, "he needs to make decisions even about the choice of the coffee we will order". Stavros says that he would prefer not to make all the decisions and to trust others to make decisions, but he is reluctant to do so. He believes that in situations where he is not involved, things do not get done properly.

Stavros recalls a situation when he decided to allocate a whole project to one salesperson and not be involved at all. He called the customer to discuss something irrelevant to this contract, and during the conversation, he realized that some important contract terms had been neglected. He was so mad, and he started yelling. That was one time that everybody in the company heard his voice. The salesperson still claims that these terms would have been included at a later stage, and he feels very insulted by this constant cross-checking. He thinks that Stavros called the customer not because he was an old friend of Stavros that used to do business with him and wanted to talk about a new business deal, but to check on him, the salesperson. Despite this incident, most of the people at the company realize that this company is up and running because Stavros is always there, working exhausting hours and trying his best to make it a success. What is often discussed in informal discussions among employees is that Stavros's leadership style, decisions, and actions have made this company what it is now. But they also discuss that from this point onwards, this style and attitude have already started to keep them behind.

The company consists of the following departments.

Technical Department

The director of this department was one of the founding members of the company who sold his share to Stavros D. but wanted to keep his job. A person who is reliable, trustworthy, loyal, and committed to the company, he values processes and focuses on quality. He comes first in the morning and leaves last, and he puts all his effort to make it a success. When there is a need, even on Sundays, he will come to the office without a second thought. He believes in Stavros and follows all his suggestions without any questions.

He manages a team of five developers. If someone wants to talk to a member of their team then they should contact him first to get permission. This ensures quality according to him. He doesn't want to be bypassed, and sometimes it gets difficult to cooperate with him as he shows no flexibility and adjustment. He often says that "the processes are here to follow them not to ignore them". When he realizes that something is not according to the processes agreed upon, he snaps, and the discussion can easily become a fight. His team members get requests, but they know that they need to ask for approval before responding. That makes the whole process very slow and bureaucratic. For instance, a salesperson could be with a customer and need to get some technical details before contract signing. It is very difficult to provide direct answers to the customer, as programmers need to discuss it with their manager first before answering. One programmer explains "at the beginning, it was frustrating not to be able to handle your own issues but then, I saw the positive side which is you don't need to worry as somebody else has the responsibility".

Sales Department

For the last four years, the department has been managed by a very experienced sales director who has previous experience in the technology sector. He is effective and low profile, and he joined the company because he was offered his first job as a director. He created a team of eight salespeople, and very soon he realized that only five could deal with the customers. The other three explicitly said that they prefer to stay in and deal with the back-office work. He was very surprised when he realized that this company was a technological one but didn't use any customer management systems or automated logistics and purchasing systems. Instead, they rely on traditional databases. He often explains that the company's strategy should expand to focus on strategic alliance development, software development, and innovative services. To implement this plan, he needs a sales force with technical skills. He finds cooperation with the technical department very difficult.

Business Development Department

The head of this department is the last and most controversial hiring. Stavros hired this director because of his work experience and his extensive business network. He came highly recommended because he had held three positions as general director before, and Stavros was very impressed. Stavros missed an important detail of his CV, the duration of these posts, which weren't longer than 18 months. During the interview, he claimed that he lost his jobs because of the economic crisis and that he could open many doors because of his business contacts and his skills. He is now over a year in this company, and he has managed to arrange meetings with many high-profile people. However, there has been no follow-up from his end, and therefore there haven't been any contracts signed. He explains that this is not his responsibility as he promised to open doors and then it is the sales department who needs to arrange the details. Stavros understands that they should cooperate, but he is very disappointed with the results of this department.

Finance Department

The finance director is very competent with numbers and attention to detail, and he managed to create a team of three people who cooperate very effectively. The climate in his team is very positive, and he is known for being fair and competent. The finance director complains about the lack of systems makes his job very time-consuming and that all the decision-making is concentrated on Stavros. He cannot do his job because he needs permission from Stavros almost every day. Stavros negotiates salaries with each person separately, and then he informs the finance director of the numbers. In these negotiating sessions, Stavros is alone with the employees without their immediate supervisor being present. That creates many problems for the finance department, and the finance director is frustrated because the processes are very slow and the customers are not being served correctly.

AN IMPORTANT INCIDENT

The company got an important deal with a bank and managed to get deals in Bulgaria and Cyprus. All staff felt pressure to offer the services they promised to their customers. There was a shortage of developers and general IT practitioners in the market, and some people who promised to join them pulled out at the last minute. The situation was very difficult.

Stavros called a meeting with the directors of sales and business development to find solutions to this situation. Stavros was very upset, and he started yelling in the meeting when the sales director and the business development director started accusing each other of causing the problems. He couldn't understand how these people who had very high salaries could not perform and deal with the situation. Instead of feeling satisfied with the new deals, he felt stressed and burned out. Stavros understood that the sales team was exhausted, and he heard some corridor rumors that his best salesperson had been approached by his competitors. When he talked to him, the salesperson said that,

> I cannot do my job here without support from the technical department. I needed some support for a deal, and nobody answered me from our technical team. I am in sales, and I haven't received any training from eight years now so you either train me or you give me direct access to one member of the technical team.

Stavros was now very upset and very sad because the sales director had handed in his notice. He hadn't expected that at all. This caused him a serious health problem that forced the sales director to withdraw his notice and act as general director in the absence of Stavros. After this serious health issue that kept Stavros away from the office for several weeks, he was convinced to appoint an HR officer who would be mainly responsible for hiring and training certification.

HR ON BOARD

Stavros interviewed people, and he finally appointed an HR person with eight years of experience. Nikos, the new HR officer, was surprised to find out that the permanent employees were 95% male and that there were no processes related to HR functions such as onboarding, performance management, rewards, or training. He also realized that there was limited communication among various departments and that each director was very protective of his "territory". Nikos decided to make suggestions to Stavros and to mainly concentrate on setting up a recruitment process enabled by technology, and he then standardized the process of training certification.

In the beginning, Nikos had a really difficult time convincing Stavros to set up HR processes. Nikos spent long hours trying to understand the tech job specifications and the tech industry, and he attended two online courses. Stavros wasn't convinced about the use of various hiring platforms and investing in employer branding and recruitment processes. Nikos explained that IT candidates and developers need to know the company to be interested in sending in their CVs. GTE started having a presence at major tech events and joined many universities and tech start-up events. Nikos set up a reliable hiring process that allowed GTE to have a database of available tech workers. That made it easier to select the right people to match each contract with their clients. The time saved from this process was invested in meeting these people in person, offering coaching, building personal relationships, arranging their training, and making them feel part of a wider team. Better matching led to fewer dropouts and to more satisfied customers.

As the months went by, Stavros realized that they had been "chasing" tech candidates for years who could drop out at the last minute, leaving the company exposed to its customers and causing delays and expenses. In some instances, they had to send GTE's internal people from the technical department to make sure that there were no delays in the projects until they filled the temporary positions. Stavros realized that Nikos had started to build a network with tech people, making it much easier to find the right people and replace people when necessary. There was a steady increase in projects, and some clients called him back to say that they were happy with the people who implemented the project. As a result, both Stavros and the sales director started inviting Nikos to meetings with customers and partnering with him to make decisions and offers.

Nikos realized from the start that one major issue in this company was its structure. Therefore, he decided to talk openly to Stavros about possible changes related to the structure. The meeting didn't go well, and Stavros defended all his past hiring decisions. Nikos managed to convince him to create a new role related to project management and secured a budget for two new hires. Nikos hired two female employees with technical backgrounds and experience in project management. When these two people came on board, the salespeople started getting the support they needed. Three big new contracts created the need for more project managers, but Stavros refused to accept this proposal. It was way out of their budget. Then Nikos found the right moment to ask for an internal restructuring, presenting performance data from each department. Stavros realized that the business development director opened doors, but his figures were disappointing. As a result, Stavros had to fire him along with another two people who didn't fit in. This allowed him to hire two more people in project management roles and one in marketing/social media.

Nikos and the sales director worked together to organize a training and team-building event for the whole company. They spent a day out of the office to build trust, cooperation, and communication, and Nikos talked to each one of the internal people to formulate a training plan. The event was a success, and everyone started feeling differently.

After three years of cooperation, Stavros thinks that it was a very good decision to hire Nikos. He is surprised about Nikos's contribution to new and existing contracts. He thought that Nikos could contribute only to the internal administration that the company needed, and he never expected to find a partner in business contract negotiations and implementation. Nikos was also very useful during the pandemic when they had to move all their staff online. Stavros now feels that he has a team that he can trust and together can create a better future for GTE.

CASE STUDY QUESTIONS FOR DISCUSSION

1. What were the reasons behind Stavros's decision to exclude HRM? Was it justifiable at the early stages of his business?
2. Identify and describe what the HRM professional did and why it was a success.
3. Compare the before and after the hiring of the HR professional and make conclusions. What are the key implications?
4. What are the main challenges that an HRM professional faces in an SME?

NOTES

1 GrandTechExpert (GTE) is a fictional name.

REFERENCES

Botero, I. C., & Litchfield, S. R. 2013. Exploring human resource management in family firms: A summary of what we know and ideas for future development. In *Handbook of Research on Family Business*, Second Edition. Edward Elgar Publishing.

Botero, I. C., Cruz, C., Massis, A. D., & Nordqvist, M. 2015. Family business research in the European context. *European Journal of International Management*, 9(2), 139–159.

European Commission. 2022. SME country fact sheet. https://ec.europa.eu/docsroom/documents/50491/attachments/1/translations/en/renditions/native

Pellegrini, E. K., & Scandura, T. A. 2008. Paternalistic leadership: A review and agenda for future research. *Journal of Management*, 34(3), 566–593.

CHAPTER 17

Israel

Redesigning the Production Floor and Reward System in a Food Production Company: HRM Considerations

Michal Biron and Hilla Peretz

CASE SYNOPSIS

Foodco is one of the largest food corporations in Israel. Netfood,[1] a multinational corporation, has a holding share of 64% in Foodco. Bamco, one of Foodco's largest production facilities, faced challenges when Netfood set new quality standards. Two problems were identified whose solution could help to increase the plant's productivity: One, relating to how employees work, and two, relating to how employees are being rewarded. This case study discusses both issues in the context of changing labor relations in Israel as well as globalization processes affecting the Israeli economy.

KEYWORDS

Organizational change, performance appraisal, rewards, union-management relations, Israel

LEARNING OUTCOMES

After reading this case, students will be:

1. Able to describe variations in rewards practices.
2. Aware of differences in the role of employees' unions.

DOI: 10.4324/9781003307099-21

3. Aware of drivers for ongoing training and development within organizations.
4. Aware of the role of HRM in multinational corporations.
5. Able to identify key HRM challenges facing organizations undergoing major change.

ORGANIZATIONAL CONTEXT

Foodco is one of the largest food corporations in Israel. It was founded in the early 1940s and now has nine manufacturing facilities in Israel, producing over 1,000 products. Foodco exports its products to other countries as well, primarily to Europe. The corporation's products constantly face competition from both locally produced and imported products. Foodco became a public company in 1992 (with 25% of its shares traded in the Tel Aviv Stock Market). Starting in 1995, Netfood, a large, multinational corporation, has gradually increased its holdings in Foodco and now has a holding rate of 64%. The partnership with Netfood set new standards of quality and excellence and instituted advanced work procedures.

The partnership afforded Foodco increased knowledge in a variety of relevant areas such as advanced technologies, management, finances, and marketing. At the same time, Netfood's management has increasingly put pressure on Foodco to improve its performance. A special team of experts and consultants from Netfood ("target-setting team"), designed to handle the challenges posed by the acquisition of Foodco, visited all production facilities in Israel and gave specific recommendations on how to improve various processes with the aim of enhancing performance.

One of Foodco's biggest production facilities is Bamco. Established in 1974, the plant produced mainly pasta products. Gradually over the years, its scope of activities broadened. The plant, located in Northern Israel, doubled in size due to extensions in 1997 and again in 2005; several baking production lines were installed, and it became the baking center of Foodco. Following the visit of Netfood's target-setting team to Bamco, two problems were identified whose solutions could help increase the productivity of the plant. The first had to do with the structure of the production floor, and the second had to do with the reward system. This case study focuses on both issues and how they relate to the changing labor relationships in Israel as well as to globalization processes affecting the Israeli economy.

NATIONAL CONTEXT: HRM IN ISRAEL[2]

From its establishment in 1948, the union movement was a dominant power in Israel, with the major trade union, the Histadrut, having strong economic and political power. Socialism was the leading socio-economic ideology during the first decades of Israel's existence, generating a strong sense of cohesion in the country and enabling it to cope with enormous difficulties such as security (which, albeit to a lesser extent, remains an issue today) and the heterogeneity of its population caused by a number of waves of mass immigration from various countries. The Histadrut represented more than 80% of all wage earners, while at the same time, it was also one of the largest employers in Israel. Thus, the Israeli industrial relations system was highly corporatist in nature (Haberfeld, 1995). The Histadrut owned the country's largest steel, chemistry, and construction industries, as well as many other basic industries. As a major employer, and the sole trade union, the Histadrut had a tremendous influence on the human resource management (HRM) function. Labor relations were a major HRM activity, dictated mainly by a very powerful union and supported by legislation and regulations. Consequently, the HRM function during this era held a lowly, administrative position (emphasis was on recruitment, record keeping, seniority-based promotions, procedures, and regulation) and had minimal influence on strategic matters.

Things began to change in the late 1970s. Global and local recessions as well as high inflation rates considerably slowed Israel's economic growth. The HRM function was facing issues of layoffs and complex compensation management, while simultaneously coping with issues of changing industrial environment, the introduction of multinationals, and a shift to private industry dominance. In particular, at the beginning of the 1980s rapid growth in the high-tech industry occurred. This was mainly due to the availability of a high-level technical workforce, resulting from the downsizing of technical professions in the defense industry and the immigration of many scientists from the former Soviet Union. This process, together with a sharp decline in union membership between 1990 and 2010, following an increase in unionization rates that is attributed to the 2011 Israeli social justice protests, had a major impact on HRM. The position of the HRM function within the organization has changed, facing new challenges of managing a multi-cultural, highly educated, strongly socially aware workforce in large and complex organizational settings, exposed to growing national and international competition. In line with these changing demands, HRM professionals are viewed more as strategic partners contributing to the development and the accomplishment of the organization-wide business plan and objectives, and also key players in enhancing the quality of work-life, promoting work-life balance, and strengthening partnerships with local communities.

BACKGROUND TO THE CASE

Industrial Relations at Bamco

Bamco employs nearly 370 employees, most of whom live in the nearby city. The plant is involved in local community life through such activities as supporting local schools and institutes for the elderly. The plant has enjoyed good relationships with its employees for many years. The last labor dispute took place in 1995 and concerned the introduction of a temporary (i.e., trial) contract for new employees (see below). Labor relationships at Bamco are based on three elements:

1. Employees are affiliated with a recognized trade union.
2. A reward system graded by level and tenure, with a productivity bonus paid upon meeting quantity targets (see criteria below – sub-section "Reward System") and with overtime working limited to 15 hours per week.
3. Nationally agreed terms and conditions of employment determined by the joint industrial council for food workers, covering all companies in this industry.

The Production Process at Bamco

Historically, the company has had two production departments: Baking and pasta. Each department produced several products. Work in the production area was organized on the basis of product lines. While there were few unique production elements (for specific products), generally there were three main stages for production. The first stage involved the blending of ingredients and flavorings to form a uniform mass. This was done within the computer-controlled preparation area, where all the ingredients required for a batch were mixed according to the specification produced by the works-order program. The mixture was then mechanically formed into various shapes (based on the product line) and placed onto a belt carrying them to the cooking area. The second stage involved baking or frying, and – for some products – coating (chocolate, salt, etc.). From the cooking area, products were again automatically placed on a belt, which transferred them to the packing area. In this final stage, products were packed in single units (auto-packing). Packed units were then manually inserted into boxes/plastic bags.

Of the manufacturing personnel at Bamco (which composes about 60% of the entire workforce of the plant), 64% are males, most are married (84%), and the mean age is 42. Work is organized in shifts, including nights and excluding Saturdays (Sabbath) and public holidays. Work schedules are organized with two days off per week. There are six to seven product lines operating simultaneously on each shift, led by foremen (one foreman per two to three product lines). The managers of the two production departments are usually in the plant during morning shifts only. They report to the plant manager.

Most production jobs are highly standardized. Four employees are assigned to each production line: One employee in the blending area, checking for and fixing problems with the mixture, cleaning, etc.; one employee in the cooking area, checking for and removing defective products, cleaning, etc.; and two employees in the packing area. In addition, there is supporting staff that provides services to all production lines in a given shift: Two employees assist with more general tasks such as transporting boxes, loading ingredients into the mixer, etc.; routine quality tests (mixture, cooked products, etc.) are performed by two members of the quality assurance department; and finally, two technicians handle mechanical problems and perform system maintenance. The structure of the production unit at Bamco is shown in Figure 17.1.

FIGURE 17.1 Structure of the production unit at Bamco

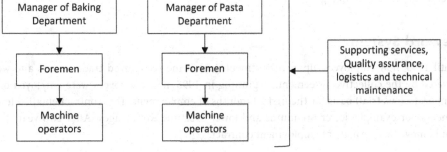

PROBLEMS FACING PRODUCTIVITY

Two problem areas were identified by Netfood's target-setting team in 2004: The inefficient structure of the production unit, and an uncompetitive reward system.

Structure of the Production Unit

The design of the production unit often resulted in conflicts and communication problems. Department managers had to change specifications during production to adjust to excessive demands, unexpected failures, or dynamic priority setting. However, foremen were primarily concerned with meeting performance targets and maintaining production schedules – for those product lines for which they were responsible. Such a design often discouraged cooperation across product lines, not to mention across departments. Further, foremen had limited authority to make changes during the production process and were thus allowed to apply only partial/temporal solutions to operational problems in the absence of the department manager. In sum, the original design of manufacturing at Bamco was very inflexible, lacking a broad, system-wide perspective for managing the shop floor.

Netfood's target-setting team recommended changing the structure of the production unit to "simplify communication channels, grow employees from within by providing opportunities to take more responsibilities, and improve work processes in order to increase the plant's profitability". To do so, the number of foremen per shift was reduced to one (instead of three), and their job description was changed to "shift managers", responsible for the entire plant's operation during their shift. This change required extensive training, which was mainly provided by department managers, and included issues such as anticipating and responding to operational problems and over/under staffing. Within this new structure, the role of department managers has shifted from administrative monitoring and technical operation (now part of the shift managers' job description) toward coaching and training. Moreover, after the change is implemented, the plan is that department managers could become more involved in strategic planning (e.g., new products), contributing their expertise and experience in relevant matters.

Finally, most production workers (machine operators) would have more power and responsibilities following the proposed change. In fact, given that there would only be one shift manager per shift, some of the tasks that were previously performed by the foremen (e.g., temperature checks) were now included in the job description of production workers. On the one hand, this would increase employee sense of worth and control. On the other hand, it also involves a higher workload and the need to coordinate efforts across product lines. The new structure of the production unit is shown in Figure 17.2.

Reward System

Until 1995, new employees, upon recruitment, joined the recognized trade unions and were covered by the collective agreement. Beginning in 1995, new employees were employed on a temporary (i.e., trial) basis for the first 24 months of employment. This contract entailed fewer benefits, for example, lower premiums and lower overtime work wages. After two years they would move to a permanent employment contract.

FIGURE 17.2 New structure of the production unit at Bamco

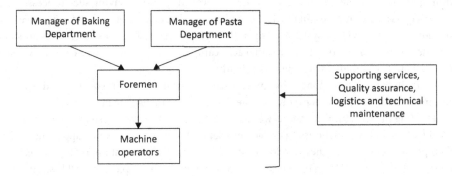

Traditionally, rewards at Bamco were based on seniority increments and shift premiums (for second and night shifts). Pay also partly varied as a function of performance. The single parameter upon which performance was evaluated was quantity: Specific targets were set for each production line (i.e., the number of units to be produced per hour), and premiums were allocated upon meeting these targets.

Rewards at Bamco have always been considered above average compared to other firms in the Israeli food industry. Yet HRM surveys from recent years indicated that employees are unhappy with their pay. In addition, while the original reward scheme seemed to enhance employee efforts and productivity, the quality of production did not improve. To address these issues, and in line with the recommendations made by Netfood's target-setting team, a new reward plan was introduced in 2005. This plan was based on the following three criteria (all of which were of equal weight):

1. Performance: An index based on the difference between the actual total time for completing all tasks in a given product line and a set criterion (i.e., standard), taking into account planned breaks, for maintenance, cleaning, etc. Performance may be increased by minimizing unplanned breaks (e.g., errors) and by taking more efficient (and thus shorter) planned breaks.

2. Efficiency: An index based on the difference between the actual number of units packed and a set criterion. Efficiency may be increased by minimizing unplanned breaks and working at a standard pace.

3. Quality: An index referring to the number of units produced without failures, out of all units produced in a given product line. Quality may be increased by specializing and minimizing failures.

THE ROLE OF THE HRM DEPARTMENT

Theo is the manager of the HRM department at Bamco. He was externally recruited for this job in 2000. Theo is well experienced with the challenges involved in globalization processes in the form of mergers and acquisitions. In his former job as the HRM manager of a steel production company, the company went into a merger with a Chinese firm. Theo is aware of the extensive planning and training needed for successfully implementing and surviving such processes – for both managers and employees. In particular, he believes that instead of the rigid, repetitive tasks and traditional supervisory systems in operation, employees at Bamco should work in small, adaptable teams with rotating tasks within each team. The new reward scheme not only fosters this model but also enhances perceptions of equity.

Zachary, Bamco's plant manager, has much trust and confidence in Theo. Theo and two other senior members of the HRM department ("the HRM change management team") were given the task of leading the structural change as well as the change in the reward system. To this end, they worked with the HRM functions at Foodco and Netfood to develop relevant supporting policies and programs. For example, they developed a training program aimed at improving the technical and managerial skills of shift managers and a two-day seminar for employees at all levels intended to introduce and discuss normative issues (including such topics as communication, the global marketplace, etc.). Similarly, together with the managers of the two production departments at Bamco, the team developed and validated the standards for the new reward system.

Creating the Proper Climate for Union Cooperation

Given that nearly 80% of Bamco's workforce is unionized, the recognized trade union tradition-ally had a lot of say in organizational change processes and was involved in the planning and implementation stages of such processes. Working with the union was more complicated this time. Netfood's growing impact in recent years (in terms of shareholdings) allowed for more direct, explicit pressures. The management of Bamco and Foodco realized that to increase competitiveness and productivity, Bamco would have to quickly adopt the changes recommended by Netfood's target-setting team. While Theo had previous experience dealing with unions and generally preferred working through dialogue-enabled rather than unidirectional solutions, the tight schedule for administrating the current changes allowed for only a little time to consult the union.

On the evening after Zachary and Theo announced the changes about to take place, the leaders of the trade union called for a special, urgent meeting. They were disappointed by the way decisions were made, with Bamco's management neglecting employee rights and needs, particularly in light of the long-lasting legacy of collaboration. Two main areas of concern were discussed: (1) The new production design, in particular with respect to increasing job demands and changing job descriptions, and (2) the ability of the new reward system to accurately capture employee efforts and consider extra job demands. At the end of the meeting, members unanimously agreed to announce a labor dispute. Theo and Zachary realized this could develop into a crisis. Netfood's management expected to see some positive results already by the second quarter of next year.

FIVE YEARS LATER: FURTHER CHANGES TO THE PRODUCTION FLOOR AND REWARD SYSTEM

Since the original writing of this case, Bamco has gone through additional changes with implications for both topics covered in this chapter. First, the outline of the production floor was once again adjusted. The two production departments ("baking" and "pasta") were integrated under a single production manager and a deputy manager. This allowed for better synergies and cooperation between production lines. For example, prior to this change, each department was primarily concerned with its own employees. In the case of early completion of a day's work in one department, no support was given to the other department, which might have needed a few extra hands. Merging the departments into one unit enabled more efficient use of resources, in this and similar situations. The structural change was also possible given that technology-wise, the operation of the production lines became more similar – across products. The change was well-received by employees because it created better (more collaborative) co-worker relationships and enabled the creation of a thicker and stronger (more autonomous) mid-level management layer – offering opportunities for internal promotions. Notably, it also enabled Bamco to be more competitive, relative to other firms in the area, when recruiting for the position of production manager, as this position was now more attractive in terms of both challenge and compensation.

Second, the premium-based reward system was canceled, and instead, a position-based reward scheme was implemented. In this scheme, each position (role) has an index consisting of three to five levels. Within each level, there are specific professional and behavioral criteria that need to be met. For example, a dough maker can specialize in two, three, or four mixers. Moving up from one level to the next is based on training and certification (professional parameters) and meeting behavioral standards (e.g., disciplinary actions and safety violations). Employees are also encouraged to engage in cross-role development (i.e., move up along more than a single-role ladder and get double the role-based rewards) – to foster versatility. Compensation in the new reward scheme is not fixed, but dependent on the employee continuously holding the specific position (on a specific level). This allows Bamco greater flexibility in the compensations it offers, without committing indefinitely to high reward levels. Notably, this change in rewards allocation corresponds with broader trends in the minimum wage in Israel. The minimum wage has increased several times in the past few years, making it hard to create meaningful premium-based incentives. The revised reward system incentivizes those who are willing to invest in learning and increase their employability. This also enhances Bamco's efforts around employee retention.

CASE STUDY QUESTIONS FOR DISCUSSION

1. What are the main changes regarding Bamco's production structure, and how are they related to training programs?
2. In what ways has the structure of Israeli labor relations affected the traditional reward system in Bamco?
3. What are the pros and cons of the new structure of the production unit for Bamco employees?
4. What are the main differences between Bamco's old and new reward systems?

NOTES

1 The names of the organizations and the protagonists are fictitious.
2 This section is based on Tzafrir, Baruch, & Meshoulam (2007). Additional information can be found in Weisberg (2010).

REFERENCES

Haberfeld, Y. 1995. Why do workers join unions? The case of Israel. *Industrial and Labour Relations Review, 48,* 656–670.

Tzafrir, S.S., Baruch, Y., & Meshoulam, I. 2007. HRM in Israel: New challenges. *International Journal of Human Resource Management, 18,* 114–131.

Weisberg, J. 2010. "Evolutionary" and "revolutionary" events affecting HRM in Israel: 1948–2008. *Human Resource Management Review, 20,* 176–185.

CHAPTER 18

Italy

Human Resource Management in Italian Family-Owned SMEs: Sustaining the Competitive Advantage through B Corp Transformation

Silvia Bagdadli and Martina Gianecchini

CASE SYNOPSIS

Romano Lana is a 50-year-old family-owned medium enterprise located in Tuscany (Italy). Notwithstanding its robust financial performance, Romano Lana is struggling to maintain its competitive advantage. Linda, one of the owner's children appointed as HR manager in the company, is convinced that getting benefit corporation (B Corp) certification will support the transformation needed to become more attractive to skilled employees, much needed to embrace the change required by the increasing competition. However, Linda needs to overcome the resistance of her father, Cecco, who strongly believes in the positive aspects of being a family firm (flexibility, reactiveness, cohesiveness) and is convinced that any kind of certification would include bureaucracy and (worthless) procedures.

KEYWORDS

HRM practices, sustainable competitive advantage, family-owned SMEs, B Corp, Italy

DOI: 10.4324/9781003307099-22

LEARNING OUTCOMES

1. Have a general understanding of HRM in small and medium-sized enterprises (SMEs).
2. Understand the process of structuration and formalization of HRM practices.
3. Understand how becoming a benefit corporation (B Corp) can enhance HRM in SMEs.
4. Understand how HRM can support a sustainable competitive advantage.
5. Develop knowledge of the Italian entrepreneurial business context.

INTRODUCTION

Linda, the HR Manager of Romano Lana,[1] an Italian wool and clothing company, was extremely excited and anxious before entering the meeting to illustrate to her father (the founder and CEO of the company) her idea to certify the family company as a benefit corporation (B Corp). Romano Lana is a 50-year-old family-owned medium-sized firm located in the province of Prato, in the Tuscany region. "Quality" and "tradition" are the keywords of the company, that encompass pursuing a product differentiation strategy based on high-quality raw materials and craftsmanship production of its 150 workers. Notwithstanding robust financial performance, Romano Lana is struggling to maintain its competitive advantage, as competitors are continuously innovating products, manufacturing processes, and customer relationships. Linda's family firm does not have qualified managers for initiating those changes to sustain the competitive advantage in the long term. Linda thought that the lane to B Corp certification might be the solution to attract and retain skilled employees. In addition, she strongly believed that the characteristics of a family-owned SME, like Romano Lana, would favor the achievement of the certification. At the same time, her "babbo" (dad), Cecco, was convinced that any kind of certification would include bureaucracy and (worthless) procedures, unfortunately so familiar to an Italian entrepreneur. In addition, the transformation may undermine the family climate of Romano Lana. With this in mind, Cecco set about meeting with Linda to discuss risks and opportunities for Romano Lana to get B Corp certification.

ORGANIZATIONAL SETTING: "ROMANO LANA" WOOL AND CLOTHING PRODUCTION

Established in 1972, Romano Lane was named after its founder (Cecco Romano) who started producing wool fabrics in a village in the province of Prato, in Tuscany. Committed to producing high-quality products, he traveled around the world in search of the best wool, setting the ground for the downstream integration of the productive process. A few years after the foundation of the company, Cecco launched the first Romano Lana men's suit line, soon transformed into a complete branded collection including knitwear and sportswear. From its inception, Romano Lana had a strong export strategy: In 2021 only 15% of the company's sales were in

Italy, while Europe and North America were the company's largest markets with 70% of sales, followed by the fast-growing Chinese market, with the remaining 15%. Romano Lana's production is dedicated to its own brand for 30% of its capacity, and for the remaining 70% the company produces for national and international fashion brands. "Quality" and "tradition" are the keywords of the company, where the intention was to maintain a differentiation strategy based on high-quality raw materials and craftsmanship production of its workers, as opposed to low-cost and growing international competitors.

Cecco – 70 years old – is the CEO and is still actively involved in all the strategic decisions and in most operational ones. Elena (Cecco's older sister) and Sara (Cecco's wife) sit on the board of directors; Roberto (Cecco's younger brother) is the production manager; Linda (Cecco's daughter) is the human resources manager. The company has about 150 employees: Many of them are experienced workers and wool artisans who have spent their entire careers in Romano Lana and who live in the villages near the company's main location.

NATIONAL CONTEXT: FAMILY-OWNED SMES IN ITALY

SMEs play an important role in the Italian business economy. As illustrated in the SME performance review annually compiled by the European Union (EU), in 2020, SMEs represented 99.9% of the total number of Italian firms, generating 64.3% of the total value added and employing 76.1% of the total workforce. The average SME has 3.1 employees, slightly below the EU average of 3.7. The average productivity of the firms, calculated as value added per person employed, was approximately EUR 38,300 in 2020, slightly below the EU average of EUR 40,000. This lower productivity rate is ascribed to higher barriers in accessing the capital needed to finance the growth, a modest role played by equity capital markets and venture capital investments. The daily operations of Italian SMEs are also hampered by burdensome administrative requirements (more than 300 hours/year spent on bureaucracy) and frequent changes in the regulatory framework. In addition, and most importantly, tax rates are up to 64% of company turnover. The cost and number of procedures required to start a business are also among the highest in the EU.

Notwithstanding these obstacles, Italian SMEs appear particularly active in introducing innovation in their businesses to remain competitive in national and international markets. Indeed, many Italian SMEs, active in sectors such as agri-food and fashion, rely on a combination of craftsmanship and manufacturing ability, along with entrepreneurial innovation and flexibility to adapt to technological and market developments. Italy scores above the EU average in SME-related innovation indicators: 39% of Italian SMEs innovate in-house, and 41% of them introduce innovative products or processes, also thanks to trademark and patent applications. Italian SMEs are also more likely to introduce marketing and organizational innovations than the EU average. Innovation is conducive to quality in products, which is the basis of SME success in international markets: 15% of firms export goods outside the EU, significantly above the EU average of 10%.

The development of Italian SMEs is intertwined with the strong family atmosphere of its entrepreneurial environment: According to the latest census of enterprises (2021), family businesses represent 75.2% of Italian firms with at least three employees and 63.7% of those with ten or more employees. Italian family businesses are known for their longevity (as are the Italian population): Of the world's 100 oldest businesses, 15 are Italian and five are among the top ten oldest family businesses still active today.

In family-owned SMEs, the family has a dominant influence on the business with the aim of sustaining family control across generations. This influence generates the so-called "familiness" (Pearson, Carr, & Shaw, 2008), a bundle of idiosyncratic resources and capabilities deriving from the interaction between the history of the family, the family members, and the business. Family members most often provide financial capital, with a long-term return orientation; human capital, as they are frequently employed in company top positions; and social capital in the form of personal relationships with relevant stakeholders. But the overlap between the family and the business has some potential drawbacks, including a potential lack of managerial skills and family conflicts that may limit the business development and managerialization of the firm.

In family-owned SMEs, it is generally considered that "informal practices predominate" in HRM (Bacon & Hoque, 2005: 1976). Employment relations are based on unwritten rules leading to informal accommodation and flexibility. As managerial resources are likely to be scarce, there may not be an HR department or professionals, with the entrepreneur directly and informally managing the employees. Therefore, SMEs face several HR challenges including difficulty in attracting and retaining key talents and skills, which in turn may undermine the creation of a sustainable competitive advantage. By contrast, "familiness" creates a sense of reciprocity in the mutual expectations of employer and employees, requiring less sophisticated HRM practices. In addition, since the family and the firm are so intertwined, family firms are sensitive to social responsibility issues because they want to maintain a positive reputation (Berrone et al., 2010).

Key aspects of HRM practices in SMEs are detailed in the following paragraphs (Cardon & Stevens, 2004). While, as mentioned above, most family-owned SMEs do not have formal HR departments, most firms have recruitment policies, even if they are only implicit. However, attracting talents may prove difficult in SMEs because of limited financial resources, lack of visibility and reputation as an employer of choice, and jobs with unclear boundaries and responsibilities. In addition, when the selection of candidates is concerned, family-owned SMEs often rely on the match of individual competencies and values with the organizational culture rather than aligning professional knowledge, skills, and abilities with the ones required for the job. Person–organization fit is, therefore, a key criterion in hiring a new employee.

In SMEs, training and development opportunities for employees are carefully selected according to their direct and indirect costs (i.e., time spent away from productive work by the participants). Consequently, sources of formal training are limited to the less expensive ones (e.g., trade associations, short college seminars, free online courses), and informal in-house training (e.g., training on the job, work shadowing) is preferred.

As for compensation policies in small companies, they are not sophisticated, and incentives are often assigned on an ad-hoc basis, creating potential issues in terms of internal consistency and fairness. By contrast, in family-owned SMEs, compensation is viewed from a total rewards perspective, including the informal working environment, good personal relationships, extensive opportunities for learning on the job, and job stability. The reduced company size and the strong connection between the family and the employees might suggest the possibility to adopt long-term pay incentives in the form of equity ownership (e.g., ESOPs or stock sharing), which are particularly effective in retaining and stimulating talented employees: However, family members may be reluctant to break apart the concentrated ownership that typically exists in such companies.

Given the key aspects of HRM practices in SMEs described above, attracting, motivating, and retaining talents and skilled employees is often difficult, and this may undermine the competitive advantage in the medium term, especially in those industries with dynamic competition.

ROMANO LANA: BECOMING A BENEFIT CORPORATION?

Linda started to play with the idea of becoming a benefit corporation (B Corp) after a business trends conference she had attended the previous year. To learn more about B Corp, she set up a meeting with Nativa, a consulting company helping Italian firms to obtain the B Corp certification.

"Becoming a B Corp, your firm will enter into a community of more than 4,000 companies worldwide sharing the common goal to change the world through their business activities", stated the consultant. "Italy is one the fastest growing B Corp community in Europe: in 2020 there were almost 170 B Corps operating in our country. B Corps use profits and growth as a means for obtaining a positive impact for their employees, communities, and the environment".

"This for sure resonates Romano Lana values: we are a family-owned medium enterprise operating in the same local community for the last five decades. We consider all employees as a large family: we help each other regardless of the immediate economic return of our actions. But… what are the requirements for obtaining the certification?"

"The first and most important step for obtaining the certification", the consultant started to explain "is to complete the so-called B Impact Assessment. It covers five areas of impact: governance, workers, community, environment, and customers. Please notice that to measure all these aspects, your firm needs to have formalized policies and practices…"

"Uhm, this might be an issue for my dad", Linda said mumbling "You know, before my appointment as HR manager five years ago, the company did not have an HR manager for 50 years. My father used to manage employees in a very informal way. We relied on a labor consultant for personnel administration and legal issues".

"I know what you mean", the consultant interrupted "but I am sure that your father will understand the advantages that the B Corp certification generally brings to companies. First of all, being a B Corp is a guarantee for investors that the company is managed with a long-term horizon. Your reputation will benefit as well: you will be recognized by customers and potential employees as a company caring not only about profit but also about environment, society, fair trade and transparency. And we all know that customers and talents are becoming progressively more sensitive to the responsible behaviors of companies".

Listening to the consultant, Linda was aware that not all the arguments were particularly convincing for Romano Lana, but some of them might be particularly relevant at this moment. The company was struggling to sustain its competitive advantage: Quality and tradition were important but not enough anymore to face competitive innovations in products, in manufacturing processes, and in the value proposition to clients and customers. Given the scenario, she was aware that Romano Lana did not have advanced HR practices for initiating and sustaining these changes in the long term and in particular was not able to attract and retain enough qualified employees.

ARE WE THE RIGHT COMPANY TO BECOME A B CORP?

Linda and her dad were in the large meeting room of the company. "How do you do *babbo* today?" Linda started off the conversation. "You know, the usual", Cecco answered in a dry tone. "I have just talked with Roberto who is complaining about suppliers' delays. The market is tight, but we are renowned as a reliable company and I do not want that our partners' faults to spill onto our reputation. But tell me about that B Corp idea of yours, I am curious".

Linda conveyed to her father what the consultant had suggested. She also showed him some websites of companies in the wool and clothing industry that had recently decided to become a B Corp: Rifo (https://rifo-lab.com/en) and Successori Reda (https://www.reda1865.com/uk/).

Cecco looked skeptically at Linda. "I talked with some fellow entrepreneurs over a dinner and I overheard some of them complaining about the rigidity that certifications introduce within the company".

"I know your concerns", Linda started patiently to explain, "but I believe that our company already possesses some of the key aspects of a B Corp. We need some adjustments, but these will be minor efforts if compared with the expected advantages. Let's see for instance what is required for getting the certification in the area of impact that is called *workers*: The certification requires that the company has in place activities for empowering and engaging people. You did this from day one of the life of our company! You are always available to talk to people, you listen to them. The certification requires us to identify some formal procedures for that, and I guess we can easily find a way. As participation is concerned, the certification requires us to report if employees participate in the ownership of the company".

"It's impossible!" Cecco abruptly interrupted Linda. "This is *my* company, that I have built with daily efforts and sacrifices. I have invested all my money into getting Romano Lana where it is right now, and I intend to keep the company in the family!"

"I clearly understand your point *babbo*", Linda continued "but we need to be realistic about the future of the company. You are not getting younger, uncle Roberto is just a few years younger than you, and I am the only other family member actively involved in the management of our firm. There are some middle-aged managers who grew up with you here: they know the business very well, you taught them everything and we do not want them leaving the company creating some competing spinoff. Why not involve them in the company ownership?" Cecco was pensive: It was true that some middle managers were like sons to him, but not for real! "And since we are talking about involving non-family members in the ownership", Linda continued, "areas where we need to work hard are related to diversity, equity and inclusion. Do not look so surprised! Try to answer these questions: How many women are involved in the management of the company, considering that they represent 70% of the entire workforce? How many workers are not originally from the village where we have the headquarters? Do you still ask candidates about their relatives to understand if you know them?"

"What's wrong with that?" Cecco asked, appearing astonished. "Shared values are important and social origins tell a lot about that. If you are going to work in *my* company, I need to know everything about you because you are becoming a member of *my* family. And in addition to that, as far as the women issue is concerned, *you* are in a management position! You know that we are in a male dominated business: diversity is not always perceived so positively…"

"I know it very well: thank you *babbo*", Linda erupted "but, if we want to remain competitive and introduce innovations, we need to attract qualified people, that probably are not living within a radius of 25 kilometers from here. And, outside our province, Romano Lana is not attractive at all. Last month I was invited as guest speaker in a lesson of the Master Program in Fashion System Design at the University of Firenze, just 80 kilometers from here. Do you know how many students were aware of our brand? None!"

"Well Linda, we've known it for many years", said Cecco condescendingly, "being a small company, mainly operating in the business-to-business we have issues in what you, HR expert, call employer branding".

"And since we've known it for many years, what have you done to solve the problem?" Linda promptly replied. "We need brilliant minds to remain competitive. And skilled people search for companies offering a stimulating work environment. I know that we are a small company, but how is it even possible that we do not have a formalized training and development plan? New entrants are given in 'custody' to Giorgio, our older worker, for the first week of their employment regardless of the department they are destinated to. The promotion criteria are not clear at all, and they are mainly based on your personal preferences. Training is quite exclusively on-the-job: when I attended the HR course program at Bocconi University in Milan four years ago, I was the first person to get an external training opportunity in the last 15 years. Getting a B Corp certification provides us the opportunity to redesign all these processes, that are mainly informal, and to make explicit some clear criteria for attracting, retaining and developing people. We care about our people and they care about our company". Linda continued with a more relaxed tone, "Providing flexible time and remote working agreements during the pandemic period was not a problem for us, because we were already experimenting with solutions to meet the requests of parents caring for their children. We are the main sponsors of many social activities in the local community, where our workers live: the renovation of the elementary school, the planning of a playground for children, the funding of a gym. But how are these activities benefiting our company? Are they really useful for attracting talented potentials?" Cecco changed his expression. Linda was hard-minded, stubborn at times, but he knew, deeper inside, she was right.

WHAT'S NEXT?

Linda and Cecco left the meeting room still thinking about the conversation they had. Cecco knew very well the business issues Linda was referring to: Without innovation in products, manufacturing processes, and the value proposition to clients and customers, Romano Lana was destined for a rapid decline. At the same time, though, the company was perfect as it was: Flexible, reactive, and cohesive. Pursuing the B Corp certification represented a strategic change with strong implications for key organizational strong points. He had resisted his entire business life the temptation of formalizing his firm's people management practices. He had always thought that writing down rules and procedures, and applying and enforcing them systematically meant rigidity and bureaucracy! In addition to that, he was scared from all the talks about diversity, sharing ownership with non-family employees, and attracting quality potential employees. He wondered how it would be possible to maintain the firm's legacy and values if people did not share a common social background.

Linda was pensive as well. In the conversation with her father, more resistance than she was expecting had surfaced. Nevertheless, she was convinced that family firms, like Romano Lana, were "physiologically" inclined to get a B Corps certification. Since they cannot compete on salary, family firms aim to create a good working environment, not only for attracting workers but also because poor employee relations can negatively affect the reputation of the firm and, consequently, of the family. In addition to that, the long-term orientation that characterizes all the firm's activities, including the development of human capital, represents a rare characteristic in the current competitive environment, which is characterized by uncertainty and volatility. Finally, people's involvement and participation are not only "formal" but based on day-to-day interactions, exchanges, and strict collaboration. In addition, getting the certification could be easier than expected. However, the doubt remains: Is the B Corp certification a good solution to Romano Lana's sustainable competitive advantage?

CASE STUDY QUESTIONS FOR DISCUSSION

1. To get the B Corp certification, Romano Lana would need to formalize its HR management practices: Recruitment and selection, training and development, performance management, and compensation. Provide company-specific suggestions about how to pursue this objective without sacrificing the company's values (quality and tradition) and business strengths (flexibility, reactiveness, cohesiveness).

2. In your opinion, why and to what extent could having a B Corp certification help an SME in attracting and retaining skilled and talented workers?

3. Develop the key aspects of Romano Lana's "employee value proposition" in order to facilitate the attraction of skilled and talented workers. In particular, refer to the work environment, meaningful work, development opportunities, and compensation.

4. In your opinion, which are the main obstacles that a family-owned SME may encounter in getting a B Corp certification? And what are the facilitating factors? Please answer these questions both in general terms and referring to the Romano Lana case.

NOTE

1 Romano Lana is not a real company, but it is inspired by several similar companies operating in the Italian SMEs entrepreneurial business context. "Lana" is translated as "wool" in English.

REFERENCES

Bacon, N., & Hoque, K. 2005. HRM in the SME sector: Valuable employees and coercive networks. *The International Journal of Human Resource Management*, 16(11): 1976–1999.

Berrone, P., Cruz, C., Gomez-Mejia, L. R., & Larraza-Kintana, M. 2010. Socioemotional wealth and corporate responses to institutional pressures: Do family-controlled firms pollute less? *Administrative Science Quarterly*, 55(1), 82–113.

Cardon, M. S., & Stevens, C. E. 2004. Managing human resources in small organizations: What do we know? *Human Resource Management Review*, 14(3): 295–323.

Pearson, A. W., Carr, J. C., & Shaw, J. C. 2008. Toward a theory of familiness: A social capital perspective. *Entrepreneurship Theory and Practice*, 32(6): 949–969.

CHAPTER 19

Saudi Arabia

Implementing the Localization Law Effectively: The Case of HMG in Saudi Arabia

Hadeel M. Alkhalaf

I am proud of our achievements this year which include the launch and expansion of our digital services and capabilities, our proactive and agile response to the COVID-19 pandemic, our continuous efforts towards growth and expanding our footprint, our continuation of talent development and education through online channels, and our commitment to our patients through innovative care and disease awareness campaigns. Our healthcare technology solutions proved vital in securing our market leadership and received the endorsement of public and private sector peers who sought our expertise to address their most urgent needs. I am proud of the dedication of our team, particularly our front-line workers, who showed great courage and played a vital role in their support of our country in its battle against the most severe healthcare crisis in recent history.

(Nasser AlHugbani, CEO, HMG Annual Strategic Report 2020)

CASE SYNOPSIS

This case focuses on how human resource management (HRM) in a healthcare organization responded to external institutional factors in general and to labor law in particular. It also shows the significance of strategic HRM and how the integration of business and HRM strategies is important for the success, growth, and resilience of the organization. Particularly, this case illustrates the effectiveness of HRM best practices and the necessity of taking the context into consideration. It starts by introducing

DOI: 10.4324/9781003307099-23

Al-Habib Medical Group (HMG) and its current position as a leading health provider within Saudi Arabia. Then, a background to the case is provided in detail, with the aim of putting the organization into its context so that students can fully understand the external factors and how they are affecting HRM in that context. The context section also explains thoroughly the localization law and reviews the reasons for its failure, the common reactions of employers, and the efforts and initiatives of the decision-makers to make it successful. Finally, the case presents how HMG responds, what HRM strategy it is taking, and its proactive solutions and initiatives that help it to implement the localization law successfully and also become a benchmark in the health sector.

KEYWORDS

Strategic HRM, labor law, HRM practices, health sector, Saudi Arabia

LEARNING OUTCOMES

1. Realize the significance of strategic HRM as a foundation for having a strong business.
2. Understand the impact of institutional factors and labor laws, in particular, on HRM.
3. Recognize the importance of analyzing the context and adopting a contextual HRM approach.
4. Appraise the ability of the universalistic perspective of HRM to achieve competitive advantage and firm performance.
5. Critique localization laws and the necessity of all stakeholders' participation in decision-making.

ORGANIZATIONAL SETTING

Al-Habib Medical Group (HMG) was launched in 1995 with a well-defined vision to be one of the most trusted healthcare providers in the Middle East. One of its main objectives is to achieve excellence in several specialties following top-level international standards in the very competitive context of Saudi Arabia, which has around 500 healthcare providers (Statista.com). HMG started with Al-Olaya Medical Complex in Riyadh as its core facility and is now considered the largest provider of comprehensive healthcare services in the Middle East. It currently operates 20 medical facilities across Saudi Arabia, the UAE, and Bahrain. It has received 38 international and national awards and accreditations, including the Middle East HR Excellence Award, and employs more than 10,000 employees, ranging from doctors to administration staff and technicians, most of whom are highly qualified. The headquarter is in Riyadh, Saudi Arabia.

Despite the fierce competition among Saudi healthcare providers, HMG has maintained a leading position, not only in the Saudi market but also in the entire Gulf region due to its several competitive advantages. It provides integrated medical services, including primary and secondary medical services and sub-specialty and support services. It also offers home services of the same high quality. This has earned it many certificates of accreditation and quality. It has invested in advanced technology solutions, including medical equipment and hospital management systems.

HMG offers its services on a daily basis in its numerous hospitals and centers. This requires a large and efficient staff who need constant training and development to deal with patients' requirements. In fact, HMG's ability to attract and train highly qualified international and local talent is one of its main competitive advantages. According to its top management, the human resource management (HRM) department functions as "a strategic partner to the business" to make HMG the employer of choice for talented professionals. HMG also has other strengths, including strategic relationships with insurance companies and suppliers, growth and larger-scale operations in comparison to rivals, and a distinguished reputation.

BACKGROUND TO THE CASE

A comprehensive understanding of HRM in Saudi Arabia requires clarification of the main factors influencing HRM practices. Previous research on the Saudi context has identified economic influences, political environment, labor market structure, and national culture as among these factors (Mellahi, 2000; Mellahi & Wood, 2002). Therefore, a PESTEL (political, economic, socio-cultural, technological, environmental, and legal) analysis of the country is presented in Table 19.1 to outline the environment within which HMG operates and how it affects HRM.[1]

CHALLENGES AND INITIATIVES

Based on the aforementioned variables, there are many challenges facing the Saudi economy, which are recognized as having an impact on HRM practices. Because of the speed of growth during the last 30 years, the Saudi economy has relied heavily on foreign workers. Foreign nationals account for around 73% of workers in the private sector (GASTATS, 2022), where managers have a widespread belief that it is more expensive to hire locals than expatriates. Individuals hired in this manner cannot change jobs or work for another organization without the permission of the initial sponsor, which keeps turnover among expatriates low (Mellahi & Wood, 2002). This leaves workers with little bargaining power, endorsing the view commonly held by employers that foreign workers are easier to manage (Elamin, 2012). However, unemployment is becoming an issue in Saudi Arabia due to its young population and the low rate of female participation in the labor force. This is exacerbated by the lack of technical and vocational skills among Saudi workers and their reluctance to accept occupations that reflect a lower social position (Varshney, 2016a).

TABLE 19.1 External factors

Political and environmental factors	Technological and economic factors	Socio-cultural factors	Labor market factors	Legal factors
- It's the largest of the GCC countries with an area of around 2 million km^2 (GASTATS, 2022) - It's a monarchy and the King rules the nation through a council of ministers. - The political and business environment is strongly characterized by masculine and tribal values and influenced by the country's conservative and religious culture	- It has a strong technological infrastructure as it strives for a knowledge economy - More than 70% of its revenue garnered from the petrochemical industry (GASTATS,2019) - Non-oil economic activities have shown an upward trend during the last four years with the new Vision 2030 - The latest financial constrictions and the fluctuation of oil prices have impeded employment in the public sector which leads to make the role of the private sector critical as a job creator	- Its population growth is among the highest in the world. Current population is around 34 million (General Authority for Statistics, 2021) - Islam is the main religion and the source of its regulations and people's values and work ethics (Budhwar & Mellahi, 2006) - Based on Hofstede's cultural dimensions (Hofstede, 1984, 1991), KSA is characterized by its high power distance and uncertainty avoidance, with strict rules and policies. Saudi culture is also collectivist, and employees tend to show a moderately masculine attitude (Bjerke & Al-Meer, 1993; Al-Gahtani, Hubona & Wang, 2007). - The education system focuses on theoretical education and less on vocational training (Harry, 2007, 2016; Baqadir, Patrick, & Burns, 2011)	- More than 100,000 graduates entering the job market every year (Ministry of Education, 2020) - The rapid growth in the economy after oil discovery created an unbalanced labor market that is heavily reliant on foreign workers (Tlaiss & Elamin, 2016) - The unemployment is 10% (GASTATS, 2022) - Employers remain more inclined to recruit expatriates than Saudi nationals	- Sponsorship "Kafeel" regulation (expatriates are granted a work permit for a specific occupation with a particular employer) results in a preference for hiring them over national applicants. - The localization (Saudization) program was established in an attempt to alleviate the unemployment rate and change the mentality regarding employment in the foreign-dominated private sector - There is a lack of collaboration between policy-makers and employers in order to achieve the optimal goals of the localization law

As a result of these issues facing the labor market, the government has undertaken many actions that have profoundly affected HRM policies within organizations. The localization (Saudization) program (which seeks to replace non-Saudi workers with Saudis in the private sector) was established in the Sixth Development Plan in an attempt to alleviate the unemployment rate and change the mentality regarding employment in the foreign-dominated private sector. The government has worked hard to implement Saudization in an effort to overcome the rentier state phenomenon (Beblawi & Luciani, 2015), with the establishment of many programs, including the Human Resource Development Fund (HRDF), which pays 75% of training costs for Saudi employees and 50% of their salaries for two years to encourage private organizations to recruit Saudi citizens (Al-Dosary & Rahman, 2005). However, the literature highlights a lack of collaboration between policy-makers and employers, as there is no participation from the private sector in training graduates and a clear dearth of studies and cooperation on the implications of this law for educational institutes, and private and public organizations (Alogla, 1990; Alhumaid, 2003; Alotaibi, 2014). Therefore, the success of Saudization in the private sector remains limited, with employers remaining more inclined to recruit expatriates than Saudi nationals for a variety of reasons, including cost savings, a desire to maintain management control, a lack of specific skills (especially in the health sector), and unwillingness to change (Al-Asfour & Khan, 2014).

Employers' resistance to this law (Saudization) takes different forms, one of which is commonly known as the "ghost workers phenomenon", whereby private firms recruit Saudis, pay them a portion of their monthly salary, and ask them not to come to the workplace (Al-Asfour & Khan, 2014). This enables employers to meet their quota of national employees required by regulation without actually having them in the workplace. This phenomenon, along with other practices such as exploitation and corruption, which companies engage in to comply with the localization law, is entirely at odds with what the localization program is intended to achieve. It also highlights the deeply engrained stereotyping of national workers as unproductive and casts doubt on the work ethics in such an environment (Tlaiss & Elamin, 2016).

In the above regard, Godard (2002) argued that a system that requires continuous monitoring and tight control is always challenging and breeds "unintended consequences". In addition, although the nationalization program has been effective in resolving some entrenched challenges, albeit to a limited extent, it has created barriers to the adoption of many of the best HRM practices. For example, in order to recruit nationals, employers are adopting a duality of standards and classify applicants according to nationality to create a pool of local candidates. They are sometimes varying HRM policies with contradicting objectives that adopt specific practices only for nationals or only for expatriates, which leads to a lack of the required internal fit (Ehrnrooth & Björkman, 2012; Jenkins & Delbridge, 2013). This has negative consequences for the equity and work satisfaction of foreign employees, which can affect their performance. It is also in opposition to the Islamic rejection of discrimination in all its forms (Taliss & Elamin, 2016). In its recently launched Vision 2030, the Saudi government is aiming to improve the skills of Saudi workers by developing several programs alongside other previously established initiatives, such as King Abdullah's scholarship program (KASP), employment regulation reform to grant foreign workers more rights, and an increased minimum wage for Saudi nationals. Many other initiatives, including privatization and an increase in the number of vocational training institutes, have also sought to reduce public sector dominance in the market and equip locals with the required skills to compete. All of these obstacles and initiatives explain why it is difficult to localize the workforce in such an environment and highlight the success of HMG in meeting the requirements of this law despite the challenges.

HMG'S STRATEGY FOR IMPLEMENTING THE LOCALIZATION LAW

Despite the highly competitive environment within the Saudi health sector, HMG has distinguished itself through the quality of its services, its outstanding reputation, and its compliance with labor law, especially the localization regulations (Saudization). It achieved this by adopting an effective HRM strategy that is supported by top management instead of superficially fulfilling the minimum legal requirements to avoid fines. Despite the difficulty of sourcing employees with the required skills in the health sector, HMG has not resorted to manipulative practices but has instead engaged in proactive planning and developed a long-term vision to implement the law. Rather than merely replacing ex-pats with national employees, its strategy is to create an integrated workforce and promote a culture of learning and knowledge sharing by appreciating the intellectual and skilled employees. Moreover, HMG has developed strong contextual policies and procedures that mesh well with Saudi labor law and the national culture and has strictly implemented them to create a healthy work environment.

The first principle of HMG's strategy is the "division of work". Detailed job descriptions are compiled and updated every two years to determine which jobs can be localized and which ones might prove more difficult to localize. For instance, it is difficult to replace physicians but it is easier to recruit local administration staff. Similarly, faced with the global shortage of nursing staff, HMG launched an initiative to attract interns and graduates from local nursing schools. Any decision to localize a post is based on an analysis of the regional labor market and the availability of skills. However, to avoid the limitations of the division of work, the Group implements job rotation to ensure that a replacement is ready whenever there is a vacancy. Second, it has created a reputation for excellence and high quality in all its services, not only among its external customers, namely patients, but also among its employees, which makes it an attractive workplace for applicants. It has focused on improving the work environment in a way that conforms to social norms and characteristics. For example, it limits night shifts for Saudi female workers and, since 2014, has implemented a five-day working week for Saudi employees instead of a six-day one. It also exercises transparent and strong performance management to reduce ambiguity in a society characterized by uncertainty avoidance. Additionally, in order to attract, motivate, and maintain talent, the compensation and benefits department has engaged in benchmarking and has updated its salary scales according to the market, offering very competitive salaries for new graduates.

Like all organizations operating in Saudi Arabia, HMG has encountered many challenges and obstacles to recruiting local employees. However, it has made proactive efforts to overcome these obstacles and to invest in recruitment and training to meet the challenge of regaining employees. To combat the scarcity of specific skills and specializations in the labor market, it has developed agreements with most Saudi universities and colleges to provide internship programs for students of medicine and other health specializations. Moreover, HMG participates in most of the recruitment fairs organized by local universities and those organized abroad by Saudi cultural bureaus to seek out talent. It also provides training programs ending in employment for fresh graduates from other specialties and has an academic career center open to all staff to promote continuous learning for all employees and engage in regular training evaluations. Thus, it is clear that adopting skills and knowledge instead of experience as selection criteria to attract new graduates, offering them the ability to develop their skills through on-the-job training, and retaining them by adopting effective HRM practices are what distinguish HMG from organizations that fail to satisfy the localization law. Even for managerial jobs requiring experience, HMG has created its leaders by setting out a career path for all its employees. This is in contrast to most organizations, which look for experienced applicants to avoid the cost of training. This makes localization more difficult for them due to the skills gap in the local labor market, as discussed in the background section above. In response to the numerous studies and reports that have identified a lack of private sector participation in training graduates and a lack of collaboration between companies and educational institutes as the main obstacles to localization in the private sector, HMG has taken the initiative to fill that gap and implement the law effectively.

Commenting on the reason for HMG's low turnover of Saudi staff compared to that of other organizations in the health sector, the HR manager reported that HMG's strategy includes monitoring the monthly indicator of turnover to ensure that it does not reach more than 1.5%. In addition, exit interviews are conducted and analyzed, and action plans are developed based on the findings. For example, if an existing employee cites a high workload or the leadership style of the direct manager as the reason for leaving, HMG takes action to tackle the problem or improve the situation. The HRM manager reported succession planning and internal recruitment and promotion to manage expectations and motivate staff, as these are among the main reasons for staff retention.

He added that investing in graduates from the time they join HMG and drawing a career path for them, as well as providing efficient performance management to specify training needs and having a specific department for compensation and benefits, promotes sustainability and stability and increases employees' loyalty in the long term. He confirmed that all recruitment and other HRM processes are transparent and free of discrimination and nepotism.

CURRENT DIFFICULTIES AND THREATS

Although HMG has succeeded in implementing the localization law, the Group has admitted that it still faces many challenges that might be considered threats to the success of its strategy for applying this law. In general, unlike the situation in other sectors, which depend on production lines and which rely more on technology and machines, human capital represents the largest cost in the health sector. In HMG, this can reach more than 60%, as HMG operates 24 hours a day, seven days a week. Therefore, anything that influences HRM planning can have a significant direct effect on the success of the organization. Additionally, up to this point, organizations in the Saudi private sector have not been able to compete with public health organizations, as the latter have lighter workloads, fewer working hours, and higher compensation, especially for health practitioners. However, the latest economic reforms have reduced the differences, especially with the recent privatization plans. In addition, because HMG provides high-quality training and has a sound reputation, its employees have become targets of public and other private sector organizations. This requires HMG to put in extra effort and funds in order to keep their professional and talented workers. Furthermore, there is another challenge that is related to changing the culture of working in the private sector and the negative stereotyping related to low job security in a way that harmonizes with the new vision of Saudi Arabia, especially in small cities and remote areas. The HRM department is working hard to change the mentality of young men from outside the large cities, who have few role models among their family or friends, as most people in these areas work in government agencies or their own businesses rather than large international companies. However, the change might be mandatory within the next few years, as the government is not recruiting at the same pace as before.

This case has focused on Al-Habib Medical Group (HMG), the largest provider of private healthcare in Saudi Arabia, and its success in implementing the localization law. As explained above, HMG has adopted strategic HRM plans that include developing long-term policies and procedures. HMG emphasized that human capital is an asset and not a cost; therefore, it has invested in employees' training and development for success and sustainability. This HRM strategy has taken into account the cultural context and the other influential institutional factors that have been clarified in the background section. Finally, this illustration has briefly described the constant challenges and obstacles to the effective application of the law with HMG's values of continuous change and improvement.

CASE STUDY QUESTIONS FOR DISCUSSION

1. In your opinion, how has adopting strategic HRM supported HMG to effectively apply the localization law? Identify and highlight the areas that indicate HMG's strategic plans including the quotation of the CEO.

2. By utilizing institutional theory, explain how institutional factors and labor laws in particular have influenced HRM in HMG and the role of organizational context in decision-making.

3. Discuss the relationship between the universalistic perspective of HRM and organizational performance in light of the best HRM practices adopted by HMG.

4. What has HMG done differently from other organizations that tried to implement the localization law?

5. Debate: Argue for or against the mandatory localization law and the possible consequences for HRM policies and procedures.

NOTE

1   Although labor market trends should be under the socio-cultural factors, they are presented in a separate column because of their significant effect on the HRM practices.

REFERENCES

AI-Gahtani, S. S., Hubona, G. S. & Wang, J. 2007. Information Technology (IT) in Saudi Arabia: Culture and the acceptance and use of IT. *Information and Management*, 44(8): 681–691.

Al Humaid, M. 2003. *The factors affecting the process of Saudization in the private sector in the Kingdom of Saudi Arabia: A case study of Riyadh City*. Ph.D. dissertation, The University of Exeter.

Al-Asfour, A. & Khan, S. A. 2014. Workforce localization in the kingdom of Saudi Arabia: Issues and challenges. *Human Resource Development International*, 17(2), pp. 243–253.

Al-Dosary, A. S. & Rahman, S. M. 2005. Saudization (Localization): A critical review. *Human Resource Development International*, 8(4), pp. 495–502.

Alogla, H. 1990. *Obstacles to Saudization in the private sector of the Saudi Arabian labor force*. Ph.D. dissertation, Michigan State University.

Alotaibi, A. 2014. *Opportunities and barriers to collaboration in addressing unemployment in Saudi Arabia*. Ph.D. dissertation, University of La Verne, La Verne, CA.

Baqadir, A., Patrick, F. & Burns, G. 2011. Addressing the skills gap in Saudi Arabia: Does vocational education address the needs of private sector employers? *Journal of Vocational Education & Training*, 63(4), pp. 551–561.

Beblawi, H. & Luciani, G. (Eds.). 2015. *The Rentier State*. Routledge.

Bjerke, B. & Al-Meer, A. 1993. Culture's consequences: management in Saudi Arabia. *Leadership and Organization Development Journal*, 14(2), pp. 30–35.

Budhwar, P. S. & Mellahi, K. (Eds.). 2006. *Managing Human Resources in the Middle-East*. Routledge.

Ehrnrooth, M. & Björkman, I. 2012. An integrative HRM process theorization: Beyond signalling effects and mutual gains. *Journal of Management Studies*, 49(6), pp. 1109–1135.

Elamin, A. M. 2012. Perceived organizational justice and work-related attitudes: A study of Saudi employees. *World Journal of Entrepreneurship, Management and Sustainable Development*, 8(1), pp. 71–88.

General Authority for Statistics (GASTATS). 2019. *Budget Data*, [Online] Retrieved on 12/07/22 from http://www.stats.gov.sa/en/1026

General Authority for Statistics (GASTATS). 2021. *Population Estimates in the Midyear of 2021* [Online] Retrieved on 10/07/22 from http://www.stats.gov.sa/en/43

General Authority for Statistics (GASTATS). 2022a. *General Information about the Kingdom of Saudi Arabia* [Online] Retrieved on 10/07/22 from http://www.stats.gov.sa/en/page/259

General Authority for Statistics (GASTATS). 2022b. *Labor Market Statistics Q1, 2022*, [Online] Retrieved on 12/07/22 from http://www.stats.gov.sa/en/814

Godard, J. 2002. Institutional environments, employer practices, and states in liberal market economies. *Industrial Relations: A Journal Economy and Society*, 41(2), pp. 249–86.

Harry, W. 2007. Employment creation and localization: The crucial human resource issues for the GCC. *International Journal of Human Resource Management*, 18, pp. 132–146.

Harry, W. 2016. 3. Society level factors impacting human resource management in the Middle East. In: Budhwar, P. S. & Mellahi, K. (Eds.), *Handbook of Human Resource Management in the Middle East*, Cheltenham: Edward Elgar.

HMG. (2020, December 25). Report 2020. HMG.COM. Retrieved on 05/10/21 from https://hmg.com/ir/en/Pages/ReportsPublications.aspx

Hofstede, G. (1984). Cultural dimensions in management and planning. *Asia Pacific Journal of Management*, 1: 81–99.

Hofstede, G. (1991). Empirical models of cultural differences. In N. Bleichrodt & P. J. D. Drenth (Eds.), *Contemporary issues in cross-cultural psychology* (pp. 4–20). Lisse, the Netherlands: Swets & Zeitlinger Publishers.

Jenkins, S. & Delbridge, R. 2013. Context matters: Examining 'soft' and 'hard' approaches to employee engagement in two workplaces. *The International Journal of Human Resource Management*, 24(14), pp. 2670–2691.

Mellahi K. 2000. Human resource development through vocational education in Gulf cooperation countries: The case of Saudi Arabia. *Journal of Vocational Education and Training*, 52(2), pp. 329–344.

Mellahi, K. & Wood, G. 2002. Desperately seeking stability: The making and remaking of the Saudi Arabian petroleum growth regime. *Competition and Change*, 6(4), pp. 345–62.

Ministry of Education. 2020. *Open Data*, [Online] Retrieved on 01/07/22 from https://data.gov .sa/Data/organization/3910a763-1829-445f-97b12bd988249b7e?groups=education_and _training

Saudi Vision. 2030. *Saudi Arabia's Vision for 2030*, [Online] Retrieved on 30/09/2021 from file: ///C:/Users/alkhalh2/Downloads/Saudi_Vision2030_EN%20(2).pdf

Statista.com. Total Number of Hospitals in Saudi Arabia from 2011 to 2021*. Retrieved on 03/11/21 from https://www.statista.com/statistics/608579/total-number-of-hospitals-in -saudi-arabia/

Tlaiss, H. A. & Elamin, A. 2016. Human resource management in Saudi Arabia. In: Budhwar, P. S. & Mellahi, K. (Eds.), *Handbook of Human Resource Management in the Middle East*, Cheltenham: Edward Elgar.

Varshney, D. 2016a. The young Saudi employee and the current labor market dynamics of Saudi Arabia: A paradigm shift. *CLEAR International Journal of Research in Commerce & Management*, 7(12), pp. 56–61.

CHAPTER 20

UAE

Improving Internal Service: Leveraging HRM to Drive Organizational Change

Scott L. Martin

CASE SYNOPSIS

The COVID-19 pandemic created financial challenges for United Bank. The human resource management (HRM) function was tasked with improving the organization's efficiency and effectiveness. Needs analysis indicated the organization would benefit from improving the quality of internal service. The organization development (OD) team led a multi-phase intervention to improve internal service. The initial phase involved a communication campaign to enhance awareness regarding the importance of internal service. The project included a study to identify the dimensions of internal customer service and the types of employee behaviors that would be most effective in impacting each of the dimensions of internal service. The final phase of the intervention was focused on helping employees be more proactive in serving internal customers.

KEYWORDS

Internal service, organization development, needs analysis, proactivity, UAE

DOI: 10.4324/9781003307099-24

LEARNING OUTCOMES

1. Explain why internal service is an important yet challenging aspect of organizational effectiveness.
2. Predict how cultural dimensions can impact the quality of internal service and proactive behavior.
3. Design an organizational intervention using needs analysis, HRM tactics, and evaluation processes to improve organizational effectiveness.

INTRODUCTION

United Bank is a private bank that was established in 1972 in Abu Dhabi, which is the capital of the United Arab Emirates (UAE).[1] The bank was one of the first in the region and played a formative role in building the nation's financial system. United Bank is one of the largest banks in the UAE and has a reputation for providing superior customer service. It has nearly 6,000 employees and operates 125 branches across 15 countries. The bank values its employees and prides itself on providing employees with competitive compensation and excellent career opportunities.

United Bank has generated strong financial results during the past decade, but the COVID-19 pandemic created serious financial challenges. The HRM function was tasked with improving the organization's efficiency and effectiveness. Needs analysis indicated the organization would benefit from improving the quality of internal service. Internal service refers to the products or services that employees provide to other employees in the same organization (excluding immediate managers, subordinates, and teammates). For instance, a loan officer must obtain information from three different departments before a loan can be finalized. This case study examines the effectiveness of a multi-phase intervention designed to improve internal service.

UAE BACKGROUND

The UAE turned 50 years old in 2021. Despite its relative youth, the UAE has a modern infrastructure and disposable income is among the highest in the world. The country's rapid development has been driven largely by oil and gas exports. The UAE has nearly 10% of the world's known petroleum reserves, which is particularly significant given that it has a population of only 10 million.

The UAE is governed by heredity rule, and the rulers or Sheikhs retain a great deal of power. For instance, unions and collective bargaining do not currently exist in the UAE. However, the rulers tend to be paternalistic and humane (Ewers, 2016). The UAE government has been rather generous in distributing its wealth among its citizens. UAE citizens enjoy a variety of benefits including tax-free income and free university education. Thus, the discovery of oil and gas has led to a dramatic improvement in the UAE lifestyle over a relatively short period of time.

Despite its wealth, the COVID-19 pandemic created serious economic challenges for the UAE. The pandemic led to massive drops in the price of oil. Petroleum exports accounted for about 30% of GDP, and the entire petroleum sector experienced a host of "knock-on" effects that impacted about half of the UAE economy. Weak oil prices contributed to problems in a host of industries including construction, real estate, and tourism. GDP dropped by about 6% in 2020.

It is true that oil prices increased dramatically a couple of years later, but this is not relevant to the economic conditions the UAE faced in 2020. In fact, such dramatic fluctuations in oil prices highlight the challenges of managing an economy that is heavily reliant on a single resource.

The banking industry also faced tremendous pressure in 2020. United Bank's non-performing loans increased by about 20%. Given the poor economic conditions, there were fewer businesses seeking new loans. It was also difficult to generate profits from any new loans that did materialize; interest rates were at or near zero percent. United Bank's profits dropped by about 30% in 2021.

HUMAN RESOURCE MANAGEMENT BACKGROUND

The UAE has two distinct cultural characteristics. First, the UAE, along with many other Middle Eastern countries, is considered a "high power distance" culture (Carl, Gupta, & Javidan, 2004; Hofstede, 2001). In such cultures, leaders are expected to make all major decisions and maintain a degree of distance from followers. This is consistent with the paternalistic leadership style. Second, the UAE tends to have a collectivistic culture (Carl, Gupta, & Javidan, 2004; Hofstede, 2001), which encourages group cohesion and discourages the recognition or punishment of individuals.

Naturally, these cultural characteristics have an influence on HRM practices. Specifically, organizations in the UAE tend to emphasize the importance of training and development and downplay other HRM interventions (Suliman, 2006). A reliance on training and development is consistent with the paternal leadership style, as it implies that employees have the underlying capabilities and motivation, and only need the requisite knowledge and skills to be successful. In other words, it has a rather nurturing and optimistic flavor.

At the same time, there is less emphasis on selection and motivational interventions. Hiring processes are heavily dependent on connections or "wasta" and tend not to rely on rigorous selection and assessment procedures. With respect to motivation, there are laws that make it difficult to terminate the employment of UAE nationals, and pay-for-performance is not common practice. When organizations decide to provide pay increases, it is common to grant an across-the-board increase to all employees (i.e., cost-of-living adjustment or COLA). Such practices clearly reflect the collectivistic culture.

Although training and development are emphasized and are largely commendable, there tends to be a lack of attention devoted to "needs analysis" (Martin, Abdulla, & Zamzam, 2018). Needs analysis is often prescribed as the initial step of the training and development process to be sure that: 1) Training is the appropriate intervention; 2) the program includes the proper content; and 3) only employees who need the training are required to attend. In the UAE, there is a tendency to develop a training program and require all employees in a given job or level (regardless of need) to participate in the training program. This is consistent with high power distance (i.e., there is a dictate from above) and collectivism (i.e., all employees should be treated in a similar manner).

IMPROVING INTERNAL SERVICE

The financial challenges at United Bank forced the organization to terminate the employment of about 250 employees in 2020. Unfortunately, as is often the case, this only placed more pressure on the existing employees to improve the organization's financial results despite having fewer employees. The HRM function was asked to help identify strategies to improve the organization's effectiveness. The head of HRM agreed but suggested that the strategies should be rooted in a proper needs analysis because a "top-down" directive was unlikely to be effective.

The OD team was tasked with taking the lead on this initiative. They conducted a few group interviews with all major functions, including branch operations, investments, and customer service. The OD team maintained a log of all serious proposals and reviewed them with two additional focus groups. Many of the suggestions were excellent but involved new strategic directions that were beyond the scope of this project. One suggestion that came up repeatedly and which appeared feasible was to improve the quality of "internal service". Internal service refers to the products or services that employees provide to other employees in the same organization. For instance, a loan officer must obtain information from three different departments before a loan can be finalized. As one employee put it: "We all tend to be very responsive to our immediate Managers, but we can be a little more casual when asked to support employees in other departments". A manager elaborated on this point: "I think this is a universal problem, but the problem is pronounced in the Middle East. We tend to have a 'high power distance' culture here so employees are very, and perhaps even overly, careful to please their own Managers. But what this often means is that they tend to have less time and energy available to support their internal customers".

The head of HRM and the OD team presented the general idea to the executive committee, which consisted of the CEO, the COO, and the heads of all departments. The CEO complimented the team for identifying an important issue that could indeed improve the efficiency and effectiveness of the organization. He asked the group to develop a plan and begin implementation within the next 30 days.

COMMUNICATION CAMPAIGN

The OD team conducted two focus groups with employees from multiple functions to determine the first step of the project. The consensus was that the plan to improve internal service was a good idea, but the issue was just not "top of mind" for most employees. This suggested that the organization should begin with a major communication campaign.

The OD team collaborated with the communications unit to develop a multi-pronged communication effort. This included discussions about the importance of internal service in town hall meetings by the CEO and departmental meetings by all department heads. Each monthly newsletter included at least one article focusing on the importance of internal service. Posters were displayed throughout the office encouraging employees to support colleagues. The communications focused on clarifying the nature of internal service. For instance, internal service has often been viewed as the support that staff functions, such as HR and IT, provide to line functions, such as sales and operations. However, in reality, all employees receive support from others and must also provide support to other employees. The communications also highlighted the costs of poor internal service including employee dissatisfaction and increased labor costs.

The communication campaign lasted for three months. To evaluate the effectiveness of the communication campaign, the OD team distributed a brief survey to all employees and conducted a few focus groups. These group interviews targeted employees who were primarily on the "receiving end" of internal service. The internal customers felt that most service providers were aware of the importance of internal service, but they were not sure that this awareness actually translated into better service. As one loan officer put it: "Everyone is very pleasant and says the 'right' thing. We have a collectivist culture so it would be unusual to find a service provider being dismissive or rude. I'm just not sure the support I receive is really any better than before."

The OD team then conducted a few group interviews with employees who were largely responsible for providing internal service to other employees. The service providers said they felt the communication campaign had helped them become more aware of this responsibility, but they felt the initiative needed to provide employees with more specific guidance. An employee from the IT department said: "Few would disagree that internal service is important, but exactly what am I supposed to do differently?"

TRAINING

The OD team met to reflect on the feedback provided by the service providers. Obviously, it would be impossible to provide specific guidance related to every service encounter. However, the team agreed they could develop a general model linking service behaviors with dimensions of internal service, but they felt they should conduct a study to do this properly (see Martin, Klimoski, & Henderson, 2021).

The first step was to identify the most important dimensions of internal service. The OD team turned to seminal research devoted to *external* customer service for guidance (Kang, James, & Alexandris, 2002; Parasuraman, Zeithaml, & Berry, 1988). The team concluded that there were three major dimensions relevant to internal service: Reliability, responsiveness, and innovation. Reliability was defined as the ability to perform promised services accurately and on time. Responsiveness was defined as the willingness to help customers and react promptly to customer requests. Innovation was defined as providing customers with new and customized services.

The next step was to capture the different types of employee behaviors. Research in the performance modeling area suggests there are three major dimensions of employee performance: Core task proficiency, adaptivity, and proactivity (Griffin, Neal, & Parker, 2007). Core task proficiency refers to fulfilling the prescribed requirements of the position (i.e., responsibilities that would typically appear in a job description). Adaptivity refers to the propensity to cope with or respond to change. Proactivity refers to self-starting behavior to change work processes or oneself.

The final step was to determine the relationship between employee behaviors and the dimensions of internal service. The OD team randomly selected 140 employees from support units (i.e., service providers). The managers of the service providers were asked to evaluate the service providers on the dimensions of behavior (i.e., proficiency, adaptivity, proactivity). About two months later, three internal customers were asked to evaluate each of the service providers on the service dimensions (i.e., reliability, responsiveness, innovation). All employees were informed that these evaluations were being collected for research purposes only.

The OD team analyzed the results using a statistical technique called structural equation modeling. There was a clear pattern of results: Being proficient was related to the reliability dimension, being adaptive was related to the responsiveness dimension, and being proactive was related to the innovation dimension (see Figure 20.1).

The next question was how to convert this knowledge into action. The head of HRM and the OD team met with the executive committee, and it was agreed that all employees would be asked to attend a half-day workshop devoted to internal service. The workshop began by highlighting the importance of internal service and allowing participants to discuss specific examples of effective and ineffective service. The workshop then examined the three aspects of internal service. Reliability was positioned as the most important dimension of internal service, and employees were encouraged to focus on this dimension (at least initially). In terms of adaptivity, employees were told that it was often important to follow the customer's lead when it came to simple requests. Participants learned that proactivity occurred more in dynamic environments; as the environment changed, employees were expected to take more independent action. The workshops were conducted over a period of six months. All employees were asked to collaborate with their internal customers to improve internal service.

The OD team conducted a series of focus groups with employees to evaluate the impact of the workshops. The internal customers felt the top 20% of employees were providing higher levels of service, but the remaining 80% of the employees did not seem to improve much if at all.

The consensus was that the intervention was too complicated for most employees. There were a few reasons at play here. First, it should be recognized that most employees have a full set of obligations related to their manager and immediate teammates, so there are limits on how much more attention they can devote to internal customers. Second, employees generally serve multiple customers, and the specific service demands often vary according to the customer and the nature of the services required. Third, service providers naturally have their own unique strengths and limitations, so it is difficult to provide a standard recommendation for all employees.

The service providers raised an additional concern. It was suggested that some customers were requesting services that might be personally beneficial but that did not appear to be in the best interests of the organization. This is a common problem with internal service because

FIGURE 20.1 Linking employee behaviors with the dimensions of internal service

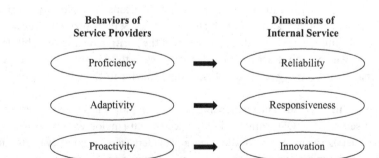

internal customers are not generally paying for the services they receive (at least not directly). The OD team concluded that a more structured intervention would be required, and they decided to leverage the performance management and talent management systems.

PERFORMANCE AND TALENT MANAGEMENT

Beginning with the next cycle of the performance management process, all employees were asked to meet with one internal customer and agree to target one service dimension for this customer. The employee was then asked to collaborate with his/her immediate manager to identify the specific behaviors that would most likely impact the targeted service dimension. These behaviors were to be included on the goal-setting form for the next six months. All managers were asked to conduct a bi-monthly coaching session to discuss progress regarding this goal. This process was then repeated with one more customer for the next six months.

The topic of internal service was also added as a dimension to the talent management process. The talent management meetings and feedback were conducted every year for all manager-level employees and above. The topic of internal service was added to the 360-feedback survey which was distributed to all direct reports and to key internal customers every year. This was perceived to be important by managers because the talent management process was used to make succession planning decisions.

At the end of the year, the OD team surveyed internal customers and collected a few objective measures (e.g., time to process new loans) to determine the effectiveness of the project. The results indicated that reliability and responsiveness had improved by about 15%. This was considered a real success. On the other hand, innovation had improved by only about 3%. Interviews were conducted with service providers who explained that reliability and responsiveness were relatively easy to impact (by being proficient or adapting to changes, respectively), but driving innovation (by being proactive) was far more difficult. A member of the OD team added: "And given our paternalistic culture, taking independent action can be particularly challenging for many employees". This suggested the need for additional guidance related to helping service providers be more proactive.

IMPROVING PROACTIVITY

The training and development team developed a two-hour training session devoted to helping service providers be more proactive. The sessions were delivered to all functions at United Bank. The sessions highlighted the fact that proactivity was likely to be more difficult than being more reliable or responsive, but that proactivity was more likely to contribute to organizational effectiveness and individual success. Employees were encouraged to not settle for the status quo and to look for ways to be more creative in providing services to internal customers.

After about six months, the OD team conducted a series of focus groups to assess the level of proactivity. The general consensus was that proactivity did not improve. In fact, internal customers mentioned that service providers were often pursuing ideas that might be creative but were probably not particularly practical. Some customers even felt that such efforts were distracting the service providers and they were ignoring simple requests (i.e., not being adaptive).

The OD team turned to the scientific literature related to proactivity to provide guidance on how to proceed (see Parker & Collins, 2010). Research related to proactivity suggests there are three major steps:

1.   Identify the problem or opportunity.
2.   Develop a plan to address the problem or take advantage of the opportunity.
3.   Take independent action to implement the plan.

The results of the literature review were discussed with a group of service providers to determine how to proceed. The employees felt that the planning and action steps were generally straightforward given appropriate resources and motivation. On the other hand, they argued that the initial identification of a potential problem or opportunity could be extremely difficult. One of the managers also argued that this responsibility should not lie solely with the service provider; she felt the responsibility should lie primarily with the two relevant management teams.

The OD team met with the executive committee, and they agreed that identifying potential problems and opportunities would be targeted during the next year. Each service provider and his/her manager were asked to meet with one internal customer to discuss likely problems or opportunities that the customer might face. Importantly, all parties (i.e., the service provider, internal customer, and the respective managers) were to identify common indicators of such problems or opportunities. For example, the internal customer might monitor the frequency of loan inquiries while the service provider might monitor the level of available resources to support loan requests. Regular monitoring of such indicators was to be included in each employee's performance management form. The talent management process was revised to indicate that managers were responsible for helping service providers anticipate problems or opportunities that customers might encounter in the future.

At the end of the year, the OD team evaluated the impact of the intervention on the quality of internal service using both objective measures and a survey of internal customers. The results indicated that services related to the reliability and responsiveness dimensions improved by an additional 5%, and, more to the point, performance related to the innovation dimension improved by about 10%. This was viewed as quite positive given that it was just the first year in which the organization was focused on helping employees to be more proactive. The HRM and OD leaders felt they had identified an important tactic for improving proactivity.

NEXT STEPS

It has been about four years since the OD team started the project to improve the quality of internal service. The OD team has reflected on the project to decide on potential next steps. One team member suggested that the project had been successful, and the organization should be able to provide effective levels of internal service without additional support from OD. The manager of OD indicated that most large-scale OD efforts take at least five years to be truly successful. Another member of the team then asked: "Why are we trying to make this decision? Why not ask employees about their perceptions and needs regarding the current quality of internal service?"

CASE STUDY QUESTIONS FOR DISCUSSION

1. Why is internal service important, and why is effective internal service often lacking in organizations?
2. How might high power distance impact the quality of internal service? How might it impact proactive behavior?
3. Provide a critique on the multi-phase intervention to improve internal service at United Bank. What do you see as its main strengths? How about its main weaknesses?
4. The multi-phase intervention relied on training, performance management, and talent management processes to improve internal service. What additional HRM interventions might you implement to further improve the quality of internal service at United Bank?

NOTE

1 The name of the organization has been changed.

REFERENCES

Carl, D., Gupta, V., & Javidan, M. 2004. Power distance. In R. J. House, P. J. Hanges, M. Javidan, P. W. Dorfman, & V. Gupta (Eds.), *Culture, Leadership, and Organizations: The GLOBE Study of 62 Societies*: 513–563. Thousand Oaks: Sage Publications.

Ewers, M. C. 2016. Oil, human capital and diversification: The challenge of transition in the UAE and the Arab Gulf states. *The Geographical Journal*, 182(3): 236–250.

Griffin, M. A., Neal, A., & Parker, S. K. 2007. A new model of work role performance: Positive behavior in uncertain and interdependent contexts. *Academy of Management Journal*, 50(2): 327–347.

Hofstede, G. 2001. *Culture's Consequences: Comparing Values, Behaviors, Institutions, and Organizations Across Nations*. Thousand Oaks: Sage Publications.

Kang, G., James, J., & Alexandris, K. 2002. Measurement of internal service quality: Application of the SERVQUAL battery to internal service quality. *Managing Service Quality*, 12(5): 278–291.

Martin, S. L., Habeeb, Z., & Zamzam, H. A. 2018. Training and development at United Bank: What do the employees think? In L. C. Christiansen, M. Biron, E. Farndale, & B. Kuvaas (Eds.), *The Global Human Resource Management Casebook*: 236–242. New York: Routledge.

Martin, S. L., Klimoski, R. J., & Henderson, A. (in press). Improving internal service: Identifying the roles of employee proficiency, adaptivity and proactivity. *Journal of Organizational Effectiveness: People and Performance*, 9(1): 50–67.

Parasuraman, A., Zeithaml, V. A., & Berry, L. L. 1988. SERVQUAL: A multiple-item scale for measuring consumer perceptions of service quality. *Journal of Retailing*, 64(1): 12–40.

Parker, S. K., & Collins, C. G. 2010. Taking stock: Integrating and differentiating multiple proactive behaviors. *Journal of Management*, 36(3): 633–662.

Suliman, A. M. T. 2006. Human resource management in the United Arab Emirates. In P. S. Budhwar, & K. Mellahi (Eds.), *Managing Human Resources in the Middle East*: 59–78. London: Routledge.

Supplementary Resources

Campbell, D. J. 2000. The proactive employee: Managing workplace initiative. *The Academy of Management Executive*, 14(3): 52–66.

Ehrhart, K. H., Witt, L. A., Schneider, B., & Perry, S. J. 2011. Service employees give as they get: Internal service as a moderator of the service climate-service outcomes link. *Journal of Applied Psychology*, 96(2): 423–431.

Johnston, R. 2008. Internal service: Barriers, flows and assessment. *International Journal of Service Industry Management*, 19(2): 210–231.

PART V

Asia and the Pacific Rim

CHAPTER 21

Australia

The Casual Employment Crisis at Australian Universities: What are the HRM Responsibilities?

Helen De Cieri and Karin Sanders

CASE SYNOPSIS

Deficiencies in the management of casual workers within Australian universities, particularly regarding underpayment, have led to complaints of exploitation. These deficiencies have been worsened by the COVID-19 pandemic, as this pandemic caused a huge reduction in international student enrollments, leading to widespread job losses. This case study describes the crisis in Australian universities regarding casual workers, the human resource management (HRM) implications, and lessons to be learned for the capability of universities to survive and thrive. Further, it illustrates the ramifications for Australia's ranking on the United Nations Sustainable Development Goals, especially on decent work and human rights.

KEYWORDS

Higher education and universities, casual employment, COVID-19 pandemic, decent work, Australia

DOI: 10.4324/9781003307099-26

LEARNING OUTCOMES

1. Understand links between the university business model and HRM.
2. Identify challenges for HRM professionals related to casual employment practices.
3. Understand links between the United Nations Sustainable Development Goals and HRM.

INTRODUCTION

In the past decade, the business model used by Australian universities has increasingly relied on casual employment (to more than 25% of the Australian workforce), which is linked to the rapid growth in the enrollment of fee-paying international students. Employers of these casual employees make no advance commitment to ongoing work, and casual employees are not entitled to paid sick or holiday leave. Deficiencies in the management of casual workers within Australian universities, particularly regarding underpayment, have led to allegations of exploitation. These deficiencies have been worsened by the COVID-19 pandemic, as this pandemic caused a huge reduction in international student enrollments, leading to widespread job losses. Lessons learned for universities include concerns about the reputational damage to institutions with both immediate and long-term implications for the ability of universities to attract, motivate, and retain talent. As well as pandemic restrictions on borders and visas, universities face obstacles including budget constraints, increased competition from online learning platforms, and concerns about educational quality. The case raises questions about whether the HRM practices in Australian universities can be viewed as sustainable.

Australia is governed through a federal parliamentary constitutional monarchy. In 2021, the population of Australia was over 25.5 million people (Australian Bureau of Statistics [ABS], 2021a). The cultural and linguistic diversity of Australia's resident population has been reshaped over many years by migration. In 2021, almost 30% of Australia's population had been born overseas (ABS, 2021b). Australia has a long-established history of international education, with an increased reliance on income from international students. "Where in 1989 universities derived more than 80% of their operating costs from the public purse, now it is estimated to be less than 40% – a figure well below the OECD average for public investment in tertiary education" (Horne, 2020).

AUSTRALIAN UNIVERSITIES AND THE INFLUENCE OF THE PANDEMIC

Australian universities are very important for the Australian economy. Before the COVID-19 pandemic, education was Australia's fourth-largest export. "Australia's education exports totaled $40 billion[1] in 2019. This included $17 billion in tuition fees paid by international students and $23 billion in international students' living expenses while they studied in Australia"

(Grozinger & Parsons, 2020: 39). Australian universities "contribute enormously to national research and development – international student fees help sustain this" (Horne, 2020).

Around the beginning of this century, Australian universities moved to a corporate model of strategic focus, structure, and operation (Parker, 2020). In this model, senior management, revenue growth, brand recognition, university prestige, and profit became the dominant elements (Parker, 2011). This resulted in a situation in which 20% to 50% of the student enrollments were fee-paying international students, constituting up to 30% or more of the total revenue. This business model is however at risk when the international students predominantly come from one (China) or two (India) countries (Hewett, 2020). Changes in governance and regulation in these countries directly affect the revenue for Australian universities. The business model of Australian universities effectively shifted the risks of the international student fee market onto insecurely employed staff with few entitlements or employment rights (that is, casual workers).

The COVID-19 pandemic hit Australian universities hard (Baré, Marshman, Beard, & Tjia, 2021). On February 1, 2020, the Australian government introduced restrictions on non-residents arriving from mainland China in response to the outbreak of COVID-19; this affected Chinese international students planning to commence their studies in February and March (when the Australian teaching year begins), as well as continuing students who had traveled back home for the Chinese New Year. From March 20, 2020, all overseas travel was banned, with only a few exceptions (Grozinger & Parsons, 2020). Despite efforts to switch university classes to online formats, closed international borders and limited online study options have reportedly carved $13.6 billion from Australia's overseas education exports since 2019. Based on ABS statistics, Adams (2021) reports that the annual value of tertiary education exports, accounting for tuition, accommodation, and related travel expenses, fell from $40.3 billion over the 2019 calendar year to $26.7 billion in the 12 months to June 2021.

The government established a COVID-19 wage subsidy scheme but excluded the higher education sector, despite substantial job losses (Horne, 2020). Casual academics were not eligible for the government's wage subsidy scheme due to rules that require more than 12 months of continuous employment with an organization that has lost between 30–50% of its revenue, effectively ruling universities out. Harris et al. (2020) report that many universities responded with clear policies and support in response to COVID-19. For example, executive staff at some universities, such as La Trobe University and the University of Wollongong, took a 20% pay cut and froze any non-essential travel. Other universities offered voluntary redundancy packages with two to three years' salary for tenured academics. The Australian National University extended benefits to their casual and contract staff; these benefits include honoring existing contracts, paying sessional tutors despite reductions in teaching hours, and paying casual staff to attend online professional development. While these are positive examples, casual staff were and are still in a vulnerable situation.

CASUAL WORKERS WITHIN AUSTRALIAN UNIVERSITIES: THEIR VULNERABLE SITUATION

Australian universities employ approximately 130,000 academic staff and another 130,000 professional (administrative and support) staff (Baré et al., 2021; Department of Education,

2020). Between 2009 and 2019, academic staff (headcount), including academics employed on a continuing or a fixed contract as well as casual workers, increased by 37%. However, the number of academic staff with tenure or continuing employment with generous conditions and job security is decreasing. Casual workers are essential for the delivery of teaching and work regularly on short-term, hours-based contracts. The number of casual workers has been estimated at 70% of the teaching staff in some universities (Harris et al., 2020). While the employment is casual, much of the work casual staff are expected to do is regular and stable over time. Student enrollments, for example, which drive teaching work, were quite steady in the years before the COVID-19 pandemic (Cahill, 2020). Job insecurity is not the only threat to casual workers. Casual workers may find it difficult to determine what are their entitlements or even to ask questions about their entitlements and job conditions (Cahill, 2020).

Allegations of underpayment. In June 2021, the University of Sydney published a report titled "The Tip of the Iceberg: A Report into Wage Theft and Underpayment of Casual Employees at the University of Sydney" based on the results of a semester-long audit (see Boncardo, 2021). Twenty-nine casual workers participated in this study, and they tracked each hour they worked, before comparing these hours to those for which they were paid. The report findings showed that 90% of the 29 casual workers were performing unpaid work: On average almost half an hour of extra work for every hour they were contracted to work.

The Australian government launched a senate inquiry into unlawful underpayment in universities and found that around half of Australia's universities had been involved in the underpayment of casual academic and professional staff. Major Australian universities were therefore in the news in 2021, with stories potentially damaging to institutional reputations. The University of New South Wales (UNSW) estimated it has a "potential liability to the casual academic workforce" amounting to tens of millions (CMM June 3, 2021), and the University of Melbourne announced it owed over 1,000 past and present casuals $9.5 m for work they had not been correctly paid for (CMM September 10, 2021). The University of Sydney announced it owed $12.75m mainly to professional staff, while the University of Queensland has a review underway (CMM 14 and 22, 2021). The Tertiary Education Quality Standards Agency has become involved – convening a webinar for universities "on the subject of wage underpayments" (CMM September 2, 2021). Policymakers and senior management within Australian universities have responded in different ways. University managers typically downplay the problem of underpayment. For instance, the Australian Higher Education Industrial Association (AHEIA), an employer group representing universities, claimed wage theft is not a systemic issue in Australian universities (Cahill, 2020).

Next steps: Repayment. In 2020 at Macquarie University, the NTEU negotiated about $50,000 in back payments (retrospective payments that were owed to workers) for casual staff whose tutorials had been reclassified as "small group teaching activities" with a lower rate of pay (Cahill, 2020). By the end of 2021, over a quarter of the 39 public universities in Australia were making repayments, undertaking audits, or in dispute with their casual workers over unpaid wages (Boncardo, 2021). Legal actions are underway in most of the leading universities (Maslen, 2020). Several vice-chancellors and senior university managers have been required to appear before the Australian Senate inquiry to explain their employment practices.

KEY LESSONS LEARNED

What are the major HRM lessons learned from the case of casual employment in Australian universities?

Skill shortages and reputational damage for Australian universities. The universities have for several years raised concerns about their ability to attract the best researchers from across the globe. Before the pandemic, concerns had already been raised about plans of the national government to increase restrictions on the professions open to skilled migration, and the lack of a pathway to permanent residency and citizenship. Adding to concerns in Australian universities about the attraction of talent, the reduction of international enrollments during the COVID-19 pandemic and the revelation of casual employment arrangements such as underpayment for casual workers have created a crisis in the Australian higher education sector. These factors are likely to affect public perception and have negative implications for the reputation of institutions; there are both immediate and long-term implications for the ability of universities to attract, motivate, and retain staff. This all raises the question: Should Australian universities reconsider their business model?

Failure to demonstrate sustainability. There is increasing societal expectation and pressure for HRM scholars and practitioners across all industries and sectors to demonstrate action and commitment to sustainability (Stahl et al., 2020) and human rights (Wettstein et al., 2019). Over the past decade, drivers for this pressure have included corporate scandals and the growth of stakeholder activism. The COVID-19 crisis has heightened the relevance and urgency for employers to act. For firms that are seeking to engage in sustainability, the United Nations Sustainable Development Goals (SDGs) offer a framework to guide their efforts (WHO, 2021). The SDGs reflect a broad view of sustainability that includes economic, environmental, and humanitarian aspects. Some SDGs, specifically gender equality and reduced inequality, health and well-being, and decent work and human rights, may be most relevant to HRM. Australia has adopted the SDGs, yet there has been criticism about the progress to date (www.unaa.org.au/sdg/). In the past four years, Australia's ranking on the SDGs decreased on the World SDG Index from 17th in 2016 to 38th in 2019 (United Nations, 2019).

It is undeniable that in some cases the HRM function has been actively engaged in exploitative practices, or at least is silent, insensitive, or slow to act on humanitarian crises, human rights abuses, and inequality, all of which are areas that have been hard-hit by the pandemic (Bapuji et al., 2020). For the HRM function to demonstrate sustainability, employers should adopt HRM strategies and practices that are designed and implemented with a focus on achieving long-term economic, environmental, and humanitarian goals, both inside and beyond the firm (Ehnert et al., 2016). However, research to date shows that the HRM function has largely failed to be involved in the design and implementation of such strategies and has failed to deliver on sustainability goals (Stahl et al., 2019). In many organizations, the HRM function now faces a critical juncture: Either contribute to sustainability or be complicit in (and even responsible for) the exploitation of labor. There are some examples of universities focusing more on sustainability. For instance, the University of Melbourne installed a sustainability team to promote a sustainable, equitable community through its campus operations, environments, and engagement activities. The UNSW Business School has special scholarships for incoming indigenous students and students from a lower social-economic status. It can be argued that universities have a special role and responsibility in confronting the challenges of global sustainability in a changing climate through humanitarian and environmental stewardship, which should become visible by implementing sustainable HRM practices.

Wage theft affects casual workers who have been underpaid, as well as students. Many of the casual workers within Australian universities are vulnerable immigrants on visas, research students, and early career academics who may be re-considering their aspirations for academic careers. Where staff are undervalued, underpaid, and working under pressure exacerbated by the COVID-19 pandemic, the quality of education is likely to suffer. In addition to the individual who has been underpaid, there may be negative effects on the students and the reputation of Australian universities.

THE WAY FORWARD

There are possible ways forward to resolve the HRM challenges we have identified in the previous section. We summarize five "opportunities for change" as identified by Baré et al. (2021) and build on these by adding suggestions for Australian universities. The first opportunity for change is the removal of impediments to flexibility in employment. For example, changing employment contracts to allow fixed-term engagement for teaching duties would provide more job security than has been available in casual employment. The second opportunity for change is focused on improving employment for casual academic staff and includes creating new employment structures such as a reward/career structure that would offer long-term career pathways for casual teaching staff. The third opportunity is to consider the development of a cross-sector collaboration to assist workers to have their previous experience at another institution recognized by a new employer. This might include formal accreditation for academic staff in teaching roles, which could contribute to quality enhancements in education. The fourth opportunity in universities is to create career paths for professional (administrative) staff, which would include recognizing university administration as a professional career path, with accreditation, and reviewing the professional staff classification structure. Finally, Baré et al. (2021) note the opportunities to recognize and support important roles performed by third space professionals in universities, such as educational designers, librarians, and student learning support staff.

From casuals to salaried employees. Cahill (2020) argues that the solution to the problems of casual workers within Australian universities is very simple: "end the over-reliance of universities on casuals". Moving casual workers into salaried positions with greater security and employment rights would be good for staff (both academic staff and casual workers), good for students, and good for the broader community. Although we agree with the suggested move from casual work to salaried positions, we argue that more is needed. When implementing this proposal, it seems inevitable that many current casual workers would move to so-called education-focused or teaching-focused positions. Education-focused teaching members of staff are employed by universities in a salaried continuing position with allowances such as paid personal leave and holiday leave. Most of these positions comprise 80% teaching and 20% service. Education-focused roles are already being used in many Australian universities, with appointments and career pathways up to the level of professor.

While we applaud these developments, we see two concerns. First, education-focused contracts lack flexibility and are largely invisible to people outside the university. Having an 80% teaching contract means that there is very limited scope for an incumbent to undertake research, which in turn hampers any opportunity to transfer to a combined research and teaching contract. It is also difficult for education-focused employees to gain international recognition, which is typically required in academic appointment and promotion applications. Solutions to this problem might be to simply remove the international recognition requirement or to revise requirements to include activities that education-focused employees are engaged in. The second concern we have is that there is a danger of creating different groups of academics whereby the education-focused members of staff are seen or treated as lower, or second-class citizens. This will create "cohesiveness" challenges for everyone, from senior managers and line managers, to HRM, and academic work groups.

Sustainable HRM practices for Australian universities. The HRM function could and should be actively addressing structural inequalities and the quality of employment conditions throughout the workforce (Bapuji et al., 2020; Soundararajan et al., 2021; Wettstein et al., 2019). Sustainable HRM practices target social, economic, and environmental aims. As an umbrella concept, sustainable HRM plays a fundamental role in achieving companies' sustainable goals (Renwick et al., 2013) by influencing employees' attitudes and behaviors. Sustainable HRM practices aim to minimize the negative impact of firms on the natural environment and acknowledge the critical enabling roles of senior managers, HRM, and line managers. For Australian universities, this means that the role of casual workers should be reconsidered. Many casual workers have been working in universities for a long time and have built up valuable expertise. Unless changes are made in Australian universities, valued expertise could be lost, and the reputation of Australian universities is at risk.

CASE STUDY QUESTIONS FOR DISCUSSION

1. Describe the business model used by Australian universities. Should Australian universities reconsider their business model?

2. Describe the situation of casual workers within Australian universities, with reference to various HRM theories.

3. Explain the relationship between the United Nations Sustainable Development Goals and HRM.

4. Which HRM practices could be implemented to improve the situation of casual workers at Australian universities?

NOTE

1 All money amounts in this chapter are provided in Australian dollars. June 2022: one Australian dollar is .70 US dollar.

REFERENCES

Adams, D. 2021, August 6. The pandemic has carved $13.6 billion from Australia's education sector as international student numbers fall. *Business Insider*. Accessed November 29, 2021 from https://www.businessinsider.com.au/australia-education-export-value-collapse -border-closure.

Australian Bureau of Statistics. 2021a. *National, state and territory population.* Accessed November 10, 2021 from https://www.abs.gov.au/statistics/people/population/national -state-and-territory-population/latest-release#key-statistics

Australian Bureau of Statistics. 2021b. *Migration*, Australia. Accessed November 10, 2021 from https://www.abs.gov.au/statistics/people/population/migration-australia/latest-release

Bapuji, H., Patel, C., Ertug, G., & Allen, D. G. 2020. Corona crisis and inequality: Why management research needs a societal turn. *Journal of Management*, 46: 1205–1222.

Baré, E., Marshman, I., Beard, J., & Tjia, T. 2021, February 23. COVID hit casual academics hard. Here are 5 ways to produce a better deal for unis and staff. *The Conversation*. Accessed November 17 2021 from https://theconversation.com/covid-hit-casual-academics-hard -here-are-5-ways-to-produce-a-better-deal-for-unis-and-staff-155357

Boncardo, R. 2021, June 16. Wage theft in higher education and how to stop it. *Overland*. Accessed November 28 from https://overland.org.au/2021/06/wage-theft-in-higher-education-and -how-to-stop-it/

Cahill, D. 2020. Wage theft and casual work are built into university business models. *The Conversation*. Accessed November 29, 2021 from https://theconversation.com/wage-theft -and-casual-work-are-built-into-university-business-models-147555

Department of Education. 2020. *Higher education statistics*. Canberra: Australian Government. Retrieved on 05/10/21 from https://www.education.gov.au/higher-education-statistics

Ehnert, I., Parsa, S., Roper, I., Wagner, M., & Müller-Camen, M. 2016. Reporting on sustainability and HRM: A comparative study of sustainability reporting practices by the world's largest companies. *The International Journal of Human Resource Management*, 27: 88–108.

Grozinger, P., & Parsons, S. 2020, December 10. The COVID-19 outbreak and Australia's education and tourism exports. *Reserve Bank of Australia*, December, 38–44. Accessed November 10 2021 from https://www.rba.gov.au/publications/bulletin/2020/dec/the-covid -19-outbreak-and-australias-education-and-tourism-exports.html

Harris, J., Snithers, K., & Spina, N. 2020, May 15. More than 70% of academics at some universities are casuals. They're losing work and are cut out of JobKeeper. *The Conversation*. Accessed December 5, 2021 from https://theconversation.com/more-than-70-of-academics-at-some -universities-are-casuals-theyre-losing-work-and-are-cut-out-of-jobkeeper-137778

Hewett, J. 2020, June 10. Time's up for universities facing China risk. *Australian Financial Review*. Accessed December 1, 2020 from https://www.afr.com/policy/health-and-education/time -s-up-for-universities-facing-china-risk-20200610-p55192

Horne, J. 2020, May 22. How universities came to rely on international students. *The Conversation*. Accessed November 10 2021 from https://theconversation.com/how-universities-came-to-rely-on-international-students-138796

Maslen, G. 2020, September 1. Universities face legal action over wage theft claims. *University World News*. Accessed December 21 2021 from https://www.universityworldnews.com/post.php?story=20200901140618585

Parker, L. D. 2011. University corporatization: Driving redefinition. *Critical Perspectives on Accounting*, 22(4): 434–450.

Parker, L. D. 2020. Australian universities in a pandemic world: Transforming a broken business model? *Journal of Accounting & Organizational Change*, 16(4): 541–548.

Renwick, D. W. S., Redman, T., & Maguire, S. 2013. Green human resource management: A review and research agenda. *International Journal of Management Reviews*, 15(1): 1–14.

Soundararajan, V., Wilhelm, M. M., & Crane, A. (2021). Humanizing research on working conditions in supply chains: Building a path to decent work. *Journal of Supply Chain Management*, 57(2): 3–13.

Stahl, G. K., Brewster, C .J., Collings, D. G., & Hajro, A. 2020. Enhancing the role of human resource management in corporate sustainability and social responsibility: A multi-stakeholder, multidimensional approach to HRM. *Human Resource Management Review*, 30: 100708.

United Nations. 2019. UN sustainable development solutions network. *Sustainable development report 2019*, p. 20, 69, cited in https://www.unaa.org.au/sdg/.

Wettstein, F., Giuliani, E., Santangelo, G. D., & Stahl, G. K. 2019. International business and human rights: A research agenda. *Journal of World Business*, 54: 54–65.

World Health Organization. 2021. *World health statistics 2021. Monitoring health for the SDGs, sustainable development goals*. Geneva: World Health Organization. Accessed August 1 2021 from https://www.who.int/data/gho/publications/world-health-statistics.

CHAPTER 22

India

Gender Diversity and Inclusion: Strategies and Practices at ICICI Bank

Radha R. Sharma

CASE SYNOPSIS

The case encapsulates innovative diversity and inclusion practices adopted by ICICI Bank, a leading private bank in India. It garners significance in the backdrop of the COVID-19 pandemic when a countrywide lockdown was declared in India, but the banks, coming under the Essential Services Act, had to function with strict adherence to the COVID-19 protocol of the government. ICICI Bank adopted several innovative, i-centric (digitally enabled) practices in human resource management and banking services, surging ahead in the banking sector even in the new normal. Its work culture supports merit-based gender equity policies and practices for talent management.

KEYWORDS

Gender diversity, gender equality, gender equity, innovative D&I practices, digitalization of HR, India

DOI: 10.4324/9781003307099-27

LEARNING OUTCOMES

1. Develop an understanding of diversity and inclusion in the workplace.
2. Appreciate the role of leadership in creating a gender-inclusive organization.
3. Differentiate between gender equality and gender equity.
4. Gain insight into innovative digital HR and organizational practices for D&I.

INTRODUCTION

Ruma,[1] with her brilliant academic record and career aspiration, had joined ICICI Bank on October March 18, 2020, and was still familiarizing herself with the new role when the news about the countrywide lockdown flashed on Indian television news channels on March 24, 2020, that the surge of hospital cases caused by the global pandemic, COVID-19, needed to be controlled. It came as a bolt from the blue; she became worried about her performance for career progression in a high-performing organization. A phone call from Nitish Singh, the manager of a New Delhi branch, enquiring about her and her family's health on March 25, was like music to her ears. He spent a good 15 minutes explaining to her the entire process and assured her of all possible support in her onboarding. She had met him once for a courtesy call and was surprised at this caring gesture of a senior officer toward a new employee. Thereafter, she got introduced to other colleagues and found the work culture to be very inclusive, and people- and customer-centric.

As per the Indian Government's instructions, banks were exempt from the lockdown and were allowed to remain open with limited functioning, and staff with strict adherence to the COVID-19 protocol announced by the government. While digitalization, online functioning, fear and anxiety, and social isolation stress were being experienced by people at large, Ruma observed that the ICICI Bank staff went the extra mile to reach out to employees at large and offered emotional support. Most organizations had implemented salary cuts due to the slowing down of economic activities as a result of the pandemic, but ICICI Bank decided to reward over 80,000 of its frontline employees (over 80% of its workforce) with a salary hike of up to 8% in recognition of the services rendered by them in the functioning of the bank during the COVID-19 pandemic (Press Trust of India, 2020). Female employees who worked double shifts (Hochschild & Machung, 1989) felt more assured and resilient with this support (Chawla & Sharma, 2019), something that also resonated with Ruma. ICICI Bank has an open culture where employees can interact with the senior leadership team enabled by technology and facilitated by a formal engagement forum, viz., "Engage your Leader" and "E-Branch Visits". These sessions are conducted over iStudio, an in-house application that is a two-way communication platform capable of connecting all employees across locations. This helped ICICI Bank become more inclusive, innovative, i-centric (digitally enabled), and effective, surging ahead in the banking sector even in the new normal.

ORGANIZATIONAL SETTING

ICICI Bank is the second largest private sector bank in India offering a diversified portfolio of financial products and services to retail, SME, and corporate customers. It is a leading private sector bank with a presence in 15 countries. Its subsidiaries include India's leading private sector insurance, asset management, and securities brokerage companies, and among the country's largest private equity firms. ICICI Bank has consistently strived to be a future-ready organization and accordingly has developed its capabilities to ensure agility and value creation in its businesses, which is reflected in the several pioneering initiatives taken by the bank.

ICICI Bank was formed in 1994 as a subsidiary of the Industrial Credit and Investment Corporation of India Limited (ICICI), which was incorporated at the initiative of the World Bank, the Government of India, and representatives of Indian industry in 1995, to create a development financial institution for providing medium-term and long-term project financing to Indian businesses. Once established, ICICI undertook normal banking operations, viz., mobilizing deposits and offering credit cards, car loans, and other bank products. After a series of mergers (with the Bank of Madura) and a reverse merger, ICICI was transformed from an industrial project finance institution into India's most comprehensive financial services powerhouse with interests in retail banking, insurance, online trading, and BPO among others, thereby transforming the Indian banking industry. ICICI Bank's equity shares are listed on Indian stock exchanges at Chennai, Delhi, Kolkata, Vadodara, Bombay, and the National Stock Exchange of India Limited, and its American depositary receipts (ADRs) are listed on the New York Stock Exchange (NYSE).

HRM IN THE INDIAN CONTEXT

India, the largest democracy and the second largest country in the world had an estimated population in 2021 of 1.39 billion. More than 65% of the population of India is below the age of 35. Consisting of 28 states and 8 union territories (centrally administered) spread over 3.3 million square kilometers (www.india.gov.in/india-glance/profile, December 12, 2021), India is one of the oldest civilizations in the world with a kaleidoscopic variety of cultural, linguistic, religious, and ethnic diversity with a pluralistic worldview, synthesizing mindset, and high context sensitivity.

HRM in India has evolved over the decades from a purely statutory *labor welfare function* to *strategic HRM* and *digital HRM*. The central government has enacted 44 labor-related statutes dealing with minimum wage, accidental and social security benefits, occupational safety and health, conditions of employment, disciplinary action, formation of trade unions, industrial relations, etc. New labor codes and reforms were introduced during 2019–2020. Accordingly, central and state governments have taken various legislative, administrative, and e-governance initiatives to generate employment and to facilitate ease of doing business (Ministry of Labour, Govt. of India). Service sector organizations like IT and ITES, banking, and insurance have adopted e-HRM in India, and COVID-19 accelerated the pace of digitalization of HR. Digitalization has been adopted even in traditional organizations in the automobile, energy, and

FMCG sectors (Sharma & Shukla, 2013; Sinha, 2017). Interpersonal relations are important, and social, cultural, economic, and political factors seem to influence HRM policies and practices.

India ranked 112th among 153 countries in the Global Gender Gap Index 2020 (Sharma et al., 2021). The process of reducing gender inequalities has slowed down due to the impact of the COVID-19 pandemic. Though the Indian constitution grants gender equality and Indian women have been prime ministers and presidents of the country, gender equity is an ongoing workplace issue (Sharma & Chawla, 2021). Few women make it to the top due to socio-economic hurdles, prejudices, and covert discrimination (Sharma, 1982; Sharma & Sharma, 2015, Chawla & Sharma, 2016). A historic new company law was enacted, with the President of India giving his assent to the Companies Bill, 2013, which made it mandatory to have women on the board of directors for certain classes of companies. This was a landmark decision for the inclusion of women in decision-making roles on corporate boards. Research by Catalyst (2021) reports that when women hold at least three seats, "this critical mass" is good for corporate governance. Research in India has revealed that boards of directors having three or more women in at least four of five years significantly outperformed those with sustained low representation by 84% on return on sales (ROS), 60% on return on invested capital (ROIC), and 46% on return on equity (ROE) (Tripathi, 2021). According to Catalyst (2021), 16.6% of companies in India had women directors in 2020, of which 18.6 % had three or more women directors.

ECONOMIC REFORMS AND THE GLOBALIZATION OF INDIA

After independence in 1947, India planned its strategy for development through five-year plans and has seen 12 "five-year plans". This led to setting up state-owned industries in all major fields, including banks, to provide large-scale employment. Socialism, the dominant ideology of the government, later resulted in low productivity and caused problems of balance of payment. This necessitated economic reforms, and in July 1991, the first wave of globalization and liberalization commenced, comprising economic liberalization, consumer focus, market orientation, and competition. Realizing the importance and strengthening the link between social development and economic growth, the Planning Commission of the government brought out National Human Development Report, 2001. Consequently, banks were required to play a major role in accelerating the country's socio-economic development. Therefore, banking reforms constituted a major part of the economic reforms to bring about "operational flexibility" and "functional autonomy" to enhance "efficiency, productivity, and profitability". Recently some additional reforms have been made to address the new developments by integrating technologies for enhancing the reach and ease of banking. This has impacted HRM policies and practices to strengthen the foundations of the banking system for greater stability, customer centricity, efficiency, performance, and profitability.

ICICI BANK: ALIGNING WITH THE BUSINESS ENVIRONMENT

Since its inception in 1994, ICICI Bank has made phenomenal progress in a short span under K.V. Kamath as its managing director and CEO in its embryonic stage in 1996 to 2009, and later under Ms. Chanda Kochhar as MD and CEO from 2009–2018. Kamath's aggressive plans got ICICI Bank listed on the NYSE in 1999, the first-ever Indian financial institution to go the ADR route. In 2007, ICICI Bank made history by raising USD 5 billion in the largest-ever public offering with total bids worth over USD 25 billion from across the globe (Sharma & Abraham, 2011a & b).

Meritocracy and performance were the most important criteria in recognizing leaders, and this strategy facilitated the identification of the top 5% of the bank's talent who were treated differently for opportunities for development and leadership roles, etc. With a view to enhancing market share, Kamath focused on identifying and nurturing leaders in the bank who could foresee business opportunities, and he believed that women were more likely to articulate and take a stand on corporate matters than men. With the sustained strategy of leadership development, ICICI Bank came to be known as a "CEO factory" and produced leaders, including women, who have headed businesses within ICICI Bank and top management roles in other banks/financial institutions.

GENDER DIVERSITY AND INCLUSION AT ICICI BANK

Gender diversity has been the focus of ICICI Bank since the 1980s. K.V. Kamath is credited with empowering women, who constituted 30% of the staff during his tenure. He consistently selected women rather than men to realize his vision for ICICI as diverse and inclusive. "It's clearly a result of merit and of not distinguishing between a man or a woman", said Kamath. His criteria for selection had been "leaders with ability, intellect, and the entrepreneurial ability to lead teams", and he valued women's "ability to think in a much more detached manner than men" (Elliott, 2006). "Almost all the leaders we have picked have succeeded, and most have been women", said Kamath (Elliott, op. cit.). He created a business culture that was not only free from gender bias but also provided a working environment where women felt comfortable (Elliott, op. cit.). Many women served in leadership roles, viz, Lalita Gupte as joint MD who played an important role in transforming ICICI; Kalpana Morparia, later another joint MD, who was considered by her peer bankers as the backbone of ICICI; and Shikha Sharma, another high achiever, who contributed to different segments of the bank and believed that women had smaller egos that made them agile. The HR department of ICICI practiced gender equity (Sharma, R & Sharma, 2015) and supported women taking time off during the day for important family duties, as the head of HR believed that this helped women return to work with much vigor.

In 2009, Ms. Chanda Kochhar, the then joint MD and group chief financial officer of ICICI Bank succeeded Kamath as CEO and managing director. Being a woman leader, she had a better understanding of gender issues and introduced several gender-sensitive policies and practices as will be evident from the following paragraphs. Kochhar opined "It gets the benefits of a different perspective of gender diversity because of the different mix of ways women look at things, not just at numbers but more passionately on the impact on customers and employees".

Gender diversity, gender balance, and women in leadership roles have been important considerations at ICICI Bank not only for diversity and diverse perspectives but also in providing a greater talent pool for years. The bank consistently adopted meritocracy and fairness-based approaches for performance assessment (ICICI Careers). For retention of women employees who very often choose to drop out from the workplace at key life stages, in 2016, the bank introduced a technology-enabled initiative called iWork@home, a first-of-its-kind program providing access to work applications in a safe and secure manner for an extended period of time depending on requirements. Kochhar said that,

> "We wanted to create a stronger support system for women to ensure that they do not leave the workforce at key life stages. We decided to use technology to make life simpler for women managers."

This also facilitated effective functioning of women employees in their dual role. The following three quotes are from *India Times* (2016).

"Niambari Bahadkar, an operations manager at ICICI Bank, realised that increasing responsibilities towards ageing parents were making it tougher for her to pursue her job."

But she was not the only one finding it difficult to handle her duties at home along with work. Other employees had other challenges:

> "Tinaz Jokhi, assistant manager operations, was dealing with the pressure of changes in life owing to her recent marriage."

and

> "Vishakha Chauhan, who was in the final stages of her pregnancy, felt that though she was fit enough to work, the commute to work was just not possible for her at this stage."

The bank's leave policy includes maternity leave, childcare leave, fertility leave, and adoption leave, which supports the needs of women employees at different life stages. The women who avail of maternity/other special leaves are appraised differently, with due consideration, to ensure fair and unbiased performance appraisal (Sharma & Mukherji, 2012). Women managers – with young children – who undertake business travel can take their children along, and the cost of travel and stay of young children and their caregivers is covered by the bank. When women employees are required for official work until the late evening, special arrangements are made to ensure their safety getting home. ICICI Bank has set up a Quick Response Team (QRT) to assist women employees who might experience distress while commuting. These QRT teams are equipped with GPS, medical equipment, and medically trained staff to deal with medical emergencies, if any. These are effective, not to mention innovative, gender-equitable, and gender-inclusive practices that very few organizations adopt. Ruma, the new employee, was absolutely thrilled with the gender-sensitive policies and inclusive work practices, as she dreamed of her future career being at the bank.

These gender-equitable policies and practices have produced strong women leaders for senior roles not only for ICICI Bank but, in the process, provided a galaxy of strong women leaders to the corporate sector in India. A national daily of India, *The Economic Times* (2014), stated that

> "The results of such support have been ... over the years, ICICI Bank has emerged as a CEO factory of sorts."

Gender diversity is embedded in the culture of ICICI Bank with its gender-sensitive policies and practices. The bank is an equal opportunity employer and has policy and practices to ensure respect and dignity for everyone.

> "ICICI's leadership in the space of gender parity speaks loud and clear with the number of women leaders the bank has sent out to the world."
>
> *(Saundarya Rajesh, Founder of Avtar Career Creators and*
> *FLEXI Careers India;* India Times, *2016)*

ICICI Bank has mechanisms for dealing with complaints of discrimination or harassment. If any case of sexual harassment is reported, it is handled as per the guidelines set under PoSH Act. Complaints, if any, are handled with the utmost sensitivity and confidentiality at the earliest and are resolved within a specified timeframe. Prevention of Sexual Harassment at Workplace (PoSH) Act 2013 is an Indian law enacted with the objective of making workplaces safer for women by preventing, prohibiting, and redressing acts of sexual harassment against them in the workplace. The law came in effect in India on December 9, 2013, by the Ministry for Women and Child Development. In order to generate awareness, ICICI Bank makes all employees go through mandatory e-learning on the PoSH Act.

WORK CULTURE AT ICICI BANK

Since 2018, Mr. Sandeep Bakhshi has been the CEO of ICICI Bank. In March 2020, women constituted 32% of the bank's workforce. People practices have been the strength of the bank and have further evolved over the years. Its work culture is highly business oriented and agile, which allows it to adapt to market opportunities and changing business environments. This requires innovation and execution, strategic alignment between people and processes, capability development technological support, and synergy among employees as "one team" with sensitivity and responsibility. The inclusive culture has been created through extensive communication meetings with leadership teams, workshops, induction programs, and leadership development workshops. In addition, senior leadership periodically share their business perspective in the form of short videos through "Huddle".

ICICI Bank took the initiative in 2019 to redesign its workplaces to blur hierarchies and create an "open office culture" to strengthen and develop synergy. In line with the above process simplification, in 2020 a singular performance objective was adopted by the leadership team aligning with market opportunities. In order to "embed the essence of One Bank, One Team, One Goal, the Bank created 'Ecosystem team'" (Human Capital at ICICI). These ecosystem teams facilitated cross-functional collaboration and have been instrumental in enhancing focus on servicing the customers as one team. To quote a customer:

> "ICICI Bank is continuously partnering with us in our transformation journey of digitising banking across our entire ecosystem."
>
> *(Mr. Rajendran Arunachalam, Exe. VP/CFO. Thermax Global;*
> *www.economictimes.com, Vol. 49, no. 263, p.1, Nov. 22, 2021)*

Observance of professionalism and ethical standards and upholding the principles of integrity and compliance are mandatory for all employees. The bank has a "Group Code of Business Conduct and Ethics", which articulates the desired behavior, values, principles, and standards of professional conduct expected from each employee. The new employees are required to go through training modules relating to the code of conduct, information security, anti-money laundering, and other compliance-related areas, which are necessary for banking-related work. Information about other compliance issues is shared periodically with the employees.

THE ROAD AHEAD

ICICI Bank was adjudged as "Best Company to Work For" by *Business Today* (national magazine) in 2020, on the basis of a nationwide survey conducted in collaboration with PeopleStrong. ICICI Bank won this award in the "Banking, Financial Services and Insurance" sector consecutively for the fourth year. The parameters considered for selection of awardees were: Culture of inclusion, work environment, culture of innovation, challenging work opportunities, communication, work-life balance and flexibility, job security and company stability, leadership's commitment to the business, learning opportunities, career growth path, fairness, and objectivity. Leveraging its human capital of both genders and with a focus on its customers, ICICI Bank rechristened all the corporate offices and central functions as ICICI Service Centres, where there is close to 25% women participation in frontline sales offices.

Gender parity is a business case, as women in India constitute 48% of the population; they are decision-makers in the family, customers, and talent that should be leveraged for the growth of the economy. Above all, gender parity and inclusiveness are needed for optimizing women's potential and personal growth. ICICI Bank has exemplary policies for gender diversity and inclusion along with an enabling environment supported by technological innovations and meritocracy for career and business growth. However, this requires women to be ambitious and have self-confidence, resilience, and the desire to excel and overcome the stereotype of being only a homemaker. HR policy regarding recruitment, selection, training, learning, growth opportunities, and women empowerment plays a significant role in creating a culture of diversity and inclusion in the organization, which is evident from the case of ICICI Bank.

With all the positives at the bank and its inclusiveness, Ruma observed that some junior women colleagues found it hard to cope with high-pressure target-driven work, particularly in the marketing function. She found that gender played a subtle role in their effective functioning, as many customers preferred to deal with male rather than woman officers from the bank. This made her reflect that while merit, inclusive organizational culture, and equal opportunity were important for career progression, societal culture was also important in women's career progression in non-traditional roles, but the good news was that the situation was improving with government policies. She thought of creating a WhatsApp group of women managers across sectors for discussing what more could be done to accelerate a shift in the mindset of people at large and considered reading some international HRM on D&I policies and practices in other countries.

CASE STUDY QUESTIONS FOR DISCUSSION

1. Think about diversity and inclusion experience at the workplace in your cultural context. Based on your personal experience during the past two years, share one thing that you consider should have been in the HR policy for diversity and inclusion for talent management and compare it with the policy of ICICI Bank as given in the case.

2. In your view, do you think leadership can influence HRM practices such as recruitment, selection, training, and career development in promoting gender diversity and inclusion in an organization?

NOTE

1 Ruma and Nitish Singh are pseudo protagonists used in this case. The case has been written using secondary data available in the public domain.

REFERENCES

Chawla, S. & Sharma, R.R. 2019. Enhancing women's well-being: The role of psychological capital and perceived gender equity, with social support as a moderator and commitment as a mediator. *Frontiers in Psychology*, 10, 1377. Doi: 10.3389/fpsyg.2019.01377

Chawla, S., & Sharma, R.R. 2016. How women traverse an upward journey in Indian industry: Multiple case studies. *Gender in Management: An International Journal*, 31(3), 181–206.

Economic Times. 2014, March 9. How ICICI Bank has emerged as a 'CEO factory' of primarily women leaders. https://economictimes.indiatimes.com/how-icici-bank-has-emerged-as-a-ceo-factory-of primarilywomenleaders/articleshow/31682254.cms?utm_source=content ofinterest&utm_medium=text&utm_campaign=cppst

Elliott, J. 2006. The women of ICICI bank. Oct. 9, *Fortune Magazine*. https://money.cnn.com/magazines/fortune/fortune_archive/2006/10/16/8390326/index.htm

Hochschild, A., & Machung, A. 1989. *The Second Shift. Working Parents and the Revolution at Home*. New York: Viking.

Human Capital at ICICI. https://www.icicibank.com/aboutus/Annual-Reports/2019-20/AR/human-capital.html. Retrieved on 14.12.21.

ICICI Careers. https://www.icicicareers.com/website/know-us/women-at-icici/2016/Nov/women-at-icici-bank.html. Retrieved on 14.12.21.

India Times. 2016, March 8. *ICICI Bank Has Given Its Female Employees the Option to Work from Home for A Year*. https://www.indiatimes.com/news/india/this-women-s-day-icici-bank-gifted-its-female-staff-the-option-to-work-from-home-for-long-durations-251688.html. Retrieved on 14.12.21.

Ministry of Labour, Govt. of India New Labour Codes for New India. https://labour.gov.in/labour-law-reforms. Retrieved on 16.11.22.

PoSH Act. 2013. https://legislative.gov.in/sites/default/files/A2013-14.pdf Retrieved on 19.12.21.

Press Trust of India. 2020, July 7. https://www.business-standard.com/article/finance/icici-bank-to-give-80k-employees-up-to-8-pay-hike-for-work-amid-covid-19-120070701244_1.html. Retrieved on Dec. 19, 2021.

Sharma, H., & Shukla, S. 2013. Human resource management in digital age: Trends in Indian corporate HR practices. *IRC's International Journal of Multidisciplinary Research in Social & Management Science*, 1(3), 66–77.

Sharma, R.R. 1982. Education of women in India: Inequalities and bottlenecks. *Education Quarterly*, 3, 20–27.

Sharma, R.R., & Abraham, P. 2011a. *Leveraging Human Capital for Business Growth in The Global Human Resources Casebook*, (Eds.) J. Hayton, M. Biron, L.C. Christiansen, & B. Kuvaas. Rutledge, USA: Academy of Management.

Sharma, R.R., & Abraham, P. 2011b. ICICI bank: The emergent bank of emerging economies. In *Spitzeck; Pirson, Michael & Dierksmeier, C. Banking with Integrity: The Winners of the Financial Crisis?* London: Palgrave Macmillan USA, 115–128.

Sharma, R.R., & Chawla, S. 2021. Gender equality & gender equity: Strategies for bridging the gender gap in the corporate world, Springer books. In: J. Marques (Ed.), *Exploring Gender at Work* (chapter 0, pp. 197–212). New York: Springer.

Sharma, R.R., & Mukherji, S. 2012. Women in India: Their Odyssey towards equality. In S. Groschl & J. Tagaki (Eds.) *Diversity Quotas, Diverse Perspectives-The Case of Gender* (pp. 91–118). UK: Gower.

Sharma, R.R., & Sharma, N.P. 2015. Opening the gender diversity black box: Causality of perceived gender equity and locus of control and mediation of work engagement in employee well-being. *Frontiers in Psychology*, 6, 1371.

Sharma, R.R., Chawla, S. et al. 2021. Global gender gap index: World economic forum perspective. In E.S. Ng, C.L. Stamper, A. Klarsfeld, & Y.J. Han (Eds.), *2021 Handbook on Diversity and Inclusion Indices A Research Compendium* (pp. 150–163). Cheltenham, UK; Northampton: Edward Elgar Publishing Limited.

Sinha, B.C. 2017. *Impact of e-HRM: A study of select systems, 107(9), 1257 1275*. Indian organizations (doctoral dissertation). Lovely Professional University, Phagwara, India. Retrieved from http://hdl.handle.net/10603/148304

Tripathi, A. 2021. Women on board: An analysis of companies act, 2013. https://taxguru.in/company-law/women-board-analysis-companies-act-2013.html. Retrieved on 12.12.21.

CHAPTER 23

Japan

The Quest of Pasona for Employees' Work-Life Balance: Relocation of Headquarters from Tokyo to a Remote Island

Azusa Ebisuya, Tomoki Sekiguchi, and Gayan Prasad Hettiarachchi

CASE SYNOPSIS

This case study introduces Pasona Group Inc. (hereafter referred to as Pasona), which is making courageous attempts to relocate some of its headquarters' functions from Tokyo to Awaji Island and transfer its core employees accordingly. Pasona was established in 1976 as an HRM service provider firmly grounded in the noble corporate philosophy of "solutions to society's problems". Although many Japanese companies have their headquarters in overcrowded Tokyo, which is Japan's administrative and economic center, Pasona has made a bold move to leave Tokyo. This case study discusses both the opportunities and challenges of relocating Pasona's headquarters to a rural area. It also considers whether such relocation is a feasible and realistic strategy for large corporations in Japan.

KEYWORDS

Urban overconcentration, headquarters' relocation, work-life balance, Japan

DOI: 10.4324/9781003307099-28

LEARNING OUTCOMES

By reading this case, the readers will be able to:

1. Understand how overconcentration in big cities affects the working environment and employees' work-life balance.
2. Understand the role of headquarters' HRM practices in large Japanese companies.
3. Understand how relocating headquarters' functions from big cities to rural areas influences the work styles and employees' work-life balance.
4. Understand how companies can improve their employees' working environment and the border society on the same footing.
5. Identify the pros and cons of relocating headquarters from big cities to rural areas from both HRM and business perspectives.

CONTEXTUAL BACKGROUND OF THE CASE

In Japan, the headquarters of government agencies and corporations have traditionally been concentrated in and around Tokyo. Many companies that originally operated outside of Tokyo have moved their corporate headquarters to Tokyo. Thus, the city has been serving as a convenient knowledge and resource hub providing unique opportunities for executives and other personnel known as "core employees" or "core personnel" (Dedoussis, 1995) that oversee critical operations of the entire company to form networks and expand their operations in new directions. Tokyo has become an attractive location for headquarters for a multitude of organizations that are actively seeking new knowledge, markets, and resources. This trend is expected to continue based on PricewaterhouseCoopers' projections that rank Tokyo as the largest agglomeration by population and economic size by 2025 (UK Economic Outlook, 2009).

From an operational standpoint, maintaining headquarters in a city such as Tokyo is extremely expensive due to real estate prices. The labor costs are also expensive due to the high cost of living in Tokyo. From an HR standpoint, the "overconcentration of Tokyo" has resulted in negative effects on the living and working environment and employees' work-life balance. Specifically, the rise in prices of commodities and real estate due to the influx of population brought by companies, the unhealthy living environments (cramped rooms, dense residential areas, safety issues, etc.), and the extended commuting time on packed trains and buses during rush hour are negatively affecting employee well-being. There are also secondary effects on individuals, families, and the entire country. The increasing number of unmarried couples and declining birthrates due to financial insecurity and the difficulty in ensuring a healthy child-rearing environment are at the top of the list (Honjo, 1998).

In light of these concerning issues, an increasing number of companies are contemplating relocating or partially dispersing their headquarters' functions away from Tokyo. According to a survey conducted by the Japan Business Federation, the number of companies headquartered in Tokyo reporting they will relocate their headquarters' functions from Tokyo, or are considering doing so in the future, rose from 7.5% in 2015 to 22.6% in 2020 (Newswitch, 2021).

THE BIRTH OF PASONA

In February 1976, just one month before graduating from college, Yasuyuki Nambu, the current chief executive officer (CEO) of Pasona Group Inc./the Chairman CEO of Pasona Inc., launched a company called Temporary Center Inc. in Osaka, Japan's second-largest commercial city. Temporary Center Inc., Pasona's predecessor, developed a temporary staffing system that allowed individuals with various circumstances to choose from a wide variety of employment options. In 1993, the company changed its name to Pasona Inc. and moved its headquarters to Tokyo. In the 1990s, Pasona expanded to become a group company by acquiring subsidiaries that provided various types of HR services, enabling Pasona to provide a diverse range of staffing options for various industry sectors (Yamamoto, 2021).

Pasona's corporate philosophy that endeavors to provide "solutions to society's problems" is founded on three supporting pillars: "a society in which every person is able to find work that they like and a career that complements their personal goals", "a society in which people are free to exercise their talents through an egalitarian relationship between the workplace and the individual", and "promoting diversity and continually create opportunities for individuals to achieve their dreams". In harmony with its philosophy, Pasona has worked diligently to enable as many people as possible to experience the joy of fruitful work (Pasona Group Corporate Philosophy, www.pasonagroup.co.jp/english/company/philosophy_e.html. Accessed: July 12, 2022).

One of Pasona's pioneering efforts since its establishment has been the advancement of women in the Japanese workplace. In Japan, wives were traditionally expected to stay at home to take care of children and house chores while the husbands focused on their secular work. Thus, it was difficult for women to pursue a career after marriage or childbirth. As a result, most large Japanese companies had a majority of male employees as core permanent employees. In an effort to address such issues, Pasona has been actively promoting the advancement of women into the workplace by considering women's life stages and providing various employment opportunities, for instance, temporary staffing that meets individual circumstances.

Pasona also envisions revitalizing local communities to bring joy to people's work. Pasona aims to achieve this by creating jobs in the agricultural sector. Although Japan's rural areas have vast stretches of land and fertile soil ideal for farming, many farmers find it difficult to sustain productive farming due to a decrease in the number of young workers who wish to endure physical labor. Pasona has been implementing various projects since 2008 aimed at supporting the revival of agriculture on Awaji Island, a small island in Japan with which they share a strong and long relationship. Beautiful Awaji Island is situated in the Hyogo Prefecture, 600 km from Tokyo, in western Japan. It has an area of about 595 square kilometers, 65% of which is covered by mountainous and hilly terrain, with 60,201 households and a population of 131,474 as of 2021 (Yamamoto, 2021).

PASONA'S RESISTANCE TO THE OVERCONCENTRATION IN TOKYO

Pasona's recent announcement to relocate its headquarters away from Tokyo is a somewhat surprising and bold decision. Pasona sent 120 employees, excluding new hires, to Awaji Island in the spring of 2021 after announcing a partial relocation of its headquarters operations in the fall of 2020. Since June 2021, Pasona has been planning further relocations, which include constructing a new office building by spring 2023 that can accommodate about 800 employees. Pasona plans to relocate approximately 1,200 of its 1,800 headquarters jobs by May 2024, with the possibility of more relocations in the future (Yamamoto, 2021).

Several factors guided the decision to relocate, including the need for risk reduction, ensuring work quality, and improving the quality of family life. The choice to relocate specifically to Awaji Island was influenced by some of Pasona's prior prosperous experiences there.

DIFFICULT TIMES, BOLD MOVES: WHY RELOCATE HEADQUARTERS' FUNCTIONS?

The massive earthquake that struck eastern Japan in 2011 shocked many companies in Tokyo, including Pasona. The fear of losing control of the headquarters' important functions during a disaster brought to mind the need to distribute geographically some of the functions as a risk-reduction strategy. Still, many companies could not gain the momentum necessary to make the bold move. Then came COVID-19, highlighting the problems associated with centralized functions of headquarters once again, especially in overcrowded cities.

To cope with the challenges of the pandemic, many companies in Tokyo resorted to remote work. However, Pasona concluded that it was difficult to develop HR adequately through non-face-to-face, virtual means. In addition, confining the key workforce into cramped Tokyo apartments for remote work could potentially hinder their work performance. The company believed it was important for employees to actually meet and work together to have a rewarding work environment. Furthermore, their view was not limited to addressing business needs during the pandemic. Pasona realized that even if the threats of COVID-19 could be eventually eliminated and employees could work together in the office again, their quality of life would not improve in this urban environment due to the reasons discussed above (Honjo, 1998). Pasona was interested in positively affecting the workforce's productivity, work-life balance, and family life. Consequently, Pasona made the bold decision to move some of its headquarters to a region with abundant space surrounded by beautiful nature. With this, the company envisions reducing remote work, providing face-to-face employment, and greatly improving the quality of life for the employees and their families during and after the pandemic.

A NEW PLACE TO WORK THAT RESISTS THE TRENDS OF THE TIMES: WHY MOVE TO AWAJI ISLAND?

Pasona's strong attraction to Awaji Island was partially due to its geographical conditions and the island's characteristics. It is a lush green island surrounded by a beautiful blue sea, with several well-maintained beaches, parks, gardens in the forest, and breathtaking waterfalls. Therefore, for Pasona, the island is a paradise having the potential to set in motion a successful tourism industry. Along these lines, Pasona has been promoting economic activities on Awaji Island since 2008, which includes a self-sustaining agricultural support project and the construction of various facilities aimed at tourism. However, the only concern was the lack of HR to help manage business activities on the island.

For Pasona, which has been successfully operating its businesses as an HR service provider for decades, this was an opportunity to further the business. Awaji Island was not simply a peaceful location to host its headquarters' functions permanently away from the negative effects of a big city, but also the ideal environment where Pasona could utilize its expertise and actively participate in the tourism industry.

THE MILK AND HONEY IN THE PROMISED LAND: MAKING HRM A SUCCESS

Pasona's transferring of headquarters' functions from Tokyo to Awaji Island has brought about major changes in the work styles and lifestyles of headquarters' employees as well as the locals. Most of these changes are bearing good fruit at this stage, pointing to the effectiveness of the HRM practices associated with the decision to relocate. Pasona's promised land, Awaji Island, is expected to provide plenty of milk and honey to the employees who willingly settle there.

IDEAL PLACE TO LIVE AND WORK: EMPLOYEES' QUALITY OF LIFE IMPROVED

One of the move's highlighted successes is the dramatic improvement in the well-being of Pasona's employees. The integrated environment where employees can work while enjoying the nature of Awaji Island has contributed greatly to maintaining a good physical, mental, and social state of mind for Pasona's employees. As its offices, Pasona used some of the facilities of the Yumebutai, a huge resort facility originally located on Awaji Island. This allows employees to experience the beautiful natural scenery of the ocean and mountains during work hours, while simultaneously interacting with various people, such as parents, children, students, and the elderly visiting the island for leisure. This enables employees to interact with nature, which is a rare experience in Tokyo, while still being able to interact with a variety of people, which is one of the big advantages of big cities like Tokyo that could have been lost due to the move (Yamamoto, 2021).

Another positive aspect is that Pasona is now able to provide specific support to its employees in maintaining a good work-life balance. The establishment of a daycare facility for employees' children is one of the highlights in this respect. Awaji Island allows for ample office space, making it easy to provide multipurpose spaces other than work areas within the office. The Pasona Family Office – an area dedicated to daycare facilities – also offers English language lessons, as well as ballet and karate lessons, among others. The employees are now able to lead a more relaxed family life in terms of both saving time (no need to travel to the daycare facility) and maintaining peace of mind (Newswitch, 2020).

Furthermore, Pasona has succeeded in improving the lifestyles of the employees' immediate families. Families that used to live in densely crowded, compact areas of Tokyo can now enjoy living in an open environment on Awaji Island that offers clean air, fresh food, and a beautiful view. Many employees and their families feel that the slightly cold atmosphere and the unspoken sense of distrust and insecurity present in the city have been dispelled. A Pasona manager, who moved to the island with her husband and child, said, "The living environment on Awaji Island is safer than in Tokyo, so I feel more secure when I send my child off to school" (Newswitch, 2020).

Family welfare is not limited to the comfortable living environment but also extends to aspects that contribute to their well-being, such as quality education and medical care. When Pasona relocated some of its headquarters' functions, it consulted the local government and schools on Awaji Island to ensure that the children of relocating employees could continue school without interruption. Pasona is also considering inviting an international school to Awaji Island in the near future, thereby endeavoring to increase the options for the education of its employees' children. For medical care, Pasona invited in-house physicians to Awaji Island to ensure that employees and their families could receive the same level of medical services found in Tokyo. With these efforts, Pasona is endeavoring to create an optimal working and living environment where employees can work comfortably and effectively while enjoying the conveniences of city life that they could potentially miss due to the move.

IDEAL PLACE TO REVITALIZE: CORPORATE SOCIAL RESPONSIBILITY

With this ongoing project of relocating the headquarters' functions, Pasona is continuing to revitalize Awaji Island's economy, which they initiated back in 2008, through implementing various business models and opportunities that could benefit the island and its inhabitants. For example, the company renovated and reused closed schools on the island to house a company that trains employees for the tourism industry. In addition, Pasona is building restaurants and various tourist facilities that go hand in hand with the island's charm, as well as an amusement park that combines animation with the island's natural beauty to boast the flow of people to the island (Newswitch, 2021).

As part of establishing an efficient work environment for the employees, a new telecommunication infrastructure has been developed that covers a wide area of the island, and it is expected to play a vital role in supporting the tourism industry as well. Communication networks have become much stronger for the residents on the island as well. These changes not only benefit Pasona's employees but also positively contribute toward improving the islanders' quality of life.

CONTINUING TO CULTIVATE AND DEVELOP THE PROMISED LAND: HRM'S CHALLENGES

Pasona has already achieved much by relocating some of its headquarters' functions. However, there are challenges that need to be addressed to attract more families to the promised land, to help them settle down, and continue to provide for them and other local residents. Some 1,200 employees' jobs are scheduled to be relocated by spring 2024. In addition to securing housing for all the migrants, guaranteeing livelihoods for accompanying family members, and arranging schools for children, Pasona needs to continue improving the infrastructures for telecommunication, transportation, water supply, waste management, and so on. This could prove to be a tall order for Pasona to handle alone; hence, it would require additional efforts to lobby the government and local authorities.

A more difficult HRM-related issue is that even if the employees responsible for the head-quarters' functions are scheduled to relocate from Tokyo, not all of them may be looking for-ward to the move. In spite of the better living and working environment, and in spite of the advanced communication networks and medical care facilities, it is hard for some to forget the lifestyles and extended networks they have established in Tokyo. In encouraging additional employees to willfully make the move to Awaji Island, Pasona will have to approach individuals on a more personal level to support their decision-making process and the subsequent reloca-tion. For example, when an employee born and raised in the city relocates, it may be effective to first live in a neighboring city where commuting to Awaji Island is possible, rather than abruptly making the move to a local town on Awaji Island. Sufficient time and effort will be needed in advance to mentally prepare and care for each employee in a unique way so that one can go through and withstand major changes taking place in and around their life. Pasona will also have to become not only a resource provider but also the actual engineer in forming a figurative bridge between the migrants and the locals during this move.

Pasona may have a bigger challenge ahead in completing its headquarters' relocation to Awaji Island. Even if the headquarters' major functions begin to operate on Awaji Island, not all the cogwheels of the business may fit into place as they did in Tokyo. As mentioned earlier, the company's headquarters plays a special role that requires it to be traditionally located in an economic and knowledge hub that provides ready access to vast amounts of information on a daily basis, spotting possible dangers and opportunities in the business arena. In this regard, Pasona may have to make extra efforts to effectively relocate and manage its existing knowledge networks with other partners outside the company. Pasona will have to maintain its presence in the network from a distance.

CONCLUSION

No doubt, moving away from Tokyo can reduce operational costs regarding both office mainte-nance and labor as the land prices and living expenses are considerably cheaper in rural areas (NEC, 2021). However, many large corporations headquartered in Tokyo have not yet realized the need to relocate their headquarters. Pasona is boldly moving against the flow, and it claims to have achieved some success. One of the reasons for Pasona's success is that it has a long and strong relationship with Awaji Island to which it relocated. Another reason is that although Awaji Island is in a rural area of Japan, it provides relatively easy access to the infrastructural requirements of a community. There are many areas where conditions are not as favorable as Awaji Island; hence, it may not be possible for other companies to imitate Pasona's relocation path as quickly and effectively.

Even if there is an ideal and attractive location to move to that is away from the bustling city, how feasible will it be for companies to relocate their headquarters from Tokyo while sustain-ably developing their existing businesses? Will such a move revolutionize the way people work for the better? Will an increasing number of companies find meaning in Pasona's quest? We do not know the answers yet. But it is safe to say that having in place a strategy to tap into the best of economic and knowledge hubs such as Tokyo, where synergistic activities evolve, will play a key role in successful relocations. To this end, the enterprise's novel digital transformation strategies become a key ingredient.

Many people are now beginning to learn how to communicate smoothly with internal and external entities through virtual means. Each company has entered a phase of creating new values for corporate operations and HRM that are not bound by the former methods. Some companies believe that the ideal environment for synergistic information sharing is no longer a place where people physically gather. Pasona believes that in-person interactions are essential, but they must be in an environment that enables the employees' work, personal, and family lives to thrive on equal footing. Only time will tell which school of thought survives.

ACKNOWLEDGMENTS

We would like to thank Ms. Kinuko Yamamoto (Executive Officer and Vice President/Director, Pasona Group Inc.), Ms. Mariko Ueki (Executive Officer, Pasona Group Inc.), and Ms. Tomoko Sudo (Pasona Group Inc.) for their generous support in writing this case.

CASE STUDY QUESTIONS FOR DISCUSSION

1. How does the nature of employees' work-life balance differ between working in a big city such as Tokyo and working in a rural area such as Awaji Island?

2. Other than the examples introduced in this chapter, what other corporate social responsibility pursuits can Pasona consider on Awaji Island regarding further improvements in the quality of life for both its employees and the locals?

3. If the employees who are asked to relocate to Awaji Island from Tokyo hesitate to do so, how could Pasona manage such a situation? What would be the potential incentives for those reluctant employees to make the move?

REFERENCES

Dedoussis, V. 1995. Simply a question of cultural barriers? The search for new perspectives in the transfer of Japanese management practices. *Journal of Management Studies*, 32(6): 731–745.

Honjo, M. 1998. The growth of Tokyo as a world city. In F. Lo & Y-M. Yeung (Eds.), *Globalization and the World of Large Cities*. United Nations University.

NEC, Orchestrating a Brighter World, April 16, 2021. Retrieved from https://www.nec-solutioninnovators.co.jp/sp/contents/column/20210416.html. Accessed: July 12, 2022.

Newswitch, November 26, 2020. Retrieved from https://newswitch.jp/p/24806. Accessed: July 12, 2022.

Newswitch, June 25, 2021. Retrieved from https://newswitch.jp/p/27745. Accessed: July 12, 2022.

UK Economic Outlook, November 2009. *UK Blogs*. Retrieved from https://pwc.blogs.com/files/global-city-gdp-rankings-2008-2025.pdf. Accessed: July 12, 2022.

Yamamoto, K. 2021. Establishment of industry in regional revitalization: Partial relocation of headquarters functions to Awaji Island and new ways of working (Japanese). Presented at the 24th Annual Conference of the Japanese Association of Administrative Science, online.

CHAPTER 24

Singapore

On Cheong's Human Resource Legacy

Audrey Chia

CASE SYNOPSIS

On Cheong Jewelry was founded in Singapore in 1936. As the business grew, it continued to value employee loyalty and retention, while adopting human resource management (HRM) practices that allowed employees to continue to learn, train, and re-train. These practices evolved to make On Cheong an age-friendly, multi-generational workplace. Some employees have worked at On Cheong for 60 years or more. In the coming years, almost half of On Cheong's employees will approach or have reached retirement age. How can On Cheong renew its workforce while holding on to its values of employee loyalty, engagement, and lifelong learning?

KEYWORDS

Age-friendly, inclusive, diversity, change and continuity, multi-generational workforce, Singapore

LEARNING OUTCOMES

1. Realize that even in a small- or medium-sized business, age-friendly and inclusive human resource management practices can be adopted.

DOI: 10.4324/9781003307099-29

2. Gain insight into how age-inclusive workplace practices can benefit the business, its customers, and its employees.
3. Consider the challenges and risks associated with culture and change during workforce renewal.

INTRODUCTION

Singapore is a city-state of 728 square kilometers, situated one degree north of the equator. A former British colony that gained independence in 1965, Singapore has steadily progressed to become a high-income country with one of the world's most competitive economies (IMD World Competitiveness Ranking, 2021).

According to the Department of Statistics in Singapore, the population of Singapore was 5.45 million in 2021. Among citizens, the proportion aged 65 and above was 17.6% and is expected to rise to 23.8% by 2030. Its three major ethnic groups are Chinese (75.9%), Malay (15.1%), and Indian (7.4%) (Department of Statistics, Singapore). The life expectancy at birth of Singapore residents is among the highest in the world. In 2020, life expectancy at birth was 83.9 years: 86.1 years for females and 81.5 years for males. Life expectancy at the age of 65 in 2020 was 23.2 years for females and 19.6 years for males.

With rising life expectancy and an aging population, Singapore's statutory retirement age – which protects employees from dismissal on grounds of age – will increase from 62 in 2021 to 65 in 2030. The Ministry of Manpower in Singapore has required employers to allow employees to continue working until the re-employment[1] age of 67 (in 2021), subject to a review of terms of employment such as job scope, hours, pay, and benefits. The re-employment age will be raised to 70 by 2030.

AN OVERVIEW OF JEWELRY RETAIL IN SINGAPORE

In Singapore, as in many other cultures, jewelry has deep cultural significance. It is given on special occasions such as births, birthdays, and weddings. The Singapore history site roots.gov .sg details Singapore's ethnic wedding customs and the significance of jewelry. In Indian and Chinese communities, gold jewelry of high purity (22 or 24 karats) is traditionally presented to the bride. Among the Chinese in Singapore, it is customary for the bride to receive "four points of gold" – a ring, bangle, necklace, and pair of earrings – from the groom's family. According to traditional Indian wedding customs, brides wear gold jewelry from head to toe; the amount and weight of jewelry are considered indicators of status. Jewelry is worn by Indian men and women on festive and religious occasions. Besides being used as adornment, gold jewelry is a store of value. It serves decorative, cultural, and economic functions, giving a measure of financial security to the owner.

As Singapore developed, so did tastes in jewelry. Traditional goldsmiths expanded their product range beyond gold, jade, and rose-cut diamonds to include jewelry with brilliant-cut diamonds and gemstones, and contemporary designs. Jewelry continued to be handed from one generation to the next as family heirlooms.

With globalization and rising affluence, Singapore saw the entry of international jewelry brands, including Harry Winston, Graff, Cartier, Van Cleef & Arpels, Tiffany, and Bulgari. These brands competed in the high jewelry segment and also produced "entry-level" products for brand aspirants. Their offerings broadened the range of jewelry choices in Singapore.

Competition for the jewelry business rose further with the online stores. Customers in Singapore can browse jewelry in magnified and rotatable detail at James Allen, Blue Nile, Leibish, and other international stores. They can also chat online with jewelry consultants. Online shopping platforms like Lazada and Shopee provide access to a host of Asian jewelry brands like Chow Tai Fook and home-grown brands like Lee Hwa Jewelry, with monthly discounts and specials. During the COVID-19 pandemic, auction houses Sotheby's, Christie's, Phillips, and Bonhams started to sell jewelry online, with much success (Financial Times, 2020).

Competition for Singapore's jewelry business has intensified and will continue to increase. How has a local, 85-year-old jewelry retailer managed to survive and thrive in such an environment? Over the decades, On Cheong has continued to adapt, re-imagine, and refresh its jewelry business, while remaining true to its founder's values.

ON CHEONG JEWELRY

On Cheong Jewelry was established on December 25, 1936. Its headquarters and main showroom are at 251 South Bridge Rd, the location it has occupied since 1941. Another showroom is on New Bridge Road, 400 meters away. Along South Bridge Road, which is part of Singapore's Chinatown, are shophouses with a range of businesses: Traditional bakeries, restaurants, traditional Chinese medicine, grilled pork jerky, cafes, pawnbroking, souvenirs, gems and minerals, and others.

On Cheong is a family-owned, family-run business. As explained on its website, the name "On Cheong" or "安昌" in Chinese is from the phrase "平安昌盛" (peace and prosperity). Its founder, Ho Yew Ping, was born in Guangdong, China. In 1925, aged 14, he moved to Malaya to seek work and became an apprentice in a goldsmith's shop. He later returned to Guangdong to marry Leung Chew Fun, and they moved to Singapore. In 1936, he founded a small goldsmith business, which he named On Cheong. He acquired two other goldsmith businesses in the 1940s, then incorporated his company as On Cheong Company Private Limited in 1949. After his death in 1965, his wife managed the business with help from her brother-in-law Ho Teck Fan and two nephews. Her eldest son Dr Ho Nai Kiong, a neonatologist, assumed the role of chairman but did not participate in day-to-day operations. This continued until 1982 when Madam Leung persuaded her youngest son Charles Ho Nai Chuen to work in the family business.

Charles Ho had graduated with an accountancy degree from the University of Singapore. He had worked as an auditor at Coopers and Lybrand Public Accountants and had been seconded to Brunei Shell Petroleum as a management consultant. Upon his mother's request, he left his position to work at On Cheong. After working for five months, he applied for a master's degree in business administration to fulfill a personal ambition and to explore an academic career in case working in the family business was found to be unsuitable.

In 1985, Madam Leung passed away, 40 days after her youngest son Charles returned to Singapore with an MBA from Aston University, UK. His mother's death prompted Charles Ho to reach a decision. He observed that his older siblings were occupied with their own careers, so he committed to continuing the family business. He obtained his professional qualification as a chartered management accountant in 1986 while learning as much as he could about the jewelry business. He studied gemology and design, obtaining a certificate from the Gemological Institute of America. He learned every aspect of the family business from the ground up, starting in retail. In 1990, he assumed the role of managing director.

Under Mr. Charles Ho's leadership, On Cheong adopted the vision: "To be the leading heritage jewelry synonymous with distinctive value and excellent relationships with customers across generations" (On Cheong Jewelry website). To realize this vision, On Cheong adopted a human-centric approach. Externally, it focused on customer needs, changing trends, and service. Internally, On Cheong focused on nurturing "long-lasting, cohesive relationships with staff". It sought to do so by "offering a conducive and satisfying working environment; and creating challenging opportunities for lifelong learning and skills upgrading" (On Cheong Jewelry website).

To adapt to changing trends and customer preferences, On Cheong regularly refreshed and rebranded its look and appeal. In the last five years, its two showrooms have been redesigned in soothing hues of green and cream. Salespersons wear smart gray suits or shirts with ties. The windows and showcases display jewelry in a variety of designs from vintage to Art Deco and modern. On Cheong's in-house designers have also created hybrid designs that combine auspicious traditional symbols such as "bi" (safety disk) or "ruyi" ("as you wish") with contemporary designs and materials. Besides gold and platinum, the jewelry pieces feature diamonds, jadeite, rubies, sapphires, emeralds, tourmalines, aquamarines, tsavorites, and other gemstones. On Cheong's customization and design services allow customers to create their own unique jewelry.

Prices at On Cheong range from $200 for a small gold pendant, to over $300,000 for high-end pieces with imperial jadeite or gemstones. For transparency, the price of gold, which varies from day to day, is displayed at the shop entrance.

EMPLOYEES OF ON CHEONG

Jewelry stores can seem forbidding, but On Cheong's stores were designed to be open and welcoming. There are no heavy doors or stern-looking guards. The stores open to the walkway. Passers-by can catch a glimpse of the retail staff as they walk by, and one who steps into the South Bridge Road store is likely to be greeted by a neatly dressed, older gentleman with a genial face: Mr. Tong Kwok Meng. Mr. Tong joined On Cheong when he was 16 and has worked there for 60 years. His father also worked at On Cheong, as a jewelry craftsman.

On Cheong has 32 full-time employees and one part-time employee. These employees work in different functions: finance, human resources, marketing, inventory, information technology and administration, design, and retail. On Cheong has more female employees (19) than male (14). Twenty-two employees are above the age of 50; five are in their 70s and one is in his 80s. The average age of On Cheong employees is 55 years. The employees' tenure at On Cheong ranges from less than five to over 60 years, with an average of 21 years.

On Cheong has been featured regularly by government agencies, Human resource management associations, and news media for creating an age-inclusive workplace and offering career opportunities and progression regardless of age or gender. In 2012, On Cheong received an

Exemplary Employer Award from the Tripartite Alliance for Fair and Progressive Employment Practices (TAFEP), for its fair, responsible, and progressive employment practices. TAFEP also recognized On Cheong as an Outstanding Workplace for Mature Employees.

In an interview, Charles Ho remarked that On Cheong retains employees

> as long as they are keen to stay on, can contribute to the company effectively, and have a clean bill of health.... Our older employees have...(a) wealth of experience...a multi-generational workforce will benefit all employees as there is much to learn from one another.
> *(The Active Age, 2015)*

On Cheong emphasizes continuous learning and training; reciprocal mentoring; and age-friendly practices.

LIFELONG LEARNING

The emphasis on lifelong learning is evident in On Cheong's twice-yearly identification of employees' learning needs by functional heads. HR managers create a learning roadmap, obtain approval from the functional heads and managing director, and then communicate the learning calendar to employees.

Employees are required to obtain a Workforce Skills Qualification Certificate in Service Excellence from Workforce Singapore. Each year, all employees attend a minimum of 16 hours training in job-related skills. For example, managers and potential leaders were enrolled in a diploma program in leadership and people management, offered by the government agency Workforce Singapore. Each employee is also required to undergo eight hours of personal development training each year, on topics such as personal grooming, business etiquette, mindfulness, and time and stress management.

Financial support is provided for employees to pursue further education to obtain a certificate, diploma, or degree. Employees are given leave to take examinations as part of their further education.

An additional three days of study leave are given to encourage employees to enroll in SkillsFuture training. SkillsFuture is Singapore's "national movement to provide Singaporeans with the opportunities to develop their fullest potential throughout life" and contribute to "Singapore's next phase of development towards an advanced economy and inclusive society" (SkillsFuture, 2015). All employees who are citizens and permanent residents are given SkillsFuture training credit by the government. On Cheong encourages employees to use their SkillsFuture credit to enhance their skills and knowledge in jewelry design, customer service, sales and marketing, productivity and innovation, accounting and finance, and human resource management.

Learning is both encouraged and rewarded. Upon completion of certified programs, employees stand a chance of being promoted, based on merit. On Cheong adopts the policies of "promote from within" and "replace from within". Mr. Lee Chim Sam started work at On Cheong in 2000 and is now the operations manager at the New Bridge Road branch. He credited the training programs for his development and preparation for his managerial role. On a personal level, he learned to project a positive and professional image, negotiate and close sales, and respond to service challenges. For his managerial role, he learned how to promote workplace diversity, manage the store's sales performance and operations, and provide guidance and direction to staff.

Career paths are created based on employees' aptitudes, potential, skills, and interests. Employees can move across functional areas to learn different aspects of the business. Some employees have roles that span more than one function, for example, jewelry design and marketing. Ms. Jenny Johnson, who joined On Cheong as a retail executive, was given the opportunity to design some of On Cheong's signature, high-end jewelry. She also had a competency for conducting training and subsequently assumed the role of internal trainer. Ms. Kek Kim Chin, On Cheong's visual merchandising leader, was first hired as a jewelry executive. Having undergone training in digital and computer-assisted design for jewelry, she now designs On Cheong's signature collections and creates custom designs. Mr. Kartono Lim originally held a retail role. He subsequently acquired certificates in information technology (IT) to support On Cheong's digital transformation. He was later promoted to assistant operations manager, overseeing administration and IT.

On Cheong received the WSQ Most Supportive Employer Award in 2015, the SkillsFuture Employer Award in 2017, and the SkillsFuture Fellowships Award in 2018.

INCLUSIVE AND AGE-FRIENDLY WORK CULTURE

Reciprocal Buddy System

On Cheong has adopted a buddy system that pairs a more experienced employee with a younger one, for reciprocal mentoring and coaching. The mature employee mentors the younger: Sharing advice, insights, and customer service skills. Younger employees assist mature employees in technology adoption. On the transition from paper-based invoicing to a computer-based Point of Sale system, Mr. Tong commented:

> Instead of imposing a fixed timeline … we were paired up with younger colleagues who assisted us in embracing new technology…On Cheong values my experience and gives me the opportunity to upgrade myself. Whether you have been with the company for 50 years or five years, everyone is given an equal chance to upgrade.
>
> *(Tripartite Alliance for Fair Employment Practices, 2013)*

He chuckled when recounting his early years, "It was not easy using the abacus! With the computer, we have the information in front of us. It is better."

Human Resource Management Practices

On Cheong's inclusive culture and practices are reflected in its recruitment practices. Their job advertisements state only the requisite qualifications, skills, knowledge, and experience. Job application forms ask only for job-relevant information. No information is sought on age, date of birth, gender, race, religion, marital status, and family responsibilities.

Interviews, tests, and role-plays are used to assess applicants' competencies. Equally important, the recruitment process aims to identify the extent of similarity between applicants' values and those of the company: Care, trust, and passion. For example, a test question related to care might ask, "You notice that one of your colleagues is not in a good mood. What would you do?" The recruitment process seeks and gives weight to the alignment of personal values with those of the company.

Employee Engagement and Well-Being

Employee engagement is explicitly mentioned as part of On Cheong's mission to provide a conducive and satisfying work environment. Ms. Veronica Lim, the retail manager at On Cheong's South Bridge Road branch recounted,

> When I first came to work at On Cheong more than 30 years ago, employees would all have a meal together on the third floor of the shophouse before starting work. After work, we would dine together again, before leaving for home. A cook was hired to prepare the meals. On festive occasions, our founder's wife would cook special dishes for us. Working here is like joining a big family.

While the twice-daily shophouse meals are no longer a feature of work at On Cheong, the sense of family persists.

On Cheong engages employees through a variety of activities: Off-site team-building exercises, lunch-together sessions, learning days, and inter-department staff meetings that keep them informed and allow them to voice their views. There are also regular dialogue sessions with Managing Director Charles Ho.

On Cheong's corporate responsibility program gives employees a chance to contribute to the surrounding community. From 2018 to 2020, employees volunteered at Yong-En Care Center, which is situated in Chinatown. The Center provides dementia care and programs for active aging to elderly residents and in-kind aid to disadvantaged families. On Cheong employees distributed bread to low-income families and helped at the dementia care center. In 2022, employees participated in a beach clean-up.

On Cheong has a Workplace Health and Promotion committee that focuses on employee health, safety, and well-being. There are programs on healthy eating, exercise, and safety and security at work. Managing Director Charles Ho also leads physical exercises as part of staff engagement.

Attention is paid to the physical aspects of work. To create a well and age-friendly workplace, On Cheong employees are encouraged to regularly change their posture at work. They can choose to sit or stand while working. Rest areas are provided for employees to take breaks and have snacks or meals. At the end of each day, all items of jewelry are scanned, removed from the showcases and windows, and placed on trolleys that are then wheeled into the strong room. Because of the sheer number and weight of pieces, the task takes some physical effort. To lighten the physical burden on older employees, the trolleys were made lighter, and the strong room was moved from the second story to the ground floor (HRM Magazine, 2015). Tasks that are more physically demanding are usually carried out by younger staff. In 2017 and 2019, On Cheong was given Singapore Health Awards by the Health Promotion Board for excellence in workplace health.

On Cheong's focus on meaningful work and productive longevity attracted Lily Chan, an experienced jewelry specialist, to join the company. She said,

> I knew about On Cheong long before I joined the team, and I admired how progressive the company seemed, so when I was given the opportunity, I leapt at the chance...we are constantly upgrading and improving ourselves – from customer service, to design, to knowledge about our gems and jewels. It is a never-ending journey of learning and growing, regardless of age.

This focus on learning also extends to customers. Before the COVID-19 pandemic, On Cheong regularly hosted workshops for both children and adults on jewelry making, its heritage, and holiday arts and craft.

On Cheong's inclusiveness and diversity are mirrored by its customers, who consist of Chinese, Indian, and Malay locals, foreign residents, and tourists. Local customers span generations. It is not uncommon to see parents with their children, or grandchildren with their grandparents. A 96-year-old regular customer, who often visited the store with her 28-year-old granddaughter, commented: "Other than trust and service, what makes me come back to On Cheong is the people...(they) are so friendly and warm-hearted" (On Cheong Jewelry Facebook). This customer referred to Ms. Yvonne Yip, a jewelry specialist whose lively personality and passion for customer service helped forge relationships with customers. Ms. Yip has worked at On Cheong for 23 years.

On Cheong's retail employees are paid a salary and bonuses. The company chose not to pay sales commissions, for two reasons. The first was to reduce the risk of unhealthy competition among employees, and instead promote collaboration and prosocial behavior. The second was to encourage staff to listen to customers' needs and preferences before making recommendations, and not engage in a hard sell.

REMAINING COMPETITIVE

Under Charles Ho's leadership, On Cheong has undergone several transformations. During the Asian Financial Crisis of 1997–1998, he made the strategic decision to focus more on custom-made, one-of-a-kind jewelry and less on mass-market offerings. He also created a niche for On Cheong in high-quality, Type A (natural and untreated) jadeite (Singapore Memory Project). The popularity of jadeite has since widened, and prices of jadeite have escalated worldwide (CNN, 27 September 2016)

To mark On Cheong's 80th anniversary in 2016 and 85th anniversary in 2021, special logos and commemorative jewelry collections were launched. On Cheong tapped into its heritage and progressive practices to position itself as a jeweler that blends modernity with heritage. Its tagline, "Crafted by time, cherished for generations" is used to position its jewelry as products of tradition and heirlooms of the future.

To engage the public, On Cheong uses social media such as Facebook, Telegram, and Instagram. Its promotions and National Day sale, held in August each year, help to drive business. During the COVID-19 pandemic, On Cheong increased the number of items in its online store and held additional promotions and sales. In 2021, On Cheong was recognized by the Singapore Tourism Board among brands that are "Made with Passion" and represent the best of Singapore's identity.

CASE STUDY QUESTIONS FOR DISCUSSION

1. In the coming years, On Cheong's loyal and mature employees will grow older and some might choose to retire. Six employees are already over 70, and 15 are over the age of 60. This means that almost half the employees are near or over the retirement age. How should On Cheong renew its workforce? Should it recruit and nurture a new cohort of younger employees? Should employees be hired early in their career, perhaps right out of school, as has been the case for many of the current employees? Should On Cheong also hire more mature employees and people with longer work experience, who may have worked in other organizations and industries? They could bring their skills, experience, and new ideas to On Cheong.

2. It also seems likely that the next generation of employees may not stay with On Cheong for decades, or for life. How might this affect or change On Cheong's culture, which has emphasized warm, long-term relationships among employees? How could the sense of belonging and familial identity be cultivated?

3. The tenure of employees also has implications for customer relations. Would it be more difficult for On Cheong to continue to foster long-term relationships with customers if its employees do not remain in the company for as many years as before?

4. Finally, how could On Cheong continue its legacy as a human-centric organization that recognizes and appreciates the diversity and potential of each employee? Could On Cheong's notion of "Crafted by time, cherished for generations" apply equally to its employees and work culture?

NOTE

1   "Re-employment refers to the re-contracting of employees who have reached the retirement age, to allow them to continue working if they are willing and able to. This is done by offering such employees a re-employment contract."

REFERENCES

Aaron, K. 2015. An ageing workforce part 5: In conversation with Charles Ho. *The Active Age*, January 6, 2015. http://activeage.co/ageing-workforce-part-5-interview-charles-ho/

About Skills Future. 2015. https://www.skillsfuture.gov.sg/AboutSkillsFuture

Best practices of on Cheong jewellery. *HRM Magazine* 15(4), April 23, 2015. https://issuu.com/hrmasia/docs/hrm_15.04_e-zine_pdf/41

Department of Statistics, Singapore. https://www.singstat.gov.sg/

IMD World Competitiveness Ranking. 2021. https://www.imd.org/centers/world-competitiveness-center/rankings/world-competitiveness/

Making of Gold Jewelry by Indian Goldsmiths. https://www.roots.gov.sg/ich-landing/ich/making-of-gold-jewelry-by-indian-goldsmiths

McCafferty, G. 2016. Fifty shades of jade: Why Chinese buyers spend millions on this stone. *CNN*, Sept 27, 2016. https://edition.cnn.com/style/article/jade-supply-influencing-style/index.html

Ministry of Manpower, Singapore. https://www.mom.gov.sg/

On Cheong: About us. https://oncheong.com/about-us/

On Cheong Jewelry Facebook. https://www.facebook.com/oncheong1936/

Singapore Memory Project. 2015. On Cheong Jewelry. https://www.singaporememory.sg/contents/SMA-58f4315b-bc69-4155-8018-ebfb92174362

Tripartite Alliance for Fair & Progressive Employment Practices. 2013. *Annual Review & Inclusive Workplaces in Singapore.* https://docplayer.net/22564034-Annual-review-inclusive-workplaces-in-singapore.html

Youde, K. Online sales success shines a light in the gloom of luxury auctions. *Financial Times*, Sept 5, 2020. https://www.ft.com/content/8e787737-e0c8-42ce-ad4f-fd7dd191305f

Supplementary Resources

Chinatown Historic District (this provides a sense of On Cheong's location and surroundings). https://www.ura.gov.sg/services/download_file.aspx?f={70ECC8CB-F09A-4F46-8137-C90573AEE3FD}

On Cheong Jewelry on Instagram. https://www.instagram.com/oncheongjewellery1936/?hl=en

Staudinger, U. M. (2015). Images of aging: Outside and inside perspectives. https://cgt.columbia.edu/wp-content/uploads/2016/03/Images-of-Aging-Outside-and-Inside-Perspectives.pdf

The new map of life. https://longevity.stanford.edu/the-new-map-of-life-initiative/

CHAPTER 25

South Korea

Selecting and Developing Senior Leaders at Company A

Huh-Jung Hahn, Joonghak Lee, and Sewon Kim

CASE SYNOPSIS

Company A[1] is one of the largest for-profit organizations in South Korea. The company has been successful in many sectors. However, recent radical changes in technology and business culture and environments have continuously threatened Company A's competitiveness and profitability. One main problem that had emerged was that an increasing number of newly promoted senior leaders were found to have non-satisfactory performances, and almost half of them were terminated following a recent annual personnel review process. This issue was primarily attributed to Company A's leadership not being aptly prepared to take on the challenges and responsibilities inherent to novel business areas. This case describes how Company A formed its current selection practices for senior leaders and developed programs aiming to help those chosen leaders flourish in new business environments.

KEYWORDS

Confucianism, high-context culture, assessment center, leadership competency, South Korea

DOI: 10.4324/9781003307099-30

LEARNING OUTCOMES

1. Describe the cultural characteristics of HRM practices in South Korea.
2. Identify the differences between high-context and low-context cultures.
3. Discuss how the country- or organization-specific cultures influence HRM practices.
4. Explain the key components of an assessment center (AC).
5. Discuss how an AC is designed and implemented.

INTRODUCTION

The atmosphere in the office has been tense over the past few months. Major news outlets have reported extensively on how Company A is experiencing major turnover in its leadership by changing more than 40% of its executives. For the past ten years at Company A, Manager Y has dealt with selecting and developing senior leaders. Previously, for him, the day of the announcement of the annual executive promotions garnered much anticipation and celebration; this year, however, he is unenthusiastic and senses the gloom. What happened to Company A? In this case, we present an in-depth analysis examining the human resource management (HRM)-related issues contributing to the current outcome, as well as the culturally transformative steps taken to resolve these matters.

TRADITIONAL CULTURAL ENVIRONMENTS OF HRM IN SOUTH KOREA

Traditionally, Confucianism is considered one of the most fundamental influences for forming organizational cultures and HRM practices in South Korea (hereafter, Korea) (Froese et al., 2018). At its core, the Confucian value system upholds abiding by seniority, maintaining collective harmony, and following a paternal hierarchy (Bae et al., 2011; House et al., 2004). Seniority is often a leading criterion in HRM practices, such as in promotion and compensation, and has even extended its reach to performance appraisal techniques. Therefore, seniority-based HRM has been widely adopted in Korean organizations. In regard to maintaining harmonious relationships throughout the organization, superiors evaluate subordinates leniently to avoid confrontation. A firm's emphasis on harmony has traditionally led to fewer layoffs and a greater focus on internal promotion and development and long-term employment. In return, strong loyalty and commitment are expected from employees. Furthermore, in the hierarchical relationship structure, top-down decision-making is very common, and the major role of managers is to support their employees and their well-being akin to a father figure in a family. Paternalistic managers tend to care about employees' personal needs and interests and consider how their decision will affect the extended family (the organization) (Chai et al., 2016). This management style is also known to boost operational efficiency, mainly by reducing the time it takes to make important decisions, leading to faster execution. Despite such merits, the paternalistic management style can result in the neglect of employees' voices in suggestions and changes, as leadership does not always involve their employees in the decision-making process and is rarely openly challenged (Choi, 2004).

In addition to the practices mentioned above, a "high-context" culture (Hall, 1976; House et al., 2004) is profoundly embedded in communication and interactions within Korean organizations (Kim et al., 1998). A "high-context" culture is characterized by indirect and implicit communication, as opposed to a "low-context" culture wherein employees frequently address each other in a more straightforward and explicit manner. Here, the main message lies in the context, which is not always verbalized, and the crux of problematic issues or behaviors is often not explicitly asserted at all (Barkai, 2008). Throughout the organization, such a "high-context" culture has a firm grasp on how employees are selected, evaluated, and developed.

In recent years, HRM practices in Korea have evolved toward adopting a mixture of traditional Eastern Confucian values and Western management principles. This change was spurred by the 1997 Asian financial crisis and the ensuing bailout by the International Monetary Fund (IMF), followed by the pervasive impact of globalization in the 2000s. These events have collectively brought on widespread pressure on Korean businesses to follow Western management principles, such as task- (versus relationship-) oriented performance evaluation and rewards and scientific- and data-based HRM practices (Bae & Lawler, 2000). As a result, Western and low-context communication styles have increasingly been adopted to boost employees' contributions and performances in many Korean companies.

ORGANIZATIONAL SETTING OF COMPANY A

Company A was founded nearly 50 years ago and is now one of the largest for-profit organizations in Korea. The company initially began in food service and manufacturing, later made the jump to the retail industry (where it was incredibly successful), and has been steadily expanding into several other sectors. Company A operates in over 30 countries with more than 50 affiliations and consists of approximately 100,000 employees worldwide. Annually, the revenue is an estimated $50 billion with approximately $10 billion in net profit. As is the case with many large companies in Korea, Company A is primarily owned and continues to be controlled by the original founder and his family members (this unique governance structure is called *Chaebol* in Korea). To this day, the founder's original management philosophy remains the strongest influence in every aspect of Company A's various businesses.

The founder's perspectives on people and work have heavily influenced many HRM practices. More specifically, these perspectives include lifetime employment, family-like organizational culture, high employee loyalty, and internal promotion policies. On the basis of Confucianism, the founder created a strong inclination toward those cultural values and principles and maintained such practices much longer than other companies of similar scale. As a notable example, while many Korean companies carried out massive layoffs during the Asian financial crisis in 1997, Company A sought to retain its employees by adhering to corporate core values and policies. The fact that nearly 90% of senior leaders are internally promoted and have decade-long tenures represents how well the company values and conducts internal development and promotion. However, after the incumbent chairman (the founder's son) took over Company A in the early 2010s, Western corporate operation practices were actively adopted throughout the organization. Nevertheless, his approach to the management of employees remains largely in line with the founder's.

HRM ISSUES AT COMPANY A

As any other commercial entity in the global economy may experience, the recent radical changes in technology and business environments have continuously threatened Company A's competitiveness and profitability. For example, the traditional retail business that had been very successful for the past decades for Company A has struggled to compete with fast-growing online retail companies. Moreover, ever since the COVID-19 pandemic, consumers have increasingly shifted their purchasing to online shopping platforms, significantly threatening the viability of most offline-centric retail businesses. Additionally, due to this consumer movement to the digital space, businesses in food service and chemicals, which have been the most profitable sectors of Company A, are constantly in need of routine restructuring and divestment. In this light, for the first time since its establishment in 1979, one of Company A's affiliates found itself needing to implement an early retirement program for older employees (approximately 40% of its total employees).

In such times of hardship, Company A inevitably needed to create new business opportunities to survive and flourish. To this point, the chairman and top leadership tried shifting the business focus from brick-and-mortar retail and chemical commodities to newer domains, such as online retail, biotechnology, and healthcare businesses. These changes have provided new streams of revenue and brought on considerable early success. However, over time, a glaring problem started to emerge: An increasing number of newly promoted senior leaders were found to have non-satisfactory performance. This issue was largely attributed to Company A's leadership not being aptly prepared to take on the challenges and responsibilities inherent to novel areas of business. The issue became strikingly evident following a recent annual personnel review process in which almost half of senior leaders were terminated – this was the highest percentage of termination ever in the history of Company A. After realizing that the company needed profoundly better ways to prepare for future opportunities, the chairman swiftly directed HRM functions to critically examine and reformulate their internal selection and development practices for senior leaders.

A major critique that arose from the reform process was the ambiguous and seemingly subjective criteria applied for assessing and developing senior leaders at Company A. In fact, it is not unusual for HRM work to be done within corporate silos without clear and shared criteria due to confidentiality reasons (English et al., 2007). These tendencies may be further bolstered by the country and the organization's culture. As mentioned above, in Confucian and high-context cultures prevalently found in Korea, there is often indirect and implicit communication among people, leaving many important points to be inferred; as a result, requests for explicit and precisely written criteria may not be easily accommodated. Moreover, due to the strong dominance of the founder or chairman (the *Chaebol* governance structure), HRM policies and actions based on objective measures could be easily overridden by the preferences, judgments, or decisions of top leadership.

It is understandable that much of present-day Korean HRM practices are firmly rooted in its cultural heritage. However, as indicated earlier, such traditional influences may also negatively contribute to breakdowns in communication and failure to reach a general consensus, thereby hindering the future success of an organization. Therefore, there is a major need to accurately identify the personal qualities and skills of highly effective leaders and broadly disseminate them for successful leadership selection and development. Below, we describe how Company A, through the adoption of Western and low-context HRM practices, developed and implemented a systematic approach that paved the path toward achieving this goal.

OUTCOMES OF ADDRESSING HRM ISSUES

Company A sought to create a new senior leadership selection and development system with an emphasis on transparent logic, data-driven criteria, and organization-specific contexts. More specifically, the company's HRM department developed a leadership competency model and designed an assessment center (AC), which utilizes a collection of performance and behavior evaluation techniques for competency assessment. The main role of the AC was to develop strategies and tools for assessing leadership competencies, such as realistic simulation exercises and psychometric tests utilized by trained assessors (Thornton & Rupp, 2006). As an application of what had been learned, the selection of the leadership pool was conducted based on the results of those assessments. Furthermore, those empirical data were continuously used to customize and improve a wide array of leadership development programs. Below, we describe in detail how the AC was implemented in the focal organization as Company A worked to address the aforementioned HRM issues.

Identification of Senior Leadership Competencies

For the proper implementation of the AC, Company A initially needed to identify the desired leadership competencies. For this, Company A's HRM department took the conventional approach to building a competency model. First, high-performing senior leaders were recruited by the HRM department for two-hour-long, in-depth interviews to identify critical success factors (e.g., behavioral characteristics, conceptual and technical skills, key work experiences, personal values, etc.) that differentiate themselves from average performers. Those high-performance leaders were identified by the chief executive officer (CEO) and the chief HRM officer along with other C-suite executives' recommendations. In addition, the high-performing senior leaders' supervisors, subordinates, and peers were also interviewed to offer their insights into the focal leaders' noteworthy qualities. Second, by utilizing a competency card approach, the relationships and patterns among the identified competencies were systematically reviewed and discussed in an in-depth manner, and those competencies found to be of similar nature were grouped into a higher-order category. Finally, all the competencies and relationships that emerged during the project were carefully verified using a two-step process: The HRM department initially distributed a validation survey to the interview participants as well as the remaining senior leaders who had not been interviewed for the project; and after the survey responses were collected by the HRM department, a modified competency model was shared with C-suite executives for final verification.

As shown in Figure 25.1, Company A's competency model for senior leaders consists of 12 competencies. These competencies are consolidated into the following four groups based

FIGURE 25.1 Leadership competency model of senior leaders at Company A

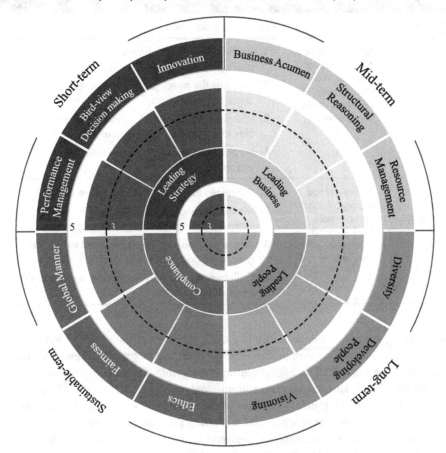

on the duration within which each competency is performed: Leading strategy (short-term), leading business (mid-term), leading people (long-term), and compliance (sustainable term). Each competency can also be assessed in the AC by specific behavioral indicators that are described in Table 25.1 (Company A permitted the disclosure of behavioral indicators for only two competencies).

Assessment Tools of the AC

Company A developed three different types of simulation exercises (in-basket, presentation, and role-play) and a comprehensive set of psychometric tests. 1) In-basket required AC participants to identify solutions to complicated tasks and conflicts within a limited timeframe. This tool was mainly used to measure the essential competencies of leaders, such as decision-making skills and business knowledge. 2) Presentation required the AC participants to first analyze a given problematic situation and then verbally communicate the main issues and key results to a group of assessors (described below). This assessment focused on evaluating how well one can pin down the cause of a problem and provide strategic advice in a logical and insightful manner.

TABLE 25.1 Definitions and behavioral indicators of competencies

Competency	Definition	Behavioral indicators
Innovation	Ability to drive organizational innovation by recognizing the need for innovation	1. Recognizes which changes are needed in the organization. 2. Spreads the need for innovation relevant to the organization's goals. 3. Identifies and eliminates resistance and obstacles to innovation in advance. 4. Introduces actions to drive innovation in the organization.
Bird's-eye view decision-making	Ability to lead the organization and promote work from an enterprise-wide perspective	1. Prioritizes the interests of the entire company. 2. Makes decisions and takes actions while considering the impact on the entire company. 3. Aligns the goals of the department to the strategies and goals of the organization. 4. Collaborates actively to create synergy with other departments.

3) Role-playing provided an opportunity to gauge interpersonal skills. More specifically, this tool was designed to assess communication, motivation, conflict management, and coaching skills, all of which are crucial for high-performing leadership. 4) Finally, the assessment of the in-house leadership quality test was also administered to the AC participants. This assessment incorporated not only the general five-factor model that assesses the general compatibility of one's traits and compositions to a potential leadership position (e.g., openness to experience, conscientiousness, extraversion, agreeableness, and neuroticism) but also additional organization-specific factors that could serve as predictive markers of leader success or derailment (e.g., innovation or excessive dominance) at Company A.

To ensure robust results, at least two simulation exercises, as well as the psychometric test, were utilized to assess each competency of senior leaders in Company A (see Table 25.2). Of note, the "X" in Table 25.2 indicates that a particular simulation exercise was used to assess the corresponding leadership competency.

Selecting and Training Assessors

The proper selection and training of assessors were imperative for the successful implementation of the AC. Company A invited a group of assessors consisting of internal members and external experts. The internal members were selected based on their past performance, job rank, age, and factors relevant to the assessment role and were often senior-level leaders with established track records. The external experts were mostly faculty from renowned national universities with academic backgrounds in business administration or industrial and organizational psychology.

Once determined, the assessors participated in a three full-day training workshop run by the HRM department and the external consulting group. They learned the role of the assessor, the

TABLE 25.2 Competency-assessment tool matrix

Group	Competency	Simulation exercise		
		In-basket	Presentation	Role-play
Leading strategy	Performance management		X	X
	Bird's-eye view decision-making	X	X	
	Innovation	X	X	
Leading Business	Business acumen	X	X	
	Structural reasoning	X	X	
	Resource management		X	X
Leading People	Diversity	X		X
	Developing people	X		X
	Visioning		X	X
Compliance	Ethics	X		X
	Fairness	X		X
	Global manner		X	X

competency model, and how to recognize high-performance indicators in each simulation and measurement. The assessors also participated in several mock assessment exercises, wherein two assessors were paired together and given opportunities to compare, recalibrate, or converge their initial scores and decisions. The purpose of the activity was for the assessors to develop shared and consistent approaches to their evaluations.

Rollout of the AC Practices

After training the assessors, Company A rolled out the AC practice sessions. In the first introductory session with the participants, the AC coordinators explained the following:

- What the competency model is and what its backgrounds are.
- Which competencies will be assessed and why.
- How each assessment session is to be conducted.
- How assessment results will be summarized and utilized.

Next, the assessors measured the participants' leadership competencies using the aforementioned simulation exercises and the in-house developed leadership quality test. In the following session, the assessors provided feedback and comments regarding the participants' performances in the test and exercises. Finally, after detailed reviews and discussions of the evaluation scores and recommendations among the assessors, the assessment results for each participant were summarized and finalized.

Applications of the Assessment Results

Selection

Prior to the adoption of the AC, the HRM department was accustomed to selecting leaders mostly based on their age, job rank, organizational tenure, reputation within the company, and the incumbent CEO's recommendation. Due to the implementation of the AC, a wealth of competency-based, empirical data has now become available for the decision-making of leadership selection. A general rule was to exclude a candidate from the pool if s/he had any competency that was two or more levels below the highest desired threshold. Additionally, the criteria for selection carried subtle differences for certain positions and industries in the decision-making process. For example, for a position that regularly required new business development in an evolving industry domain, candidates who scored low in innovation and bird's-eye view decision-making were promptly removed from further consideration, although it was the only competency below the threshold. On the other hand, those scoring high in openness to experience on the test were more positively considered in the selection process. Moreover, leader derailment factors identified by the leadership quality test were also taken into account for important selection and promotion decisions.

Development

The AC's empirical data were also used to strengthen senior leadership development programs. More content-specific and formalized training programs were designed or modified based on the leadership competency model. Individual development plans became more connected to the leadership competency model as well as the empirical data provided by the AC. An ongoing dialogue was also established between a senior leadership candidate, his/her supervisor, and the HRM department in the following areas:

- Which competencies are key to the candidate's potential leadership position.
- The gaps between the candidate's competency level and those required by the potential leadership position.
- A developmental plan that will provide the learning and experiences for the candidate to develop those required competencies.

The HRM department also arranged various developmental activities for the leadership candidates, including action learning, cross-functional rotations, project assignments, training courses, mentoring, and individualized learning. Particularly, the candidates were provided with an external executive coach upon their request after AC participation. Each candidate attended regular one-on-one sessions with the executive coach to enhance the desired leadership competencies. An HRM coordinator monitored the overall progress and made any necessary changes in coaching topics, often following consultations with the coach. Upon the completion of the first six coaching sessions, the HRM department shared reports with the candidates and designed new coaching plans if needed.

Cultural/Contextual Considerations in Implementing the AC

Despite there being standard guidelines for the implementation of any AC, particular cultural aspects (pertaining to Confucian values and organization-specific contexts) needed to be considered in a few key areas of the AC. For example, independent of their past track record, age and job rank were included as crucial factors for the selection of AC assessors – this was due to the seniority-based and hierarchical culture upheld in Confucian culture, wherein employees are much more open to and receptive to critical feedback from evaluators of higher age and rank.

Another example pertains to Company A offering a much more extensive and detailed introductory session (regarding the AC) to senior leader participants than what would be expected in Western culture organizations. This was due to the following: First and foremost, employees at Company A were largely unfamiliar with being systematically assessed by comprehensive and concrete methodologies. Additionally, as low-context communication felt foreign to the senior leaders, the successful implementation of various competency assessments was dependent on how well the HRM department provided – precisely and cautiously – instructions regarding the intricate details of the entire AC process, ranging from construction of the competency model and conducting the simulation exercises to the utilization of the results and follow-up after the AC. To this point, the HRM department dedicated a considerable amount of time in the introductory session to not only prepare the senior leaders for the AC by providing written instructions, video clips, and educational brochures but also to accommodate all questions, comments, and concerns.

CASE STUDY QUESTIONS FOR DISCUSSION

1. What are the core cultural characteristics of HRM practices in Korea? How would you compare them to those of your own country?
2. Describe the general advantages and disadvantages of an internal promotion and development system.
3. What challenges do you anticipate following Company A's recent changes to its practices for selecting and developing senior leaders?
4. What positive outcomes could emerge for Company A in the long term after the implementation of the AC for senior leaders?

NOTE

1 All names, dates, and other identifying information mentioned herein were modified with minor factual changes to preserve the privacy of Company A.

REFERENCES

Bae, J., & Lawler, J. J. 2000. Organizational and HRM strategies in Korea: Impact on firm performance in an emerging economy. *Academy of Management Journal*, 43(3): 502–517.

Bae, J., Chen, S. J., & Rowley, C. 2011. From a paternalistic model towards what? HRM trends in Korea and Taiwan. *Personnel Review*, 40(6): 700–722.

Barkai, J. 2008. What's a cross-cultural mediator to do? A low-context solution for a high-context problem. *Cardozo Journal of Conflict Resolution*, 10: 43–89.

Chai, D. S., Jeong, S., Kim, J., Kim, S., & Hamlin, R. G. 2016. Perceived managerial leadership effectiveness in a South Korean context: A qualitative study on indigenous managerial leadership. *Asia Pacific Journal of Management*, 33(3): 789–820.

Choi, J. T. 2004. Transformation of Korean HRM based on Confucian values. *Seoul Journal of Business*, 10: 1–26.

English, D. E., Manton, E. J., & Walker, J. 2007. Human resource managers' perception of selected communication competencies. *Education*, 127(3): 410–418.

Froese, F. J., Sekiguchi, T., & Maharjan, M. P. 2018. Human resource management in Japan and South Korea. In F. L. Cooke & S. Kim (Eds). *Routledge handbook of human resource management in Asia*: 275–294. Abigndon: Routledge.

Hall, E. T. 1976. *Beyond culture*. New York: Doubleday.

House, R. J., Hanges, P. J., Javidan, M., Dorfman, P. W., & Gupta, V. 2004. *Culture, leadership, and organizations: The GLOBE study of 62 societies*. London: Sage.

Kim, D., Pan, Y., & Park, H. S. 1998. High-versus low-context culture: A comparison of Chinese, Korean, and American cultures. *Psychology & Marketing*, 15(6): 507–521.

Thornton, G. C., & Rupp, D. E. 2006. *Assessment centers in human resource management: Strategies for prediction, diagnosis, and development*. Mahwah: Lawrence Erlbaum.

CHAPTER 26

Thailand

HRM Practices for Managing Age-diverse Employees in the Workplace: A Case Study of a Global Thai Company

Chaturong Napathorn

CASE SYNOPSIS

Bob, the director of Somen's human resource management (HRM) department, was very proud that his company had been selected as one of the 500 most admired companies in 2020. However, one of his major concerns during the past few years is that Somen's workforce is increasingly age diverse. Baby boomers and Generation X, Y, and Z employees have been working together, leading to higher levels of interpersonal conflict among employees due to biases and prejudices against those who have different ideas and opinions. He has thus attempted to solve the problem incurred by age diversity and help every generation of employees thrive in an age-diverse workplace of Somen.

KEYWORDS

Age diversity, aging society, human resource management, institutional contexts, culture, Thailand

DOI: 10.4324/9781003307099-31

LEARNING OUTCOMES

1. Understand why firms should adopt and implement HRM practices that are specifically designed to foster an age-diverse workplace.
2. Realize why institutional and cultural contexts may influence the adoption and implementation of age-diverse HRM practices within the workplace.
3. Propose HRM practices that should foster every generation of employees within the workplace to effectively work together.

ORGANIZATIONAL SETTING

Somen Rice Vermicelli Company Limited was established in 1930 by Mr. Somchai Somen.[1] Initially, the factory was operated under the status of a limited partnership, and its first factory was located in the Pathumwan district in Bangkok. Later, in 1959, Somen Rice Vermicelli Factory Company Limited was established with the primary objective of producing rice vermicelli and products from rice, including rice flour, glutinous rice flour, rice sticks, rice starch, and glutinous rice starch, under the "Elephant" brand. The company has been the leader in this area for a long time. Its products have been exported and sold across countries throughout the globe. The company's organizational structure can be divided into 28 functions, including production, engineering, domestic sales, international sales, and human resources. Currently, the headquarters of Somen is located in Sam Pran district in the Nakhon Pathom province of Thailand. The company is operated by the "Somen" family and has approximately 5,800 employees (as of December 31, 2021). The company has approximately 2,200 employees who are more than 50 years old. The company has no retirement age. Any employee who wishes to continue working after they reach 60 years of age will automatically maintain their full-time status. The company has approximately 990 employees who are more than 60 years of age. In fact, approximately 10% of total employees (or almost 600 employees) are more than 65 years of age.

During the past few years, Somen's workforce has been increasingly age diverse. Various generations of employees, including baby boomers and Generations X, Y, and Z, have been working together. In particular, the company has recruited newly qualified graduates from Thai and foreign universities to work at Somen. At the same time, in order to solve the problem of skills shortage in the labor market, it has also retained experienced, older employees who possess tacit knowledge and skills in several areas, such as maintenance operations and manufacturing, by offering the "no retirement age" policy to this group of employees. In fact, Somen has paid special attention to the transfer of knowledge from older employees to younger generations of employees. In this regard, older employees, especially those who are retired technicians or retired senior technicians, have to serve as advisors or mentors for younger employees. In some cases, the company has had to record (via video – VDO) how each retired technician does his or her jobs, especially jobs that require special expertise, so that other younger employees can learn from watching the VDO.

BACKGROUND TO THE CASE

Historical and Economic Background

Unlike many countries in Southeast Asia, Thailand was never colonized by European countries or the United States. However, Japan occupied the country for a brief period during World War II (Lawler & Atmiyanandana, 2003). Thailand reached a turning point in 1932 when it transitioned from an 800-year-old absolute monarchy to a constitutional monarchy (Gullaprawit, 2002). It then changed its name from Siam to Thailand. According to the current regime, the government or cabinet is divided into several levels: Ministries and quasi-autonomous agencies, provinces, districts, municipalities, communes, and villages. The ministries responsible for the country's HRM practices are the Ministry of Education (which includes University Affairs), the Ministry of Labor, the Ministry of Social Development and Human Security, and the Ministry of Science and Technology.

In terms of its economic background, Thailand has fallen into the middle-income trap, which means the country has low rates of research and development (R&D) investment, innovation, and productivity growth. In this regard, the Thai economy has been unable to continue to grow sufficiently. In fact, one of the leading industries contributing to Thailand's economic growth is the food and agro-food processing industry. Thailand's food and agro-food processing industry is substantial and one of the most rapidly internationalizing industries in the country (Thirawat, Robins, & Baume, 2012). It began internationalizing in 1970. Since then, the industry has generated double-digit annual export growth rates, except for the year 2007, when the rate declined to below 10% (9.52%). However, the overall Thai economy, including the food and agro-food processing industry, is projected to slow down significantly due to the COVID-19 pandemic. The Thai government's countermeasures, such as travel restrictions and the closure of venues considered high-risk areas to curb the spread of the virus disease, have severely impacted the growth of various industries, including the food and agro-food processing industry.

Institutional Contexts

Thailand's skills formation system has several deficiencies, including skill shortages and skill mismatches (Napathorn, in press). Regarding the skills shortage, over 50% of firms in Thailand are unable to fill vacancies within a period of three months (Siam Commercial Bank Economic Intelligence Center, 2015). In terms of skills mismatches, they result from the fact that universities in Thailand have traditionally focused on skills needed by the bureaucracy (e.g., political science, law, and education) instead of skills needed by private firms (e.g., sciences, engineering, and information technology) (Suehiro & Yabushita, 2014). Healthcare institutions in Thailand, including hospitals and clinics, nursing homes, and health maintenance organizations (Narayanamurthy, Gurumurthy, Subramanian, & Moser, 2018), are likely to face several challenges, including the burden from aging populations when Thailand is becoming an aging society. These challenges lead to increasing demand for medical services and diagnostic equipment (Siemens Healthineers, 2015). However, the medical service costs of private hospitals are quite expensive (Hfocus, 2018). Thus, most Thai people have to obtain medical services from public hospitals and face the barrier of long waiting times (Wattanapisit & Saengow, 2018). Regarding regulatory institutions, they are generally viewed as "weak" (Komutputipong &

Keerasuntonpong, 2019; Bruton, Dess, & Janney, 2007). For instance, Thailand has been viewed as a country with weak intellectual property laws (Zhao, 2006). In this regard, it is possible that explicit knowledge can be easily copied by competitors, while tacit knowledge tends to be a source of Thai firms' competitive advantage (Guo, Cai, & Fei, 2019).

Finally, regarding the welfare state regime, economic policy is perceived to be superior to social policy (Upton, 2010; Wood & Gough, 2006). That said, the Thai government has focused more on economic development strategies than on the improvement of social security systems (Tohyama, 2015). In this case, the amount of social security benefits that older employees obtain from the social security fund (so-called old age pension) (the maximum amount received by older employees is approximately 5,250 Thai baht per month or approximately USD 175 per month) (Padsuwan, 2018) and the amount of elderly life allowance these employees obtain from the Ministry of Social Development and Human Security (ranging from 600–1,000 Thai baht per month for people who are at least 60 years of age, which is approximately USD 20–35 per month) (Buranikanont, 2019) are quite low and cannot cover the standard of living among older employees after retirement given the rising costs of medical services in Thailand (Newstoday, 2017). In the past years, employees who retired did not receive any severance pay from their employers. Recently, the Thai Labor Protection Act has been amended to ensure that employees who retire are expected to obtain additional severance pay from their employers. The amount of severance pay that is paid to employees depends on the employee's years of service in a firm. However, the maximum amount employees can receive is ten times their last-month salary (Paitoonpong, 2018). Nevertheless, the Thai government expects that severance pay, benefits, and allowance obtained from employers and the Thai government are still not sufficient for older employees. In this regard, the Thai government has attempted to search for ways to urge employees across firms to start saving their money when they are young (Manager Online, 2020).

Population Sizes and Cultural Contexts

Currently, there are approximately 70.06 million people living in Thailand. The Thai population essentially consists of two main groups: Ethnic Thai people and individuals of Chinese descent. Some Chinese people are married to Thai people, and their children are "Sino-Thais" (Lawler & Suttawet, 2000). Not surprisingly, Thai family enterprises have been influenced by Chinese culture in terms of management and HRM practices (Lawler & Atmiyanandana, 2003). The Chinese management system seems to be influenced by Confucianism (Lawler & Siengthai, 1997): Managers demand loyalty from their subordinates, and the subordinates anticipate that the managers will take care of their needs.

In terms of the Thai cultural context, Thailand's high level of conflict/uncertainty avoidance and low levels of individualism and masculinity (Hofstede, 1980) are the main reasons why Thai society is quite cooperative and not so aggressive (Suthakavatin, 2005). Additionally, the high level of power distance is one of the reasons why Thai employees accept the imbalance of power and authority between managers and employees within the workplace (Napathorn, 2018). Theravada Buddhism also plays an important role in shaping the Thai culture. It is likely to encourage Thai people to be unassertive, passive, and unambitious with respect to exercising their rights (Napathorn and Kuruvilla, 2018). Thai people pay special attention to cultural values, such as "Mai Pen Rai (never mind)" and "Jai Yen (take it easy)" (Thanasankit, 2002).

These values reflect the "superior–subordinate" relationships within the workplace environment (Siengthai, Tanlamai, & Rowley, 2008).

Aging Society and Firm-Level HRM Practices

The World Health Organization has classified aging societies into three different levels: Aging societies, aged societies, and super-aged societies. Currently, Thailand is transitioning from an aging society into an aged society at a faster rate than other developing economies (Bank of Thailand, 2018). [Here, an aged society refers to a country where the population that is at least 60 years of age accounts for more than 20% of the total population or where the population that is at least 65 years of age accounts for more than 14% of the total population (World Health Organization, 2002).] Typically, this structural transformation process takes 18 to 115 years, but in Thailand, it is taking only 20 years because the proportion of the population aged over 65 years has increased very rapidly: From 7% of the total population in 2000 to 13% of the total population in 2020 (Napathorn, in press). By 2035, Thailand will be the first developing economy to become a super-aged society. However, most other countries that are super-aged societies are developed economies with per capita incomes of more than USD 12,500 per year, whereas the per capita income of Thailand is USD 5,700 per year (Napathorn, in press). In this regard, the Thai labor force is likely to become old before it becomes rich, and older Thai individuals will have to depend heavily on government subsidies (which tend to be insufficient to cover their standard of living) and support from family members. Additionally, because the proportion of Thai labor has decreased at a faster rate than in other countries (Napathorn, in press), firms, including Somen, have had to adopt several HRM strategies and practices, including the extension of retirement age, the recruitment of retired employees into their firms, and the upskilling and reskilling of labor, to cope with this situation and retain older employees over time.

HRM PRACTICES AND AGE DIVERSITY AT SOMEN: WHAT DOES THE FUTURE HOLD?

To attract newly qualified graduates and experienced job candidates, Somen primarily relies on employee referrals and, to a lesser extent, other recruitment channels in attracting potential candidates to the company. The referral recruitment strategy plays a crucial role in maintaining the family-like and informal corporate culture of Somen. Many candidates who are family members of Somen's current employees resigned from other firms located in the urban area of Bangkok to apply for jobs at Somen because they could stay with their parents when they work at Somen. Additionally, these candidates learned from their parents who work at Somen that working here should provide them with a good standard of living in terms of acceptable wages/salaries, special or festival bonuses, and various types of benefits.

On-the-job training is one of the most effective training methods at Somen. Typically, senior employees serve as mentors for younger generations of employees, so that they can transfer their firm-specific knowledge and experience to these young employees. This firm-specific knowledge and experience can thus be transferred from generation to generation of employees. This transfer has been very important for the long-term success of Somen. For instance, the invention and maintenance of machinery is considered firm-specific knowledge that is crucial to the company's success. In this regard, senior technicians must serve as mentors for younger employees. In some cases, the company records a VDO when senior technicians conduct maintenance of the machinery so that younger employees can learn directly from the VDO. The top managers of Somen believe that transferring knowledge and skills by recording the VDO is better than writing detailed processes in a manual. Somen has also implemented the policy of appointing senior technicians as advisors to the technical department after the retirement of these senior technicians so that the advisors can provide recommendations and solve problems for junior technicians. This can also facilitate the transfer of knowledge to younger generations of employees and maintain a family-like corporate culture.

Additionally, classroom training is used to equip employees with various electrical, mechanical, and electronic techniques, such as how to operate machinery, knowledge and skills about occupational safety, 5S technique (5S technique refers to a technique applied to create a workplace that is clean, uncluttered, safe, and well organized to help reduce waste and optimize productivity), and computer skills. Moreover, Somen also provides several training courses that aim to improve the quality of employees' lives, such as a financial planning course. The financial planning course helps Somen employees be free from debt, learn how to manage their money, have sufficient savings for spending, and have a better quality of working life, especially after retirement.

Furthermore, Somen provides annual health check-ups for its employees to ensure that these employees maintain good health. Every morning and afternoon, the company must measure the blood pressure of employees who have done risky jobs, such as lifting. The company offers yoga, Zumba, and fitness classes for employees, as well as jogging and cycling clubs for employees who can still do those activities. Somen has further provided a first aid room with 24-hour doctors and an ambulance in case any employees need to go to nearby hospitals. The company has also offered its employees training courses, such as occupational safety and fire extinguishing techniques, so that they can work safely at the factory level.

Older employees at Somen, especially those who are retired technicians or retired senior technicians, have also been encouraged to serve as advisors for younger employees. Additionally, Somen has encouraged its older employees to participate in the decision-making processes because these employees have accumulated extensive work experience over time. Somen has typically exempted older employees from working night shifts, and thus most work day shifts. However, Somen does not allow its older employees to work part-time because the company's management of part-time employees is quite sophisticated. In fact, most older employees at Somen do not want to work part-time. Rather, they are willing to work full-time because they are eligible to receive the same levels of wages and benefits as younger employees. Moreover, Somen's top managers have been willing to move older employees among different jobs so they can perform duties that are appropriate for their physical health conditions and ages. Overall, Somen has implemented a variety of HRM practices for managing its employees.

As several generations of employees (including baby boomers, Generation X, Generation Y, and Generation Z employees) have been working together across functions, departments, and projects to implement projects to move the firm toward a global company, Bob, the director of Somen's HRM department, expects to see the tacit knowledge exchange and transfer across generations, and several new ideas and insights incurred from such exchange and transfer should help the company achieve the goal of initiating new and creative projects to expand the customer base and diversify the firm into new types of businesses. However, what has actually happened is that higher levels of interpersonal conflict among employees have emerged due to biases and prejudices against those who have different ideas and opinions. On the one hand, the number of disputes between managers and employees or among employees across different generations has continuously increased. On the other hand, the number of new and creative ideas, insights, or projects has not increased as Bob has expected. Bob believes that one of the causes of this problem is age diversity in the workforce. He has thus attempted to solve this problem and help every generation of employees thrive in the age-diverse workplace of Somen. What would the best way to solve this problem be? Have there been any mistakes incurred from its current HRM practices? If so, what should the bundle of HRM practices that should be implemented at Somen in the future be?

CASE STUDY QUESTIONS FOR DISCUSSION

1. In your opinion, do you think the current HRM practices at Somen are still appropriate in the present situation? Why or why not?
2. Do the current HRM practices implemented at Somen respond to the institutional and cultural contexts of Thailand? Why or why not?
3. How should the bundle of HRM practices implemented at Somen be redesigned in order to help the firm leverage new and creative ideas across generations of employees and thrive in the situation of aging societies and the fierce business arena? Please explain in detail.

ACKNOWLEDGMENTS

The author would like to thank the Thailand Research Fund for partially funding this research.

NOTE

1 For confidentiality reasons, and due to the sensitive nature of the subject matter, a pseudonym is used, and certain details concerning the organization's titles, details, and activities have been altered.

REFERENCES

Bank of Thailand. 2018. Aging society and the challenge of the Thai labor market. Retrieved on November 25, 2018 from https://www.bot.or.th/Thai/MonetaryPolicy/EconomicConditions /AAA/AgePeriodCohort.pdf.

Bruton, G.D., Dess, G.G., & Janney, J.J. 2007. Knowledge management in technology-focused firms in emerging economies: Caveats on capabilities, networks, and real options. *Asia Pacific Journal of Management*, 24(2), 115–130.

Buranikanont, I. 2019. Elderly life allowance. Retrieved on June 22, 2020 from https://www
.posttoday.com/finance-stock/columnist/607539.

Gullaprawit, C. 2002. Thailand. In M. Zanko (Ed.), *The Handbook of Human Resource Management Policies and Practices in Asia-Pacific Economies*. Volume 1. Northampton, MA: Edward Elgar.

Guo, R., Cai, L., & Fei, Y. 2019. Knowledge integration methods, product innovation and high-tech new venture performance in China. *Technology Analysis & Strategic Management*, 31(3), 306–318.

Hfocus. 2018. Ministry of Commerce solved the problems regarding overpriced medical costs in Thailand (Translated from Thai title). Retrieved on June 22, 2020 from https://www.hfocus
.org/content/2018/11/16535.

Hofstede, G. 1980. *Culture's Consequences: International Differences in Work-Related Values*. Beverly Hills: Sage.

Komutputipong, N. & Keerasuntonpong, P. 2019. Accountability perception of Thai Government: To whom and what counts. *Journal of Public Budgeting, Accounting & Financial Management*, 31(1), 45–65.

Lawler, J.J. & Atmiyanandana, V. 2003. HRM in Thailand: A post-1997 update. *Asia Pacific Business Review*, 9(4), 165–185.

Lawler, J.J. & Siengthai, S. 1997. Human resource management and strategy in the Thai banking industry. *Research and Practice in Human Resource Management*, 5(1), 73–88.

Lawler, J.J. & Suttawet, C. 2000. Labor unions, globalization and deregulation in Thailand. *Asia Pacific Business Review*, 6(3–4), 214–238.

Manager Online. 2020. *Aging Societies…Old and Poor… National Agenda Without Supportive Plans (Translated from Thai Title)*. Retrieved on June 23, 2020 from https://mgronline.com
/daily/detail/9630000005397.

Napathorn, C. 2023. HR practices for managing aging employees in organizations: The case of Thailand. *International Journal of Emerging Markets*, 18(5): 1187–1215.

Napathorn, C. 2018. Contextual influences on HRM practices in social enterprises: The case of Thailand. *International Journal of Emerging Markets*, 13(6), 1969–2000.

Napathorn, C. & Kuruvilla, S. 2018. Human resource management in Indonesia, Malaysia, and Thailand. In F.L. Cooke and S. Kim (Eds.), *Routledge handbook of human resource management in Asia*, pp. 333–354. London: Routledge.

Narayanamurthy, G., Gurumurthy, A., Subramanian, N., & Moser, R. 2018. Assessing the readiness to implement lean in healthcare institutions–A case study. *International Journal of Production Economics*, 197, 123–142.

Newstoday. 2017. *The development of social security toward equivalent societies (Translated from Thai title)*. Retrieved on June 21, 2020 from https://newstoday2000.com.

Padsuwan, S. 2018. How much you will receive from the social security fund upon retirement? (Translated from Thai title). Retrieved on June 22, 2020 from https://www.finnomena.com
/wealthguru/retire-and-social-security-office/.

Paitoonpong, S. 2018. Retirement of private-sector employees. Retrieved on June 23, 2020 from https://tdri.or.th/2018/02/labor-retirement/.

Siam Commercial Bank Economic Intelligence Center. 2015. *Insight: Bridging Thailand's Labor Gap*. Retrieved on June 10, 2015 from www.scbeic.com.

Siemens Healthineers. 2015. Healthcare in emerging markets: Challenges & opportunities. Retrieved on June 19, 2020 from https://www.siemens-healthineers.com/magazine/mso -healthcare-in-emerging-markets.html#:~:text=The%20Disproportionately%20Growing %20and%20Aging,for%20New%20Healthcare%20Delivery%20Models&text=The%20heal thcare%20systems%20in%20those,adequate%20healthcare%20to%20the%20masses.

Siengthai, S., Tanlamai, U., & Rowley, C. 2008. The changing face of human resource management in Thailand. In C. Rowley and S. Abdul-Rahman, S. (Eds), *The Changing Face of Management in Southeast Asia*, pp. 155–184. London: Routledge.

Suehiro, A. & Yabushita, N. 2014. Thailand: Post-developmentalist capitalism. In M.A. Witt and G. Redding (Eds), *The Oxford Handbook of Asian Business Systems*, pp. 260–282, Oxford: Oxford University Press.

Suthakavatin, T. 2005. *Comparative Labor Relations (Translated from Thai Title)*. Bangkok: TPN Press.

Thanasankit, T. 2002. Requirements engineering: Exploring the influence of power and Thai values. *European Journal of Information Systems*, 11(2), 128–141.

Thirawat, N., Robins, F., & Baume, G. 2012. Internationalization factors of Thai multinationals and Thailand's Bilateral trade policy. *Journal of Asia-Pacific Business*, 13(2), 143–176.

Tohyama, H. 2015. Varieties of Asian welfare capitalisms and the influence of globalization. *Journal of International and Comparative Social Policy*, 31(1), 51–73.

Upton, S. 2010. The Thai welfare regime: Towards a wellbeing perspective. Paper prepared for the Symposium on Promoting Social Inclusion in South Asia: Policies, Pitfalls, and Analysis of Welfare/Insecurity Regimes, 12–14 September 2010.

Wattanapisit, A. & Saengow, U. 2018. Patients' perspectives regarding hospital visits in the universal health coverage system of Thailand: A qualitative study. *Asia Pacific Family Medicine*, 17(1), 1–8.

Wood, G. & Gough, I. 2006. A comparative welfare regime approach to global social policy. *World Development*, 34(10), 1696–1712.

World Health Organization. 2002. Active ageing: A policy framework. Retrieved on November 20, 2018 from http://whqlibdoc.who.int/hq/2002/WHO_NMH_NPH_02.8.pdf.

Zhao, M. 2006. Conducting R&D in countries with weak intellectual property rights protection. *Management Science*, 52, 1185–1199.

Supplementary Resources

Boehm, S. A., Schröder, H., & Bal, M. 2021. Age-related human resource management policies and practices: Antecedents, outcomes, and conceptualizations. *Work, Aging and Retirement*, 7(4), 257–272.

The Americas

CHAPTER 27

Canada

La Vie en Rose: Globalization Challenges for Human Resources Management in a Canadian Lingerie Leader

Sylvie Guerrero, Ewan Oiry, and Ariane Ollier-Malaterre

CASE SYNOPSIS

From its headquarters in Montreal (Quebec, Canada), La Vie en Rose sells lingerie, swimwear, and sleepwear in over 275 boutiques in 18 countries. The company has followed a growth strategy since its acquisition by François Roberge in 1996. This case study describes the international human resources management (HRM) challenges raised by its expansion. It examines HRM in Canada and in the province of Quebec. It describes the operating modes of the fashion industry. Building on this information, the second part of this case study presents a series of five challenges created by the firm's growth. Students are asked to develop international HRM solutions for each of these challenges.

KEYWORDS

Globalization strategy, international HRM, skills development, e-commerce, recruitment and selection, Canada

DOI: 10.4324/9781003307099-33

LEARNING OUTCOMES

1. Learn about the labor context in Canada and Quebec.
2. Gain HRM-relevant knowledge about the challenges of the lingerie industry.
3. Implement HRM selection and retention strategies in a labor shortage context.
4. Design an appropriate work organization to control the quality of globalized production.
5. Roll out international HRM practices for franchisees.

INTRODUCTION

La Vie en Rose is a Canadian lingerie retailer headquartered in the city of Montreal, in the province of Quebec. The firm designs and sells lingerie, swimwear, and sleepwear. The brand has become famous in Canada through its network of dedicated boutiques, where customers find quality products featuring cheerful colors and sophisticated designs. Target customers are women between 25 and 55 years old. The company owns over 275 boutiques (La Vie en Rose and Bikini Village) in Canada and around 100 boutiques operated under a franchise contract in 18 countries worldwide (www.lavieenrose.com/us/international), with a noteworthy presence in the Middle East and the Maghreb. La Vie en Rose is especially present in Saudi Arabia, with 25 stores, and in the United Arab Emirates, with ten stores. The firm plans to pursue its expansion by opening new stores in India, China, Australia, and Georgia.

PART ONE: ORGANIZATIONAL AND INDUSTRIAL SETTING

La Vie en Rose: A Jewel of the Canadian Lingerie Industry

La Vie en Rose has been an expert in lingerie, swimwear, and sleepwear since 1985. It was founded by Harry Kaner, a Toronto businessman, in collaboration with his wife, Rosemary Kaner. The couple wanted to offer personal service from well-trained salespeople in each fitting room. Unfortunately, the concept was not profitable, and the company filed for bankruptcy protection. In 1987, La Vie en Rose was sold to Algo. In 1996, after years of losses, Algo sold La Vie en Rose to a Quebec entrepreneur, François Roberge, who had previous experience in the textile industry. François Roberge moved the head office from Toronto to downtown Montreal. From this period on, the company followed a growth strategy (10% to 20% of growth each year for more than ten years). François Roberge dramatically increased the number of bra models, diversified its activities to panties and swimwear, and opened the first boutique abroad in 2004. The firm acquired complementary branches such as Ainsi Soit-Elle (another lingerie retailer in Quebec, a trademark that was then disregarded) in 2011 and the Bikini Village chain of swimsuit stores in 2015. It created its own product lines, including Aqua Swimwear in 1998, the Muse collection in 2010 (mastectomy bras), and the Sleek Back Bra in 2017 (a bra with wider wings for more comfort). More globally, La Vie en Rose's market positioning is to design "products that fit real life and provide comfort to body and soul, while making shopping for lingerie, swimwear, sleepwear fun and effortless".

A key company ambition is to pursue its growth by acquiring new boutiques. It currently owns over 275 boutiques in 125 Canadian cities, employing about 4,000 people nationwide. The approximately 100 other boutiques are located in 18 countries, with a strong presence in North Africa and the Middle East. All 100 international stores operate under a franchise contract: The headquarters in Montreal provides product descriptions and selling advice, and manages communications, budget, and strategy. Growth in the United States is projected with the explosion of online sales, and in Asia and beyond, fueled by the opening of new stores.

The Labor Market in Canada and Quebec

Canada is a decentralized country of approximately 38 million inhabitants, in which each province implements policies that regulate its economy and job market. Quebec is one of ten Canadian provinces. In many ways, work and business life in Quebec are very similar to that of the other Canadian provinces. For example, the whole country, including Quebec, must contend with an aging workforce. The percentage of people over 65 is growing rapidly and should exceed 20% by 2040.

A key factor in the Canadian labor market affecting La Vie en Rose is the persistent and worsening labor shortage. In September 2021, the Canadian unemployment rate was about 7% with a job vacancy rate of 4.6%. Canada relies heavily on immigration to pursue its economic growth. Due to its aging population, the country lacks the workforce to fill job vacancies. As a result, it positions itself as an attractive destination for immigration. A total of 284,387 people immigrated to the country between July 1, 2019, and June 30, 2020 (www.statista.com/statistics/443063/number-of-immigrants-in-canada/). Overall, almost 25% of the people living in Canada in 2021 were born in a foreign country. In Quebec, labor shortages are even worse than in the rest of Canada. Quebec reached a peak job vacancy rate of 5.6% and an unemployment rate of only 5.3% in 2021 (www150.statcan.gc.ca/n1/pub/71-607-x/71-607-x2017002-eng.htm). According to Statistics Canada, there were 731,900 job vacancies in the second quarter of 2021 in Canada, with the largest increase in Quebec. Moreover, access to professional jobs is protected by 46 powerful professional orders. On average, around 40,000 new immigrants arrive yearly in Quebec (www.statista.com/statistics/609162/number-of-immigrants-in-quebec/), and 15% of the population of the province was born in a foreign country.

Unfortunately for La Vie en Rose, retail trade is among the industries most affected by job vacancies (www150.statcan.gc.ca/n1/daily-quotidien/210827/dq210827b-eng.htm), with 30% of Canadian organizations expecting labor shortages to be an obstacle for their business. Job vacancies in retail trade increased to 84,300 in the second quarter of 2021. The occupations most in demand are retail salespersons, store shelf stockers, clerks, and order fillers. "Help wanted" signs appear in many storefronts across the country, and the competition to attract and retain employees is fierce.

Quebec has specific characteristics that make it unique in Canada. First, French is the official language and must be used at work. Second, Quebec is more highly unionized than anywhere else in North America. About 40% of employees are unionized in Quebec, compared with 30% in the rest of Canada (https://qe.cirano.qc.ca/theme/marche-travail/main-doeuvre/tableau -taux-syndicalisation-secteur-dactivite-2019). These employees are protected under elaborate collective agreements. However, in Quebec, La Vie en Rose operates in accordance with pro-vincial regulations and is not unionized. Therefore, Quebec unions and their collective agree-ments do not seriously affect the company's operating modes. Workers' rights are governed by the provincial labor code, which sets employment conditions for working hours, wages, leaves, vacation, and health and safety norms. Other standards apply to employees working in federally regulated businesses such as transportation, banking, and telecoms.

WORLD FASHION: FOR BETTER OR FOR WORSE

"World fashion" refers to a simplified version of Western clothing manufactured on a mass scale. The number of world fashion brands has grown rapidly around the world, such that now customers can buy clothes that could be manufactured and sold anywhere in the world. Among the most famous brands are Shein, Bershka, H&M, and Uniqlo. In parallel to world fashion, there are small and specialized fashion industries that cater to specific local markets and main-tain traditional methods of producing textiles and clothes (www.britannica.com/art/fashion-industry/Fashion-retailing-marketing-and-merchandising#ref296480), but their contribution to the global revenue of fashion is marginal.

La Vie en Rose is part of the world fashion industry, similar to H&M and other well-known brands. As such, it first selects fabrics to produce apparel: These fabrics can be made from natu-ral fibers such as cotton, or synthetic fibers such as nylon. The latter are less costly and have properties such as stain resistance and body heat retention that make them very attractive. There is a growing interest in eco-fibers such as hemp, and hence potential for developing a more sus-tainable fashion industry. In this regard, La Vie en Rose thus strives to use a large proportion of recycled fibers and is committed to acting in an eco-conscious manner (www.lavieenrose.com/en/eco-conscious-initiative).

Designers use environmentally friendly fabrics to create clothes including lingerie, swim-wear, and sleepwear. They work in design teams, with computer-assisted design techniques, which allow them to make rapid changes, imagine a variety of products, and share their ideas with colleagues. La Vie en Rose produces moderately priced and budget bras and panties. The company relies on manufacturing firms or contractors to produce lingerie and other apparel according to their specifications. Usually, three collections are manufactured per year in most fashion companies, but there is a lively debate about this. Some fast-fashion manufacturers pro-duce new collections more often, and La Vie en Rose found that producing new collections more frequently enabled the company to increase revenues through creativity. For example, collec-tions were created for specific events such as Halloween, New Year's, and Valentine's Day. Other opportunities lie in targeted customer profiles. La Vie en Rose has historically chosen to focus on a mix of comfort and elegance. In this marketing segment, many options exist, based on the women's body (e.g., short, thin, strong, big) and lifestyle (e.g., sports, city, work). Producing clothes in a range of sizes is a challenge for the entire fashion industry and is even greater in lingerie. Patterns cannot simply be scaled up or down uniformly from a basic template, and pattern-making is a highly skilled profession.

Another significant issue in the lingerie business is the location of assembly factories. Sewing is still labor-intensive, and this puts pressure on clothing manufacturers to seek out low-wage

countries   (www.britannica.com/art/fashion-industry/Fashion-design-and-manufacturing).
They have relocated production and opened factories in countries where workers work hard
for low wages. We all recall the Nike scandal in 1997 when the manufacturer was accused of
hiring children to work in poor air quality conditions (Carty, 2001). Like its competitors, La
Vie en Rose manufactures its products in various factories located in several Asian countries.

Once the clothing is designed and manufactured, retailers receive the products for sale in
the upcoming months. Marketers help retailers to both sell products and meet their customers' needs. Fashion shows, catalogs, special prices, and promotions help to build the brand's
reputation and increase sales. Due to the COVID-19 crisis, internet shopping has increased
significantly. Yet the move to online commerce creates new challenges for the fashion industry,
such as handling returns and defects, shipping orders to customers' addresses, and managing
stock to accommodate customers who may be located anywhere in the world. The diversity of
shopping options has increased competition among retailers and is forcing them to think about
how to organize diverse clothing displays and a new delivery network.

CASE STUDY QUESTIONS FOR DISCUSSION

1. Analyze the environment in which La Vie en Rose operates: What are the company's
    main strengths and weaknesses?
2. What are the main HRM challenges (up to five) that the company is likely to face if it
    maintains its current growth strategy?

PART TWO: IMAGINE THE FUTURE AND ITS HUMAN RESOURCES MANAGEMENT CHALLENGES

Now that we have looked at the context in which La Vie en Rose operates, let us prepare for the
future and devise potential solutions to the five main HRM challenges that the company may
face as it pursues its growth strategy.

CHALLENGE 1: DESIGN INNOVATIVE COLLECTIONS

One option for La Vie en Rose is to increase the number of product lines (collections), but this
requires the design teams to exhibit more creativity and productivity. The number of product lines has already increased with the development of new products (the Muse collection, for
example), but more could be done by adding to the number of collections per year or to product
lines. Note that pattern-making is a highly skilled profession, and the process of designing a new
collection or a new product line remains long and complex.

An HRM challenge could be to increase the design team's productivity. One idea that has
emerged in the fashion industry is the implementation of multi-skilled teams specializing in specific product lines such as swimsuits or bras. Multi-skilled teams possess skills in more than one

area of business. For example, multi-skilled teams can design, market, and sell a product line. They tend to design more innovative and original products through the exchange of expertise and ideas: Employees in these teams design products more rapidly, exchange information more often, and are collectively more productive (https://smallbusiness.chron.com/advantages-multi-skilled-labor-18280.html). They become accountable for designing products that meet customers' needs worldwide. However, changing work organization is demanding and raises many issues: Relational skills are needed, as is the ability to think globally (as opposed to thinking in silos). Moreover, knowledge of local specificities and tastes is important for international sales.

CASE STUDY QUESTION FOR DISCUSSION

Imagine that La Vie en Rose decides to implement multi-skilled teams. What impact would this decision have on recruiting new employees and training and compensating the workers in these teams?

CHALLENGE 2: INCREASE PRODUCT QUALITY

In the textile industry, including lingerie and swimwear, products must be manufactured in a variety of sizes, and must meet specific quality standards. This is particularly challenging for lingerie made with lace and featuring highly detailed designs. Quality control processes are of prime importance to guarantee product quality and compliance with manufacturing standards. Quality is usually checked by a manager or a quality control specialist at three periods: In the preproduction phase, during production, and after the product has been manufactured (https://fashioninsiders.co/toolkit/top-tips/quality-control-fashion-manufacturing/). In the preproduction phase, controls are in place to ensure the quality of raw materials (the right size, color, etc.). During production, spot checks ensure that products are made properly throughout the production line. The final quality control ensures that the product looks like it is described in the specification sheets and that it passes the required tests. Only when quality is approved can apparel be sent to storage areas.

In terms of HRM, quality control raises many challenges. One option is to hire quality control inspectors who can visit each factory, on behalf of La Vie en Rose, and perform the required checks at every stage of the production process. These inspectors would be trained by La Vie en Rose and oversee one or several factories. They could be hired and trained in Canada. However, sending these employees from Canada to factories in other locations may have significant HRM implications, especially if employees are expatriates rather than engaged in short on-site visits. Conversely, another option for La Vie en Rose would be to hire and train local employees to perform quality control; this mode also has specific HRM implications because the recruitment and training process would be beyond the firm's expertise. A third option for La Vie en Rose would be to subcontract quality control to local independent control firms. However, none of these three options would eliminate defects due to transportation. Additional inspectors might be needed in warehouses. In short, the firm needs to build a team of well-trained quality inspectors able to guarantee the same quality standards in all of La Vie en Rose's factories and warehouses.

CASE STUDY QUESTIONS FOR DISCUSSION

Which of these options would you recommend for building the strongest team of quality inspectors at La Vie en Rose? What implications does it entail for HRM?

CHALLENGE 3: BOOST E-COMMERCE AND KEEP BOUTIQUE SALES VIGOROUS

Driven by the COVID-19 pandemic, e-commerce has increased significantly. In March 2020, global retail website traffic reached an unprecedented peak of 14.3 billion visits, and online sales are expected to reach USD 6.5 trillion by 2023 (Bhatti et al., 2021). La Vie en Rose conducts business both online and in brick-and-mortar stores. The online business facilitates price reduction and allows a larger selection of products. However, in-store shopping can offer the physical experience that helps customers discover the universe around a given brand. It is preferred by customers who want to appreciate the quality of products and are worried about a perceived lack of security in online transactions (https://en.wikipedia.org/wiki/E-commerce#cite_note-830).

E-commerce is now fully-fledged. It has created entirely new occupations to serve online customers, such as community managers, and a host of new titles in such fields as website design photography and e-marketing. It helps create new job opportunities due to the high demand for information-related services, software applications, and digital products. The jobs require highly skilled workers who manage abundant information, customer demands, and production processes. Moreover, e-commerce requires sufficient stocks so that products can be delivered to customers in time. The logistics needed for product storage and distribution have become more complex: Products can be sent from any factory, warehouse, or store to a customer's personal address, which can be anywhere in the world. For e-commerce, warehouse activities require more employees to manage, supervise, and organize product distribution. Employees working in these jobs must be skilled and well-trained.

CASE STUDY QUESTION FOR DISCUSSION

With the current labor shortage, hiring employees with specific technical skills or training existing employees is a challenge for Quebec and Canada. Could you propose an HRM strategy to recruit employees who have the required new skills for e-commerce and retain them at La Vie en Rose?

CHALLENGE 4: SUPPORTING NEW BOUTIQUES WORLDWIDE

Historically, La Vie en Rose has grown as a group of retailers that can meet customers' needs for comfortable lingerie. In a franchise system, the headquarters provides product descriptions, marketing, and selling advice. The functional departments such as marketing/e-commerce, design, operations, accounting, and human resources, are located at the headquarters. In contrast, shop managers are responsible for their own boutiques. This includes hiring employees, product management, and ensuring shop profitability. La Vie en Rose must carefully hire boutique managers and assistant managers to maintain the company brand and use appropriate marketing techniques. In addition, they must provide managers with latitude to enable them to adapt the company directives to the reality of local markets.

In Canada, due to the labor shortages described in the first section of this case study, the employee turnover rate for most retailers is high, including the turnover rate of managers and assistant managers (www.hrreporter.com/focus-areas/culture-and-engagement/canada-ranks-4th-globally-for-highest-employee-turnover/2830610). La Vie en Rose, similar to many retailers, is likely to face fierce competition in attracting and retaining employees. With 4,000 employees nationwide, a high turnover means hundreds of recruitments per year. This represents large investments in time, money, and training for La Vie en Rose. Moreover, the rise of e-commerce challenges the original business model that made La Vie en Rose successful. Indeed, e-commerce puts retailers' very survival at risk. To remain attractive, stores are forced to change their sales strategies. Many companies have increased digital efforts to attract customers while closing physical shops. If La Vie en Rose wants to maintain attractive brick-and-mortar stores and avoid closures in Canada, it might need to enhance the customers' in-store experience. This implies intensifying employees' and managers' training and ensuring that managers are more skilled at marketing products. The stores must also boost the quality of their customer relationships.

On the international scene, La Vie en Rose has opened more than 100 stores in 17 different countries, especially in the Maghreb and the Middle East, and has plans to pursue its growth strategy with additional boutiques in Asia. Local boutique managers must adapt Canadian guidelines to the daily routines and values of people living in different local areas. This has direct implications for HRM regarding the recruitment of shop managers. The firm needs to hire managers and assistant managers who are comfortable with the business principles of Canada in order to develop successful and effective franchisee-franchiser relationships and to represent the brand adequately. However, these individuals must also serve local markets, which they must know well. In short, they must be able to work at the interface of their culture and the North American culture that prevails at La Vie en Rose.

CASE STUDY QUESTION FOR DISCUSSION

What HRM strategy (i.e., selection, training, compensation, assessment) do you recommend helping La Vie en Rose hire and retain loyal, well-trained, and high-performing managers in all their stores?

CHALLENGE 5: BECOMING SOCIALLY RESPONSIBLE

Like most companies in the fast-fashion industry, La Vie en Rose takes part in a global system in which clothing overproduction destroys the planet's resources, creates waste, and increases air pollution due to excessive transportation. To date, other production and distribution modes appear to be simply unrealistic and much too costly. Aware of the criticism of the fashion industry, La Vie en Rose uses organic or recycled fibers, promotes eco-friendly packaging, and encourages eco-citizen behaviors. However, the firm's social and eco-responsibility may be more a matter of discourse than a reality guiding its production and logistics decisions.

CASE STUDY QUESTION FOR DISCUSSION

What role could the HRM department play to help La Vie en Rose become more eco-responsible?

Strategic HRM

Castro Christiansen, L., & Higgs, M. 2008. How the alignment of business strategy and HR strategy can impact performance: A practical insight for managers. *Journal of General Management*, 33(4): 13–34.

Kuipers, B. S., & Giurge, L. M. 2017. Does alignment matter? The performance implications of HR roles connected to organizational strategy. *The International Journal of Human Resource Management*, 28(22): 3179–3201.

Nikolaou, I., & Oostrom, J. K. 2015. *Employee Recruitment, Selection, and Assessment: Contemporary Issues for Theory and Practice.* Psychology Press.

Oppong, N. Y., & Nisar, T. (Reviewing Editor). 2017. Exploring the importance of human resource activities-strategies alignments: Interactive brainstorming groups approach, *Cogent Business & Management*, 4(1), https://doi.org/10.1080/23311975.2016.1273081.

Snell, S. A., & Morris, S. S. 2021. Time for realignment: The HR ecosystem. *Academy of Management Perspectives*, 35: 219–236.

International HRM

Baruch, Y., Dickmann, M., Yochanan, A., & Bournois, F. 2013. Exploring international work: Types and dimensions of global careers. *The International Journal of Human Resource Management*, 24(12): 2369–2393.

El Akremi, A., Mignonac, K., & Perrigot, R. 2011. Opportunistic behaviors in franchise chains: The role of cohesion among franchisees. *Strategic Management Journal*, 32: 930–948.

Lakhani, T. 2021. Understanding human resource practices and outcomes in franchise businesses, center for hospitality research. *Cornell Center for Innovative Hospitality Labor and Employment Relations Research Brief.* 1–8, https://ecommons.cornell.edu/handle/1813/110247.

Cross-cultural HRM and Marketing

Bhatti, A., Akram, H., Basit, H. M., Khan, A.U., Naqvi, S. M. R., Bilal, M. 2020. E-commerce trends during COVID-19 Pandemic. International Journal of Future Generation Communication and Networking, 13(2): 1449–1452.

Chun-Hsiao W., Varma A. 2019. Cultural distance and expatriate failure rates: The moderating role of expatriate management practices. *The International Journal of Human Resource Management*, 30(15): 2211–2230.

Rahman, M., Albaity, M., Isa, C.R. and Azma, N. 2018. Towards a better understanding of fashion clothing purchase involvement. Journal of Islamic Marketing, 9(3): 544–559.

Corporate Social Responsibility

Carty, V. 2001. The Internet and grassroots politics: Nike, the athletic apparel industry and the anti-sweatshop campaign. *Tamara: Journal for Critical Organization Inquiry*, 1(2): 34–48.
Fuentes-García, F. J., Núñez-Tabales, J. M., Veroz-Herradón, R. 2008. Applicability of corporate social responsibility to human resources management: Perspective from Spain. *Journal of Business Ethics*, 82(1): 27–44.

Garment Manufacturing

Gersak, G. 2013. *Design of Clothing Manufacturing Processes. A Systematic Approach to Planning, Scheduling and Control*. Woodhead Publishing Series in Textiles, 306 p.

Supplementary Resources

Borden Ladner Gervais. 2018. *Labor and Employment Law in Quebec: A Practical Guide*, 82 p. downloaded from www.blg.com.
Rauturier, S. 2021. What is fast fashion? July 26, retrieved from: https://goodonyou.eco/what-is-fast-fashion/ on November 26, 2021.
Vidéo: https://montreal.ctvnews.ca/higher-wages-bonuses-quebec-employers-change-their-approach-as-worker-shortage-continues-1.5613912.
Website of the chartered professionals in Human Resources Canada and in particular studies and reports: https://cphr.ca/resources/original-studies-and-reports/.
Website of the Quebec Commission on workplace standards, fairness, health and safety (Commission des normes, de l'équité, de la santé et de la sécurité du travail (CNESST): https://www.cnesst.gouv.qc.ca/en.
Website of the Québec technical textiles industry: https://www.technitextile.ca/en.

CHAPTER 28

Chile

Developing a New Organizational Culture at SKY Airline

Andrés Raineri

CASE SYNOPSIS

This case describes the transformation of an airline from a local family business into a regional low-cost carrier. The case focuses on the development and communication of a new organizational culture. At the end of the case, the airline faced a harsh social crisis in Chile and the spread of the COVID-19 pandemic throughout Latin America. Managers must decide if and how to continue with the organizational culture changes.

KEYWORDS

Organizational culture, change management, low-cost strategy, HRM function, Chile

LEARNING OUTCOMES

The case pursues three learning objectives related to the formulation and implementation of an organizational culture.

1. Understand the impact of new strategy implementation on an organizational system, with particular emphasis on the organizational culture and HRM practices.

DOI: 10.4324/9781003307099-34

2. Discuss some of the determinants of an organizational culture and its alignment with the business strategy and external environment.
3. Suggest changes to an organization's culture and its implementation in an uncertain and turbulent environment.

BACKGROUND TO THE CASE

Chile's continental land is a long, narrow strip that for more than 6,400 km borders the Pacific Ocean, yet its average width is only 177 km. In 2020, it had a GDP of approximately USD 292.9 billion, ranking 43rd in the world and 5th in Latin America. It has a population of 19.1 million people, including 1.5 million immigrants from other Latin American countries that arrived mostly during the last five years. Its economy is distributed as follows: 56.5% in the services sector, 31.4% in the industry sector, and 3.9% in agriculture. Chile is the world's largest copper producer. Minerals comprise 53% of Chilean exports. Other leading exports are fruits, fish products, wood pulp, and wine. From 1990 to 2015, Chile's per capita GDP almost tripled, becoming the second-largest GDP in Latin America in 2021. Over the same period, university enrollment grew by 500%, and income inequality fell below the regional average (*The Economist*, 2021). Such achievements led many to consider Chile as a Latin America success story, due to its democratic stability, economic growth, and social peace.

Nevertheless, during the last decade, an ever-increasing sense of social disconformity grew out of multiple causes, including corruption of the political class, frequent economic collusions of firms in many industries, loss of peoples' trust in the country's institutions (e.g., the justice system), and growing concerns about unfair healthcare, education, and pensions systems (*The Economist*, 2021). The outbreak of COVID-19 further contributed to the hardship and uncertainty, imposing prolonged local and worldwide flight restrictions due to security and health concerns. The disruptiveness of the social outburst and the pandemic forced SKY Airline's executive team to decide whether to continue or reconsider the implementation of a new organizational culture in the face of the new reality.

THE PASSENGER AIR TRANSPORT INDUSTRY IN CHILE

In 2018, three airlines competed in the Chilean local market. SKY Airline, a low-cost carrier (LCC), was Chile's second-largest airline with 25% of the market. Its main competitor was LATAM (59.2% of the market), which operated a mixed model, combining practices from a "legacy model" offering additional services (e.g., first-class seats, airport lounges, complimentary cabin services), with an LCC model in the local market. A third player, JetSmart (15%), entered Chile in 2017 as an ultra-low-cost carrier, where revenue depends on consumers purchasing ancillary products, such as hotel and tour packages. In 2019, domestic passengers in Chile grew by 17% annually, and trips-per-capita was expected to increase.

THE ORIGINS OF THE COMPANY

SKY Airline began operations in 1981 when Jürgen Paulmann, a Chilean businessman, created a company for on-demand flights with a Piper Aztec plane. In 1999 Paulmann and a partner began operating charter flights from Cuba to different Caribbean countries. In 2001, two airlines left the Chilean market, leaving a single local operator, a scenario that required adding an alternative competitor to avoid anti-monopoly laws. Taking advantage of this opportunity SKY decided to operate in Chile. In 2002, SKY made its first flight within Chilean territory, with a Boeing 737-200 and only one passenger. Destinations to Chile's main cities were initiated in the following years. In 2007, it began operating international flights to Peru, Bolivia (2009), Argentina (2010), and Brazil (2018).

During its first decade, SKY was managed from the corporate headquarters of a family business group, which involved more than 40 companies created by Jürgen Paulmann, including supermarkets, processed foods, and wholesale distribution. The corporate culture was marked by the founder's management style. He personally led each company with teams of managers. When the company's founder passed away in 2014, his son Holger Paulmann took over management. Holger had worked in the family business since 2007, learning the ropes by holding various positions including chief operations officer.

By the end of 2014, Holger proposed to the board a complete separation of SKY from the rest of the group's businesses. A new management team was formed, with responsibilities for strategic decisions. The new organization was grouped into six areas: finance, sales and marketing, people, technology, operational safety, internal control, and operations.

TRANSFORMING SKY INTO A LOW-COST CARRIER

With the collaboration of a consulting firm, the possibility to follow the LCC model in Chile was assessed in 2015. An executive at SKY commented on the consulting team's recommendations:

> they concluded that, in the Chilean market, there was room for the development of an LCC airline..., they went further and said that if it wasn't us, it was going to be someone else... if a third low-cost competitor arrived and LATAM was there, we would be crushed in the middle. That was how the decision was made very quickly.
>
> *(Halpern & Minzer, 2018)*

To develop long-term sustainability and anticipate the threat of LCC airlines entering the regional market, SKY announced its LCC strategy in 2015. Soon the executive team concluded the need to realign the organizational system components with the new business model.

Holger became the driving force behind the company's transformation. To guide the LCC model implementation, a new company's mission was formulated: "Putting the sky within everyone's reach by providing a reliable and simple service". As Holger pointed out, "we wanted to democratize air transport" (Paulmann, 2016). In addition, a new vision was created, "Being the best Low-Cost airline for South America". Four principles supported the new model: Customer focus centered on "pay what you use", performance improvement led by technology, efficiency and reliability, and simplicity in processes and services.

SKY's commercial division led changes in service design, sales, profitability, and customer support throughout the travel process. Sales migrated from commercial offices to e-commerce. There were so many changes during the transformation that the idea of "turning everything around" became part of the local language. The commercial division represented the latter by changing, in the company's logo, the direction of the letter "K" in SKY, as in "SʞY". A new corporate image was developed to emphasize a youthful and rebellious attitude (Halpern & Minzer, 2018). However, being an airline, the new image should also convey efficiency and safety, so the idea of "being boldly logical" was emphasized to guide the new strategy implementation. Green and purple were chosen as the new institutional colors. It was decided that these colors better reflected the new spirit and had not been used by other airlines (Halpern & Minzer, 2018). An online media campaign to promote the new image and strategy was launched (for an example, see the video at: www.youtube.com/watch?v=kacVlPzv7wc).

Changes were made throughout the organization during 2017–2018. SʞY's airplane fleet was upgraded with more efficient, less contaminant A320neo Airbus planes. Operational and administrative processes were streamlined. ERP cloud tools were implemented, manual processes were eliminated by 80%, monthly procedure closing times were reduced by 50%, the use of paper was minimized, and a decrease in time of "aircraft turnaround" in airports was reduced to an average of 29 minutes, from the moment a plane landed until it was ready to take off again.

SʞY's HRM function, created in 2014 when the LCC transformation began, was the only unit that started from scratch in the new structure (Tirado, 2023). Previously, HRM processes were shared with the other group businesses at corporate headquarters. Headquarters provided basic HRM services (i.e., employment contracts and salaries payment). Personnel requests were attended to through a corporate HR manager who visited SʞY's operations twice a week. Labor relations were also handled at a corporate level. Francisco Tirado became the new HRM director. One of the first tasks addressed by HRM was the development of a vision: "Our HRM vision is to achieve a committed, agile, and proud organization aligned with our values. We seek to attract and retain the best talent for SʞY's teams".

People management was one of the few areas that increased its workforce during the LCC transformation, instead of experiencing layoffs, as occurred in most of the organization. In September 2019, 35 people worked in the HRM function, distributed in four areas: Personnel administration, labor relations, compensations, and organizational development. This last area included teams dedicated to internal communications, personnel selection, talent development, and change and organizational culture.

DEVELOPING A NEW ORGANIZATIONAL CULTURE

The disciplined and frugal management style and culture that successfully led the first years of the firm needed to change. To allow SʞY to face the challenges that the LCC strategy brought, management recognized the need for a new set of company values. HRM led the change and organizational culture initiatives in the company. Soon it became clear that developing a new organizational culture would require employees' participation. Leading a co-construction process, HRM coordinated several activities with employees and management, to develop a new set of values for SKY (Hartmann, 2019). Meetings, focus groups, and surveys were organized to facilitate the discussion. More than 33% of employees participated in the process. In the final stage of formulating the new culture, a group of employees who were recognized by their peers as representatives of the desired SKY culture as well as being highly motivated by the cultural change, representing the wide variety of employees, joined in a two-day retreat where the new values and associated behaviors were defined (Tirado, 2023). Simultaneously, other firms' organizational cultures, and best practices in culture transmission, were benchmarked.

Four core values were selected and presented to employees through what became known as the "Log of Values and Behaviors" (in reference to a "Flight Log"). These core values were also converted into concrete guidelines for employee behaviors: To **Act Correctly**, by planning, acting, and using time properly to fulfill promises. **Courage**, to make the right decisions for the company, even if they are difficult. **Closeness** to others, to generate a respectful and constructive dialogue with workers and clients. **Committed** to facing changes and difficulties with a positive and collaborative attitude to achieve goals. A code of ethics described the company values clarified unacceptable behaviors, defined a crime prevention model, and specified employees' responsibilities with a fairness culture and law compliance.

The company's digital transformation was not directly addressed in the new cultural values, but it effectively drove a cultural transformation. Referring to the impact of digital transformation, an executive at SKY commented that "we have incorporated technology into the DNA of our organizational culture... it is a requirement for success in an industry like ours".

ALIGNING HRM PROCESSES WITH THE NEW STRATEGY AND CULTURE

SKY's HRM director described that "after defining the new values, the main challenge for the HRM function was to modify all HRM processes and activities, placing the new values at the center of each practice" (Tirado, 2023). It was essential to ensure alignment with the strategy and consistency across HRM practices. The physical work environment was redesigned. At the corporate building and airport locations the color purple, the signature of the new corporate image, was highlighted. New spaces for recreation, relaxation, privacy, and to facilitate creativity and innovation, were developed. Thematic settings, related to the world of airlines, were built. For example, next to the open-floor offices, enclosed telephone booths were created, with nicknames associated with the language of aviation (i.e., Charlie), to facilitate private conversations. Airplane seats were added to some rest areas. An internal branding campaign to promote the new culture was held throughout the firm. In meeting rooms and common spaces, phrases referring to the new culture were installed. Soon, the company consciously decided to refer to employees as "SKYERS", promoting a sense of identity and belonging. A social media campaign was launched to announce the new company values and corporate building changes (for an example, see the video at: www.youtube.com/watch?v=In0Y3EDvf2U).

HRM practices were redesigned to support the new strategy and culture. Personnel selection processes were completely transformed, incorporating an assessment of job candidates' alignment to the newly defined values and behaviors as a central part of the personnel selection guidelines. Line managers made decisions on the technical competencies of candidates (Tirado, 2023). Available positions, and first contact with applicants, were conducted through the company's website and social networks (LinkedIn, Indeed, Laborum, etc.). After filtering applicants according to job competencies, candidates' "fit" to the organizational culture was assessed through interviews (Hartmann, 2019). Candidates with previous training or experience in project management were highly valued for many managerial positions. Similarly, the performance evaluation process, originally designed to assess generic corporate competencies, was redesigned at all levels to include the evaluation of values and behaviors.

Several training and development initiatives were implemented during the strategy change. Culture workshops promoting corporate values and strategic principles were held throughout the organization. In "Our Values Stories", a successful annual initiative, SKYERS were asked about real-life stories experienced by themselves or their colleagues, which reflected the new set of values at work. These stories were used as examples communicated throughout the organization via more playful activities (e.g., small puppet theaters), facilitating SKYERS' identification with the new values and comprehending how they transferred to their daily work (Tirado, 2023). Other training programs in topics related to accident reduction, professional and mental health, teamwork, and continuous improvement were contracted for all levels of employees, including senior management.

A milestone event in the transmission of the corporate culture was the onboarding process, an in-house managed program, prided by company members (Hartmann, 2019). Its highlight consists of a half-day retreat at corporate headquarters held once a month. Every new entrant to the company is invited. The retreat is directed by the CEO and starts with a socializing breakfast, followed by a welcome motivational speech, where the CEO transmits the company history, corporate values, and the importance of collaborators for the company. Other executives follow with presentations about specific topics. The process communicates to new workers the warm, inclusive, open-door leadership style they should expect. SKY seeks to promote and develop leaders who can create close and respectful relations with their team members, have a strategic and global vision of the business, possess ethical standards to serve as models to others, and hold the technical knowledge necessary to achieve company goals.

People from more than 20 different nationalities work at the company, making diversity inclusion an essential part of its culture. Consistently, SKY's compensation strategy is based on an equal pay policy for men and women. Initially, the policy was implemented for managerial positions and later was extended to all positions. Francisco Tirado, SKY's HRM director, noted:

> We are a tremendously inclusive company. Our rate of foreign workers is higher than the industry average. We live in a very specialized industry so borders disappear when it comes to finding the best. SKY was founded by German immigrants, so it is our essence to work in a multicultural team… We make efforts to simplify the process of obtaining a work visa for foreigners with a professional degree or technical qualification who see Chile and our company as an attractive destination where to develop.
>
> *(RH Management, 2016)*

The company's inclusion practices have also sought to protect the elderly. "The challenge we have for the future is to improve the quality of life of the elderly… we have a tremendous opportunity to contribute by generating initiatives that promote an active and healthy aging" added Francisco (Valdés, 2019). Benchmarking and search for best practices in diversity and inclusive management are frequently carried out in collaboration with the International Labor

Organization, governmental offices, and minority rights advocate organizations. The company's diversity and inclusion policies have been transmitted to 100% of employees. The topic has also been incorporated into the "onboarding" program, leaders' training, organizational climate studies, job analyses, and company regulations. To reinforce the centrality of people at SKY, the board decided that the local results obtained at the organizational climate survey are some of the key performance indicators in the incentive system for all SKY's managers and supervisors' positions, data which is collected every month.

To promote the company's regard for local communities, a social media campaign communicated the "democratization" of flying and promoted SKY programs that facilitate air travel to communities that previously did not have the opportunity to fly (for example, see this video: www.youtube.com/watch?v=3BkPKgAFIwg). In 2018 and 2019, the new strategy implementation paid off when SKY received Skytrax recognition for being the best low-cost airline in Latin America.

THE 2019 SOCIAL OUTBURST AND THE COVID-19 PANDEMIC IN CHILE

On Friday, October 18, 2019, a series of demonstrations took place in the country, where citizens raised their voices for different social demands, unfortunately accompanied by riots, looting, and fires, triggering a social crisis. Many industries were affected, including airlines. In the first hours, control over flights was lost, airport food establishments were unable to cope with stranded passengers, and flights were rescheduled again and again. Discontent at the airports was enormous. Within hours, SKY reinforced its call-center team and communicated to passengers its high flexibility for rescheduling flights at no cost. The next day, airport security and sanitary conditions became uncertain. Pilots and other crew members were stranded on highways, unable to reach the airport on time for their flights due to traffic disruptions by protesters. Most flights were canceled or rescheduled. SKY had to cancel 144 flights, affecting about 24 thousand passengers.

The problems would only worsen with the soon-to-come COVID-19 pandemic. On March 3, 2020, the first case of COVID-19 was confirmed in Chile. The outbreak spread throughout the country. Soon, the government closed the country's air borders and prohibited international flights. In April and May 2020, only 5% of scheduled domestic flights were made. SKY Airline asked the government for financial help to protect employees. This aid was temporary, and over the months a more drastic decision was needed. By September 2020, dismissals had reached more than 300 employees, about 35% of the total headcount.

The pandemic forced SKY managers not only to face the financial and operational crisis. New health and safety requirements were introduced (e.g., disinfection, temperature checks, viral tests). Moreover, passengers expected carriers to provide protection from flight uncertainty and health concerns. Similarly, employees' concerns about job stability and health security at work grew exponentially. In early 2020, the company prioritized working from home (WfH). Obviously, the latter policy was not possible for airport personnel, pilots, and cabin crews.

The level of disruptiveness of the social outburst and the pandemic surprised SKY Airline's executives. A path of economic uncertainty and instability could last for several years to come.

SKY's HRM team has had to face a new reality and decide whether to persevere with the HRM strategy and cultural changes or readjust.

CASE STUDY QUESTIONS FOR DISCUSSION

1. How would you characterize the environment and challenges faced by SKY when making the decision to transform the airline into a LCC? Do you think that SKY took a correct strategic decision when adopting a LCC strategy?
2. How prepared was the organization for the new business strategy?
3. What roles did the HRM function played in the LCC business model implementation?
4. How would you describe the new culture?

REFERENCES

Halpern, P. & Minzer, V. 2018. *Comunicación Estratégica*. Ediciones UC.

Hartmann, R. 2019. Presentation "Cultura Sky" at MRH PUC, May 30, 2019.

Paulmann, H. 2016. Revista a bordo. September 2016, page 4.

rhmanagement. 2016. https://rhmanagement.cl/fuerza-laboral-emergente-inmigrantes-en-chile/

The Economist. 2021. https://www.economist.com/the-americas/2021/10/28/chile-once-considered
-latin-americas-finland-is-in-trouble

Tirado, F. 2023. SKY airlines HRM Director. Personal communication.

Valdés, P. 2019. https://www.lacuarta.com/cronica/noticia/conocida-aerolinea-se-compromete
-inclusion-laboral-personas-mayores/397556/

CHAPTER 29

Colombia

Sustainable Human Resources Management: Balancing Profitability and Talent Well-Being in an Insurance Company[1]

Jaime Andrés Bayona and Luisa Fernanda Maya

CASE SYNOPSIS

Valor Insurance Company (VIC) began its operations more than 40 years ago. Since then, it has been acknowledged as one of Colombia's best firms to work for due to recognition of its family-focused corporate culture. In 2014, Star Insures (a multinational reinsurance company) bought 51% of VIC, generating the opening of new lines of business. This purchase brought insecurity and instability for employees, and due to financial situations, during 2018 and 2019, some layoffs were made.

The case analyzes how sustainable human resource management (HRM) practices can help to keep talent within the organization and help the company achieve its new strategic objectives. For this, the case lays out the story of Alexandra, the HRM of VIC, who needs to advocate for the retention of talent that maintains the family spirit of the company, but at the same time, has concerns about how to keep VIC economically sustainable. In this case, students are expected to identify sustainable HRM practices of VIC and evaluate the impact of such practices on worker turnover. This analysis should consider the national and organizational cultures and the current financial challenges facing VIC after its acquisition by the multinational company.

DOI: 10.4324/9781003307099-35

KEYWORDS

Sustainable HRM, talent management, well-being, Colombia

LEARNING OUTCOMES

1. Identify sustainable HRM practices in an organization.
2. Identify internal corporate social responsibility practices in an organization.
3. Evaluate the impact of sustainable HRM practices on worker turnover.

ORGANIZATIONAL CONTEXT

VIC was founded in 1979, as a family firm, and its shareholders were direct family members or close friends. Thus, the organizational culture was formed around family, where those hired were referred by relatives or close friends. Regardless of the position, individuals held a great closeness that always prevailed, with no significant power distance (Calderón et al., 1990).

HRM IN COLOMBIA

Colombia is a country with 50 million habitants that has recently joined the OECD, which has led to a series of economic, political, and cultural transformations. The country's GDP in 2021 was USD 295.610 billion, with a GDP per capita of USD 5,752 (International Monetary Fund, 2021) and a Gini coefficient of 51.7, placing it as one of the most unequal countries in the world (World Bank, 2021). The unemployment rate was around 9.5% before the pandemic (DANE, 2019); 62% of workers in the country are in the service sector, 21% in industry, and 17% in agriculture. Most Colombian companies (~90%) are small in term number of workers and profitability, but they generate around 80% of employment in the country and 35% of its GDP (Mintrabajo, 2019).

In the cultural sphere, Colombia has been traditionally seen as a country ranking high in collectivism, power distance, and uncertainty avoidance (Hofstede, 2001). However, more recent data have indicated that the country is much more individualistic, possibly due to its entry into the global market, where this trait is highly valued in the business environment (Bayona, 2021).

Regarding HRM, since most of the companies are family-owned and small or medium-sized, their HRM practices tend to follow a traditional administrative approach. However, with increasing globalization during the last 20 years, HRM processes need to be aligned with organizational strategy. Currently, different HRM associations promote such alignment among their associated companies. Furthermore, some consulting firms assess companies' branding in terms of excellence. This has caught the attention of companies since they have seen these listings as a way to enhance their reputation and attract and retain talent (Calderón et al., 2010).

ORGANIZATIONAL CULTURE

The organizational culture of VIC has always been characterized as being people-oriented; this culture has transcended decades, regardless of changes in CEOs or the arrival of new shareholders. Due to its flat hierarchy, top management seeks to focus on providing lower-level positions such as professionals, technicians, or operatives with the sense that VIC is their second home. This is a culture where employees feel comfortable sharing ideas with their colleagues and managers. In the same way, such a culture is intended to provide security, stability, and support for their financial and vocational needs. VIC, from its origins, has been a company that has focused on employee well-being. Although it is not a corporate policy, the practice is that every employee is considered a fundamental part of the organization, whose development and happiness are key to firm success.

With positive reviews in employer branding surveys, the organization has positioned itself and generated visibility in the labor market as a great place to work. These reviews evaluate the most promising companies in various categories, including employee–supervisor relationships, connections between teams and functions, and a sense of belonging (Great Place to Work, 2021). In 2011, VIC was selected among the 50 best companies in this survey. In 2013, the firm was ranked 8th, in 2014, it ranked 28th, and on the last survey, carried out in 2016, VIC was not included as a finalist, which triggered a work plan to regain trust and credibility.

ACQUISITION BY STAR INSURES

In 2014, the European company Star Insures (a reinsurance company) bought 51% of VIC, generating the opening of new business lines and more significant support for customers.[2] At the time of purchase, Star Insures highlighted the importance of generating greater profitability. However, the CEO, Álvaro Rodríguez, made it clear that VIC was in a good position thanks to its employees. As such, it was essential to avoid personnel restructuring under the merger. The acquisition generated great fear of losing their jobs among employees, especially those with high tenure, which sometimes led to decreased productivity.

Following the acquisition, the corporate mission statement and values were modified. The current mission is: "We are a leading provider of corporate insurance solutions. We apply new perspectives, expert knowledge, and financial capacity to support our clients in anticipating and managing risks, protecting their assets, and thus supporting Colombia's development, renewal, and progress" (Valor Insurance Company, 2018). Regarding values: "We act with integrity and rectitude of conduct, honesty, transparency, impartiality, and personal responsibility, we are consistent with what we think, say and do" (Valor Insurance Company, 2018).

CHALLENGES OF VIC

Current financial situation. After being purchased by Star Insures, it was thought that the company's economic situation would improve. However, the numbers were contrary to expectations. In 2014 the company's net profit was USD 6.5 million, in 2015, USD 20 million, and in 2016, USD 3 million; in 2017 and 2018, the numbers were red, with losses of USD 2.5 million

FIGURE 29.1 Percentage of turnover at VIC from 2016 to 2019 by quarters

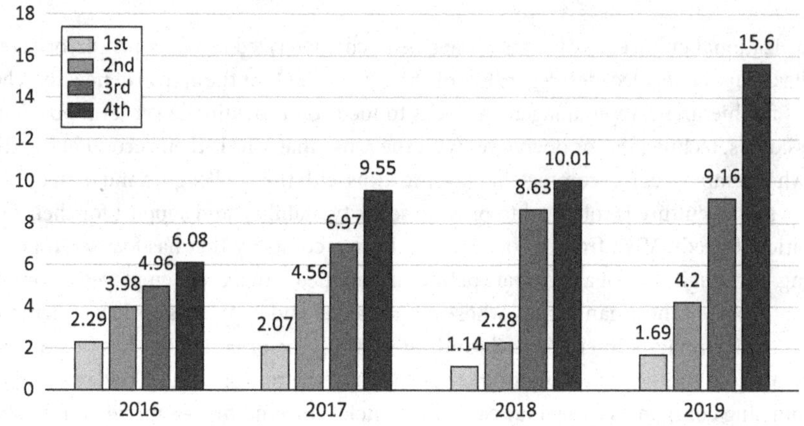

Source: VIC HRM department

each year; finally, in 2019 the losses were estimated to be around USD 6 million. These downward trends generated emotional stress in the collaborators, as well as a decrease in the commitment and turnover of staff.

Staff turnover. Year after year, the HRM department meets with the planning management and the operations VPs, to establish the maximum percentages in which the turnover indicator can be moved (i.e., rotation policy). However, the total population of the company has been decreasing year after year due to the restructurings that have been made. In some cases, after the person retires, the need to rehire is evaluated, and in other cases, due to process optimization issues, outsourcing is used to carry out the work.

Figure 29.1 shows the accumulated turnover level for each quarter from 2016 to 2019. The end of 2019 was not favorable since the indicator ended at a turnover level of 15.6%, exceeding the previous years and exceeding the maximum level established by the rotation policy, which is 13% per year. The reason given by employees for resigning was a better job opportunity in 47% of the cases.

Alexandra Vargas, HRM at VIC, is concerned because next week she will have a meeting with the CEO, who informed her that the new majority shareholders of the company had requested an action plan to deal with the current turnover problem: The company is facing a significant talent drain (in technical positions requiring a university degree and specialized certifications) but at the same time facing financial difficulties. How do we remain responsible to workers in times of financial problems? VIC has been recognized as an excellent workplace, offering its employees many additional benefits than those required by law. How do we deal with increased staff turnover due to job insecurity? Alexandra is expected to offer "economically viable" alternatives to reduce staff turnover without modifying the family culture that has characterized the organization.

SUSTAINABLE HRM PRACTICES AT VIC

Following the change in organizational culture, a series of practices that are aligned with talent management have been implemented. In a recent seminar on current HRM tendencies,

Alexandra learned that sustainable HRM involves actions organizations should implement to guarantee constant access to quality HR (Müller-Christ & Remer, 1999). This definition implies that: (1) Sustainable HRM focuses on daily practices; (2) its objective is to attract and retain talented workers; and (3) the concept of sustainability is understood as maintaining a workforce that allows compliance with organizational goals, so its emphasis is on vertical alignment. This last component is critical, as sustainable HRM should align with the firm strategy without compromising the company's ability to meet current and future business needs. Sustainable HRM has two horizons of action, the present and the future, so it focuses on required resources and how scarce they may be in the future (Mariappanadar, 2003).

Alexandra also remembered from a course on sustainable HRM that

> the human resource management practices are based on three principles. First is the organization's ability to attract and maintain talents and be considered a company where professionals would desire to work for (to be more attractive than the competitors). Second, the workforce should remain healthy and motivated. Third, the organization should invest in the employees' qualifications, aiming for current and future scenarios.
>
> *(Macke & Genari, 2019, p. 812)*

VIC focused its HRM practices around the concept of internal corporate social responsibility (Mory et al., 2016), meaning that the firm must go beyond regulatory compliance, applying practices that precisely seek the development of its workers. These practices are a point of contact between corporate social responsibility and HRM insofar as they are traditional practices in some types of HRM systems, such as talent management or high-performance practices. During the last couple of years, VIC has implemented seven basic practices to improve talent retention: Job stability, work environment, skill development, workforce diversity, work-life balance, substantial worker involvement, and empowerment.

Job stability. VIC provides stability to the collaborators who are part of this company. Employees hired under a long-term contract amount to 94%, and the remaining 6% are fixed-term contracts due to the need to cover transferred positions for some projects being developed in the company. In addition, there is a temporary services company, with whom the holiday replacement is handled.

Work environment. The work environment has much collaboration among colleagues. Employees can communicate directly with all kinds of positions. They can contribute and be heard to make improvements, either in their work area or contributions to different areas. Everyone is heard; even the CEO has a designated space to listen to employee concerns.

Regarding occupational health, this area depends directly on HRM, it operates following legal standards, but at the moment, there is no occupational health and safety management system (SG-SST). However, the company is carrying this out. This situation arose because, due to the company's financial issues, its implementation remained on standby, as non-execution could have led to even more expensive penalties.

Skills development. VIC uses the practice of job rotation, which allows collaborators in an area or those who have had better performance in the company to go to different parts of the world to receive training and return to train their work team. This activity provides greater recognition and the possibility of growing and getting better positions in other countries.

Training used to have a reasonably large budget (around USD 250,000 per year) and provided opportunities to acquire and improve soft skills and other aspects that could contribute to performance. At the end of 2018, the budget in this area was cut. For 2019, the budget allowed was USD 100,000, which may be for English courses and two operational schools. The subscription school teaches subscribers new lines of business that they will be working on soon, including tools for a better examination of insurance policies. The portfolio school teaches them how to utilize new and better tactics to recover their arrears. The rest of the training that had been developed for the rest of the employees remained on standby.

Workforce diversity. VIC has always been an inclusive company. Women hold most senior management positions; three out of five VPs and 24 of 32 managers and directors are women. In total, 64% of the company's positions are held by women. Similarly, the company has two Afro-descendant race employees, and one of them occupies a middle-high position.

Work-life balance. Although the firm would like to improve employees' work-life balance, it constantly asks its employees to "go the extra mile" and to commit to working extra hours (without pay), even during weekends.

Tangible employee involvement. Every employee can access financial information and the organization's performance if managers download the information to their subordinates. However, several times, employees report wanting to know the organization's performance, but their leaders do not constantly prioritize the activity. They think sharing this information could generate some alarms, decreasing performance and even prompting the employee to seek a new job. In previous years, when the company's situation generated a higher level of profitability, all employees were recognized for their excellent performance at the end of the year. In addition, the annual wage increment was a few points above the legal requirements, and the extra-legal premium was divided into June and December.

Empowerment. Each employee in the organization has a level of empowerment in the processes they manage. This can be high, medium, or low, depending on their position. At the highest levels, such as CEO, VPs, managers, and directors, decision-making is faster, and no more incredible protocol is required to execute new action plans, as long as they do not generate budget expenses. At medium levels, such as professionals, a protocol of greater monitoring in terms of decision-making must be followed, and authorization to execute a new process must be requested. Finally, more monitoring of their day-to-day work is required for low-level positions, such as assistants. In these types of positions, they have no possibility of making proposals for innovation or improvements.

RESPONSES TO INTERNALLY RESPONSIBLE HRM PRACTICES

Employees have responded differently to these talent management practices. Although these practices are intended to improve the quality of working life of all workers at VIC, some have shown to be more successful than others. For job stability, as almost all employees are under long-term contracts, their satisfaction with the company is high, and it functions as a robust retention process. For the work environment, as the family-oriented culture is shared at all levels of employees, it is a valuable feature of the organization. However, since the acquisition of VIC by Star Insures, the perception of this family-oriented culture has declined among the employees, as they feel that the new management is reinforcing more individualistic values.

Regarding skills development, the training programs were quite popular among all employees. However, as programs' duration declined over time, so did an essential motivator to stay in

TABLE 29.1 Relation between ICSR factors, turnover, and strategy

Factor	Turnover reduction	Strategy compliance
Job stability	Maintains talent Expensive, especially temp agency	Low
Work environment	Talent maintenance An occupational health system is necessary If not implemented can lead to lawsuits	Medium
Development possibilities	Expensive Talent retention You can look for trained talent in the market	Medium-high, depending on the training objectives
Diversity	Maintenance and attraction of talent Cheap	Medium
Work-life balance	Half price Talent retention improvement	Low WLB: High High WLB: Low-medium
Tangible participation	Expensive attraction and retention	Low
Empowerment	Retention and attraction Inexpensive training related	Medium

the organization, resulting in more turnover. In terms of diversity, although still highly valued in VIC, some concerns arise due to new hires being paused and the rise in turnover, particularly among women with family responsibilities. The case for work-life balance is more complicated, as the insurance sector is highly demanding in terms of time, and generally, there is an overlap between work and family spaces. Although VIC does not explicitly require its workers to work extra hours, implicit requirements for strategic workers are based on projects that sometimes run under tight deadlines, which, de facto, entails extra hours and high stress. As the current financial situation of VIC is not good, all extra monetary incentives have been paused, causing employees' motivation to decrease. Employees do not receive any additional compensation for their intense work (significantly since some of the positions have been expanded, including more tasks and responsibilities to cover employees who left the firm). Finally, regarding empowerment, some workers experienced an increase in the level of responsibility, yet this has led to stress due to overload. Table 29.1 shows the relationship between ICSR practices, turnover, and strategy related to the financial situation.

CASE STUDY QUESTIONS FOR DISCUSSION[3]

1. Which sustainable HRM practices are available to organizations, in general? Which among these practices contributes to minimizing employee turnover, in particular?

2. How are the sustainable HRM practices you chose in Question 1 aligned with the organization's strategic objectives?

3. After reviewing the company's background, it is time to propose sustainable HRM practices that maintain the spirit of commitment to VIC in its employees and respect its budgetary limitations. What should the main components of this proposal be?

4. HR manager Alexandra must focus on those HRM practices that could help to address the turnover problem. However, simultaneously, she must keep costs at bay and ensure that the selected practices enhance compliance with the company's strategic objectives. Which practices should she select and why?

NOTES

1 The case is based on a real organization. The names of the organization and the protagonists have been changed.

2 An insurance company protects the client from risk directly; a reinsurance company protects an insurance company from risk.

3 In order to properly answer these questions, it is advisable to first read the following articles: Macke and Genari (2019), and Mory et al. (2016).

REFERENCES

Bayona, J.A. 2021. *Global Work Design: Colombia* [Manuscript in preparation]. Department of Business, Pontificia Universidad Javeriana.

Calderón, G., Naranjo, J.C., & Álvarez, C.M. 2010. *Human Resources Management in Colombia: Roles, Practices, Challenges, and Limitations*. Bogotá, Colombia: ACRIP Bogotá and Cundinamarca.

Calderón, M. Leiva, G., & Cortés, M. 1990. Confidence, surety insurance company. Available in the archive of the area of the Legal Vice Presidency and Corporate Affairs. Taken on August 2, 2019.

DANE. 2019. Large integrated household survey, December. https://www.dane.gov.co/index .php/estadisticas-por-tema/demografia-y-poblacion

Great Place to Work. 2021. Best Workplaces in Colombia 2011. https://www.greatplacetowork .com.co/es/listas/los-mejores-lugares-para-trabajar-en-colombia/2011

Hofstede, G. 2001. *Culture's Consequences: Comparing Values, Behaviors, Institutions and Organizations Across Nations*. London: SAGE Publications, Inc.

International Monetary Fund. 2021. World economic outlook database: Colombia. April 2021. https://www.imf.org/en/Countries/COL

Macke, J., & Genari, D. 2019. Systematic literature review on sustainable human resource management. *Journal of Cleaner Production*, 208: 806–815. https://doi.org/10.1016/j.jclepro .2018.10.091

Mariappanadar S. 2003. Sustainable human resource strategy: The sustainable and unsustainable dilemmas of retrenchment. *International Journal of Social Economy*, 30(7–8): 906–923.

Mintrabajo. 2019. Press release: MiPymes represent more than 90% of the national productive sector and generate 80% of employment in Colombia. https://www.mintrabajo.gov.co /prensa/comunicados/2019/septiembre/mipymes-representan-mas-de-90-del-sector -productivo-nacional-y-generan-el-80-del-empleo-en-colombia-ministra-alicia-arango

Mory, L., Wirtz, B. W., & Göttel, V. 2016. Factors of internal corporate social responsibility and the effect on organizational commitment. *The International Journal of Human Resource Management*, 27(13): 1393–1425. https://doi.org/10.1080/09585192.2015.1072103

Müller-Christ, G., & Remer, A. 1999. Umweltwirtschaft oder wirtschaftsökologie? Vorüberlegungen zu einer theorie des ressourcenmanagements [Environmental economics or economic ecology? Preliminary considerations on a theory of resource management]. . In: Seidel, E., editor. Betriebliches umweltmanagement im 21 Jahrhundert: aspekte, aufgaben, perspektiven [Corporate Environmental Management in the 21st Century Aspects, Tasks, Perspectives] Berlin, Heidelberg: Springer.

Valor Insurance Company. 2018, May 14. Who we are. http: // srvvmshp: 9005 / SitePages / QuienesSomos.aspx

World Bank. 2021. Gini index: Colombia. https://data.worldbank.org/indicator/SI.POV.GINI ?locations=CO

CHAPTER 30

Mexico

HRM Experiences from a Danish Firm in Mexico: "Changing" Mexican Culture

Jacobo Ramirez and Laura Zapata-Cantú

CASE SYNOPSIS

This case relates to the challenges faced by a Danish multinational healthcare corporation (Global Care) in implementing its human resource management (HRM) system in its Mexican subsidiary. We present a cross-country comparison of management styles and HRM systems in Denmark and Mexico based on the differing institutional backgrounds and discuss the challenges and potential solutions for adapting HRM practices for the Mexican context. The key problem faced by Global Care is the adaptation of its people management system. Global Care's HRM system features three subsystems: People flow, appraisal and rewards, and employment relations. We examine the distinctions between the Mexican and Danish (Scandinavian) managerial models with regard to national and corporate cultures for people flow, appraisal, and rewards subsystems.

KEYWORDS

HRM system, MNC, institutional context, Denmark, Mexico

DOI: 10.4324/9781003307099-36

LEARNING OUTCOMES

1. Describe and discuss HRM strategies that MNCs can use when entering Mexico.
2. Discuss the various institutional settings related to HRM in Mexico, as well as implications for the development and implementation of HRM systems in Mexico.
3. Discuss contextualization and adaptation processes in the design and implementation of HRM systems in Mexico.

ORGANIZATIONAL CONTEXT

Global Care[1] is a Danish healthcare corporation and global industry leader. The company offers a broad portfolio of healthcare products including hormone systems. According to Global Care's reports (2021), they have over 45,000 full-time employees in nine countries (Algeria, Brazil, China, Denmark, France, Japan, Russia, UK, and the United States), research and development centers in five countries (China, Denmark, India, UK, and the United States), and 96 office locations in 82 countries. The company's internationalization plan is to expand into Latin America and other emerging markets. They opened a pharmaceutical commercialization and distribution branch in Mexico in 2004, which currently employs about 200 full-time staff.

Global Care's HRM system includes a people management framework that incorporates its core principles, policies, and practices. The HRM system is adopted by all its subsidiaries as standard. However, in emerging countries such as Mexico, the presence of foreign direct investment (FDI) makes it challenging to attract and retain young and highly educated managers with international business management experience (Ramirez & Søderberg, 2021; World Bank, 2020). This case examines the operations of Global Care in the Mexican context, specifically how Mexican management styles have been shaped by the legacy of cultural traits and political, economic, and environmental crises in Mexico, and how management styles have changed with the introduction of new HRM policies and practices to embrace global trends. The purpose of this case is to examine the extant institutional environment in Mexico and how it affects management styles and HRM systems compared to those in Denmark.

NATIONAL CONTEXT

Mexico is the tenth most populous country in the world, with indigenous people accounting for 15.1% of its 130 million inhabitants. Mexico has achieved economic development since the late 1980s, aided by consistent and stable macroeconomic policies that mitigate investment risk.

HRM ISSUES IN MEXICO: HISTORICAL PERSPECTIVE AND CURRENT STATE

The Mexican business culture and management style are deeply rooted in Mexican society and remain so despite the implementation of "modern" HRM systems. Researchers addressing HRM systems in Mexico have highlighted the perceived importance of values such as family, dignity, and loyalty, as well as cultural dimensions such as high-power distance, collectivism (Chhokar, Brodbeck, & House, 2007), and hierarchical (top-down) decision-making.

The traditional workplace environment in Mexico is based on strong family values. Everyone works together according to their designated roles, and employees develop strong allegiances to their company, which they view as an extended family. CEOs and firm owners are considered paternal figures and use an autocratic management style (Elvira & Davila, 2005). Supervisors tend to be understanding (*compresivo*) and assist subordinates when the need arises while keeping their distance and addressing workers formally. Workers seem to appreciate and respond warmly to such formal and dignified treatment, as long as the authority is not abused. In this context, it is common to encounter a business culture of "boss worship" (*una cultura del culto al jefe*) in which authority (*autoridad*) plays a distinctive role in management (Ramirez & Søderberg, 2021). Decision-making is generally based on status, and workers avoid questioning decisions – it is not acceptable to contradict a supervisor's opinion in public, especially across hierarchical levels (e.g., Stephens & Greer, 1995). Further, Mexican workers tend to expect instructions and have little individual control over their tasks or work processes.

The influence of the *machismo* ethic in Mexico means that many Mexicans are inclined toward face-saving, that is, they tend to avoid openly disclosing a lack of knowledge, admitting mistakes or failures, or communicating bad news out of fear of how their bosses will react. This might be explained by the lack of unemployment insurance in Mexico, which means most employees make every effort to keep their jobs. Nevertheless, these dynamics are being challenged by younger generations, who expect and demand open-door policies where employees' questions and complaints are welcome. Younger employees also favor inclusive workplaces (e.g., Paludi et al., 2021), which has led to a growing need to consider diversity (gender, sexual orientation, and other traits) and personalization of HRM systems (e.g., Ramirez & Søderberg, 2021) to attract and retain key employees. In addition, the so-called "*mañana*" syndrome (where deadlines are always pushed to "tomorrow") appears to be in decline (e.g., Elvira & Davila, 2005).

Recurrent financial crises and the institutional context of security risk have rendered non-monetary compensation an important motivator for Mexican employees. Methods of improving employees' commitment and decreasing staff turnover, such as by integrating flexible work schedules, are not new in Mexico. In addition, an egalitarian and humanistic leadership style – which aims to balance the individual and economic perspectives of an organization (Davila & Elvira, 2012) – has emerged alongside globalization and increased FDI (World Bank, 2020). This growing humanistic leadership style attempts to boost individual performance by emphasizing training (Ramirez & Søderberg, 2021), providing care and social support, and ensuring gender equality in the workplace (Paludi, Barragan, & Mills, 2021). In addition to humanistic policies and practices, the institutional context of security risk means that Mexican companies and subsidiaries must invest pragmatically in security hardware and implement calculated policies and practices based on strict candidate and employee control. This presents an inherent dual-ity: HRM systems must have 1) strong and strict employee protection and screening; and 2) a humanistic orientation, such as flexibility. Thus, the balance between stability and flexibility is a strategic dilemma when designing HRM systems in Mexico. Mexican workers respond well to monetary and non-monetary rewards that emphasize emotional appeals, family support, and social support, such as healthcare and counseling programs for employees and their families, a canteen and hot meal when working, and premiums for good attendance, punctuality, and over-time. Indeed, many Mexican employees now expect firms to provide such benefits, and they are key to building loyalty. This corresponds to the paternalistic nature of employers.

HRM ISSUES IN THE CONTEXT OF GLOBAL CARE MEXICO

Global Care Denmark's HRM System

Global Care Denmark's people management framework aims to help its managers and employees act in accordance with the firm's core values, particularly in relation to diversity and inclusion. According to a manager in Denmark, "The people management framework... combines mod-ern value-based management with traditional control [e.g., a respectful, healthy, and engaging working environment; optimized way of working; ambitious goals; and pursuit of excellence]". The people management framework was implemented in Mexico through a series of high-per-formance HRM practices, as presented in Table 30.1 (Bamberger & Meshoulam, 2000, p. 66–67).

The HRM manager of Global Care Mexico commented that "The Charter for companies in the Global Care Group and the people management framework established a new way of think-ing and working across the company". The HRM department has four employees in the fol-lowing functional areas: Recruitment; selection and career development; operational personnel management; and communication and general service. The corporate building is in Lomas de Chapultepec, an exclusive area of Mexico City, and the workplace is spacious, creating an open and pleasant atmosphere. The coffee bar has fresh fruit, water, and tea.

HRM subsystem: People flow. Global Care Mexico has adapted its recruitment and selection processes to the Mexican business environment. For example, in Denmark, the main recruit-ment channels are firms' websites, university fairs, and specialized recruitment agencies. Global Care's brand was not well known in Mexico in 2009; thus, the firm faced challenges in attract-ing employees. The HRM manager commented, "We are new in the Mexican market [and] very small in comparison to our competition, e.g., Eli Lilly. It was difficult for applicants to understand Global Care's philosophy". Thus, employees' personal networks were an important resource for recruitment. Such "word of mouth" recruiting is a powerful channel in Mexico (Elvira & Davila, 2005), which is characterized by strong relationships between friends and fam-ily members that assist them in handling work- and non-work-related issues. An employee of Global Care Mexico commented, "Global Care is a very open organization. This openness helps us to learn from each other and the environment".

To avoid discriminatory practices within the hiring process, Global Care Mexico's managers' recruit and select employees based on their job profile. The recruitment and selection manager explained,

We have access to the main HRM operational processes of the firm; however, we needed to adapt it to Mexican legislation. Global Care's philosophy is completely different from [that of] other companies that I have worked for (in the USA and Mexico). Now, I have to make sure that there is no discrimination in any of our HRM subsystems.

According to the HRM manager, demographics such as age, gender, and marital status all influence hiring decisions in Mexico. Global Care Denmark views this as discriminatory and geared toward employees with a "submissive" profile who fit the Mexican tradition of compliance.

A distinctive feature of the selection process is an online psychological test. The recruiting supervisor sends the candidate a web link, and the candidate can then complete the test anytime and anywhere. This is relatively unique in Mexico, as most psychological testing is still strictly supervised by firms' recruitment and selection departments because of the low-trust society (e.g., Kühlmann, 2005). Global Care Mexico's approach manifests basic values of trust and honesty, in line with the firm's policy of equal opportunity, which features absolute respect for individuals as human beings. As a manager in Mexico commented,

TABLE 30.1 Configuration of high-performance HRM practices in Mexico[2]

HRM subsystem	Resource and control-based HRM practices	Sample HRM practices at Global Care Mexico
People flow	Staffing	• Selective training
	Training	• Developing broad-based skills and tailoring training and development to the individual based on their level of personal autonomy
	Mobility (internal and external)	• Broad career paths
	Job security	• Guaranteed job security
	Diversity and inclusion	• Scheduling to circumvent problems caused by the security risk context, with a focus on women and people with lower socioeconomic status • Teleworking/work-from-home schemes
Appraisal and rewards	Appraisal	• Long-term, results-oriented appraisal
	Rewards	• Extensive, open-ended rewards
Employment relations	Job design	• Broad job description; flexible work assignments
	Participation	• Encouragement of participation and teamwork
	Welfare (physical and mental)	• Integral, personalized programs for physical, mental, financial, and social health

There is a complete lack of trust in some firms in Mexico, and of course when you arrive at an organization like Global Care Mexico, you say "Can this really be true?" You have to pinch yourself to make sure you're not dreaming.

Global Care Mexico's training and development program comprises an induction process followed by manager training/coaching and assessment based on competencies and feedback using a balanced scorecard approach. Employees are responsible for their own development and training, requiring a notable change in mindset. According to the HRM manager, "The biggest challenge in Mexico is to 'erase' the types of behaviors that contradict the Danish culture and Global Care people management framework. We need to de-skill our 'old' Mexican skills [and teach them] the 'new' method of management". In this sense, Global Care Denmark considers its employees as one of three types. The first type has worked at other firms that share Global Care's values to some extent. For this type of employee, the Global Care management framework is not completely "new". The second type of employee has worked only in Mexican firms and is thus more likely to need to unlearn old work habits based on "typical Mexican" management styles. The firm needs to coach these individuals to understand and perform their work according to Global Care's principles. The third type of employee has no work experience. For these employees, it is relatively easy to learn Global Care's management framework. As the HRM manager commented, "Across Global Care, we are working hard to implement a learning culture to help people build new competencies quickly". Global Care's challenge in Mexico seems to be getting employees to believe in and practice the firm's values. A manager in Mexico explained,

We cannot tolerate double or false standards. We cannot use certain values at work and others at home. The goal would be that after we start [using these values in our work], it affects our daily life at home, with friends, etc.

Global Care Mexico has implemented work-from-home schemes for its employees. The advantages of this include women being able to apply for higher-paying jobs because they can balance their careers and childcare, thus bridging the wage gap. Furthermore, remote working benefits climate change imperatives and the environment by reducing commuter journeys.

HRM subsystem: Appraisal and rewards. At Global Care Mexico, employee performance is appraised based on a balanced scorecard approach. Everyone is evaluated with the same procedure: Employees set their own goals, together with their supervisor, which they are then measured against at the end of the assessment period. This process encourages open communication and fair goal-setting for both the employees and the firm. Regarding rewards, the HRM manager noted, "Our compensation system is competitive in the local market. In addition, all employees have the right to a productivity bonus, from an office assistant to the director of the Mexican subsidiary".

Global Care Denmark is working to ensure its employees worldwide can maintain a natural balance between work and leisure time. To help employees achieve this, Global Care Mexico has implemented policies such as telecommuting, flexible scheduling, and extended maternity/paternity leave. Such policies are not common in Mexican business culture; however, they are becoming more common because of Mexico's changing institutional context. The development of personalized HRM practices, with a focus on physical and mental well-being, autonomy, flexible arrangements, and increased networking and interaction among employees, has helped to maximize productivity, innovation, and change (Zapata-Cantú, 2022).

HRM subsystem: Employment relations. Global Care's Denmark HRM department aims to encourage employee participation and open communication. One manager in Denmark commented, "On our team, there is no way to avoid participation in decision-making processes. This is a typical characteristic of Danish culture". However, another employee in Denmark noted, "Here, everything takes time. Perhaps [allowing] too much democracy is not right for all processes. We have several rounds of discussions, trying to reach a consensus and consider all opinions. This slows down all processes and makes decision-making difficult". In contrast, one person typically makes decisions in Mexico: The (typically male) boss, who represents "masculine society" (Chhokar et al., 2007). One of the most significant challenges faced by Global Care Mexico is the openness and freedom given to Mexican employees, as these characteristics seem to be in direct opposition to the traditional modes of functioning, direction/delegation, organizational structures, decision-making, and control in HRM in Mexico.

Distinct Scandinavian Management Model and Implications for Global Care Mexico's HRM System

Culture is a dynamic concept, and it is difficult to make a single statement about Mexican business culture due to its constantly changing nature. Denmark has a more stable business environment and is generally a more stable society in terms of political and economic development (e.g., Schramm-Nielsen, 2000). Global Care Mexico's HRM system (see Table 30.2) is derived from the Scandinavian model, in which managers downplay their authority, prefer egalitarian practices, delegate responsibility, and involve employees in idea generation; this is often termed a "participative" leadership style. Additionally, institutions (e.g., Scott, 2014) play a key role. In particular, the Scandinavian model is characterized by 1) stable labor relations, 2) reforms of work culture, and 3) strong governments that, in alliance with trade unions, are committed to supporting an extensive welfare and social security system with an absolute objective of full employment (Davila & Elvira, 2012; Grenness, 2003).

Although Denmark is an individualistic society (Chhokar et al., 2007), Danes tend to be group-oriented when it comes to decision-making, paying little attention to rank and status and respecting everyone equally. At work, Danes enjoy a high degree of flexibility, such as flexible start times and the option of teleworking. Danish workplaces typically do not feature the highly hierarchical structures or gender inequality found in Mexico; rather, they tend to be "flat" organizations and empower gender minorities. The distance between the boss and employees is thus short, and in principle, everyone – regardless of their education, position, or social status – is regarded as equal. Employees are not commonly under tight control. Finally, asking colleagues for advice is not considered a sign of weakness. The ability to cooperate is regarded highly, and people across status and professional categories help each other. Criticism typically focuses on one's work rather than personality, and it is acceptable to make mistakes.

Summary of the Case's Main Features

Mexico is unique in its economic development, social dynamics, and patterns of relationships within organizations. Nevertheless, there is evidence of the strong influence of Global

TABLE 30.2 Configuration of high-performance HRM practices at Global Care Mexico

HRM subsystem	Resource and control-based HRM practices	Sample HRM practices
People flow	Staffing	• Online psychological test • Panel interview based on competencies
	Training	• Employees are responsible for career development
	Mobility (internal and external)	• Opportunities for worldwide mobility within the firm
	Job security	• Job security based on employee performance
	Diversity and inclusion	• Zero discrimination • Teleworking/work-from-home schemes • Gender equality
Appraisal and rewards	Appraisal	• Based on a balanced scorecard
	Rewards	• Productivity bonus given to all employees irrespective of hierarchical position
Employment relations	Job design	• Job design based on competence
	Participation	• Encourage participation in decision-making processes
	Welfare (physical and mental)	• Based on the Global Care management framework

Care's Denmark people management framework in establishing a management style that is somewhat contradictory to the Mexican context. Implementing HRM practices has been a challenge for Global Care Mexico because the institutional context differs vastly from that in Denmark.

The case suggests that employers can develop strategies to attract and retain employees, as well as gain their trust and loyalty. For example, in modern Mexico, HRM systems are more open to diversity and inclusion. The main insight from this study is that firms must acknowledge the contextual factors at play when implementing a model of high-performance HRM practices. Nevertheless, firms do not necessarily need to change their core values to implement HRM subsystems, if they can encourage employees to adapt to an existing framework. However, Global Care's HRM system is not a completely new method of management in Mexico, as other organizations operate under similar universal values and management strategies. Thus, this case invites us to rethink the configuration of HRM practices designed elsewhere and implemented in Latin America.

CASE STUDY QUESTIONS FOR DISCUSSION

1. Given the Mexican and Danish business cultures:
   (i) What are the key institutional and cultural differences between Mexico and Denmark?
   (ii) What are the most important HRM challenges faced by Global Care Mexico? What does the company need to do to succeed?
2. What are the key strengths of Global Care in implementing its management framework in Mexico? How did the firm leverage these advantages given the current and historical state of HRM in Mexico? Draw on relevant HRM frameworks and debates where relevant, e.g., convergence/divergence and MNC HQ-subsidiary transfer and relations.
3. What is the "right" HRM strategy for Global Care Mexico – hybrid or centralized? Why? Evaluate the different options (with pros and cons).

NOTES

1 For reasons of confidentiality and sensitivity, a pseudonym is used, and certain details concerning the organization's titles and activities have been altered.
2 Adapted from the high-commitment model developed by Bamberger and Meshoulam (2000: 66–67).

REFERENCES

Bamberger, P., & Meshoulam, I. 2000. *Human Resource Strategy: Formulation, Implementation, and Impact.* London: Sage.

Chhokar, J. S., Brodbeck, F. C., & House, R. J. 2007. *Culture and Leadership Across the World: The GLOBE Book of In-depth Studies of 25 Societies.* Mahwah, NJ: Lawrence Erlbaum Associates.

Davila, A., & Elvira, M. M. 2012. Humanistic leadership: Lessons from Latin America. *Journal of World Business*, 47(4): 548–554.

Elvira, M. M., & Davila, A. 2005. Special research issue on human resource management in Latin America. *International Journal of Human Resource Management*, 16: 2164–2172.

Grenness, T. 2003. Scandinavian managers on Scandinavian management. *International Journal of Value-Based Management*, 16: 9–21.

Kühlmann, T. M. 2005. Formation of trust in German–Mexican business relations. In K. Bijlsma-Frankema & R. K. Woolthuis (Eds.), *Trust Under Pressure: Empirical Investigations of Trust and Trust Building in Uncertain Circumstances*: 37–54. Cheltenham, UK: Edward Elgar.

Paludi, M. I., Barragan, S., & Mills, A. 2021. Women CEOs in Mexico: Gendered local/global divide and the diversity management discourse. *Critical Perspectives on International Business*, 17: 128–147.

Ramirez, J., & Søderberg, A.-M. 2021. Talent management in the interface between cultural heritage and modernity: A case study of younger Mexican middle managers in a regional office. In J. Trullen & J. Bonache (Eds.), *Talent Management in Latin America: Pressing Issues and Best Practices:* 45–62. New York: Routledge.

Schramm-Nielsen, J. 2000. How to interpret uncertainty avoidance scores: A comparative study of Danish and French firms. *Cross Cultural Management: An International Journal,* 7(4): 3–11.

Scott, W. R. 2014. *Institutions and Organizations: Ideas, Interests, and Identities.* Thousand Oaks: Sage.

Stephens, G. K., & Greer, C. R. 1995. Doing business in Mexico: Understanding cultural differences. *Organizational Dynamics,* 24(1): 39–55.

World Bank. 2020. Foreign direct investment, net inflows (BoP, current US$)—Mexico (1970–2019). Retrieved October 1, 2020, from https://data.worldbank.org/indicator/BX.KLT.DINV.CD.WD?locations=MX

Zapata-Cantú, L. 2022. The evolution of knowledge transfer in Mexico, from physical to virtual spaces. In C. Machado & J. Paulo Davim (Eds.), *Organizational Innovation in the Digital Era.* Switzerland: Springer Nature.

Supplementary Resources

OECD. 2012. *Human Resources Management Country Profiles: Mexico.* Retrieved December 17, 2021 from https://www.oecd.org/gov/pem/OECD%20HRM%20Profile%20-%20Mexico.pdf

Secatero, S., Williams, S., & Romans, R. 2022. A pathway to leadership for diverse cadres of school leaders: Honoring indigenous values in a principal preparation program in New Mexico. *Leadership and Policy in Schools,* 21(1): 81–94.

World Bank. 2021. Mexico. Retrieved December 17, 2021 from https://www.worldbank.org/en/country/mexico

World Economic Forum. 2021a. Mexico. Retrieved December 17, 2021 from https://www3.weforum.org/docs/TT15/WEF_Mexico.pdf

World Economic Forum. 2021b. *Global Gender Gap.* Retrieved December 17, 2021 from https://www3.weforum.org/docs/WEF_GGGR_2021.pdf

CHAPTER 31

United States

What About Me? When Diversity, Equity, and Inclusion Efforts Result in Unintended Outcomes

Shelia A. Hyde,[1] Marla L. White,[1] and Wendy J. Casper

CASE SYNOPSIS

In the summer of 2020, George Floyd, an African American male, lost his life at the hands of Minnesota police officers. In the aftermath, the Black Lives Matter (BLM) movement, whose goal is to abolish white supremacy, grew stronger than ever in the United States. In response to BLM protests, many US organizational leaders issued statements expressing zero tolerance of racism in the workplace and implemented anti-Black racism initiatives. Senior leadership at a mid-sized technology company, MSW Technology, seeks to develop strategies to combat anti-Black racism at work and in the wider community as well as to implement best practices in their existing diversity and inclusion policies. However, some employees, in particular some non-Black employees, are not appreciative of the company's targeted initiative addressing anti-Black racism. The purpose of this case is to identify strategies to help MSW Technology with its anti-Black racism efforts while also ensuring an equitable and inclusive work environment for all employees.

KEYWORDS

Diversity management, turnover intention, employee relations, United States

DOI: 10.4324/9781003307099-37

LEARNING OUTCOMES

1. Understand the challenges of managing diversity, equity, and inclusion initiatives.
2. Explain the difference between access discrimination and treatment discrimination.
3. Make recommendations for improving retention and employee relations in relation to diversity, equity, and inclusiveness in an organization.
4. Explain the multicultural organization development (MCOD) process.

NATIONAL CONTEXT

It has been over 150 years since slavery ended in the United States. However, discrimination and racism against African Americans, who are descendants of enslaved people in the United States, still exist. When Barack Obama was elected as the President of the United States in 2008 and re-elected in 2012, many Americans thought that anti-Black racism was no longer an issue. Nevertheless, since the conclusion of his presidency in 2016, white supremacy groups have reemerged into the mainstream, police and vigilante killings of African Americans (e.g., Ahmaud Arbery, Atatiana Jefferson, Breonna Taylor, Eric Garner, George Floyd, Michael Brown, and Philando Castile) have increased, and the political divide in the United States has drastically grown. These mega-threats, defined as "negative, large-scale, diversity-related episodes that receive significant media attention" (Leigh & Melwani, 2019: 564) may impact individual (e.g., negative emotions) and group (e.g., emotional sharing) attitudes and behaviors.

The United States' long-standing racial history is complex and intertwined into the fabric of the nation. As such, race can have major implications within the workplace. As the workforce has become increasingly diverse, laws (e.g., Title VII Civil Rights Act of 1964) have been implemented and governmental organizations (e.g., Equal Opportunity Commission; EEOC) erected to prevent both access and treatment discrimination. *Access discrimination* occurs when there are barriers to obtaining employment based on factors such as race and gender. *Treatment discrimination* occurs when people receive differential outcomes (e.g., rewards, compensation, promotion) for doing the same work. In spite of legislators' efforts, discrimination still persists, especially for African Americans. For example, researchers have found that African Americans with a "Black" sounding name (compared to White Americans with a "White" sounding name) must send out 50% more resumes to obtain a job interview. Once hired, research has shown that African Americans (compared to White Americans) were rated lower in subjective performance ratings and received lower salaries (Bertrand & Mullainathan, 2004; Castilla, 2012).

The summer of 2020 was the beginning of a racial reckoning within the United States. On May 25, 2020, George Floyd, an unarmed African American man, lost his life after a police officer kneeled on his neck for 9 minutes and 29 seconds. Although there were other times when African Americans lost their lives due to police violence, this tragedy was videotaped and occurred when employees worldwide were relegated to quarantine and work-from-home protocols due to the COVID-19 pandemic. Thus, many Americans had the opportunity to witness this event as the video went viral, and they became more informed about racial injustice. Following George Floyd's unnecessary death, many Americans from all racial groups and all walks of life participated in protests to support the BLM movement, demanding justice, and police reform, and calling for organizations to make systemic changes. As a result, many company CEOs and organizational leaders issued statements expressing support for African American employees and social justice. They also pledged to combat anti-Black racism by donating to causes benefiting African American communities.

ORGANIZATIONAL CONTEXT

MSW Technology (MSW Tech)[2] was founded in the early 1990s. The company is headquartered in Dallas, Texas, but has locations in several major US cities with technology hubs, including Austin, Texas, and Santa Clara, California. MSW Tech has become a major competitor in manufacturing parts for electronic storage devices, from large data centers to personal computers. Their yearly annual revenue is approximately USD 6 billion, and the company is expected to continue to grow as the need for data storage increases.

MSW Tech currently employs 10,000 employees and serves approximately 1,000 customers domestically and internationally. MSW Tech hires employees from a variety of backgrounds (e.g., racial, gender, age, etc.) and strives to support all its employees by implementing inclusive policies and practices. MSW Tech's goal is to have a workforce that reflects the US population at large; however, they currently lag behind. Additionally, investors and legislators demand more transparency about the demographic composition of their workforce. As of the 2020 census (United States Census Bureau, 2020), there were approximately 331 million people living in the United States, and the racial/ethnic demographics were as follows: 60.1% White, 18.5% Hispanic, 13.4% African American, 5.9% Asian, and 1.5% Native American and Pacific Islander. Like many other technology companies, in 2018, MSW Tech began publishing a Diversity Annual Report. According to the most recent report, the racial/ethnic make-up comprises 53% White, 35% Asian,[3] 6% Hispanic, 5% African American, and 1% Native American and Pacific Islander. Most of the non-White employees are in entry- to mid-level professional roles. So not only is the company currently lagging in the representation of minority groups from a recruitment perspective, but they are also lagging in the representation of minority groups at the upper leadership levels of the organization.

MSW Tech has 13 senior leaders comprised of the chief executive officer (CEO), chief financial officer (CFO), five strategic business entities' chief operating officers (COOs), chief human resources officer (CHRO), chief sales and marketing officer (CSMO), chief technology officer (CTO), chief IT officer (CIO), chief communications officer (CCO), and chief legal officer (CLO). The senior leadership team is primarily male, with the exceptions of the CHRO and CCO, and primarily White, except for the CTO (an Asian male). Similarly, the senior leadership's direct reports are primarily White and male too.

MSW Tech has an internal human resources department. The department comprises the following functional areas: Talent management (diversity, equity, and inclusion (DEI), recruitment, onboarding, employee training, and development); strategic business partners (SBP); compensation and benefits; and ethics. Talent management is responsible for recruitment, including developing initiatives to recruit candidates from underrepresented backgrounds, and onboarding activities. SBP is responsible for executing the business entity's strategy (performance management). Compensation monitors and implements total rewards programs. Ethics ensures employees are trained in ethical standards and that guidelines are followed.

The HRM department endeavors to work with leaders to cultivate a diverse, equitable, and inclusive working environment. As such, over the years the DEI director, Ebony Jackson, within talent development, has assisted the company in developing and implementing several initiatives, policies, and practices. For instance, since its inception, MSW Tech has partnered with immigration and refugee organizations to help new immigrants secure entry-level positions in their manufacturing facilities. Before the United States legalized same-gender marriage in 2015, MSW Tech provided insurance benefits to same-gender couples. In 2010, a program was introduced for employees wishing to adopt children, providing educational and partial financial resources. Furthermore, the HRM department critiques and offers guidance in succession planning to ensure that all employees are being considered in the pipeline to leadership. With Ebony's oversight, employee resource groups (ERGs) have initiated mentoring and coaching programs. The company has 11 ERGs focusing on women (Women's Employee Initiative), race (Black Employee Initiative, Hispanic Employee Initiative, Asian Employee Initiative), religion (Muslim Employee Initiative, Christian Employee Initiative, Jewish Employee Initiative), former military (Veterans Employee Initiative), sexual orientation and identity (Pride Network), parenting (The Parent's Network), and new hires (The New Employee Initiative). HRM must approve the creation of new ERGs. These initiatives are instrumental in offering employees with similar interests and backgrounds safe spaces and support for their career growth and aspirations.

MSW Tech also supports the communities in which they are located. Business units are encouraged to participate in at least one day of volunteering per year. This includes serving meals to the elderly, reading to school children, and partnering with local nonprofit agencies (e.g., Salvation Army, Food Bank) to provide needed services. MSW Tech has a foundation that donates to worthy causes. For instance, during the 2020 BLM protests in the United States, MSW Tech pledged to donate USD 1 million to several Black organizations, including Black Lives Matter and several historically Black colleges and universities (HBCUs).

THE CASE AT MSW TECHNOLOGY

Coming into 2020, the United States was already gearing up for a turbulent year. Due to stark differences in political party views, the presidential election was getting heated. In March of 2020, as COVID-19 cases and deaths increased, the global pandemic caused a total shutdown of workplaces for many employers, while those who remained open required non-essential employees (e.g., administrative staff) to work from home to curb the spread of COVID-19. In line with this direction, at MSW Tech, non-essential workers were required to work at home until further notice; however, essential workers (e.g., manufacturing staff) were required to report to work on-site. The company implemented stringent cleaning procedures and safety protocols (e.g., wearing masks, washing hands, checking temperature, random testing) to mitigate risks of COVID-19 exposure. MSW Tech's HRM leaders recognized that employees were dealing with a lot of changes. Hence, they implemented several well-being policies and procedures, including funding to set up home office spaces (e.g., USD 1000 employee credit), offering flexible work schedules to manage home and work, and expanding benefits such as the Employee Assistance Program (EAP) (e.g., mental health services), and offering additional paid sick time and paid family medical leave.

As soon as the racial reckoning hit in the summer of 2020, MSW Tech's CEO, Greg Decker, directed the CHRO, Amy Meyer, and the CCO, Laurie Andersen, to develop a plan for the senior leadership team to get in front of potential issues both inside and outside of the organization. First, Laurie crafted messages for Greg. These messages were public statements issuing intolerance of racial injustice, and support for the Black Lives Matter movement and the company's Black employees. Additionally, Laurie's communications team helped company leaders craft similar email messages to send to their respective organizations. Amy's HRM team elicited the help of the Black Employee Initiative to host open forums for leaders to listen to African American employees' concerns. This allowed leaders to learn about African American experiences and what support was needed. Additionally, the HRM team implemented implicit bias/discrimination training for all employees. At Greg's direction, the foundation pledged monetary support to the local BLM chapter and three HBCUs that have a history of developing strong engineering talent – Tuskegee, North Carolina A & T, and Prairie View A & M. Lastly, Greg pledged that his leadership team would work to increase racial diversity in the pipeline to senior leadership. The HRM leadership team directed Ebony to implement an anonymous employee engagement and DEI survey. Ebony conducted the survey and reviewed the following results with the leadership team. The survey had a 90% participation rate and revealed some negative views. As some of the results in Figure 31.1 show, while 90% of White employees reported being satisfied with their work at MSW Tech, less than 30% reported feeling included in the company's DEI efforts. The reverse pattern was reported by non-White employees. On the other hand, close to 30% of Black employees reported satisfaction with their work, and approximately 80% reported they felt included in DEI efforts at MSW Tech. Non-Black minority employees were less satisfied with work (Asian = 40%, Hispanic = 30%, and Native American/Pacific Islander = 15%). Non-Black minorities felt less included in DEI efforts (Asian = 60%, Hispanic = 60%, and Native American/Pacific Islander = 50%) than African American/Black employees did.

FIGURE 31.1 Excerpts from MSW Tech survey results.

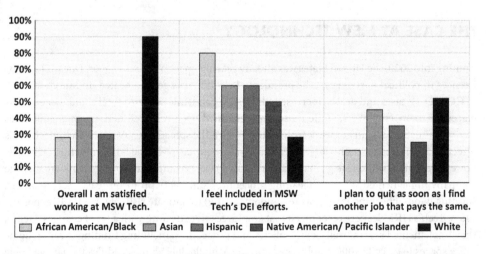

Note: The figure shows percentage of MSW Tech employees who strongly agree/agree with survey statements

Regarding overall satisfaction and career development opportunities, men at MSW rated higher levels of satisfaction and awareness of career opportunities relative to women. Women, however, felt more included in DEI efforts than men and felt that MSW Tech should speak more publicly about race and social justice issues. When asked about their intention to quit, 52% of White employees agreed or strongly agreed with the statement "I plan to quit as soon as I find another job that pays the same." In response to that statement, only 20% of African American, 45% of Asian, 35% of Hispanic, and 25% of Native American/Pacific Islander employees agreed or strongly agreed. Surprisingly, a large number of employees (39%), who had ten or more years of employment at MSW, were considering leaving the company.

Open-ended comments (see Table 31.1) at the end of the survey revealed that several employees felt recent promotions were not based on merit but on race. Some from non-Black minority groups expressed feelings that the company only cared about making Black employees feel included but was not making efforts to be inclusive of other minority groups. Several female employees remarked that efforts to promote women into management positions had weakened and they were afraid MSW Tech no longer cared about tackling this problem.

Unfortunately, soon after the survey review, Ebony left the company, and no one took on the responsibility to address the survey results. Now, MSW Tech is at a critical juncture and seeks to improve employee relations and create an environment where everyone feels valued and supported. Frustrated with the lack of progress that had been made, Greg hired a chief diversity, equity, and inclusion (CDEI) leader, Shanice Washington, an African American female, to report directly to him at the beginning of 2022. Shanice was charged with implementing sustainable change that would lead to a diverse, equitable, and inclusive workplace environment. Shanice was given a USD 100 million yearly budget to allocate to needed resources, including support staff.

CONSIDERATIONS FOR RESOLUTION OF ISSUES

Once Shanice arrives and begins her new position as CDEI officer, she reviews the survey results, but she is concerned because the data is a bit old and had not been acted upon. So, she questions whether to address issues related to this older data or collect an updated set of data. She decides to use the older data as her starting point but considers that it is also important to collect new data as well. She begins by utilizing the multicultural organization development (MCOD, Jackson, 2014) framework at MSW Tech to develop an equitable and inclusive workplace. The MCOD combines social diversity interventions, which focus on inclusion efforts, with social justice interventions, which focus on eliminating social injustice – forms of racism, sexism, classism, etc. MCOD practitioners recognize the individual changes necessary for change but also know that organizational policies and practices must be adjusted. MCOD views organizations on a six-point developmental continuum of stages from mono-cultural to multicultural stages, listed below:

1. *Exclusionary organizations* (or units) openly wish to maintain the dominance of the majority group and are hostile toward change.
2. *Club organizations* support the maintenance of privileges of the dominant group through policies and procedures that support the "correct" (i.e., dominant demographic) perspective.

TABLE 31.1 Sample responses to open-ended questions

Is there anything else you would like to share about diversity, equity, and inclusion at MSW Tech?

1. There is plenty of issues with race as it is in the world. The workplace is no place to continue those issues. *(White female)*

2. I am seeing a change in my team, especially my supervisor. I believe it is because of MSW Tech's diversity efforts. For example, my supervisor, who is a White man, mentioned that he's constantly learning about matters of race and inclusion and encouraged me to call him out if he ever slipped up. I think the company is moving in the right direction. *(Hispanic female)*

3. Minorities are represented well in our company and not discriminated against so I don't feel any further DEI efforts needs to be done at MSW Tech. *(White male)*

4. The company is only focused on hiring and promoting blacks. They do not care about relevant experience and education, and it really shows in the insane decisions management makes, and the disastrous consequences. Ironically, I am not only discriminated against because I am Hispanic, but also because I am disabled. I am not allowed to talk to anyone about my disabilities; clever way to not have to deal with accommodating the disabled, eh? *(Hispanic male)*

5. They shouldn't feel obligated to say something about race because its trendy. It is something that should be done independent of that. I want to be treated fairly regardless of my race. *(Black male)*

6. I think MSW Tech needs to do more to make sure women are treated fairly and developed for career advancement. There are only a few senior level women leaders. Women are getting left behind in the diversity, equity, and inclusion efforts. *(White female)*

7. They have fired white males – and hired more Blacks, women, and LGBTQxyz personages over having the best workers on-site. *(White male)*

8. I finally feel seen and supported at MSW Tech. I am grateful that the company is acknowledging what is happening outside of its walls and attempting to make work and opportunities more equitable. *(Black female)*

9. During this last year, I have applied for several managerial roles and didn't even get an interview. I believe I was overlooked because I am Asian and a woman. *(Asian female)*

10. I don't care either way what MSW Tech thinks about the protests and race. They do not need to be in the middle of it. Management should not look at race or gender, but experience and education, when it comes to hiring people to do a job. *(White male)*

11. Work is not the place for these things to be discussed. We are there to do a job. *(White female)*

12. Diversity stuff is a controversial issue that needs to stay away from work. It only causes more tension. *(Asian male)*

13. I do not believe MSW Tech cares about diversity. I think they are doing this diversity stuff because they are being pressured to do so. *(White male)*

14. I am Native American. Not heard a word about my people. *(Native American female)*

3. A *compliance organization* focuses on removing barriers to access discrimination without adjusting the structure and culture of the organization.

4. *Affirming organizations* take compliance a little further by addressing treatment discrimination. This includes developing non-majority employees and initiating programs that increase opportunities for them.

5. *Redefining organizations* are in transition to becoming an MCO. They examine the limitations of relying on one cultural perspective and proactively pursue the development and implementation of practices that provide resources to all socially and culturally diverse groups.

6. A *multicultural organization* represents a vision of the ideal for which to reach:

    The multicultural organization reflects the contributions and interests of diverse cultural and social groups in its mission operations, products, and services. It acts on a commitment to eradicate social oppression in all forms within the organization. The MCO includes members of diverse cultural and social groups as full participants, especially in decisions that shape the organization. It follows through on broader external social responsibilities, including support of efforts to eliminate all forms of social oppression and to educate others in multicultural perspectives (Jackson, 2014, p. 182).

After assessing where MSW Tech lies on the continuum, Shanice will begin the four components of the MCOD process, summarized below.

1. **Identify change agents.** In addition to the members of the leadership team, the team should include no more than 12 connected, supportive, employees from the organization who are trusted by their peers and understand this will be part of their job for at least two years. The change team can either be led by an external agent or someone within the organization. Since MSW Tech has recently hired Shanice, they have decided that she will lead the change team.

2. **Determine organization readiness.** Although Shanice received some information from the initial survey, additional questions need to be answered before moving forward. This step involves collecting data from the membership team, the change agents, and a sample of employees. Typically, six questions are asked in the readiness inventory (Jackson, p. 187):

    i. How are manifestations of social oppression (sexism, heterosexism, classism, and so forth) handled when discovered or reported?

    ii. Is support for diversity a core value in this organization?

    iii. Is there a clearly expressed commitment to social justice in this organization?

    iv. Does the leadership express or demonstrate its support for social justice?

    v. How well does the leadership model a value for diversity and social justice?

    vi. Is the commitment to diversity and social justice clearly stated in the mission and values of the organization?

    At least half of the data gathered from the readiness inventory should be considered positive to indicate that the organization is ready for the next component in the MCOD process. If half of the data is not positive, additional work should be done to prepare the organization. The specific work to be done is based on the data collected and could include harassment training and/or correction of long-standing social injustices.

3. **Assess the organization.** In order to identify where the organization is on the MCOD continuum, the change team collects data through three methods: Surveys, interviews, and auditing. First, survey data following the descriptions of the developmental stages are gathered from everyone in the organization. Next, interview data are gathered via focus groups to clarify survey data. Finally, the change agents collect organizational records (e.g., data for audit) and organize them for presentation to everyone in the company. This includes HRM data such as hires, terminations, promotions, grievances, and performance evaluations and associated organizational unit identification and available social identity groups (i.e., race, gender, physical and/or developmental ability, sexual orientation, and religion). Data is not analyzed but simply organized. Steps should be taken to protect the anonymity of respondents. The purpose of presenting the data is for the organization to hear the results of the assessment and to come to an agreement that the data represents the organization.

4. **Change planning and implementation**. The change team helps each unit identify changes and improvements in order to move the organization toward becoming an MCO. The focus should be on addressing issues that will result in measurable changes. After changes are made, the process should be reassessed and continued to internalize MCOD within the organization.

CASE STUDY QUESTIONS FOR DISCUSSION

1. Discuss the strengths and weaknesses MSW Tech has displayed when it comes to avoiding discrimination, managing, and valuing diversity.

2. Refer to Table 31.1. Which of the employee quotes illustrates access discrimination? Which illustrates treatment discrimination?

3. Imagine you are working for a consulting firm and have been hired by MSW Tech to help implement the MCOD process. Where do you think MSW is on organization readiness? At which stage on the MCOD continuum is MSW Tech?

4. Which areas of HRM should be involved in responding to the employee survey and/or implementing the MCOD process? In what ways should they be involved?

NOTES

1 Shared first authorship
2 MSW Technology is a fictional company. Any similarities to an existing company are purely coincidental.
3 Asians are disproportionately represented in the technology sector (BLS, 2020b).

REFERENCES

Bertrand, M., & Mullainathan, S. 2004. Are Emily and Greg more employable than Lakisha and Jamal? A field experiment on labor market discrimination. *American Economic Review*, 94(4): 991–1013.

Bureau of Labor Statistics [BLS]. 2020b. *Labor Force Statistics from the Current Population Survey.* Available at https://www.bls.gov/cps/cpsaat18.htm (accessed on November 6, 2022).

Castilla, E. J. 2012. Gender, race, and the new (merit-based) employment relationship. *Industrial Relations: A Journal of Economy and Society*, 51: 528–562.

Leigh, A., & Melwani, S. 2019. #Black employees matter: Mega-threats, identity fusion, and enacting positive deviance in organizations. *Academy of Management Review*, 44(3): 564–591.

United States Census Bureau, 2020. *Quick Facts*. Available at https://www.census.gov/quickfacts/fact/table/US/PST045219 (accessed on November 6, 2022).

Supplementary Readings

Article on BLM protests. *New York Times*. July 2020: https://www.nytimes.com/interactive/2020/07/03/us/george-floyd-protests-crowd-size.html

Article on Top 4 reasons diversity and inclusion programs fail. *Forbes*, March 2021: https://www.forbes.com/sites/forbeseq/2021/03/29/top-4-reasons-diversity-and-inclusion-programs-fail/?sh=4c6701787c84

Kramer, M.R. June 1, 2020. The 10 commitments companies must make to advance racial justice. *Harvard Business Review*, Boston, MA. https://hbr.org/2020/06/the-10-commitments-companies-must-make-to-advance-racial-justice

National Association for the Advancement of Colored People (NAACP) resource: https://naacp.org/know-issues

Society for Human Resource Management (SHRM) resource: https://www.shrm.org/resourcesandtools/tools-and-samples/how-to-guides/pages/how-to-develop-a-diversity-and-inclusion-initiative.aspx

Society for Human Resource Management (SHRM) article. August 2020: https://www.shrm.org/hr-today/news/hr-news/pages/a-new-approach-to-diversity-equity-and-inclusion.aspx

U.S. Civil Rights Act: https://www.eeoc.gov/statutes/title-vii-civil-rights-act-1964

U.S. Equal Employment Opportunity Commission best practices: https://www.eeoc.gov/initiatives/e-race/best-practices-and-tips-employees

Index

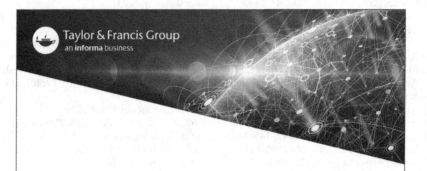

Printed in the United States
by Baker & Taylor Publisher Services

Printed in the United States
by Baker & Taylor Publisher Services